"Two of the world's leading border scholars have produced an important text focusing on the cultural dimension of borders. Unlike most border texts which focus on the political and the security dimensions of the lines which divide us, this book reflects the important cultural and social dimensions of borders as they impact upon us individuals and as groups, and play an important role in the way in which human identity is formed and is perpetuated through varying levels of exclusions and inclusions along a continuum of physical and social separation. The book highlights the fact that any form of border, at whatever social or spatial scale, is much more complex than the simplistic notion of lines on maps, or fences and walls in the landscape. The ways in which borders and their images leave an indelible imprint on our understanding of local spaces and environments enables us to understand the more complex and richer meaning of what actually constitutes a border and how this impacts upon our lives."

David Newman, *Professor, Ben-Gurion University of the Negev, Israel*

"In *Border Culture*, Victor Konrad and Anne-Laure Amilhat Szary bridge the gap between cultural theory and border studies, providing an engaging and smart contribution that deepens our understanding of how borders have implications on culture well beyond the borderlands. Highly recommended."

Reece Jones, *author of* White Borders *and* Nobody is Protected, *Professor, University of Hawaii, USA*

"While borders are consubstantial with globalization, border culture is at the heart of geopolitics in this transnational world, and is rooted in border experiences of globalization. The authors thus guide us in the mesh of these processes, at the junction of nations, where the suture is performed between and within border cultures, for they are manifold. An essential book as we may be entering, as the authors state, an era of post-globalization."

Élisabeth Vallet, *Director, Center for the Studies of Geopolitics, Raoul-Dandurand Chair, Université du Québec à Montréal, Canada*

"With *Border Culture,* Konrad and Amilhat-Szary are inviting us to reflect on the theory, imagination, and geopolitics or borders. A 'tour de force' into the border literatures, imaginaries and narratives, it is a superb book. A must read for cultural geographers."

Emmanuel Brunet-Jailly, *Professor, University of Victoria, Canada*

"This book is the first of its kind in the emerging field of Cultural Border Studies, an intriguing study of global border culture. Offering an extensive approach to the multiple intersections of borders and cultures, it will open up a much-needed debate on the roles of borders and the politics of culture."

Astrid M. Fellner, *Professor, Saarland University, Germany*

"Our world has become more bordered than at any time in human history. This sophisticated interrogation of international borders as culture offers a set of tools to help us understand, interrogate and look beyond the cartographies of our often-dismal age."

Nick Megoran, *Professor, University of Newcastle, UK*

"In a completely new perspective, Victor Konrad and Anne-Laure Amilhat Szary explore the relationship between borders and cultures. As creators of culture and cultural diversity, borders are home to new cultural forms, as well as being cultural productions involving particular imaginaries, which in turn are capable of transforming borders."

Patrick Suter, *Professor, University of Bern, Switzerland*

"Bridging border and culture studies, the authors of this captivating book invite us to overcome modern oppositions between theories and narratives, and between representations and experiences, by highlighting instead how their interplay can produce new interdisciplinary knowledge capable of reconceiving border cultures as mobile, relational, and multidimensional entities, having different symbolic and material forms, functions, and locations."

Chiara Brambilla, *Professor, University of Bergamo, Italy*

"To understand borders, you need to understand their cultural dimension. This indispensable book gives pressing arguments for including culture in any study of borders in geopolitics and everyday life, along with a thorough and insightful overview of ongoing research in the field."

Johan Schimanski, *Professor, University of Oslo, Norway*

BORDER CULTURE

This book introduces readers to the cultural imaginings of borders: the in-between spaces in which transnationalism collides with geopolitical cooperation and contestation.

Recent debates about the "refugee crisis" and the spread of the COVID-19 pandemic have politicized culture at and of borders like never before. Border culture is no longer culture at the margins but rather culture at the heart of geopolitics, flows, and experience of the transnational world. Increasingly, culture and borders are everywhere yet nowhere. In border spaces, national narratives and counter-narratives are tested and evaluated, coming up against transnational culture. This book provides an extensive and critical vision of border culture on the move, drawing on numerous examples worldwide and a growing international literature across border and cultural studies. It shows how border culture develops in the human imagination and manifests in human constructs of "nation" and "state", as well as in transnationalism. By analyzing this new and expanding cultural geography of border landscapes, the book shows the way to a fresh, broader dialogue.

Exploring the nature and meaning of the intersection of border and culture, this book will be an essential read for students and researchers across border studies, geopolitics, geography, and cultural studies.

Victor Konrad is Adjunct Research Professor at Carleton University, Canada, and formerly Director of the Canadian-American Center at the University of Maine, USA, and founding Director, Canada-U.S. Fulbright Program.

Anne-Laure Amilhat Szary is Professor at Grenoble-Alpes University, France, and head of the CNRS Pacte research unit, a pluri-disciplinary social sciences research centre.

Routledge Borderlands Studies

Borderlands are spaces of transition between cultures, societies and states. Often, like in the case of the US and Mexico, they are understood as static territorial lines and buffer zones, subservient to the development of states and state territories. However, borderlands can also be fluid and ambiguous spaces, moulded by processes of economic and political integration or shifting geopolitical dividing lines. Moreover, borderlands cultures can be found far from borders, in cities, multicultural neighbourhoods and diasporic communities. They also exist as both future-oriented geographical imaginations and imaginaries with profound historical roots. Today, globalisation, integration and new transnational forms of communication change the complex interrelationships between state, society, space and borders. Consequently, borderlands become more and more places in their own right, reflecting broader supranational patterns of political, economic and social change.

With this series we encourage inter- and multidisciplinary investigation on borders and borderlands throughout the world. We engage with the political, social and historical richness of borderlands, reflecting their unique (geo)political and cultural significance in contexts of colonial rule, nation-building and integration. The Series will explore, among other things, shifting social and political relations and place-related identities that emerge in borderlands, as well as cross-border interaction and the historical memories of every-day life at borders. With this series, we will both contribute to the rich tradition of North American and European borderlands studies and provide a forum for new growing interest in research on borderlands in Africa, Asia and Latin America.

For more information about this series, please visit: https://www.routledge.com/Routledge-Borderlands-Studies/book-series/BORDERLAND

Refugee Encounters at the Turkish-Syrian Border
Antakya at the Crossroads
Şule Can

Remapping Security on Europe's Northern Borders
Edited by Jussi P. Laine, Ilkka Liikanen and James W. Scott

Border Ireland
From Partition to Brexit
Cathal McCall

Post-Soviet Borders
A Kaleidoscope of Shifting Lives and Lands
Edited by Beate Eschment and Sabine von Löwis

Border Culture
Theory, Imagination, Geopolitics
Victor Konrad and Anne-Laure Amilhat Szary

BORDER CULTURE

Theory, Imagination, Geopolitics

Victor Konrad and Anne-Laure Amilhat Szary

Routledge
Taylor & Francis Group
LONDON AND NEW YORK

Designed cover image: "Nouvelles frontières" by Dominique Taleghani: dominiquetaleghani.com

First published 2023
by Routledge
4 Park Square, Milton Park, Abingdon, Oxon OX14 4RN

and by Routledge
605 Third Avenue, New York, NY 10158

Routledge is an imprint of the Taylor & Francis Group, an informa business

British Library Cataloguing-in-Publication Data
A catalogue record for this book is available from the British Library

ISBN: 978-1-032-29410-0 (hbk)
ISBN: 978-1-032-29411-7 (pbk)
ISBN: 978-1-003-30148-6 (ebk)

DOI: 10.4324/9781003301486

Typeset in Bembo
by Deanta Global Publishing Services, Chennai, India

CONTENTS

ILLUSTRATIONS

FOREWORD

The study of borders has undergone dramatic transformations in recent years. This has broadened our understanding of where borders are found, how they are made, what purposes they serve, and why they function as powerful cultural artefacts. Border studies thus reflect the centrality of borders and border-making to everyday life. The now widely used bordering and borderscapes approaches reflect profound transformations of social, political, and territorial relationships since the end of the Cold War as well as the often disruptive impacts of globalization on national societies. Within this context the present volume is a highly salient and timely addition to the Routledge Borderlands Studies Series. In their book, Victor Konrad and Anne-Laure Amilhat Szary seek to "decode the meaning of border culture" as a means to better understand and appreciate border complexity.

Today, Russian aggression and the brutal war in Ukraine understandably tend to direct the attention of researchers, politicians, media, and ordinary people to the security function of borders. It is, however, important to remember that even in this situation it is not just the armed defense of state sovereignty and territorial integrity that are at the core of the crisis. Questions of ethnicity, language, identity, historical legacies, memory politics, and culture in broad terms are fundamental elements of the conflict—and in the longer perspective are also its solution. In this situation, the book of Konrad and Amilhat Szary is a vital reminder of the multi-layered complexity of borders and how culture and its artistic manifestations are constantly embedded in processes of bordering at times of both conflict and cooperation— and not just on the level of every-day human interaction but within political relations as well.

The authors write (in Chapter 6) that "border culture is culture imagined and produced at boundaries, and in an increasing array of sites where visions, values, identities and other facets of human distinction meet and increasingly collide". To illustrate this idea, Konrad and Amilhat Szary guide us across nations, regions, cities, and places where the cultural dimensions of borders are reflected in imaginaries, border-crossing narratives, multiple identities, and allegiances and a multi-dimensional sense of "in-betweenness". Suggesting that cultures and borders are closely linked might meet with some suspicion and even trepidation, given an increasing propensity worldwide to exploit cultural difference in the struggle for political power. The bounding of culture, for example as part of a geopolitical strategy, is often appropriated as a political project of control as it reflects everyday needs for orientation and a sense of stability in the world. Moreover, the idea of "culture" often evokes exclusively bounded spaces and communities, Bordered culture can indeed be something highly constraining, and following Amartya Sen, violent if we insist on a singularity of culture in terms of something unambiguous and defined according to immutable categories of identity, values, and belonging.

As the authors point out, culture is a battlefield. But they also indicate that culture is not of necessity an exclusive process of bounding, it can also involve cooperation, dialogue, and evolutionary and non-finalizable processes of becoming something new. Consequently, the authors call for moving away from what they see as a "border culture trap", where culture is reduced to something that expresses otherness vis à vis mainstream, majority and/or ruling societies. As they argue, one alternative to essentializing cultural difference is to recognize and engage with borderland spaces which defy unambiguous definition or categorization. Consequently, the authors' central objective is to exemplify the significance of culture in contemporary border studies by linking political understandings of borders to socio-cultural processes, states of being, political discourses, and everyday practices.

The research upon which this book is based is also significant as a "post-disciplinary" perspective on border-related issues facing society, and it encourages greater interaction and exchange between individual disciplines themselves. The approach elaborated by Konrad and Amilhat Szary brings diverse forms of social, cultural, and political life into more holistic frames of analysis, indicating that while borders can be semi-permanent and formal in nature, they are also products of continuous border-making practices. These practices are made visible and legible through different forms of cultural appropriation and social contestation. Furthermore, with their approach, the authors also connect the realm of high (geo)politics to the situations of communities and individuals who are affected by and negotiate borders. Linking together social science and humanities traditions of border research with an appreciation for the relevance of other research fields, such as cultural psychology, Victor Konrad and Anne-Laure Amilhat Szary provide a rich cross-section of culture at borders. Among the examples developed in the book are those of border cultures expressed by place-making practices of Lhotsampa refugees in Halifax, Canada, separations and intersections of Afghanistan's many ethno-linguistic areas, cultural expression and art at border cities, mental maps of borderlanders, the performance of border guards at the Wagah border where India and Pakistan meet, and the complex border-transcending geographies of the Akwesasne Mohawk Territory.

In addition to these concrete illustrations the book also invites us to embrace the complexity of cultural, social, and political borders. As part of their theoretical considerations Konrad and Amilhat Szary explore the concept of "border thinking" as a way of seeing the world and social reality from the vantage point of being at *and amidst* social, cultural, and political borders; here, diversity, the co-existence of many different social worlds, and the daily negotiation of border-crossing rituals are the norm. Being at the border can also mean having very different places simultaneously as central reference points in everyday life. Alternatively, border thinking promotes an understanding of social borders as central to "being in the world" and the fact that we are all creating and crossing borders in one way or another. Border thinking counters the fiction of immutable border realities, meanings, and identities that is a source of misunderstandings of borders but also populist appropriations of them in terms of "taking back control". Understood in this way, border thinking completely breaks with monological obsessions and suggests that we can undertake a move from a thought-stopping to a thought-propelling consideration of borders as spaces of possibility.

Ilkka Liikanen and James W. Scott,
Editors of the Routledge Borderlands Studies Book Series

PREFACE

The Prevailing Engagement of Cultures and Borders

Borders today remain as important as ever in both differentiating and integrating nation-states, and the cultures that reside within these states and also extend across their boundaries. What border culture is, where it lives, how it works, and why it changes are all important considerations in comprehending borders, and why they continue to prevail, and loom even larger in the increasing number of walls and fences in our ostensibly borderless world. Like the walls and fences, border culture is a manifestation of the engagement of peoples at the border. Border culture, however, is more than a construction; it is an ongoing process replete with imaginaries of the border, narratives of barriers and crossings, multiple identities and states of being, and expressions of plural belongingness and multi-dimensional in-betweenness. Border culture may be difficult to compartmentalize, because by its nature, border culture is something both beyond and in-between in time and space. Yet, it emerges as something that is embraced across boundaries, and border culture is often portrayed with artistic flourish to convey the essence of cross-border engagement. Also, border culture conveys the despair of conflict and violence at borders and in borderlands.

The current reminder that cultures collide and clash in borderlands is found in the battle for Ukraine. Whereas the Ukraine emerged as a small nation-state only in the seventeenth century, it has grown substantially next to Russia since then. The Russian empire and the following Soviet Union dominated it, and, assured of this domination, the Soviets added to the Ukraine parts of Eastern European countries annexed during WWII, and then, in 1954, attached the Crimea. In 2014, Russia's President Putin re-claimed Crimea and backed Russian-leaning separatists in Ukraine's eastern regions of Donets and Luhansk. In late February 2022, a full invasion of the Ukraine began with incursions along all of the Ukraine's northern, southern, and eastern boundaries. The war, now in its seventh month, grinds on with thousands of casualties among Ukraine's civilian population and its armed forces, thousands of Russian military dead or wounded, and massive devastation throughout the Ukraine, particularly in border regions adjacent to Russia. No resolution or end to the conflict is in sight.

The entire Ukraine has become a borderland: a political space in-between East and West, a nation-state between Russia and the NATO allies, a confrontation zone between ideologies, and a social and cultural entity stranded in a global chess match. Here, the resolve of Ukrainian nationalism and identity stands firm in its attempt to resist the Russian invasion. Also, it is in this space in-between where Ukrainian culture, in all of its facets, has become emboldened and expressed in multiple symbolic actions and manifestations to forge a united front against Russian aggression, and engage the recognition and support of most of the world. The Ukraine portrays at once a heroic and demonstrative culture of a beleaguered nation fighting to sustain its territory, and a border culture rising to prominence in a global context. All "Western" nations, with NATO members of this strengthened coalition at the core, are "fighting" for the Ukraine with donations of all kinds ranging from weapons to relief aid. Whereas Russia remains intent on erasing the border with the Ukraine, the Ukrainian resistance has re-established the boundary between the nation-states, and enhanced the gulf between Ukrainian and Russian cultures. In this conflict, a virile border culture has infected Russians convinced that they are fighting "Nazism" at the edge of their country and repatriating the "Little Russians". Meanwhile, Ukrainians, with the attention and substantial support of many countries around the globe, have enlivened and bolstered the image of a border between democracy and autocracy at Ukraine's boundary with Russia. Will this border become the renewed dividing line in a new "Cold War" between Russia and Europe and its allies? Are we witnessing the formation of the ultimate wall in global relations, one that may extend to encircle China, North Korea, and former Soviet republics in the East? What kind of border culture may evolve in this scenario? How can an understanding of border culture help us to comprehend what is happening in the Ukraine, and, more broadly, to recognize the meaning of cultural engagement at borders?

In this book, we explore the substance and meaning of border culture. In order to achieve this goal, we examine, critically, the essence of both the concept of border and the concept of culture. This seemingly straightforward approach is immediately complicated by the recognition that "border" and "culture" do not reside intuitively or naturally in the same space. This recognition leads us to unpack the concepts of border and culture before we link them in our extensive discussion of border culture theory. Building on a more comprehensive and detailed examination of border culture theory than in previous studies, we approach four main themes encountered in the study of border culture. Our first consideration is focused on imaginaries of the border, and how these imaginaries inform human ideas, perceptions, attitudes, and actions related to borders. The purpose is to reveal the imaginaries of the border that help to form border culture. Next, we proceed to the narratives of the border that contribute to or result from imaginaries and discourse. These narratives are primarily nationalist although in some cases they originate from sub-national or separatist groups. Invariably, these narratives contribute to border culture, and help to shape the border milieu. From well-illustrated considerations of imaginaries and narratives, the discussion of border culture moves to a detailed assessment of how borders activate culture. This extensive examination of border culture production and border crossings draws from our border research between China and Myanmar, Laos and Vietnam, Finland and Russia, Canada and the U.S., Peru and Chile, Korea, Israel, Cyprus, and, of course, the iconic Mexico–U.S. border. The discussion of border culture production and border crossings also encompasses the insights of many other border scholars to provide an inclusive and diverse appreciation of border culture manifestations and meanings. The concluding focus of the book is on borders with/in transnational culture. This outlook addresses border culture in the era of globalization, and the current period of post-globalization. Border culture is at the heart of geopolitics in this transnational world, epitomized by plural cultures of diasporas, and the flows and objects of culture in transnational space. A profusion of border culture experience is evident in "transcultural placemaking" which results in border culture that is at once imaginary and manifested.

How do we resolve border culture in post-globalization times, and in a world where new borders are now produced by nature's re-alignments in a post-humanistic environment? Several imperatives are evident and compelling. The dynamics of border separation and integration in transnationalism have shifted, and the shifts have impacted border cultures and created new ones. Feminization of the border is evident on a global scale, and specifically in the transnational border cultures of migrant domestic workers. During the COVID-19 pandemic, and the human migrations and dislocations of the early twenty-first century, the imperative to find and stay home is evident everywhere. Border culture becomes scaled-down and personal for many with homes, but for many others without a home migration is often aligned with dispossession. The border cultures of dispossession are usually associated with violence as we see daily in the news reports from the war in Ukraine. The devastating conflict in the Ukraine is a compelling and resounding call for the need to resolve and reinstate a positive and productive border culture, not only between Russia and Europe, but in numerous other instances where territorial aggression is imminent. Ideally, cultural landscapes in transnational space, as well as in the borderlands between states, convey the mutual engagement of cultures and the resolution of border culture. Accomplishment of this goal appears elusive, certainly as we view the violence, desperation, and death in Ukraine, yet, as we have shown in this book, border culture does work, as it needs to, in our world that sways between transnationalism and definitively bordered national spaces.

Westport, Ontario, Canada, and Grenoble, France

ACKNOWLEDGEMENTS

This book has emerged, albeit slowly, from decades of reflection about what border culture means and how it works. In 2011, at the Border Regions in Transition conference in Grenoble and Geneva, we decided to embark on a project to situate border culture within the broader context of border theory, and to explore the extensive geopolitics of border culture. Not realizing the magnitude of what we had undertaken, we were naive about goals and timelines for research and writing. Also, other more immediate and compelling research and writing would intervene and conspire to constantly shift our attention elsewhere. Both of us had projects and commitments demanding our time, and of course the responsibilities of teaching and administration captured most of our moments. During the last two years, however, some circumstances have changed, and we have found the large blocks of time to commit to completing this project. Also, we have become aware of the growing interest in border culture and the need to address the topic in a critical and comprehensive way. This imperative has guided our efforts to complete the book.

Another incentive has come from our colleagues and students who have urged us on with this work. Foremost among them have been James W. Scott and Ilkka Liikanen, the editors for the Border Studies Series published by Routledge. They have encouraged us from the outset. We would also like to acknowledge the support of the following people who have helped and responded in many ways including reading the manuscript, offering illustrations, supporting our research, commenting on text, providing advice, and sharing insights: Don Alper, Pierre-Alexandre Beylier, Chiara Brambilla, Alessandro Brasile, Emmanuel Brunet-Jailly, Stan Brunn, Anna Casaglia, Jean Cristofol, Michael Darroch, Astrid Fellner, Matti Fritsch, Anne Gillo, Frederic Giraut, Todd Hataley, Lucy Hinton, Zhiding Hu, Norma Iglesias Prieto, Reece Jones, Melissa Kelly, Joel Konrad, Tuulikki Kurki, Aili Kurtis, Jussi Laine, Justin Langlois, Yuli Liu, Evelyn Mayer,

Andrea Masala, Nick Megoran, Srimoyee Mitra, David Newman, Eva Nossem, Jopi Nyman, Cedric Parizot, Ignacio Pereyra, Guilliaume Poiret, Tom Ptak, Lee Rodney, Laetitia Rouvière, Johan Schimanski, Gianlluca Simi, Patrick Suter, Laurie Trautman, Dhananjay Tripathi, Elisabeth Vallet, Martin van der Velde, Randy Widdis, and Brenda Yeoh. Also, we would like to acknowledge the helpful insights and comments of two anonymous reviewers. Their suggestions have helped us to focus and strengthen the book.

An overview and critical assessment of border culture requires the perspectives of experts in various disciplines and fields. We have drawn extensively on the expertise and insights of graduate students, post-doctoral fellows, and faculty at universities worldwide. Furthermore, we have engaged the perspectives of contributors in curatorial, cultural policy, and heritage management fields. Our intention has been to integrate the perspectives on border culture from Hispanic and Francophone literatures as well as the extensive scholarship published in English. Also, we have accessed research on border culture originating in other areas such as China and Turkey. A comprehensive global approach to conveying border culture remains a formidable and daunting task. Yet, our aim has not been to document all border culture, but to develop a better and more inclusive overview of the meaning of border culture and its geopolitical impact. This aim has led us to appreciate the incredible diversity and amazing contribution of border culture research emerging from all parts of the world. We would like to acknowledge the innovative and significant contributions of scholars who have enlivened border studies with their often unique and always compelling discoveries.

This book is also a tribute to the scholars in many fields of inquiry whose formative work laid the foundations for understanding border culture. We will not name them all here, but rather refer the reader to Chapter 2, in which we examine critically the basis for understanding border culture, and how this basis has shifted during the nineteenth through the twenty-first centuries. The early thinkers about border culture populate the "who's who" of formative anthropology, geography, political science, and sociology, among other disciplines. More recent contributors to shaping our emerging understanding of border culture are scholars in the generations immediately before us, including many of our teachers. Again, we identify them and their contributions throughout the book. We do, however, wish to identify and honour two prominent scholars who contributed to the conceptualization of border culture. First, is Jean Gottmann whose immense contributions transcended the borders of the Francophone and Anglophone worlds and far beyond. Second, is David Lowenthal, who passed away recently, in his nineties, after a career spanning more than seventy years as a leading scholar in geography, history, and heritage studies. We honour their work, and cherish the interactions we have had with them.

We acknowledge the support of the funding agencies and institutions that have supported our research in the field of border culture. Foremost among the granting agencies is the Social Sciences and Humanities Research Council of

Canada (SSHRC) through its Partnership Grant Program (Grant 895-2012-1022). The SSHRC grant, *Borders in Globalization*, was directed by Dr Emmanuel Brunet-Jailly (University of Victoria, Canada). Dr Victor Konrad (Carleton University) was co-director and lead for the culture theme. Dr Anne-Laure Amilhat Szary (Université Grenoble-Alpes) was lead for the France international partnership. For seven years (2013–2020), the SSHRC grant and matching funding from our home institutions, and other host institutions worldwide, enabled our border culture research and the work of colleagues and students. Carleton University also provided funding for Victor Konrad's work in China, Canada, the U.S., and Europe. This research was supported as well through visiting professorships for Konrad at the Karelian Institute, University of Eastern Finland, Radboud University in the Netherlands, and Yunnan Normal University and Eastern China Normal University, in Kunming and Shanghai, respectively. At Grenoble-Alpes University, the funding of the Performance Lab (https://performance.univ-grenoble-alpes.fr/) dedicated to structuring practice-based research in France was decisive in many ways. Last, but not least, the companionship with the 'antiAtlas of borders' collective (www.antiatlas.net/en/), a science-art project founded the year this book project was launched, was decisive in helping us frame and discuss this book's structure and contents.

Finally, we are honoured as well that we have had an opportunity to work with the exceptional publication team at Routledge. Helena Hurd expressed her enthusiasm for our project in 2019, after she read early drafts of several chapters. Her colleague Alexandra de Brauw has taken over stewardship of our manuscript while Helena is on maternity leave. Our editorial assistant, Rosie Anderson, has worked closely with us during the manuscript preparation and production phases. We would also like to acknowledge the efforts of Shanmugapriya Rajaram of Deanta Global who handled the copy-editing and proofs, and the others in the Routledge team who worked behind the scene on this project. It has been our privilege to work with the Routledge team to publish *Border Culture: Theory, Imagination, Geopolitics.*

Victor Konrad, Westport, Ontario, Canada
Anne-Laure Amilhat Szary, Grenoble, France

1

INTRODUCTION

Border culture on the move: Bridging border studies and culture theory

Culture shifts its shape at borders by sneaking across the line, healing division, and revealing the value of difference.
Border culture can't stop; it is always becoming.
Theories of the border and culture need a bridge to connect obvious yet elusive alignments.
Border culture theory emerges from the convergence of imagination and politics.
Border culture is culture at the edge of being and on the bridge to meaning.

1.1 Border culture on the move

In Halifax, Nova Scotia, Canada, recent immigrant families were awarded community gardens in 2014 (CBC 2014). This piece of news could appear as a mere sign of a new trend of urban nature management at the turn of the twenty-first century, or a more significant acknowledgement of human constraints in nature, allowing inhabitants to collectively redesign a role for non-built areas within our expanding cities, if it were not for one specific characteristic that binds the people concerned with these Halifax gardens together. The people are Lhotsampa refugees displaced from Bhutan, and encouraging them to grow their own seeds in their new place of life is not only about providing themselves with cheaper and sustainable food (Figure 1.1). Also, it is about enabling maintenance of traditional diets and culture through the reconstruction of past "gardenscapes" and solidifying identities as gardeners. Mainly, it is about connecting the Lhotsampa to the soil of their new haven and planting them there. Moreover, it is about the feeling of being at home. This is about healthy adaptation and nourishing traditions in Canada. The gardens are a hub for building and strengthening different forms of social capital and easing transition into life in Canada. Gardening allows these women, men, and children to enact their possible re-rooting in a different country, and could be the basis for activating their new citizenship (Hinton and Schnurr 2021).

DOI: 10.4324/9781003301486-1

FIGURE 1.1 Lhotsampa Glen Garden, Halifax, Canada. Photo reproduced with permission from Lucy Hinton, Wilfrid Laurier University.

At the world's busiest border, between the United States and Mexico, volunteers from San Diego regularly cross the line to provide care to the other, poorer side, notably by helping to grow food in the segregated *colonias* of Tijuana that spread out at the foot of the infamous wall (Solamani 2013). One of the main obstacles to launching this initiative without external support is that the land of these neighbourhoods is highly contaminated by previous industrial use and lack of waste management. This initiative therefore relies on a certain know-how about the techniques of hydroponic urban agriculture, but mostly the initiative depends on land—ground—availability. So, the activists involved in the projects have for a few years crossed the border with bags full of soil, a gesture that would be illegal if it were operated in reverse, because the United States of America prohibits the entry of all agricultural material into its territory. Should this be qualified as smuggling when the soil is heading south? Nearby, the San Diego–Tijuana Friendship Garden was located on both sides adjacent to the border wall, and served as a bi-national garden sanctuary for native plants (Casey and Watkins 2021 [2014]) (Figure 1.2). In January, 2020, the garden was bulldozed on the American side by the U.S. Border Patrol citing security concerns (YouTube 2020). After considerable local criticism, the Border Patrol apologized and allowed a re-planting of the garden destroyed on U.S. soil, but the garden is now lopsided with well-established native plants on the Mexican side and seedlings on the American side. Also, whereas the American side is bordered in a steel

FIGURE 1.2 San Diego–Tijuana Friendship Garden. The View from the United States. Photo reproduced with permission from Norma Iglesias Prieto, San Diego State University.

cage, the Mexican side is freely accessible to the public. The paradox is enticing, and revealing about culture at the border.

At first glance, these little stories both deal with agriculture and boundary crossing but they reveal much more and may help to advance our reflections on culture and borders. The stories at once enlarge our comprehension of the nature and attributes of border culture, illustrate how culture works in dividing and connecting human political space, provide clues to explain patterns of border culture, and, yet, sustain the ever-changing, shape-shifting, and quixotic aura of culture in border contexts.

> Border writing is the trace of the coyote/shaman...[in which] the writer... [is] a shaman who writes in order to cure the reader—If the border is a machine, then one of its elements is the *bicultural smuggler*, and to read is to cross over into another side where capital has not yet reduced the object to a commodity, to a place where *psychic healing* can occur.
>
> *(Hicks 1991)*

At a time when cultural studies have made it clear that culture is much more than lifestyles linked to regional specificities, how do we build tools to understand the spatiality of culture? If we agree upon understanding culture as a process, as "something which both differentiates the world and provides a concept for understanding that differentiation" (Mitchell 1995, 103), then it may appear intriguing to understand how this process interplays with the major dividing lines of the globe, the international borders and other boundaries that humans construct to stripe our planet. How are cultures bordered? How are borders cultured? These are two unusual questions to which this book seeks answers. One of the common points between the two terms is that they are commonly defined through binaries, culture being opposed to nature, border being considered as partaking territories into exclusive realms of sovereignty. In this book we build on recent scholarship that seeks to characterize the processual dimension of social facts, and to acknowledge the fluid spatialities that help fight the "crisping" of identity and the clashing of civilizations.

1.2 Culture and politics

Appreciating this point implies going beyond two facts: first, that borders are defined as arbitrary political lines that separate distinct yet connected social environments; second, that if culture goes beyond identity (Leresche and Saez 2002), it should be considered as more than a territorial construct, constituting a "geopolitical unconscious that helps to enframe and inform foreign policy debate" (Tuathail and Dalby 1998, 10). Although the legal definition of borders presents them as very stable institutions, they constitute in fact representations and imaginaries (and practices that these sustain) that have evolved in unacknowledged ways (Schimanski and Wolfe 2010, Rodney 2017, Amilhat Szary 2020). The recent renewal of border studies has shown that international dyads are not merely linear projections of political intentions, but also areas that open and close at the same time, through simultaneous and sometimes contradictory debordering and rebordering processes (Newman 1999, Popescu 2011, Parker and Vaughan-Williams 2014, Van Houtum et al., 2005, Wastl-Walter 2012, Wilson and Donnan 2012, Amilhat Szary and Giraut 2015, Casaglia and Laine 2017). Also, recent scholarship has indicated that borders are socio-political realities which proceed from a constant reshuffling of the link between an abstract idea of power and its contingent materiality (De Genova 2012, Diener and Hagen 2009, Walters 2002). We offer here to focus on the interaction between a certain type of place (understood in its plural spatialities), the political border, and cultural processes. We build on the hypothesis that assessing what borders are doing to contemporary cultural transformations could not only contribute an "understanding of geopolitics as a broad social and cultural phenomenon" (Tuathail and Dalby 1998, 4), but also establish the complex political role of culture in contemporary societies. Borders and culture offer two ways of gaining a sense of human spatiality, and in this book we witness their rapid and complex transformations in recent times.

1.3 Centres, peripheries, and the "turns" of power

This choice of analyzing borders is by no means a casual selection, because in wishing to deepen our understanding of culture as a collective component of social structures, it is generally understood that traditional identities, and notably ethnic identities, are built on spatial extensions that reside on a centre–periphery dynamic (Barth 1969). Whereas cultural groups are defined traditionally by the central common grounds which make their identity, the question of their boundaries is usually both taken for granted (groups do exist within specific territorial extensions), and left aside for reasons of clarity (cultural boundaries do not necessarily need to be demarcated). This notion of common "grounds" also needs to be considered literally. From the point of view of traditional sedentary communities, the soil is not something to be shared and the earth is what soldiers die for. This may not have been the case in all eras, but since the Renaissance, thought in modern times has reinforced considerably the interpretation of an Earth as a grid of contiguous entities, yet entities exclusive to one of the other (Elden 2013, Migdal 2004). In the framework of the nation-state, borders have acted as containers of identities, acknowledging prior identities that they contributed to and essentialized (Agnew 1994).

However, at the turn of the twenty-first century, in a globalizing world "fixist lenses" (Lapid 2001), that is conceptual tools that make us focus on social phenomena as if they were stable and bounded, are slowly left aside to acknowledge a generalized "mobility turn" (Sheller and Urry 2006). What becomes of our links to the land? And, do we reformulate these links to the land? What is the cultural sinew? Geographers and anthropologists have helped to illustrate how producing places was essential for enacting identities. These scholars have established that agriculture was the first economic mode of production and place building, inducing territorial identifications that have carved the basis for the imposed norm of territorial identities that were to be melted into the national mould during the modern era. Yet, we also realize now that globalization has allowed for the multiple identities of human beings to be expressed again, and that these multiple identities more or less intersect across a variety of borders, and are hybridized. Not only does this suggest a "cultural turn" in international relations, but also it forwards analysis of the border identity, and it offers directions for a renewed understanding of cultural spatialities. This contradicts the current thought that "Studies of transnationalism and globalization emphasize the diminishing importance of territoriality, and, consequently, posit the detachment of culture, politics and economy from any fixed borders. Borders and borderlands feature, if at all, as zones of displacement and deterritorialization" (Hoehne and Feyissa 2013). Borders, and territoriality, have in fact not diminished in importance (Agnew 2008, Paasi 2003) in transnationalism and globalization, and they may indeed be contributing to a "border turn" acknowledging their renewed visibility and significance, and perhaps their symbolic power (Konrad 2021).

Our focus on borders is thus based on a comprehensive contextualization of the bordering and de-/rebordering processes, both in time and space; it aims at reconstructing a narrative of border studies that escapes the common discourse on the "lost and found" line, considering that borders are manifest of the modern nation-state which, after having vacillated because of globalization, are now reconsolidated for security reasons. Considering borders as economical tools of the capitalist system as much as political technologies (Amilhat Szary 2020), we are able to envision a theory of border culture that goes well beyond what happens on the site of the boundary line itself.

1.4 Beyond organic culture and out of the border culture trap

Locating culture today (Low and Lawrence-Zuniga 2006) appears as a complex challenge, implying more-than-territorial approaches that question the methods and concepts of all social sciences. In this context, the notion of border may appear as problematic because cultural studies in a postcolonial context have used the "border" in many metaphorical ways, calling for a widened "border thinking" (Anzaldúa, 1987, Mignolo and Tlostanova 2006) defined as an "epistemology of the exteriority; that is, of the outside created from the inside" (Mignolo and Tlotstanova 2006, 206). We acknowledge this widened border thinking, and we will link with it in the continuum of border thought and epistemology, but we will focus on examining culture at political borders. This focus is based on the hypothesis that these political borders, at all scales, constitute a kind of space that allows very well for grasping tensions and links through both their symbolic and material existence.

Concerning both borders and culture, we will be attentive to not build upon Western conceptions of culture, notably by trying to overcome the nature/culture divide that, after having played a fundamental role in the structuring of rational occidental knowledge (Descola 2004), is profoundly questioned today, notably through the notion of the agency of the non-human (Latour 2005). Our perspective is informed by, and builds on, the notion of the post-humanistic border (Nail 2019). In this respect, our work takes into account as well the renewal of culture theory. This theory has recently moved beyond its original opposition between ordinary and extra-ordinary (notably artistic) cultural practices (Schimanski and Wolfe 2017), which used to consider that the notion of culture encompassed all that gave meaning to human lives (Cosgrove and Jackson 1987). This traditional approach often implicitly involved a degree of differentiation between the occidental world where the theorization originated and was taking place, and the rest of the world. This opposition not only was grounded on racial prejudices, but also derived from the opposition between arts and craftsmanship that arose with modernity. Throughout the book, we will work with a notion of culture that is embedded in everyday life. In so doing, we meet border studies at a point in their development which assesses how much of their existence is due to mundane border work (Rumford 2008, Cooper et al. 2014, Jagetic-Andersen et al. 2012, Jones and Johnson 2014) as much as to the performative action of the state. Accordingly, we acknowledge that when the political borders of the nation-state are drawn, if they are meant to circumscribe a set commonality of identities within a territorial frame, they also actively contribute to hardening this differentiation. As places where control is enacted and flows are monitored, they can be made to express split identities. As regions of connection and exchange, they can be taken reversely as examples of cultural continuums. This duality is never simple to handle simultaneously, and, for those who live on the border, this perpetual process of "differance" (Derrida 1972) bears considerable violence (Amilhat Szary 2013).

Cultural analysis is always taken within the contradiction of the singular and the plural, working its way between two pitfalls: culture is not an overarching notion as such, but neither can it be defined as an addition to multiple cultures which globalization ostensibly melts together. To navigate between cultural relativism and absolutism, one can choose to look at cultural production more than examining cultures *per se*. Arjun Appadurai (1996) highlights processes to explain the evolution of cultural relationships, better known as "culturation" or acculturation trends. By examining expressions of cultural identity, Appadurai contradicts the idea of a global culture and demonstrates how global trends are spatially anchored and then reformulated by flows. Cultural theorist Mieke Bal (1999, 11) stresses how the spatial component of culture is essential to understand the concept dynamically, and she programmatically expresses that she "would like to make a more important place for the spatial coordinates that define culture not as a collection of things but as a process".

If we base ourselves in geographical and multiscalar analysis to deconstruct the link between culture and power, we understand the international divide as a nexus of international and transnational, territorial and extraterritorial, political and socio-cultural (Fein 2003). In so doing, we call for moving away from the "border culture trap" which is inevitable when "'culture' is a representation of 'others' which solidifies" (Mitchell 1995, 108) and sterilizes the "self" in the same process. In order to avoid the pitfalls of essentializing cultural differences that have led to the very powerful idea of the "clash of civilizations" (Huntington 1993), and to learn from opposed works like those of Edward Said (1978), works that have taught us how much the framing of otherness expresses relations of power, we propose a renewed framework for thinking about power and its representations.

> Hence, culture was a concept deployed to stop flux in its tracks, creating stability and 'ways of life' where before there had been change and contest. The idea of culture demanded a mapping of boundaries and edges, the specification of a morphology: culture had to become a bounded object that ultimately differentiated the world.
>
> *(Mitchell 1995, 107)*

As we move towards a proposal to analyze the politics of culture, we leave aside what the field of cultural politics (Darnovsky et al. 1995) had established, and the necessary acknowledgement of cultural multiplicity. Culture is not a luxury, but of shared interest to all, rich and poor, and culture is found in the growing crossings of cultural forms and productions (Becker and Horowitz 2017). Even the dispossessed cannot be dispossessed of all of their culture.

Whereas we may assume and accept this diversity of culture, we need to acknowledge and stress that one should by no means forget how much culture is a battlefield, made of domination processes and resistance initiatives. Cultural expressions may be very powerful tools of oppression and we must not forget that if culture is often associated with the idea of mutual respect, as well as with products that escape the market economy, these common ideas have been proven false by Antonio Gramsci's (2012) analysis. Gramsci demonstrates how much the capitalist system imposes its norms through the dissemination of cultural products that make it very difficult to resist and oppose the system. In essence, the oppressed are induced into internationalization by the means of the hegemony that is imposed upon them (Houssay-Holzschuch 2020).

1.5 Bringing together theories of border and culture

In the Gramscian perspective, culture is a means of representation of power relations. It performs domination but also it underlines the possibilities of emancipating processes. There is no summary culture, no neatly aggregated and contained assemblage, but multiple representations becoming in everyday life, engaged in nature and replete with complexities and paradoxes. Throughout this book, we will be looking at material and immaterial expressions of the border, considering both practices and representations, and how these bring people together and set them apart. We seek to appreciate culture in a perspective that takes into account the post-representational turn of geography, meaning that we do not only take cultural expressions as elements that express a given reality of the border, but rather we aim to understand them as actively performing the de-/rebordering processes. In this sense, for example, border art works, either from the visual or living arts, or from literature or poetry, do not slow political situations, they contribute to transforming them. Paradoxically, these may alternatively convey a view from the dominating actors and alternative visions of borders.

Moving out of the nationalist cultural trap also implies that border culture may be everywhere, yet nowhere: it certainly contributes to questioning strongly the centre–periphery dynamics of political space. If we consider that borders are the limits of national containers, then they ostensibly form a space of confrontation between two cultural entities. This is very often summarized and simplified by the idea that national identities conflict at the border. Concurrently, since most borders are not considered as impermeable, it is often acknowledged that some kind of mingling may appear and open the space to a cross-boundary relationship. The hybridity that ensues depends on different factors that characterize the degree of openness of the border as well as on the fact that the border regions' history and languages are older than that of the state authority which divides them (Brunet-Jailly 2005). Whether this mingling is the expression and imposition of centre-based identities, or the place of negotiation of hybridity, the interaction would imply that the culture of the borders can only be expressed and perceived on site, thus condemning border culture to a marginal position. Yet, this is not borne out by the evidence. The intersections that are induced at the border travel, either because the women and men who carry them are mobile, or because artifacts and constructs are transported by a diversity of means, including a rapidly growing digital dissemination, and also because we work with an idea of the everywhere border. Cultural expressions and processes appear essential to the borderscaping—"a wider understanding of the contemporary spatiality of politics—based on a multi-sited approach at different levels"—of places and regions (Brambilla 2015, Brambilla et al. 2015, 2). Also, culture could constitute an important component within the individualization of contemporary regimes and borderities—being in an intermediate position or state (Amilhat Szary and Giraut 2015). With so much of the world caught in-between and becoming, this is what makes the analysis of border culture so important today.

Borders are spatial signifiers and culture is a process of semantization of human environments: border culture is a site where the perception of meaning is made spatially available. Border culture is an evolving framework for encoding the meaning of border (Konrad and Nicol 2008). Our aim in this book is to decode the meaning of border culture. Analyzing border culture could therefore be a way of revisiting our understanding of how cultural meaning relates to activate the boundaries of being for everyone of us (Shweder et al. 1984). Border culture both underlines the power of dominating representations and relations that encapsulate us into hegemonic frameworks, which strongly restrict our political clout, and, yet, border culture hints at tracks to follow that allow for the renegotiation of meaning through place. This direction calls for a theoretical re-engagement of border studies and cultural psychology (Muscarà 2020, Konrad 2020).

Throughout our book, the discussion between border theory and culture theory tackles the border as a specific type of place, but the discourse also extends to consideration of the border as a metaphor (Schimanski and Wolfe 2007). Gender, race, or ability/disability barriers, for example, are other kinds of barriers (and everywhere borders) that challenge and allow for cultural renewal. Although these metaphorical borders are not the central focus of this book, we acknowledge the intersectionality of evolving border thinking. Intersectional approaches, therefore, are mobilized throughout our reasoning and writing because our project is a step in the direction of stepping out of a nationalist mould of thinking, and the methodologies that accompany this constrained thought. In effect, we tell a story of "competing universalities" (Butler 2004), and we offer ways of thinking about emancipatory frameworks to deal with the dehumanization processes that are currently evident at our countries' borders.

1.6 Border culture: Theory, imaginaries and production, national narratives and counter-narratives, border crossings, and transnational border culture

Our engagement with theory in this book is not only fundamental to establishing a framework for our study, and positioning our thinking within the epistemologies of border studies and cultural studies, but also to relate theories of border and culture that do not necessarily reside comfortably in the same space. Accordingly, we begin Chapter 2 with a detailed assessment of the foundations of thought about border culture. The challenge is to situate border culture in border theory, an incomplete and unresolved theoretical framework of logical, ethical, and metaphysical components of justified beliefs and knowledge about borders (Konrad 2021). Epistemological advances in understanding "dissensus" versus consensus at borders, power, belongingness, borderscapes, and a-territoriality (or more-than-territoriality) are "ridges of knowledge" in a topographic understanding which remains incomplete for explaining interstitial components of borders and bordering.

> At best, linked approaches employing multiple perspectives, engaging with borderlands, portraying borderscapes, and articulating agency and mobility have set the stage for a recalibration of borders in globalization, and an approximation of post-globalization borders. In a post-humanistic era, in which we have encountered the limitations of nature and sparred with natural laws, states have propped up borders and emphasized boundaries. The "border turn" is reactionary, and antithetical, a time when we need to be mindful of the branded border and anxious of our belongingness both within and beyond borders.
>
> *(Konrad 2021, 1)*

Within this framework, and acknowledging new directions at the post-globalization border, we step back in time to review and examine critically the foundations of border culture theory. This retrospective involves tracing the thought of Friedrich Ratzel, Franz Boas, and Fredrik Barth, among other pioneers who explored the relationship between borders and culture. Although their research and thought built a foundation for successive theory construction, the thought about borders was relegated to political geography whereas culture was assumed the domain of anthropology. This bifurcation of attention devoted to borders and culture was to prevail until Fredrik Barth (1969) re-engaged *Ethnic Groups and Boundaries.*

The re-engagement of borders and culture emerged in a time of intellectual anti-disciplinarity during which scholars sought bridges across the divides between evolved paradigms of thought within silos of disciplines, particularly in the social sciences. Echoes of this crossing of disciplinary boundaries continue within academe and a sustained disciplinary framework which operates to structure and institutionalize research and instruction while allowing and even applauding interdisciplinarity. The point of this digression is to describe the preconditions and to emphasize the importance of the "Barth moment" in situating border culture in border theory. Yet, the integration of thought about borders and culture would require more moments of realization to form a corpus of thought to inform the theory of border culture. Chapter 2 examines these momentous steps to reveal how and why border culture operates at borders and in borderlands. Among these steps are the acknowledgements that borders are socially constructed, and that culture is political. But many less-heralded realizations have contributed to advancing our thinking about borders and culture, and these are examined in detail in Chapter 2. One of the most significant setbacks in border theory was that border theory had not addressed the border *per se*, but rather focused on the nation-state container, and, consequently, theorizing border culture remained incomplete. To address this problem, as defined earlier in the introduction, is one of the reasons that we are writing this book.

Another reason is to explore the potential for understanding border culture through imaginaries of the border. Imaginaries are "unceasing and essentially undetermined creation of figures, forms and images" (Castoriadis 1997, 3) and they become the basis of something that is expressed as reality and rationality. In our reasoning, imaginaries of all kinds combine with identities to construct border culture. Border imaginaries are spatial, social, and inherently cultural thoughts and ideas (Rodney 2017, Schimanski and Nyman 2021). They may be supposed, insubstantial, and even unreal, but these border imaginaries are often powerful thoughts and ideas that influence border interaction, governance, and policy. Border imaginaries may be unfulfilled manifestations of culture, yet they may become framed thought and expressions of cultural production. In Chapter 3, we examine how border imaginaries are formed and revealed through maps, bodies, and everyday cultural production. Border culture imaginaries are evaluated according to their thresholds of development, the nature and extent of hybridity, and the states of transition. Following Randy Widdis (2015), we consider the parallelism, parallax, and paradox of border imaginaries in order to characterize how imaginaries produce border culture. We explore some expressions of border imaginaries—life securing, life sustaining, life enriching—in order to convey how these forms of border culture impact human activity at the border and in the borderlands. Border imaginaries offer a springboard to realization and understanding of borders in globalization because they expand the discourse of possibilities and populate this discourse with figures, forms, and images of border culture. Border imaginaries take us from unresolved forms to essentialized and materialized borders, and back again to more unresolved figures and images in the production and reproduction of borders. Border imaginaries are the circulatory systems and the connective tissue generated at the border, and generating the border. Imaginaries of the border also perform the border to create and align with national narratives and counter-narratives at the border.

Stories of the border tell us who we are and confirm where we are, as well as inducing us to define precisely who "we" is and what "us" means (Schimanski and Nyman 2021). In this way, national narratives help to create and shore up the border. One could visualize national narratives building momentum within their territory, and feeding on the edge of territory to make it conform, and characterize it as different than the borderland it has become. We may know that we live in borderlands and meshed territories, but national narratives create the boundaries between what we know and what we are told. Border narratives help to establish a sense of belonging, and this belonging contributes to further border building. In Chapter 4, we engage with national narratives and counter-narratives at the border in a more detailed and extensive discussion based on the rich texture of empirical discovery recorded worldwide. We seek to reveal the nuances of national narration in order to unravel how national and official cultures of the border evolve, are challenged, and change. In this context, identity construction is a key process in building both national narratives and borders. Linked with identity construction is the process of othering, as epitomized in the anti-migration narratives rampant notably in the Americas and Europe, but also evident elsewhere and anywhere populations on the move encounter fortresses of nationalism. Accordingly, counter cultures of border control and resistance stand off or conflict, and in so doing, they inciseborders in globalization. Border cultures become complex with multiple identities and transformations. Citizenship is at once reinforced and devalued as national narratives are exported. Yet, national narratives have prevailed in globalization and they constitute a legacy component of border culture in post-globalization.

In Chapter 5, we focus on the substance of border culture production and border crossings. Border culture is most evident at crossings and in the borderlands. Here, cultural production is anchored in imaginaries of the border wherein people are both connected and divided. This border culture in the border zone is mobile and characteristically in a state of becoming. The border is constantly differentiating people, and so if you are different you become the border. This connection and collusion of difference requires new approaches and tools to unravel. The process and the product of border culture need to be theorized separately in order to understand and appreciate border culture production. This production, or more accurately productions, is comprised of powerful activators and re-activators of culture. In order to grasp the complexity of cultural productions and border crossings, we must acknowledge their intersectionality, and, concurrently, that cultural productions and border crossings are unequal, variable and protracted, and repetitive. Border cultural production is at once apparent and also least visible among ethnic and linguistic minorities living at borders and in borderlands, because these groups partly escape the dominant state narrative. As such, they are both examples and counterexamples of border culture. In Chapter 5, we draw extensively on examples of experiences among ethnic minorities at the border to explore notions of liminality and in/visibility among other aspects of border culture expressed exquisitely in minority border experiences. Border culture production is relentless and constantly fluid and in motion, thus creating a mobile border discourse cycle of national, local, and international narratives. Also, this fluidity creates eddies—detached vortexes outside the flow, or spaces of exception, where specific, usually national, narratives predominate as in offshore detention centres and holding places where status within the state is unresolved. Sometimes local narratives prevail as in tribal enclaves along the Myanmar–China border. Border culture production, concomitant with the growth of border walls and fences, has grown substantially during the twenty-first century (Amilhat Szary 2012). This expansion of border culture production is one major reason to focus our attention on who the actors are, the proliferation of actions, and, ultimately what this increased border culture production looks like, and what it means.

The final chapter in our book engages borders both with and in (with/in) transnational space. Border culture is no longer culture at the margins but rather it is culture at the heart of geopolitics. Today, we find borders in a bewildering array of contexts including the binary cues embedded in barcodes of goods crossing the border that enable the goods to be identified as compliant and allow them to cross the border expeditiously. These barcodes and other digital identifiers comprise borders in transnational space. Yet, many people may not gain access to this transnational space because they simply do not carry the digital identification that would allow them to enter. Do they have a home in transnational space? Where is home in transnational space? What is their culture at this digital border? Is it their former national culture? Is it the culture that they have negotiated throughout their journey? Is it the new hybridized culture that they attain? Or, is it a diasporic culture that spans all of these possibilities and draws from them differentially? Although we have made the point, earlier in this introduction, that even destitute migrants are not stripped of all of their culture, dispossession of some aspects of culture does occur at the border whereas other aspects of culture may be gained. Unfortunately, this dispossession may be complete and prove final as the dispossession of culture begins in migration and ends in violence at the border.

Transnationalism has occurred in concert with several significant turns in thought in globalization. As we have discussed in this opening chapter, we have veered in our thinking about culture, space, and territory, and now borders. Yet transnationalism has achieved only an incomplete turn, and this directional variation may ultimately prove counter to the turns in realization of culture, space, and the border. The transnational imaginary is unfulfilled, and so we find borders with transnational culture, borders in transnational culture, and borders with/in transnational culture. These are complex, multidimensional relationships. In the mobile world of globalization, and now post-globalization, border culture is more elusive in its dispersal of imaginaries and production, and more expressive in resistance to the recidivism of nation-states. Also, border culture is not just out there, and everywhere, but border culture works according to epistemologies of human discourse, narration, spatial behaviour, and social construction, all inclined towards geopolitics. Border culture may be dispersed in the profusion of border experience in transnationalism, yet it impacts the meanings of home and community. Also, border culture draws attention to dispossession, gendering, and violence in transnational space, as it retrieves our comprehension of the nature in and the nature of landscapes in bordered geography.

The continuity of landscapes and borderscapes is central to our capability to navigate the expanded intersectionality of the contemporary world, with its attendant proliferation of production, and intensified interaction of stages and fields of engagement. Also central is our sustained ability and commitment to making meaning in the world (Spillman 2020).

> Meaning-making is a fundamental human process and a generic human capacity. ... Meaning-making can help us understand better what we share in our interactions and our groups, and how complex social organization is accomplished on a daily basis. It can help us understand cultural differences better. And, by analyzing cultural processes, we can recognize and explain more about explicit social power, implicit social domination, difficult social conflict, and pressing social problems.
>
> *(Spillman 2020, 118)*

Lyn Spillman's concluding exhortation to her colleagues in sociology also resonates for those who study border culture, and engage in border studies more widely. The meaning of the border is inextricably cultural and political. In this book, we aim to comprehend the nature of this meaning, and we invite you to join us in this exploration.

References

Agnew, John. 1994. "The territorial trap: The geographical assumptions of international relations theory." *Review of International Political Economy* 1, (1): 53–80.

Agnew, John. 2008. "Borders on the mind: Reframing border thinking." *Ethics and Global Politics* 1, (4): 175–191.

Amilhat Szary, Anne-Laure. 2012. "Walls and border art: The politics of art display." *Journal of Borderlands Studies* 27, (2): 213–228.

Amilhat Szary, Anne-Laure. 2013. "Cultura de Fronteras." In Beatriz Nates Cruz, ed. *La frontera, las fronteras. Diálogos Transversales en Estudios Territoriales Contemporáneos.* Manizales, Colombia: Editorial Universitaria de Caldas, 43–60.

Amilhat Szary, Anne-Laure. 2020. *Géopolitique Des Frontières. Découper La Terre, Imposer Une Vision Du Monde.* Paris: Le Cavalier Bleu.

Amilhat Szary, Anne-Laure, and Frédéric Giraut, eds. 2015. *Borderities: The Politics of Contemporary Mobile Borders.* Basingstoke: Palgrave Macmillan.

Anzaldúa, Gloria. 1987. *Borderlands/La Frontera: The New Mestiza.* San Francisco: Aunt Lute Books.

Appadurai, Arjun. 1996. *Modernity at Large: Cultural Dimensions of Globalization.* Minneapolis: University of Minnesota Press.

Bal, Mieke. 1999. "Introduction." In Mieke Bal, and Bryan Gonzales, eds. *The Practice of Cultural Analysis: Exposing Interdisciplinary Interpretation.* Stanford: Stanford University Press, 1–14.

Barth, Fredrik. 1969. *Ethnic Groups and Boundaries: The Social Organization of Culture Difference.* Oslo: Universitetsforlaget.

Becker, Howard S., and Irving Louis Horowitz. 2017. *The Culture of Civility.* New York: Routledge.

Brambilla, Chiara. 2015. "Exploring the critical potential of the borderscapes concept." *Geopolitics* 20, (1): 14–34.

Brambilla, Chiara, Jussi Laine, James W. Scott, and Gianluca Bocchi, eds. 2015. *Borderscaping: Imaginations and Practices of Border Making*. Aldershot: Ashgate.

Brunet-Jailly, Emmanuel. 2005. "Theorizing borders: An interdisciplinary perspective." *Geopolitics* 10, (4): 633–645.

Butler, Judith. 2004. "Competing Universalities." In Sarah Salih, and Judith Butler, eds. *The Judith Butler Reader*. London: Blackwell, 258–277.

Canadian Broadcasting Corporation (CBC). 2014. "Halifax refugee families farming in the heart of the city." http://www.cbc.ca/news/canada/nova-scotia/halifax-refugee-families-farming-in-the-heart-of-the-city-1.2746251. Accessed August 25, 2014.

Casaglia, Anna, and Jussi Laine. 2017. "Towards a re-articulation of the relationship between state, territory, and identity through a situated understanding of borders: conclusion." *Europa Regional* 24, (1/2): 93–96.

Casey, Edward S., and Mary Watkins. 2021 [2014]. "Prelude to part 2. Friendship park: First encounter." In Edward S. Casey, and Mary Watkins, eds. *Up Against the Wall: Re-imagining the U.S.-Mexico Border*. Austin: University of Texas Press, 115–120.

Castoriadis, Cornelius. 1997. *The Imaginary Institution of Society*. Cambridge: MIT Press.

Cooper, Anthony, Chris Perkins, and Chris Rumford. 2014. "The vernacularization of borders." In Reece Jones, and Corey Johnson, eds. *Making the Border in Everyday Life*. Aldershot: Ashgate, 15–32.

Cosgrove, Dennis, and Peter Jackson. 1987. "New directions in cultural geography." *Area* 19: 95–101.

Darnovsky, Marcy, Barbara Epstein, and Richard Flacks, eds. 1995. *Cultural Politics and Social Movements*. Philadelphia: Temple University Press.

De Genova, Nicholas. 2012. "Border, scene and obscene." In Thomas Wilson, and Hastings Donnan, eds. *A Companion to Border Studies*. New York: Wiley-Blackwell, 492–504.

Derrida, Jacques. 1972. "La differance." In *Marges de la philosophie*. Paris: Editions de Minuit, 396.

Descola, Philippe. 2004. *Beyond Nature and Culture*. Chicago: University of Chicago Press.

Diener, Alexander C., and Joshua Hagen. 2009. "Theorizing borders in a 'borderless world': Globalization, territory and identity." *Geography Compass* 3, (3): 1196–1216.

Elden, Stuart. 2013. *The Birth of Territory*. Chicago: University of Chicago Press.

Fein, Seth. 2003. "Culture across borders in the Americas." *History Compass* 1, (1): 1–6. https://doi.org/10.1111/1478-0542.025.

Gramsci, Antonio. 2012. *Selections from Cultural Writings*. London: Lawrence and Wishart.

Hicks, D. Emily. 1991. *Border Writing: The Multidimensional Text*. Minneapolis: University of Minnesota Press.

Hinton, Lucy, and Matthew A. Schnurr. 2021. "Newcomers and belonging: Community gardening as a tool to ease transitions." In Victor Konrad, and Randy W. Widdis, eds. *Borders and Bordering in Atlantic Canada*. Victoria: BIG Books series" #1, 102–118.

Hoehne, Markus Virgil, and Dereje Feyissa. 2013. "Centering borders and borderlands: The evidence from Africa." In Beneddikt Korf, and Timothy Raemaekers, eds. *Violence on the Margins: States, Conflict, and Borderlands*. New York: Palgrave Macmillan, 55–84.

Houssay-Holzschuch, Myriam. 2020. "Hegemony." In Audrey Kobayashi, ed. *International Encyclopedia of Human Geography*. New York: Elsevier, 357–362.

Huntington, Samuel. 1993. "The clash of civilizations." *Foreign Affairs* 72, (3): 22–49.

Jagetic Andersen, Dorte, Martin Klatt, and Marie Sandberg, eds. 2012. *The Border Multiple: The Practicing of Borders between Public Policy and Everyday Life in Re-scaling Europe*. Aldershot: Ashgate.

Jones, Reece, and Corey Johnson, eds. 2014. *Making the Border in Everyday Life*. Aldershot: Ashgate.

Konrad, Victor. 2020. "Belongingness and borders." In James W. Scott, ed. *A Research Agenda for Border Studies*. Oxford: Edward Elgar, 109–128.

Konrad, Victor. 2021. "New directions at the post-globalization border." *Journal of Borderlands Studies* 36, (5): 713–726.

Konrad, Victor, and Heather N. Nicol. 2008. *Beyond Walls: Re-inventing the Canada-United States Borderlands*. Aldershot: Ashgate.

KPBS Public Media. 2020. "San Diego Tijuana Friendship Garden Bulldozed, Border Patrol Apologizes", January 17th, 2020. https://youtu.be/bAyqJ_SjFXo.

Lapid, Yosef. 2001. "Introduction: Identities, borders, orders: Nudging international relations theory in a new direction." In Mattias Albert, David Jacobson, and Yosef Lapid, eds. *Identities, Borders, Orders: Rethinking International Relations Theory*. Minneapolis: University of Minnesota Press, 1–20.

Latour, Bruno. 2005. *Reassembling the Social: An Introduction to Actor-Network-Theory*. New York: Oxford University Press.

Leresche, Jean-Philippe, and Guy Saez. 2002. "Political frontier regimes: Towards cross-border governance." In Markus Perkmann, and Ngai-Ling Sum, eds. *Globalization, Regionalization and Cross-border Spaces*. London: Palgrave Macmillan, 77–99.

Low, Setha M., and Denise Lawrence-Zuniga, eds. 2006. *The Anthropology of Space and Place: Locating Culture*. Oxford: Blackwell.

Migdal, Joel, ed. 2004. *Boundaries and Belonging: States and Societies in the Struggle to Shape Identities and Local Practices*. Cambridge: Cambridge University Press.

Mignolo, Walter D., and Madina V. Tlostanova. 2006. "Theorizing from the borders: Shifting to geo- and body-politics of knowledge." *European Journal of Social Theory* 9, (2): 205–221.

Mitchell, Don. 1995. "There's no such thing as culture." *Transactions of the Institute of British Geographers* 20, (1): 102–116.

Muscarà, Luca. 2020. "The great swindle of nationalist sovereigntism: On territory, psychology, and communication technologies." In Sami Moisio, Natalie Koch, Andrew E. G. Jones, Christopher Lizotte, and Juho Luukkonen, eds. *Handbook on the Changing Geographies of the State: New Spaces of Geopolitics*. Cheltenham: Edward Elgar, 96–106.

Nail, Thomas. 2019. "Kinopolitics: Borders in motion." In Simone Bignall, and Rosi Braidotti, eds. *Posthuman Ecologies: Complexity and Process after Deleuze*. New York: Rowman and Littlefield, 183–203.

Newman, David, ed. 1999. *Boundaries, Territory and Postmodernity*. London: Franck Cass.

Paasi, Anssi. 2003. "Region and place: Regional identity in question." *Progress in Human Geography* 27, (4): 475–485.

Parker, Noel, and Nick Vaughan-Williams, eds. 2014. *Critical Border Studies: Broadening and Deepening the "Lines in the Sand" Agenda*. New York: Routledge.

Popescu, Gabriel. 2011. *Bordering and Ordering the Twenty-First Century: Understanding Borders*. Lanham: Rowman and Littlefield.

Rodney, Lee. 2017. *Looking Beyond Borderlines: North America's Frontier Imagination*. New York: Routledge.

Rumford, Chris, ed. 2008. *Citizens and Borderwork in Contemporary Europe*. New York: Routledge.

Said, Edward W. 1978. *Orientalism*. New York: Vintage/Penguin Books.

Schimanski, Johan, and Jopi Nyman, eds. 2021. *Border Images, Border Narratives: The Political Aesthetics of Boundaries and Crossings*. Manchester: University of Manchester Press.

Schimanski, Johan, and Stephen Wolfe, eds. 2007. *Border Poetics De-limited*. Hannover: Wehrhahn.

Schimanski, Johan, and Stephen Wolfe. 2010. "Cultural production and negotiation of borders: Introduction to the dossier."*Journal of Borderlands Studies* 25, (1): 38–49.

Schimanski, Johan, and Stephen Wolfe, eds. 2017. *Border Aesthetics: Concepts and Intersections*. Oxford: Berghahn.

Sheller, Mimi, and John Urry. 2006. "The new mobilities paradigm." *Environment and Planning A* 28: 207–226.

Shweder, Richard A. and Robert Alan LeVine, eds. 1984. *Culture Theory: Essays on Mind, Self and Emotion*. Cambridge: Cambridge University Press.

Solamani, Sara. 2013. "Wicking the line: The garden as a site for rethinking collective critical practices of bottom-up intervention in Colonia San Bernardo and San Diego." https://www.academia.edu/4790966/Wicking_the_Line_The_Garden_as_a_Site_for_Rethinking_Collective_Practices_of_Bottom-up_Intervention_in_Colonia_San_Bernardo_and_San_Diego. See also: http://loslaurelesgarden.blogspot.com/?m=1.

Spillman, Lyn. 2020. *What Is Cultural Sociology?* Cambridge: Polity Press.

Tuathail, Gearoid, and Simon Dalby, eds. 1998. *Rethinking Geopolitics*. London: Routledge.

Van Houtum, Henk, Olivier Kramsch, and Wolfgang Zierhofer, eds. 2005. *B/Ordering Space*. Aldershot: Ashgate.

Walters, William. 2002. "The power of inscription: Beyond social construction and deconstruction in European integration studies." *Millennium: Journal of International Studies* 31, (1): 83–108.

Wastl-Walter, Doris, ed. 2012. *Companion to Border Studies*. Farnham: Ashgate.

Widdis, Randy. 2015. "A spatial grammar of migration in the Canadian-American borderlands at the turn of the twentieth century." In Benjamin Bryce, and Alexander Freund, eds. *Entangling Migration History: Borderlands and Transnationalism in the United States and Canada*. Gainesville: University Press of Florida, 47–76.

Wilson, Thomas, and Hastings Donnan. 2012. *A Companion to Border Studies*. New York: Wiley-Blackwell.

2

FOUNDATIONS

Situating border culture in border theory

Culture is often bounded in space, and this condition binds culture to boundaries.
Borderlands are mobile spaces of political and cultural engagement.
Yet, there are ambiguous borderlands, and these landscapes convey the differential, diverse, and changing nature of border culture.
Borders and culture are on the move and intertwined in relational processes.
Border cultures are at the edge of national space and in the centre of transnational space.

In September 2021, as we complete our manuscript, the main news story on the international stage is about the American and allied departure from Afghanistan, and the reinstatement of Taliban control. After more than twenty years in Afghanistan pursuing the war on terror, troops from the U.S. and its allies are leaving and joining other military and civilian units who have already departed from their Afghanistan missions (Cathey 2021). A massive rout is taking place of foreign nationals and Afghanis who fear the Taliban. Nation, identity, law, civility, community, and borders are all in flux and in question. On September 10, 2021, at the Torkham border crossing in the Khyber Pass between Afghanistan and Pakistan, National Public Radio reporter Steve Inskeep observed who is allowed to cross (Inskeep 2021). Whereas local Pashtun males cross the border with relative ease, Afghanis from Kabul and further regions of the country are delayed, if they are allowed to cross at all. Border controls are exercised by Taliban authorities on exiting Afghanis, and then by Pakistani officials fearing a surge of refugees. Afghan children attempting to sneak across the border in the wheel-wells of trucks are extricated and sent back. Although most of the children are only engaged in local trade activities, the border that once enabled their livelihoods now stands in their way as officials exercise stricter controls. Informants tell Inskeep that the border now works in stark contrast to the situation in the early 2000s when there was practically no border enforcement.

DOI: 10.4324/9781003301486-2

Despite the formidable terrain, a fence now marks the borderline to help define and enforce one of Afghanistan's most contentious borders, and defy cultural continuity and integrity.

At Torkham and other crossing places, the Afghanistan–Pakistan border is performed through the implementation of identification cards as a tool of population surveillance (Alimia 2019). This surveillance embraces Afghans in a postcolonial trajectory as they approach the border. The surveillance employs identity documentation at key junctures of border cultural power, thus rendering the Pakistan–Afghanistan borderlands a space of cultural geopolitics (Raza and Shapiro 2019), captured in the continuity of colonial worldview (Chishti 2014). Here, the legacy border, the Durand Line surveyed and imposed by the British in 1893, prevails to confront the political and cultural entities of "Pashtunistan, Tribalistan and Talibanistan" (Schetter 2013, 47). Culture intertwines with politics in motion against the law of the Durand Line (Norchi 2010). Although postcolonial border culture may be starkly evident at the Afghanistan–Pakistan border, David Slater (1998) suggests that in global times, all cultures are border cultures that stand on the shifting margins of cultural displacement to express a cultural and historical hybridity of the postcolonial world.

The borders between Afghanistan and the world, recently focused and diminished to the airport in Kabul, are now effectively closed to "Westerners". Meanwhile, borders with Pakistan and Iran, and the "stans" to the north of Afghanistan—Tajikistan, Turkmenistan, Uzbekistan—are evolving as potentially enlarged conduits for arms, drugs, and terrorist groups. For centuries, Afghanistan's borders have been mobile, porous, transitional, and contested sites of political and cultural engagement (Gregory 2004, Maley 2009, Isby 2011). The internal borders of Afghanistan are manifested in a jumble of 34 provinces when they are portrayed without an ethno-linguistic and geomorphological context (Figure 2.1a). Language and ethnicity divide the Afghan people (however,

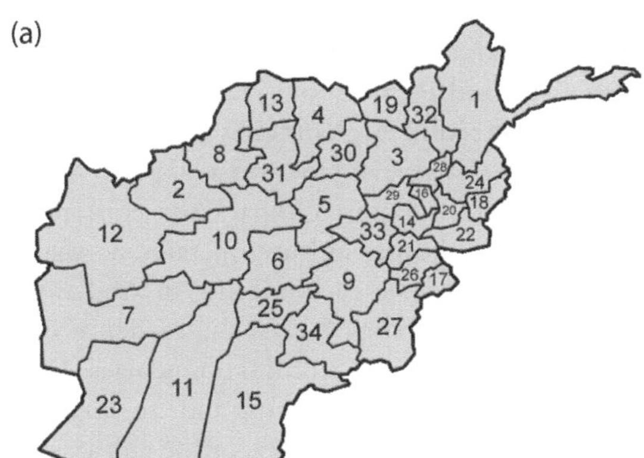

FIGURE 2.1 a: Outline Maps of Afghanistan Provinces; b: Afghanistan Map of Language and Ethnicity; c: Afghanistan Terrain. All images in the public domain. CC BY-SA 3.0, https://commons.wikipedia.org/w.

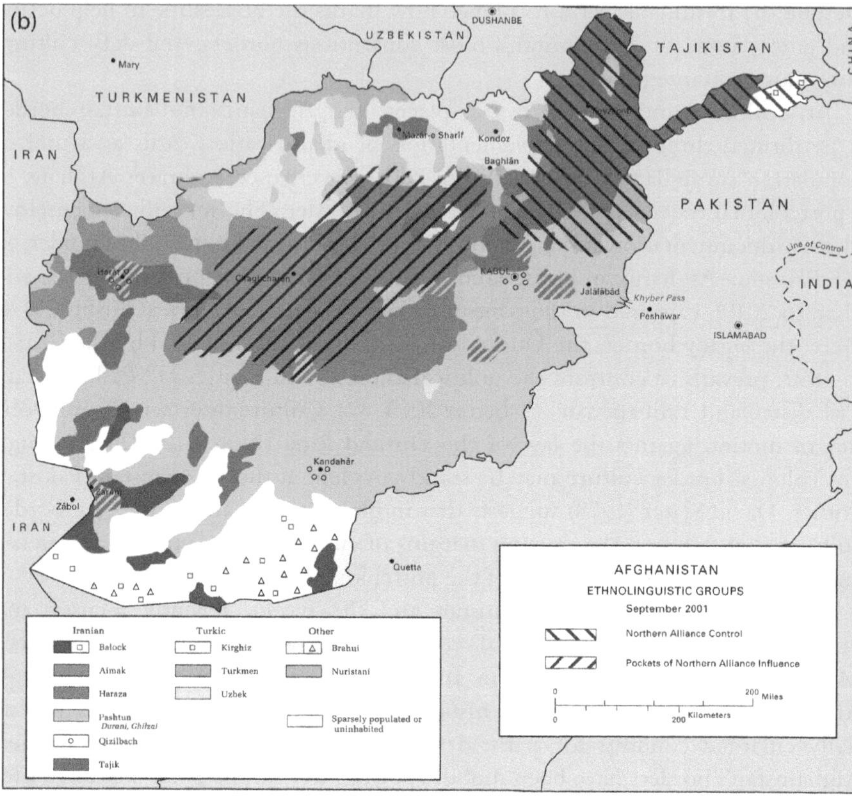

FIGURE 2.1 (Continued)

mapping these divides is extremely difficult) yet also sustain connections with all of the country's international neighbours (Figure 2.1b) within a formidable terrain of converging mountain ranges and strategic passes (Figure 2.1c).

Afghanistan is an international and intra-national borderland where culture is constantly on the move and intertwined with politics in relational and powerful processes (Mortenson and Relin 2006). The border cultures imagined and produced are at once localized in Afghanistan's multiple provinces, constructed within an imagined national space, and focused as a global icon of negative transnationalism. In this chapter, we aim to unpack the concepts and theories that enable us to understand how border culture operates, so that we may comprehend more fully situations like the re-bordering in Afghanistan. Whereas the continuity of the colonial worldview boosts the credence of borders, political borderlines increasingly do not match cultural boundaries. Nevertheless, culture uses political borders by simultaneously closing and crossing borderlines. Culture motivates borders, yet borders define cultures, refine cultures, and filter cultures. In order to understand this interaction of borders and culture, we maintain that border culture needs to be theorized as a juncture wherein human imagination and geopolitics converge in the space and time of the border. In Afghanistan, this

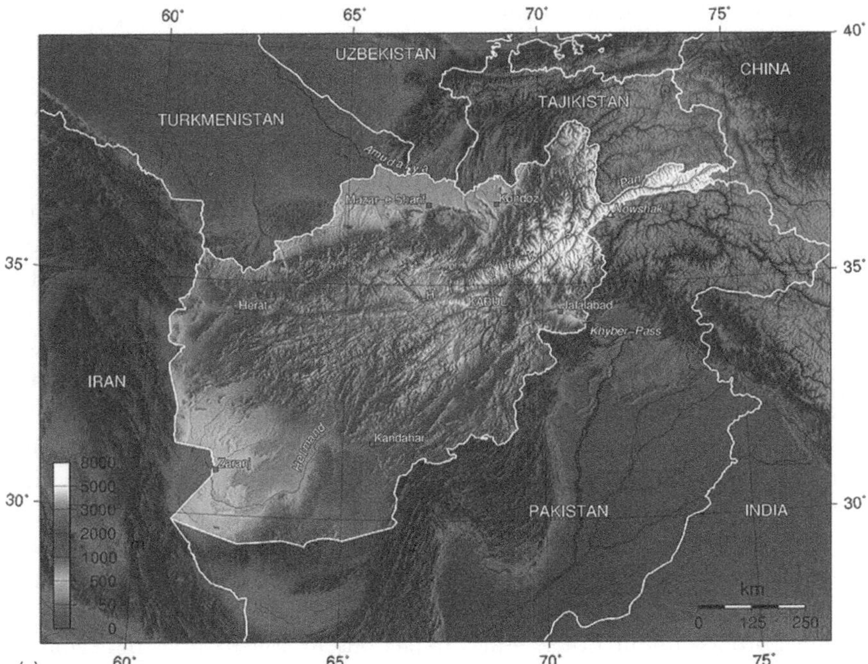

(c)

FIGURE 2.1 (Continued)

knot is evident as a crossroads of cultures, nationalities, societies, and polities in a landlocked postcolonial country at the convergence of east and west, in a remote yet strategic region at the top of the world.

As we explore the theory of border culture, we will illustrate our journey with reference to numerous examples informed by research in border culture contexts around the globe. Yet, it will be instructive to recall how border culture operates in Afghanistan as we address the theory of border culture in the main sections of this chapter: classical border culture theory, border culture in spatial and cultural "turns", emerging border culture theory, and towards integration of border culture theory. Furthermore, understanding border culture in Afghanistan requires acknowledgement and engagement of advances in border culture theory consistent with a renaissance in wider border theory, which is based in classical border theory yet integrated with post-globalization and post-humanistic thought. Before we begin this exploration of border culture theory, we aim to introduce, differentiate, and connect borders, border theory, and border culture theory.

2.1 Borders, border theory, and border culture theory

In our contemporary world, borders continue to demarcate territory and sustain boundaries around nation-states, but humanistic borders are now viewed as existing between societies, groups of all kinds, and phenomena originated through human interaction Accordingly, we envision borders as processes, and both of us have explored this vision and the components of de-bordering and re-bordering that contribute to the mobile geography of the border (Amilhat Szary and Giraut 2015, Konrad 2015, Ptak et al. 2022, Amilhat Szary 2020). Borders, in our estimation, are fundamentally territorial in their expression as lines, zones, points, and networks (Amilhat Szary 2020) in motion and constantly in flux (Konrad 2015, Nail 2016). Yet, since borders are socially constructed (Paasi 1998), and constituted through an expanding array of bordering practices (Yuval-Davis et al. 2019), then both territory and borders have also been deemed a-territorial or extending in realms of interaction beyond territory (Konrad and Brunet-Jailly 2019). More recently, in an effort to understand the relationship of borders with and beyond territory, we have tried to define borders as "space-time that materialize norms" (Amilhat Szary 2020), an approach to stress the difference with other kinds of limits and boundaries. Sergio Peña (2021) views border studies moving away from fundamental territoriality without agreement or a paradigm to understand the extended spatialization of borders. Concepts envisioned by theorists to expand and illuminate understanding of borders—borderscapes, mobile borders, among others—may in fact obscure the basic spatial evolution of borders. Some concepts, "borderities" for example, do convey the politics of mobile, contemporary borders (Amilhat Szary and Giraut 2015). These facets of borders reveal, among other characteristics, the cultural dimension of borders and bordering. Border culture is engaged, altered, produced, materialized, and removed in this dynamic border interaction of human society, politics, and space.

Among recent efforts to capture and convey the theory of the border are suggestions that societies and states are products of bordering processes as opposed to societies and states building borders, that borders are forms of social motion (kinopolitics), and that a new methodology of "critical limnology" is required to address emerging, contemporary border politics (Nail 2016). This renewed approach to border theory does not, however, encompass explicitly the intersection and integration of culture at the border. To theorize the cultural dimension of borders, we contend that a re-engagement with classical border culture theory needs to be integrated with more recent theorization about borders and culture in the social sciences and the humanities, and then linked to emerging inquiry and theory construction in cultural psychology.

Psychological perspectives have long impacted theory construction in geography, and thought about borders. Jean Gottmann (1952) in his theory of the state explains clearly the double function of the border based on psychological criteria. According to Gottmann, the border functions to defend the self, both individual self and collective self. The line is protective of self. The other function of the border is to open up possibilities for access to resources and enable crossing the line. Gottmann considered this security/access contradiction inherent to all borders. In his theory, he shows how, when the collective self feels threatened, notably by movement and migration, this collective self develops a common iconography to stabilize its identity. Whereas mainstream geographical thought engaged with psychological theories in building a geographical epistemology (Lowenthal 1961), the focus in behavioural geography (Gold 1980) either gravitated towards environmental psychology (Spencer and Blades 1986, Aiken 1991) or aligned with analytical behavioural geography (Golledge et al. 1972, Golledge and Stimson 1987). David Lowenthal was influenced by John K. Wright (1947) and his thought on the place of imagination in geography (Billinge 1977). Lowenthal also knew Jean Gottmann, who persuaded him to study geography at Berkeley with Carl Sauer (Barnes 2020, Muscarà 2022), thus broadening Lowenthal's appreciation of the engagement of culture, imagination, and place. Yet, Lowenthal's thought about borders focused on temporal divides more than spatial divides (Lowenthal 2000). Although there have been recurrent calls to engage in behavioural research on borders (van der Velde 1997), assessments conclude that this focus remains under-developed (van Houtum 2000, Paasi 2005).

Current research in cultural psychology establishes that borders are a structural component of daily life, they function in the mind and in society, they cannot exist without people experiencing them, and they exist as long as they have meaning for humans (Marsico and Varzi 2016, Marsico 2016, Valsiner 2014). The challenge in border culture theory development, then, is to secure the common ground in "mereotopology" (theory of parts and boundaries) (Smith 1996), engage with critical thinking in geopolitics, limnology, and border studies, and link border theory with theory in cultural psychology and culture studies more broadly defined. Both of us (Amilhat Szary 2015, Konrad 2020) have explored the cultural psychology of collective self and belongingness as they relate to borders. A more extensive discussion of the promise of research in cultural psychology and geography for expanding knowledge of border culture is found later in this chapter.

Whereas this book encompasses the extensive interplay of borders and culture, this chapter explores the theoretical underpinnings of this interplay. This is a very full and complex discussion. Border culture is an enticing dialectic because borders and culture do not intuitively reside in the same space. Once viewed as diametrically opposed, borders were considered the limits of territory and the edges of space, and culture was considered as integrative of the space. Franz Boas (1932, 612) concludes that "the various expressions of culture are closely interrelated and one cannot be altered without having an effect upon all the others. Culture is integrated." Social scientists of the time saw borders as containers of the nation-state and finite lines that separated people who could be differentiated by language and other characteristics related to nationality. In their view, culture either stopped or changed at borders or it should. These were strong and resilient ideas that permeated modern thought and underpinned the ideas of nation, state, and nation-state.

Yet, culture, imagined, produced, and refined constantly, is now viewed as the evolving knowledge, civility, and aesthetics shared by a group of people who may or may not be spatially proximate. Borders are socially constructed, multi-scalar, and variable in their durability and permeability. Furthermore, both borders and culture are interacting more extensively and constantly. The interplay of a broadened, more malleable, more elaborately scaled, more demonstrative, and more accessible array of cultural ideas, with a more extensive and intensive display of borders, prevails around the globe. This heightened interaction of borders and culture suggests that capturing the imagination and materialization of culture across boundaries may provide a rich insight to how borders work, how people deal with the boundaries, and how humans create and reconstruct borderlands. The culture that we produce not only meets at borders, but also borders become cultural constructions that are often more evident and demonstrative of the act of dealing with boundaries. In an ostensibly borderless world, the evident processes of bordering, de-bordering, and re-bordering, and the boundaries, barriers, fences, and walls themselves, combine to produce complex and sometimes conflicting manifestations of border culture. The porous and selective nature of borders to flows of goods, people, and ideas plays differentially with an array of cultural expressions that are encountered at and near the boundary. Understanding this interplay is the broader goal of this book; understanding the relationship between the components of this interplay is the basis of this chapter.

One objective of this chapter is to examine critically the interaction of borders and culture. Another aim is to evaluate how notions of border culture, cultural borders, and borderlands culture emerged in the establishment and successive development of anthropology, geography, and geopolitics. We begin with a re-reading of classical border culture: from Ratzel to Boas to Barth. The discussion explores how borders and culture have dominated early thought and migrated vicariously between the fields of anthropology and geography. The chapter traces how borders and culture were viewed in studies of spaces and places, in evaluations of the cultural landscape, and in early thought about borderlands. It assesses the impact of the cultural turn, postcolonial studies, and the initial focus on transnationalism on thinking about the intersection of borders and culture. Then, symbolically, with the beginning of the twenty-first century, borders and culture are situated in a more political cultural geography, in landscapes of domination, power relations, identity, and the politics of difference, and viewed through lenses of critical geography and anthropology. Borders and culture are acknowledged in motion, as edge places and spaces that emerge as more prominent, and often as locations for resistance. An aesthetic turn in border culture becomes apparent; culture at the border becomes ritualized. Yet, theories of culture and border remain grounded in an essentialist view of culture and border, in both a "territorial trap" and a "cultural trap", and, increasingly, challenged in multicultural society because intense contacts between various cultural carriers blur the clarity of demarcation lines.

2.2 The interaction of culture and borders and the emergence of border culture

In his brief polemic, "Culture across borders in the Americas", Seth Fein (2003) situates the border at the nexus of the international and transnational, territorial and extraterritorial, and political economy and socio-culture. True, borders divide territory but they do a lot more in a globalizing world of contact zones, asymmetrical relationships, increasing flows, and displacements. Fein views culture as related to and influenced by power. In this sense he follows Don Mitchell (2000, 74–75), who states that

> there is no culture in the world, only differing arrays of power that organize society in this way, and not that. Hence there is only a powerful idea of culture, an idea that has developed under specific historical conditions and was later broadened as a means of explaining material differences, social order, and relations of power.

Yet, according to Fein, the cultural turn in the social sciences has intensified scholars' needs to problematize and define how power and culture interrelate and what they are. It may be that "all politics is cultural, and all culture is political" (Fein 2003, 4), but we are left unfulfilled in our understanding of how and what culture manifests as it intersects with borders. The transnational regimes of knowledge (Krige 2019), identified by Monika Nerland (2010) in her study of international standards and practices in computer engineering, are based on transferable and sustainable discourses. In a Foucauldian perspective, these discourses incorporate relations of power and knowledge that have a productive function upon the social world, and these standards operate as soft regulation that crosses borders (Foucault 1972, 1980, 1994).These discourses and the knowledge that they encompass are key forms of international power, and they are also key elements in defining border culture (Konrad and Nicol 2011). Understanding border culture entails relating international forces operating between nations to transnational forces produced by the presence of one nation within another (Fein 2003), to capture both the "essential" and the "imagined" qualities of hybridization and differentiation at borders and in borderlands (Shimoni 2006).

Border culture is a "poly-semantic term" that has many different meanings which include "a transcultural friendship and collaboration among races, sexes and generations", "a way to analyze critically all that lies on the current tables of debates", and "hybrid art forms for new contents-in-gestation" (Gómez-Peña 1986). Border culture, then, may lead us beyond borders, and this is certainly the aim of many artists like Guillermo Gómez-Peña who recognize the borders in everyday life and how multifaceted they actually are, while they attempt to break these borders down. Whereas our aim is more academic, it still engages with the intricacies of border culture. Consequently, border culture as viewed and defined in this book embraces the polysemic variability of the term while the focus is grounded in its emergence and understanding in the social sciences.

Numerous scholars have enlarged the conception of culture as a social construction, and they have related culture to borders by exploring the link between identity and spatiality. In Francophone geography, Paul Vidal de la Blache's (1896) regional geography is based on the quest for the correspondence between a physical environment, from geomorphology and biogeography, to human settlements and "styles de vie". Jacques Ancel (1938) expands this thought and relates it specifically to borders. Claude Raffestin, a pioneer in the study of relational spaces, has worked extensively on borders since the 1970s (Raffestin 1974, 1977, 1980, 1986, 2012). The contributions of Raffestin and other Francophone geographers, and the limits to the circulation of ideas within Francophone political geography, and between Francophone and Anglophone dialogues in political geography, are assessed by Juliet Fall (2007, 2012), Juliet Fall and Stephane Rosière (2008), and Francisco Klauser (2012).Although the dialogue between Francophone and Anglophone schools of thought on borders has been enhanced in the last decade of border research, the challenge remains to engage a global exchange of border theory to include insights from the Luso-Hispanic, Asian, and other perspectives. Understanding border culture theory offers a bridge in this regard.

Border culture theory re-emerged as a focus of attention in border studies during the 1980s. Among the leading proponents, Gloria Anzaldúa (1987) and Jose David Saldívar (1997) identified and positioned border culture in contemporary thought about borders and culture by foregrounding the concept of borderlands and illustrating how culture engaged people with borders. Arjun Appadurai (1996) and David Held et al. (1994), among many other authors, have evaluated the cultural dimensions of globalization, and in so doing they have acknowledged at least to some degree, and commented on, the intersection of culture and borders. In a more focused way, Scott Michaelsen and David Johnson (1997) have explored the limits of cultural politics at borders and at borderlands, and offered among the first major statements on border and culture theory. At this early point in the theorizing about borders and culture, Anssi Paasi (1999) ascribed boundaries as social practice and discourse, and Thomas Wilson and Hastings Donnan (1998) explored border identities. Social practice encompassed identity and borderland identity crystallized social practice at the border. In recent decades the research and writing about borderland identities has burgeoned (Bonnemaison and Crambrézy 1996, Grimson 1999, Prokkola 2009).

Ramón Saldívar (2006) has moved thought on border culture from identities in another direction to examine borders and borderlands as transnational imaginaries. Also, recently, theorists in border studies have situated culture into emerging border theory (Brunet-Jailly 2005, Kramsch 2010, Konrad and Nicol 2008, 2011). Current research on borders and culture is exploring how walls and other border barriers are intersecting with cultural flows and expressions (Alvarez Perez and Berger 2009, Schimanski and Wolfe 2007, 2017, Dear et al. 2011, Dear 2013). Among these research trajectories, three directions of study require more exploration and reflection. The first direction is to situate the intersection of culture and borders in theory, and to evaluate how the theory emerged. Arising from this investigation are two research directions that require more attention and thought. They are the illumination of border culture in the spatial and cultural turns of the social sciences, and then in emerging globalization.

In the twenty-first century, both culture and borders remain over-determined concepts in human efforts to imagine and comprehend a world that is increasingly characterized by both flows and barriers. In this world, culture is everywhere yet nowhere; culture is an idea ever more produced and re-produced by society (Mitchell 2000). Similar to culture, borders are often more or less than they appear to be. In the twenty-first century, borders are emerging as filters and conduits, and simultaneously as more insurmountable barriers. More borders are being established, and the walls and fences at an increasing number of these boundaries are becoming more evident and effective as barriers, particularly to those without the means and proper identity confirmation to transit the borders (Brown 2010). Contemporary societies are situated and expressed at the intersection of culture and borders in globalization wherein de-bordering and re-bordering, borders that open and close at the same time, and borderities predominate (Amilhat Szary and Giraut 2015).

2.2.1 Classical border culture theory

This kind of thinking about border culture and cultural borders, as somehow intersecting, needs to be located within the evolving thought about territory, borders, and culture that has vicariously migrated between the fields of anthropology and geography since their inception, under the auspices of what was to be called "national methodologism"; i.e. a way of framing scientific investigation within the boundaries of a national knowledge in which the perimeter would be taken for granted (Derin, 2014). This is a timely investigation introduced in Stuart Elden's (2013) recent exploration of *The Birth of Territory* as a "political technology", a concept introduced by Michel Foucault (1984). If the emergence of territory may be conceptualized as a "political technology", then perhaps it may be valid to conceptualize culture operating at borders as an agency of political technology enabling both territorial delimitation and convergence.

In hindsight, one of the great misconceptions in both classical geopolitics and cultural anthropology was to view the nation and the state as bounded territory, both by nature and by culture. In this conceptualization, the significance of borders was underestimated and diminished immediately by Friedrich Ratzel (1940) and his contemporaries and followers in their visualization of "raum" or space, because this political and cultural space was viewed as a container of the organic state, which would ultimately spread organically and grow beyond its boundaries, including on cultural proximity criteria. This thinking, first organic state theory and then successively notions of "lebensraum" (life space) and "weltmacht" (world power), was influenced by the powerful mobile and evolutionary thought of Malthus, Darwin, Turner, and their acolytes. In the late nineteenth century, culture became interpreted as "superorganic" by Herbert Spencer and his followers (Gray 1996, Francis 2007) whereas borders became less significant, and receded before the flow of organized, enlightened, resourceful, and entitled people. The frontier was viewed as a zone of transition and a peripheral organ of the state (Cahnman 1944), and "kultur" (culture) was viewed as the embodiment of the state (Ratzel 1940).

It is in Ratzel's intertwining of anthropology, politics, and geography that the notions of border culture and cultural border are born. These ideas were then extended by his students, among them Rudolf Kjellen (1917), who emphasized the importance of social culture (Gesellschaft) as an organizing factor in forming the nation-state, and nationalism as the driving force for the nation-state (Tunander 2005). Karl Haushofer (1938) linked geopolitical concepts of "lebensraum" and frontier with ideas of strategic control and struggle for hegemony. Whereas these concepts did help to shape the ideology of the Third Reich, they also have influenced other world powers to expand cultural dominance and territorial control (Weigert 1942). During this formative period of thinking about territory, borders, and culture, Nicholas Spykman (1938, 1942) focused his conceptualization of geopolitics on the rimlands introduced by Halford Mackinder (1904, 1919). Focusing on the global powerplay in WWII, Spykman re-established the base for integrating frontiers and borders into the discourse of geopolitics, although the preoccupation with post-WWII containment theory (Kennan 1991) largely diverted attention from borders and borderlands. Whereas Saul Cohen (2003) developed concepts of gateways and shatterbelts, and introduced a hierarchy of geopolitical scales from the subnational to the geostrategic to the global, in geography it was Julian Minghi (1963) who re-built the groundwork for cultural border studies. Although his work did not offer a theory of borders, it did place culture within an emerging framework for understanding borders in a geopolitical context, and Minghi did focus on culture as a way to grasp border realities anew. On the other hand, Donald Meinig did relate culture and territory without dealing explicitly with borders although his model of the Mormon culture region acknowledged margins and borderlands (Meinig 1970). On his side of the argument, Robert David Sack (1986, 6–10) defines explicitly how culture operates among the Chippewa to enable a conception of shifting territory and mobile borders. Most geographers, however, particularly in the Anglophone world, would not revitalize border studies until the 1980s and 1990s with the advent of a changing world order and the imperatives of transnational forces, at once calling into question the relevance of borders and establishing their significance as social constructs (Foucher 1984, 1986, 1991, Newman and Paasi 1998). More recently, there has emerged a virtual worldwide obsession with borders (Foucher 2007).

Let us now step back into the realm of anthropology where we find Franz Boas, influenced by Ratzel and attributed with establishing academic anthropology (Stocking 1974, Cole 1999), defining cultural boundaries as coterminous with "nation" and ethnic delineations (Boas 1938, 1940). Boas conceptualized borders as separating culture areas and, concurrently, differentiating cultural traits across and between culture areas. Diffusion occurred when a cultural trait crossed a border, since the border was visualized as a permeable boundary, allowing some cultural traits to cross but altering others or filtering them out (Boas 1940, 250–252). Yet, Boas distanced himself from the deterministic and evolutionist ideas prevailing in emerging anthropology, and initiated the theoretical basis of modern cultural relativism (Lewis 2001). His work and professional papers need to be re-read to explore just how far he ventured beyond thinking about cultures as "A" and "B", and his allowance for a richer understanding of transition and hybridization. The idea of culture "still displays …Boas' meandering footprints" and it is this "workable ambiguity that was to be one of the ingredients of his, and our, concept of culture" (Livon 2003). One of Boas' many students, and a colleague of geographer Carl Sauer at Berkeley, Alfred Kroeber asserted that culture develops its own unique style patterns, and that culture is organized symbols expressive of underlying values. The resulting cultural goals, ideals, and orientations become fixed, and if the style pattern becomes fully realized a cultural climax would occur, with eventual fatigue and the decline of the culture (Kroeber 1944). Territories and borders are implicit if not explicit in Kroeber's work, just as the sense of cultural boundary as coterminous with nation was acknowledged in Boas' work. Few anthropologists explored cultural borders during the following decades. It was as if the cultural boundary was implicit and taken for granted in foundational anthropological studies of cultures around the globe.

In the 1960s, Fredrik Barth (1969) again drew attention to boundaries and culture in his hallmark work *Ethnic Groups and Boundaries: The Social Organization of Culture Difference*. The book is often touted as the transition to a new era of ethnic studies, but it is also the seminal work on borders in anthropology. In it, Barth and his colleagues initiate attention to the boundaries of ethnic groups, examine interdependence and symbiosis across boundaries, evaluate the persistence of cultural borders, explore differentiation, dichotomization, and integration across boundaries, assess identity maintenance across the border, and more. All of these considerations about borders and culture appear contemporary, but, whereas this collection of essays would persevere as an acknowledged turning point in ethnic studies, the work did not inspire a shift in attention towards borders in anthropology, in part because the discipline, only recently parted from its sibling geography, was not ready to contend with territory. Yet, Barth did establish an important insight that would become significant in all fields of border studies: the border is not a fixed line but rather a zone of transition.

2.2.2 Spatial and cultural turns

It was not until the 1980s and 1990s with the spatial turn that the relationship between culture and territory became more dominant in the discourse of anthropology (Geertz 1973, Goodenough 1981, Erickson 1997, Lugo 1997). A new understanding emerged. If cultures are separate long enough, a border will form

(China and Taiwan); if cultures are separate enough a border will form (Russia and Ukraine). Some borders are porous and conducive to interrelationship (U.S. and Canada), whereas others stand firm to differentiate cultures and nation-states (Spain and Portugal). Also, the border is viewed as a symbol of power, which differentiates it from a boundary (Erickson 1997). This conceptualization of symbolic power continues to resonate in contemporary explorations of cultures and borders in anthropology (Bromberger and Morel 2001, Chang 2010).

After the cultural turn of the 1980s—a moment when the national level as an *a priori* semantic horizon was being overtaken, and as the possibility of acknowledging multiple and multiscalar identities was again possible—cultural studies in the humanities and the social sciences envisioned social reality as constructed linguistically and socially, and phenomena explored as representations through narrative, discourse, rhetoric, and visual arts (Jameson 2009). Scholars began differentiating the cultural border and border culture on the basis of imagination as well as power (Johnson and Michaelsen 1997). It became understandable that imaginaries of the border contributed to the social construction of borders as well as the power wielded by the state and other agents. Transnationalism cued borderlands (Schiller et al. 1992), and the borderlands of culture emerged as a transnational imaginary (Saldívar 2006). Cultural studies evolved from a focus on migration and identity formation in borderlands to the literature and art dedicated to borders and borderlands *per se* (Anzaldúa 1987, Alvarez 1995).

Borderlands were visualized as liminal and hybrid spaces (Bhabbha 1994, Kraidy 2005) inhabited by cultures that could not revert into previously existing forms (Gupta and Ferguson 1992, 1997). These cultures—hybrid, in-between, transitional, sometimes ephemeral, energized, innovative, transnational—provided laboratories for studying identity formation, cultural hybridity, Indigeneity, migration, and power relations. The studies were influenced by post-structuralist thinkers like Foucault (plurality of knowledge and discourse as power), Derrida (deconstruction and differance), Butler (power of gender differentiation, sexuality, and language), Lacan (intersubjectivity and organizational identity discourse), Deleuze (recreation of the boundaries of life), and others who provided new insights into power, discourse, and the construction of difference. The overall achievement of the cultural turn as it relates to border studies has been to liberate the concept of border culture from its anthropo-geographical anchoring at the intersection of classical geopolitics, emergent geography, and incipient anthropology, and to refresh the conceptualization of culture at borders with re-vitalized exploration of identity, affinity, and imagination in the borderlands (Konrad 2012).

2.2.3 *Colonial and postcolonial borders: The shift to postcolonial border culture*

Oliver Thomas Kramsch (2002, 169) recognized that "territorial dynamics of European cross-border regionalism were embedded within a larger geo-historical framework including imperialism overseas", and that border studies were obliged to "engage with broader post-colonial debates". In a sense, postcolonial resistance retroactively constructs European metropolitan cultures. Yet, Matthew Sparke (2002, 203) asks: "How do cross-border regions crystallize novel post-national and postcolonial forms of state making when, all the while, they remain haunted by national and colonial patterns of en-framing?" The shift to postcolonial border culture is a graded, uneven, incomplete, and unsettling shift in exchanges and intersections across ethnic and cultural lines, and a shift to new cultural forms enshrining both *Hybridity and its Discontents* (Brah and Coombes 2000). Moreover, Chiara Brambilla (2014) has noted shifting Italian–Libyan borderscapes, and a blurring of historical borders along all of geopolitical, socio-cultural, economic, and ethnic lines as the colonial era evolved into postcolonial scenarios. This shift has resulted in a multiplicity of material and epistemological borderlands. Whereas most postcolonial scholars have acknowledged the importance of understanding postcolonial intersections (Hawley 1996, Childs and Williams 2014 [1997], Darian-Smith 1996, Ashcroft 2001, Featherstone 2005), these intersections are more explicitly inter-cultural rather than engaged in the exploration of culture at or across boundaries. The key concepts attributed to postcolonial studies do not generally include postcolonial border culture (Ashcroft et al. 2013), although Walter Mignolo (2000) argues for the contribution of subaltern knowledges to border thinking.

More recent engagements with postcolonialism, however, do note the focus of a new generation of postcolonial scholars on unstable yet productive cultural borders (Jazeel 2019). Inherent in this approach is a determination to develop an integrated perspective on geography and encounter, that is to relate bodies, borders, and difference (Wilson 2017). Border culture is increasingly about the troubling of authority, the definition of rightful presence, and the exercise of power, and this produces materially separate cultural spaces. There is a postcolonial alternative to national identity, and this identity is expressed beyond borders in incipient forms of cosmopolitan identity. However, as Riad Nasser (2019) illustrates in a study of identities in Jordan, Israel, and Palestine, the Western notion of identity formation remains logocentric and binary, rooted in the relational self and other. Understanding postcolonial border culture requires rethinking the time and space of "resilience" beyond the West (Wandji 2019).

2.2.4 Culture and borders in globalization

This book addresses culture and borders in the context of globalization in an effort to position our approach to the study of social construction of culture and borders, and the intersection of borders and culture in a changing, globalizing, and now apparently post-globalization world (Konrad 2021). We view culture as an "evolving framework for encoding the meaning of border" (Konrad and Nicol 2008, 292). Border culture is coded geopolitically into popular as well as "high" culture representations, among other forms of codes such as time/space models of the world, national myths, territorial narratives, active/passive approaches to international relations, and reactions to international crises (Dijkink 1998). "Culture is now a verb to signify the struggle to establish value for the borderlands spaces and places in between" (Konrad and Nicol 2011, 86). In one sense the interplay of culture and borders in globalization is creating or sustaining cultural islands within a cultural mosaic. The cultural components may be spatially distinct, contiguous, or arrayed in transition, yet in all instances bordering a globalizing world. Also, borders, like culture, are in constant motion, produced, adjusted, and re-produced by the societies that share these edges and interact across them (Konrad 2015). Yet, "teichopolitics", the building of walls and barriers at borders, has intervened to reduce, modify, and even halt differentially the flows of globalization across and through boundaries (Rosière and Jones 2012). The response, far from seeing culture neutralized or stopped at the border, has often been strident and resonant, with representations of culture and expressions of resistance marked on the walls and barriers themselves (Amilhat Szary 2012).

Culture in the twenty-first century increasingly is inhabiting the borderlands as well as the borderlines to display and express extended zones of transition beyond borders between states, regions, and communities (Konrad 2014). In some instances, the contemporary Ukraine for example, borderlands appear to be reverting to bordered lands (Zhurzhenko 2010), whereas in the case of the U.S.–Mexico border this situation has prevailed for 50 years. These borderlands landscapes convey the dialectic of cultural continuity and cultural discontinuity, and confront the meaning of border in a zone of interaction that is neither here nor there. These are geographies of in-betweenness and grey zones, very much present in the global south where many borders are less (or used to be less) demarcated (Meier 2020). In these borderlands, as elsewhere around the world, identity is formed and re-formed among those who claim Indigeneity, and others who cannot claim their roots in a place. In the borderlands, pressures towards homogeneity in cultural identity vie with the more extensive forces of heterogeneity to diffuse identities (Chaturvedi 2005). The borderlands culture, as illustrated in the American and British Virgin Islands, conveys at once plural expressions of identity and singular imperatives of belonging (Konrad and Everitt 2011). Long-time residents of both the British and American Virgin Islands are all Virgin Islanders, and they share common ancestries and lifeways. Yet, the border between American and British descent and citizenship is emphasized boldly. Even more emphatic boundaries are drawn between "belongers" who trace roots in the British Virgin Islands to the founding slave population (but not the autochthonous inhabitants who were decimated), and the waves of expatriates from elsewhere who now call the islands home. In the Virgin Islands, belongingness is even more important than the international border between the United Kingdom and the U.S. The intersection of borders and culture is scaled yet set in place and time, ambiguous to outsiders, yet profoundly clear to those who belong in the borderlands.

2.3 Emerging border culture theory

Border culture is important to border specialists who need to understand the role of culture in how borders work. Furthermore, social analysis in general requires a grasp of border culture because unitary "one-state-one-territory" and "one-society-one-culture" conceptualizations have been challenged (Rosaldo, 1989) and now displaced (Heyman, 2012), and this questions the nation-state narrative. Therefore, this brings forward the idea and construction of border culture, and it establishes border culture as a subject for theoretical scrutiny since, clearly, in globalization, borders and culture do not align, if they ever did. Key ideas and debates about border cultures have originated in border contexts worldwide, and this diversity has enriched the development of border culture theory, and theory in border studies more broadly (Donnan and Wilson, 1999). Yet, one border region—the U.S.–Mexico border—in particular, has contributed most substantially to the main debate which engaged theorists embracing and celebrating border cultural hybridity (Anzaldúa 1987, Rosaldo 1989) with respondents who focused on cultural and identity separation, distinction, and polarization (Villa, 2000, Vila 2003).

Josiah (Joe) Heyman (2012, 48–50) critiques these positions and calls for an understanding that both hybridity/resistance to boundaries and polarization/embracing of state boundaries are emergent features of "deep socio-historical processes". He offers a perspective on this debate which essentially removes the stand-off based on binary assumptions such as that national interiors are unitary whereas border areas blend and combine, that there are distinctive non-state or even anti-state cultural formations at borders, and that borders characteristically polarize. Heyman (2012, 51) offers three culture forming processes. First, he suggests that some processes reinforce borders as they differentiate and underscore established powerful polarizations. He cites nationalistic education and massive border security build-ups to illustrate such processes. Second, Heyman acknowledges that there are border defying and hybridizing processes especially in the borderlands. Examples include elites who collaborate and do business across the border, and, at the other end of the social spectrum, the poor who cut across the border, or at least try to access the other side. Finally, there are processes of combined and uneven development that pervade the border region. These processes have differentiated, unequal social components that are usually in an unbalanced relationship of exchange, or an asymmetry. The results are neither separation nor blending but are expressed in cultural connection, mutual recognition, sometimes sharing, and a perpetuation of inequalities and distinctions. So, according to Heyman, the debate distracts from the complexity of intertwined processes that, in reality, characterize the borderlands. We would add that the debate also questions the binaries that have always defined border and framing, and by extension, the theorizing of border culture. In addition, the typology is limiting and perhaps too caricatural to convey the complexity and fluidity of border culture processes.

An important essay by David E. Johnson and Scott Michaelsen (1997) published more than twenty years ago, and another by Alejandro Lugo (1997), in the same book, assemble the theoretical insights about border culture just before the turn of the century, at a time when border studies were still largely being pursued independently in traditional disciplines. Yet, the "reflections" of these authors recognize the emerging anti-disciplinarity of border studies that challenges border dominations, and by extension the domination of one culture over another (Lugo, 1997). Titled as "Border secrets", the essay by Johnson and Michaelsen points to borderlands as a privileged locus of hope for a better world, a space of crossroads, new ground for determining and securing relation, a place for celebrating difference that counts, and othering in a constructive sense (Johnson and Michaelsen, 1997, 2–5). In the borderlands, radical inclusivity, a kind of being in common among "peripherals" operates in concert with the limit of culture and the border of its possibility. Here there is acknowledgement if not acceptance of cultural difference, and an understanding that border crossing is necessary to cultural survival (Johnson and Michaelsen, 1997, 5–6). In retrospect, given what we have learned during recent decades about the durability of nation-state ideals and the vitality of nativism, these pronouncements appear optimistic if not naïve. Indeed, the "Limits of Cultural Politics" have been exceeded and expunged. The borderlands in many places around the globe, and certainly between Mexico and the U.S., are contested spaces populated with disenfranchised people, many originating from outside the borderlands, and scenes of violence, dislocation, and pathology. Border culture is as much about the contestation and trauma as it is about the newfound commonalities and the celebration of difference. Johnson and Michaelsen (1997, 2) do acknowledge that, amidst all of the discourses of border culture, the entry point of the border and the borderlands goes unquestioned. Border theory has not addressed the border, and, consequently theorizing border culture remains incomplete.

Social scientists engaged in border studies in the late twentieth century, and drawing from the advances in culture studies, envisioned the border as socially constructed (Raffestin 1986, Paasi 1996). This understanding and outright insistence that the border was not necessarily what it seemed to be, but could convey many perceptions by different people both in the borderlands and beyond, became one of the major contributions to border studies in the 1990s and early 2000s (Newman and Paasi 1998, Van Houtum et al. 2005, Popescu 2011). For researchers of border culture, this revelation initiated a focus on border and borderland identity studies that would weather the diversion into border security research in the wake of the events of 9/11, and extend into current research (Prokkola 2009).

Yet, culture is more than identity, and border culture encompasses imaginaries of all kinds, "popular culture and/at the border", Indigenous cultures and borders, literature, art, performance, and much more (Roberts and Stirrup 2013). Border culture is produced at the interface of imaginaries, languages, narratives, and the border. Evelyn P. Mayer (2014, 27–63) views this border culture through combined poetic and border prisms, or lenses that break up and differentiate closely combined border culture attributes. The poetic prism is situated in the cultural and literary turns in border studies, and the border prism is in the spatial turn of literatures and cultures. Our inclination is to further the conceptualization offered by Mayer, to link perspectives from the humanities and the social sciences, and, in keeping with Lugo (1997) to seek an anti-disciplinary contextualization for border culture (Bal 1999). Essentially, this approach builds on the model offered by Emmanuel Brunet-Jailly (2005) but it emphasizes the scaling of border culture within the wider framework of border theory. As outlined by Victor Konrad and Heather N. Nicol (2008, 55, 2011) it becomes possible to view multiple levels of cross-border culture linked with socially constructed and reconstructed identities. All of these dimensions of culture and identity are associated with cross-border political clout, market forces and trade flows, and political activities of multiple levels of government, and with power as an operative force. Whereas we continue to see the value of this conceptualization, it cannot encompass the various and diverse insights revealed recently as border culture is evaluated in the context of form, medium, genre, and aesthetical strategy. Theories of border culture need to acknowledge the border and make space and place for the cultural production. Furthermore, theories of border culture must grapple with social and political currents within and affecting the borderlands. Ultimately, theories of border culture must acknowledge and engage broader theoretical advances in border studies. The border is more than a line, and this book encompasses much more than the cultural becoming of cross-border regions that hybridize. The next part of this chapter addresses these concerns as it evaluates recent thought on border culture.

2.4 Border landscapes, borderscapes, dissensus, borders and cultural psychology, border culture in globalization, and the search for a theory of border culture

In her recent book *Looking Beyond Borderlines* Lee Rodney (2017, 200) concludes:

> The ambiguity of the Canadian border continues to surface as a point of contention in American politics as it is bound up in the ambiguity of Canadian culture and fraught with the tension between the unfinished narratives of past-settler colonialism and the recognition of contemporary de-colonial struggles. The US–Mexico border unambiguously cleaves the continent in half, and its unresolved tensions remain even stronger than they were in the 19th century. In this light, it is more important than ever to see borderlines as shifting and impermanent representational constructs, porous and permeable interfaces that offer the possibility of political change and negotiation.

This view of ever-increasing borderlines in globalization is optimistic because it conveys plurality of effort and experimentation, and it offers some hope of mediation between the lines delineated by culture and the spaces occupied by cultural representations. The key is in the title *Looking Beyond Borderlines* because, despite all the invocations to do so, border studies remain focused on the boundary with at least one eye. Keeping one eye on the borderline limits the binocular vision required to see like a border (Rumford 2011, 67). Instead of "seeing like a state", a constraining lens given the increasing heterotopia of contemporary borders (Scott 1998), seeing like a border allows us to conceptualize the multiple actors, sites, and cultural variables of "borderwork". Seeing like a border is visualizing and comprehending the multiscalar and multidimensional components that constitute borders and border cultures. Etienne Balibar (2002, 8–85) emphasizes that borders may be found "wherever selective controls are found", and we cannot comprehend seeing like a border by "being on the outside looking in". Bordering processes permeate everyday life, and as we pass through public spaces we encounter and experience the "frisk society" (Urry 2007). Seeing like a border is comprehending the constitutive nature of borders in social and political life (Rumford 2011). This constitutive nature of borders in social and political life is also the basis for shaping a sense of border culture.

In the search for theoretical grounding for the notion of border culture, several conceptual explorations have grappled with the cultural production accompanying borders and bordering. Some of this exploration has focused on border landscapes, and elided borderscapes, whereas other investigations have ventured into the post-functionalist debate on dissensus and the role of culture in the reconfiguration of borders in globalization. Let us focus on these theoretical explorations first, before we venture into the renewed theoretical territory in cultural psychology.

Border landscapes are repositories and reflections of border culture imagination, production, and representation (Prescott 1965). James Prescott builds this assessment on the insights of the Vidalian school in France and the cultural landscape trajectories in British and American geography during the early to middle twentieth century. Explorations of central European frontier regions by Emmanuel de Martonne, who drew the borders of central Europe at the Versailles Peace Conference (Hallair 2007, Bowd 2012), and the making of the English landscape by William George Hoskins (1955), are among the formative works on border landscapes in Europe. David Lowenthal (1991) expands this perspective with his work "British national identity and the English landscape". In North America, research by Wilbur Zelinsky (1959) on walls and fences cued numerous studies over several decades on border cultural indicators in border space. For example, certain barn types and woodpile configurations were established and sustained in the border regions between French Canada and New England as markers of culture that moved across the border, and in some instances these markers were hybridized (Konrad and Chaney 1982).The cultural landscape focus in geography during the 1960s through the 1980s also conceptualized frontiers and border regions such as the bounded Mormon culture region (Meinig 1970), and, addressed through elegant and compelling prose, the *Landscapes of Fear* apparent in border regions (Tuan 1979).

Yet, the concept of the border landscape or borderlands landscape is not sufficient to convey the rich interplay of border and culture that occurs at various scales in time and space. Borderscapes is an epistemological and methodological re-conceptualization of borders that is able to grasp the complex border landscapes of an era of globalization and transnationalism. Its aim is to promote the liberation of geopolitical imaginations from the straitjacket imposed by the pervasive methodological nationalism of the territorial trap (Brambilla 2015, Brambilla et al. 2015). The notion of borderscapes emerges from the writing of Arjun Appadurai (1996), the adaptation of the concept in geographical context by Rajaram and Grundy-Warr (2008), and the distilling and convening of this thought by Elena Dell'Agnese (2016) and others, especially within the collaborative framework of one successful research project funded by the EU, called EUBORDERSCAPES (Bordering, Political Landscapes and Social Arenas: Potentials and Challenges of Evolving Border Concepts in a post-Cold War World #FP7-SSH-2011), a consortium of twenty partners under the direction of J.W. Scott at the University of Eastern Finland in Joennsu. According to the researchers, borders are spaces of struggle, contest, and negotiation where socio-spatial identities emerge to question or re-frame territorial accounts of political belonging/exclusion. To understand these spaces, they argue, we must look beyond the identification of transnational flows and new geographies emerging from these "borderscapes" to a more relational account of the emergence of new forms of political belonging and reworked territorial practice and the concepts inherent in it. This will allow us to grasp more effectively the complexity of the modern political imaginary that underlies the production and representation of border culture. Borderscapes is an approach to bordering processes and borderlands. The concept is understood to be local configurations of bordering processes connecting different communities. These case-specific reflections convey how notions of border and perceptions of identity are conditioned by the interplay of historical, socio-cultural, geographical, and political narratives, as well as by the experience of living at and with borders. Borderscapes also reflect local politics of borders understood as framing of social arenas and political landscapes and strategies of accommodation, adaptation, and contestation. Borderscapes challenge the top-down geopolitical control of borders and privilege bottom-up perspectives (Brambilla 2015).

The borderscapes concept, moreover, forms an analytical angle to develop a wider understanding of the contemporary spatiality of politics, urging a political imperative in critical border studies based on a "multi-sited" approach at different levels or scales. This approach first requires an understanding of borders in space, and then projects the multiplicity of social spaces in which borders are negotiated by different actors, and also as border of sites for potential counter power and struggle (Brambilla and Jones 2019). Borders, as multidimensional entities, are then constituted in various symbolic and material forms and functions as well as socio-political and cultural practices. The borderscapes lens also allows us to grasp the dynamic nature of borders in space and time because borders are constantly moving (Balibar 2003, Amilhat Szary and Giraut 2015, Konrad 2015). "Thus, the borderscapes concept registers the necessity to investigate borders not as taken-for-granted entities exclusively connected to the territorial limits of nation-states, but as mobile, relational and contested sites, thereby exploring *alternative border imaginaries 'beyond the line'*" (Brambilla 2015, 17).

How can the borderscapes concept advance our understanding of border culture? First, the concept is intersectional: that is, it forms a nexus for understanding aspects of citizenship, identity, and otherness in the context of relationships between borders, forms of power, territory, and political systems. From this nexus, there may be critical questioning of the normative border as well as struggles and strategies of adaptation, contestation, and resistance surrounding it. There may also be interrogation of the interaction of in/visibility (Mountz 2011), space and power associated with each border regime, and how this interplay is reflected in border culture. Intersectionality also extends to the interconnection between the local and the global (Mignolo 2000), where even a small change in local border culture may have a global impact notably through social media (Balibar 2003). Second, the borderscapes concept is relational in that it accounts for the interaction of political visions and socio-cultural practices, social representations, and artistic imaginaries. Borderscapes enable complementary viewpoints on contemporary borders that consider the dialogic nature of bordering processes and imaginaries, and the tension between institutional and formal modes of political agency and social non-formal modes of agency that inhabit the borderscape (Dittmer and Gray, 2010). Third, borderscapes help us to clarify the relationship of the geopolitical imagination (as liberated from the territorialist (Agnew 1994) and colonialist (Gregory 2004) imperatives, with the social imaginary, and to illuminate the material basis for imaginary transformations and on the politics of the imagination as a concrete social practice (Appadurai 1996, 31). Finally, the borderscapes concept helps to bridge the metaphorical–material border gap whereby we may conceive of borders as active and contentious zones where ongoing, dialectical processes generate multiple borderlands spaces, both at and away from the boundary, and inhabited by multiple cultural imaginaries, productions, and representations.

> The major ongoing social shift in modernity has been one of democratization, in which peoples have been given voice, people made visible and social hierarchies leveled. This caused major political shifts such as nation-building and cultural shifts such as the creation of mass-market cultural production. In a postmodern, post-colonial, post-national and post-soviet era, we have seen a tendency to fragmentation and hybridization of cultural canons, nations, grand narratives, ideologies, materialities, identities, etc., simultaneous with (and perhaps dialectically connected to) a paradoxical

> resurgence of social differences and hierarchical control. These changes are clearly manifested in public discourses on multi-culturalism, neo-liberalism, migrant crises, electronic surveillance, sub-cultures, epidemics, social media, terrorism, cheap travel, climate change, etc. In line with these shifts, borders have shifted away from the edges of clearly defined national territories, been externalized or internalized, become both erased and spectacularized in the form of walls and security fences, etc. The academic response has been to develop concepts of borders such as bordering and borderscapes which are distributed, flexible and aware of the connections between borders on many different levels and scales. The challenge is to remain aware of the material violence and injustice present in many border situations and to create analytical tools which are resistant to being pre-opted in order to continue this violence and injustice.
>
> *(Laine et al. 2017)*

This excerpt from the final report of the EUBORDERSCAPES project contextualizes conceptual and theoretical development to show the active role of cultural production in bordering processes including representations and values in its potential to transform borders into creative spaces, build counter-hegemonic borderscapes in which other subjects are given visibility, mediate between private experiences of borders and the public imaginaries, form practices and norms through the political/aesthetic nexus, experimentally develop new border concepts through border figures, and de-spectacularize political and medial narratives of border crises by introducing new levels of discourse to the public sphere.

One role of cultural production is to de-familiarize the level of discourse in the public sphere. The de-familiarization may be accomplished by offering discursive bridges or geopolitical border crossings between the private and public spheres associated with borders. Personal and private experiences with the border need to link with public rhetorics. In this way, creative collaboration between performative cultural production and research extends the role of cultural production. Yet, there are ethical paradoxes and political ambivalences of border culture production, and these may contribute to hegemonic and counter-hegemonic borderscaping. Specifically, EUBORDERSCAPES mapped a wide array of border figures accessible in art, film, and literature to confirm and enlarge border concepts. Among these are distributed narratives of multiple border crossings on different levels to illustrate the disseminated border, border spaces of captivity, limbo and panic, borders as places of negotiation between tradition and modernity, sonic and culinary borderscapes, and borderscapes as memoryscapes, traumascapes, gothic dystopias, and utopian idylls (Ristoleinin 2014). Clearly, the borderscape is "plurivocal" and "multi-agential", and also in keeping with the space encompassing border culture, it is both top-down and bottom-up, and both human/institutional and material/discursive.

Narratives and images are among the many expressions of border culture production that are part of borderscapes, in which bordercrossings and bordering processes take place and contribute to the negotiation of borders in the public sphere. These aesthetic forms are central to the political process characterized by Jacques Rancière (2015) as a "partage du sensible", or a splitting, redistribution, and partaking of the sensible. This division and sharing, according to Rancière, is disaggregated through numerous forms of othering, bordering on a ubiquitous anomie, or an instability and breakdown of standards and values. To unpack this idea we need to follow Rancière's logic, which begins with the notion that the ways in which human communities are spontaneously counted as wholes are divisible into their constitutive parts and functions. Rancière wants to tear these bodies from their assigned places, and to cut across forms of culture, identity, and belonging to introduce new subjects and heterogeneous objects into the field of perception. The aim is to reorient perceptual space and disrupt belonging. Rancière sees this disruption as a process of equality in which there are two forms of exceptionality. Consensus, in the context of border culture, is the agreement on the territorial boundary, matching *poeisis* (way of doing) with *aesthesis* (horizon of affects). In consensus, the political and social are meshed, as are culture and commerce, and proper places and proper functions are attributed to all. Dissensus demonstrates the impropriety which disrupts identity and reveals a gap between *poeisis* and *aesthesis* thus calling into question the border and cultural constructs associated with it. Dissensus is about blurring the boundaries that are permeated and suffocated by the notion of consensus and creating aesthetics that are relational.

As Jane Helleiner (2016) implies in her study of borders and everyday nationalism in Niagara Falls, border culture is indeed personalized and disaggregated. We could, perhaps, view border culture as many points of multi-coloured light within a borderland. In her work on Niagara Falls, Helleiner articulates the complex ways in which everyday nationalism at the border works across region, class, race, and gender. It also disconnects between elite border projects and the concerns of ordinary citizens, and essentially, it results in differing views on national belonging. Clearly, borders mean different things to different people. Those who have the occasion to cross and inhabit the border gain a variety of insights about how the border works, the impact that the border has on residents, occasional crossers, and those who do not cross at all. They all are associated with and relate to different border cultures. Sandra Vandervalk (2017, 2021) found that Canadian residents of Stanstead, Quebec, ascribe different meanings to border landmarks and practices than Americans in adjacent Derby Line, Vermont, whereas borderlanders on both sides of the line hold common understanding of cross-border community and shared facilities. Borderland inhabitants of these towns construct a border "game" to establish their intimate knowledge of the border and their "ownership" of cross-border territory and practice. The game brings them together across the border divide because, as border security is enhanced, the meaning of the border becomes increasingly divergent, and the game underscores that the locals own the border by right of occupancy and continuity.

May we then view the border as an agent of dissensus and the borderlands as a zone of consensus as in any other type of region? The possibility of this simplification is appealing, yet, when we examine cultural production at borders and in the borderlands, we discover that the border both connects and divides, and that the borderlands are spaces and places of connectivity and commonality yet concurrently separation and estrangement. Also, border culture ameliorates occupancy and levels the space in both instances. Perhaps it is most constructive and contributive to conceptualize border culture as a meta-form in border contexts. In some instances, it acts as a metaphor, in some instances it is metabolic, in some instances it is meta-genetic, in some instances it is metamorphic, and so on. This condition of metastasis (transformation, inversion, transference, trope) combined with the condition of metayage (joint possession) captures, in our minds at least, some of the very elusive nature of culture at the edge.

As we discussed in the beginning of this chapter, understanding border culture requires a psychological perspective in border studies. This perspective has roots in Francophone and Anglophone geographical research on territory and borders by pioneers including Jean Gottmann (1952, 1973, 1980) who consistently sought explanations for why humans partition space. Luca Muscarà (2020) has re-engaged with Gottmann's work in order to unpack the intertwining of territory, psychology, and communication technologies to expose what Muscarà terms the "great swindle of nationalist sovereigntism".

Also contributing to our understanding of border culture is recent research in the field of cultural psychology. The underlying premise of this work is that "psychological phenomena take place at the border between person and environment", and the central question becomes "how do humans deal with such transitions throughout the course of their lives?" (Marsico and Varzi 2016, 327). Giuseppina Marsico (2011) conveys a concept of a "non-cuttable" cultural space in between, which is naturally fluid. In border studies we call these spaces borderlands, and this conceptualization of borderlands has now entered the theory and vocabulary of cultural psychology (Marsico 2016).

> From a cultural psychological standpoint, borders are conceived as a way of creating distinctions in the fluid flow of events, and therefore, as a psychological tool for structuring personal relationships with the environment. The moment it is created and starts to regulate the world outside us, it is also internalized and acts to modulate our minds as well. Yet, the distinctions produced by the border-making process are not always so clear. Hence ambiguity remains a fundamental aspect of borders. The richness of the concept resides in this characteristic. The inherent ambivalence of the border creates a space for negotiation and dialogue, but also it creates a space where misunderstanding and possible confusion may arise.
>
> *(Espanol et al. 2019, 123)*

Franco La Cecla (2002) adds that misunderstanding is indeed a condition for the existence of a functional borderland. Border culture is formed and displayed within a

> triadic system (inside<>border<>outside) that emerges, exists and vanishes together. This provides us with an innovative conceptual apparatus based on a triadic, co-genetic, epistemological approach that enables us to overcome the binary oppositions still very much present in contemporary debates in the field of border studies.
>
> *(Espanol et al. 2019, 123–124)*

Elise Pestre (2021) explores a dialogue of geopolitical borders and psychic borders in her research on cross-border migrants. Borders recur and enduringly affect psyches and bodies of migrants. For migrants, the border experience de-subjectivizes as much as it opens up the possibility of re-subjectivation. Accordingly, de-territorialization and re-territorialization become locked in a permanent dialectic and borders in the mind keep coming back. The theoretical re-encounter of contemporary border studies and cultural psychology has just begun (Konrad 2020), and it remains to realize the potential of this interaction.

Clearly, more thought is required on this enduring dilemma of the interaction of culture and the border, but some of the facets of this relationship are becoming more evident as theorists explore the intersection and proliferation of culture and borders in globalization (Konrad and Kelly 2021). In our estimation, more thought needs to focus on the meaning of border culture because, as demonstrated by Saleebey (1994), culture gives meaning to action by situating underlying states in an interpretive system. Our continuing goal needs to be to discern the meaning of culture at the border, and to articulate and understand the border culture or interpretive system that evolves.

2.5 Integrating border culture themes and theory

The practice of cultural analysis requires a definition of present culture, and, according to Mieke Bal (1999, 1) present culture may be summarized as "cultural memory in the present". Cultural analysis seeks to understand the past as part of the present, as what we have around us, and without which no culture would be able to exist. This makes cultural analysis inherently self-reflexive. "[Marshall] McLuhan's view of contemporary culture as a degenerative vortex into which the great myths of romanticism tumble like fragments of a shipwreck caught in the maelstrom may seem too overheated as a portrayal of the post-semiological critic's field of operation". But, "there still remains the necessity of defining the historical viewpoint in relation to the dialectic of loss and desire which romanticism set in place" (Bann 1999, 127). In contemporary border studies, and particularly in border culture analysis, the historical viewpoint needs to be constantly at hand.

Bal also acknowledges that cultural analysis is accomplished through situation in space/place, and that a more important place needs to be made for the spatial coordinates that define culture not as a collection of things but as a process. This manifestation of space/place extends beyond the distinction between linguistic and visual or aural artifacts (Bal 1999, 6–11). We suggest that it follows that cultural analysis of borders places self, memory, and space in between and on a live edge of process. Also, it is at the border where cultural analysis encounters "double exposures" (Bal 2012) and where currents of cultural process encounter change and resistance.

In border culture, there are cross-currents everywhere, because that is the condition of culture, and the intersection of borders and culture. Imaginaries and productions of culture at the border are intertwined at all scales and linked to memory, and what is essentially local may at the same time be viewed as global in its significance. Consider, for example, the artistic renditions on the Israeli–Palestinian Security Wall (Figure 2.2). These drawings focus on place and locality but espouse universals of human rights and freedom (Falke 2012). In another illustration not shown, but widely recognized, the renowned artist Banksy conveys the buoyancy of resistant spirit with a figure of a girl and balloon ascending on the Security Wall meant to contain and control the resistance, yet local inhabitants do not all like or accept Banksy's murals as reflective of their border reality, claiming that they do not wish to be taken beyond the ugly reality of the fence, since that would take them away from fighting it.

FIGURE 2.2 Imagining Beyond the Wall between Israel and the West Bank. Photo by Anne-Laure Amilhat Szary.

Within the borders and culture theme, there are, however, some clusters of cultural representation evident at borders and in borderlands. Prominent among these clusters are expressions of popular culture found in music (Valenzuela Arce 1998) and film (Dell'Agnese 2005). In art,

> Awareness of the precariousness and contingency of popular culture should counteract another danger that is always present when attention concentrates on artistic forms of expression, especially visual representations such as painting. This danger is the possibility that political experience, as well as critique, may be aestheticized and thereby removed from practice on the ground level. Actually, this raises two questions. One is whether a given interpretation aestheticizes expressions of popular culture, and the other is whether popular culture itself aestheticizes experience. As I see it, it is necessary to voice such concerns, but it would seem that the lessons we have learned, say, from studies of fascism and its aesthetics should make it impossible to entertain notions of pure, apolitical aesthetics (or art, or culture). Conversely, it does not follow that the political critique aesthetically expressed and institutionalized in the medium of popular painting is politically of no consequence.
>
> *(Fabian 1999, 254)*

In this book, we continually explore the representation of art at and of borders as political critique aesthetically expressed.

"Border art" (Berlowitz 2003), an expression from the Border Art Workshop/Taller de Arte Fronterizo formed in 1984, may be envisioned in its more comprehensive and encompassing expression as containing both border imaginaries and border artistic expression including literature, poetry, theatre, dance, painting, performance art, architecture, graffiti, and much more. A great deal of this art is expressed as visual border culture to question and even interrogate bordering and re-bordering trends (Rogoff 2000, Grison 2002, Amilhat Szary 2012). Even trash may be considered creative border culture as seen in the garbage jettisoned by migrants crossing the desert astride the U.S.–Mexico border (Sundberg 2008).

Another cluster of cultural representation at borders is found in the study of hybridity, which has been informed to a large degree by research into "Chicanxs" interactions at the Mexico–U.S. border (1994, Saldívar 2006, Villa 2000). Indigeneity forms a cluster in part as an opposition to hybridity, and, moreover, as a conceptual framework for both Indigenous peoples who either reject imposed borders, or make these borders work for them (see the example of the Akwesasne Mohawks in Chapter 5). Indigenous may also mean long and continuous occupation, and the concept may be annexed by long-time borderlands residents like the Hispanos of New Mexico and Colorado who never considered Mexico as a homeland. This study of Indigeneity and hybridity requires a sensitive ethnography at the border (Vila 2003). Other clusters form at the intersection of culture, identity, and region, as in, for example, the Euro regions emerging within and across the European Union (Perrin 2010a, 2010b, 2011). Similarly, borderlands are forming regions elsewhere around the globe to transcend political and cultural boundaries (Wastl-Walter et al. 2004). In this book, we engage with the unique opportunity to interrogate the intersection of borders and culture in regions at various scales ranging from the assemblages within communities, provinces, and states, to those encompassing entire continents and world regions (Sadowski Smith 2002). In this chapter, we review and analyze the theoretical basis of the intersection of borders and culture, and then align these with themes to be examined in subsequent chapters.

Culture, and its expression and embodiment at borders and in borderlands, may lead to strong resistance of territorial imperatives, security primacy, and economic aims, and result in intense political and social impacts that resonate in and beyond the borderlands. Some authors have begun to explore this relationship and its implications in the European Union and in South America (Kramsch 2010, Leresche and Saez 1997, Faure 1997, Marie 2020) but there is substantial opportunity and space to explore this cultural basis of borderland as a platform for developing policies of cooperation across borders in North America and in other world regions. This may mean that we need to return to the North American Free Trade Agreement-inspired constructs like the Commission for Environmental Cooperation, for example, to find a framework within which to view and construct a model of cultural cooperation and policy making across borders in North America. Strong cooperation in sport (Howell and Leeworthy 2010) already exists to inspire and inform our thinking and policy building for cultural resource management, not only within provincial and state borders in which it currently thrives, but also across these boundaries (Cafarella et al. 2021). Culture at the border and in the borderlands still remains far from being viewed as a resource, and it remains even further from being idealized as a creative force in cultural imagination and production. The idea of the "creative border" remains to be realized and articulated (Wasko and Erickson 2008).

A cluster somewhat removed and perhaps more ethereal than the clusters already mentioned is the emergence of border aesthetics, where performative power gained through the extraordinary vision, established skill, and effective practice raises the cultural imaginary and the production of culture to an exemplary level of accomplishment artistically as well as in response to the meaning of the border (Vidar Holm et al. 2011). These creations of border art are strong statements of reaction to borderland dynamics and transformative of border representations, practices, and politics (Gómez-Peña 1986, 1987, Birringer 2000, Amilhat Szary 2012, Schimanski and Wolfe 2012, 2017). Also, ethics need to be considered in artistic border representation and appropriation (Buchanan and Moore 2003). The border itself then becomes a stage for performance, representation, creation, and even ritualization (Amoore and Hall 2010). A magazine article asks: "Can architects do for borders what they've done for embassies?" (Atlantic Cities 2013). Explicitly, can architects interpret, reconstruct, and fashion borders, in ways such as those explored by Ronald Rael and Virginia Fratello, notably in their "Teeter-Totter Wall" (Rael 2017)?

There are numerous facets of the transformative nature of borders and the subsequent contribution to border culture. One exquisite example of the border as stage and ritualization is found in the Wagah "stand-off" ceremony (YouTube 2014). Although the border edge is abrupt and raw, the stand-off performed at Wagah is both serious and infused with pomp, pageantry, humour, and, ultimately, cultural display of the highest order. Art enters politics at borders (Fox 1999), and hidden geographies become "borderscapes" of cultural expression as well as political realities at the edge of territory (Rajaram and Grundy-Warr 2008). The explicit show of territorial control at Wagah also cues the intersection of other themes in the study of borders with border culture. The ceremony conveys how the role of governance in the control and management of territory up to and at its edges engages with border culture to develop imaginaries of the border relationship (Konrad 2015). Increasingly, borders in globalization, and the Canada–U.S. boundary among these, are governed with a softer touch than at Wagah, even in an era of security primacy. Imaginaries of border governance are produced by governing authorities and by people living near and interacting with the border in order to comprehend the changes at the border, and, increasingly, changes related to the border, away from the border. Border governance is not just the articulation of power and control of the border; it also engages border stakeholders in the borderlands who develop their imaginaries of how the border works and how it falls short of meeting their needs. These imaginaries lead to resistance and in some instances dialogue among the stakeholders. In the case of the International Mobility and Trade Corridor project (IMTC 2009) in the Cascade Gateway between Washington State and British Columbia, border governance actually manifests in part as cross-border governance infused and informed by border culture. The expression of territorial control at the border remains yet border governance has also advanced to engage government and non-government stakeholders, at federal to local levels, within a cross-border region, acknowledging cultural imaginaries at all scales.

The intersection of culture and governance also extends to the examination of political cultures across borders such as the Cascadian and now Salish Sea imaginaries prevalent in the borderlands and border waters of the Pacific Northwest (Artibise 2005, Groc 2011). These imaginaries, in turn, link to the ecotopian imaginary expressed as part of the environmental sustainability ethic of the cross-border region. In fact, the cross-currents of border culture are evident in their intersection with flows of people and goods, security imperatives, and sustainability and governance, in our contemporary world as well as in the past. The identification of explicit cross-currents of culture with other thematic realms in border studies, and the assessment of the theoretical significance and public policy implications of these cross-currents provide additional dividends for the readers of this book. Imagining and experiencing boundaries does not just result or end in border culture, but rather it manifests in the connections and linkages that articulate, describe, and sustain our cultural relationships across borders in globalization.

Before we conclude our consideration of border culture theory, it is important to connect and attempt to align the diversity and variety of border culture within a unifying philosophical context. Louis Dupre (1999, 255), in his essay "Cultural variety and metaphysical unity", states that "Culture consists of symbols that preserve and direct the life of a society. Through culture, humans subdue the otherness of nature, rendering "present" what previously had been absent. Incorporating all things within a single temporal vision, culture integrates them with human existence." Emmanuel Levinas' (1986, 75) formula captures the essence of all cultural activity: "La culture c'est le sens venant à l'être" ("Culture brings meaning to being"). "But meaning may be conveyed in many ways. The first domestication of primitive otherness occurs when we name things, as Adam did in Paradise. One unduly restricts the meaning of culture, however, when defining it in purely theoretical terms." Dupre goes on to say that "culture does far more than equip a society with the norms and values needed for coping with the material conditions of its existence". There is a "spiritual surplus" that takes us beyond immediate needs according to Georg Simmel (1968, 27–28), and culture raises the "phenomenally transient to ideal permanence" (Dupre 1999, 256). The spiritual surplus of culture becomes apparent at borders and it may shine more brightly in the border space. Also, border culture, by its inherent plurality is not a homogenous system of symbols but rather an irreducible multiplicity of symbolic systems to enable border crossing and existence.

2.6 Conclusions

Imagine a world where instant communication, supersonic travel, access to the latest technology, and availability of goods and services is universal. Also, imagine that this world is divided into about 200 political units that are separated by sophisticated borders and bordering systems that are being enhanced constantly to manage flows of some people, some goods and commodities, and some information. Fed by the flows, society and culture in each political unit are interconnecting with societies and cultures in all of the other units to form transnational societies and transnational cultures. What happens at the borders?

Well, as we know from our studies of contemporary border regions and cross-border zones, the results are highly variable because of different political, economic, social, and cultural circumstances in these borderlands. Culture, we now realize, is constructed both within and across boundaries, on the one hand to galvanize nationalism, and on the other hand to extend beyond nationalism. Culture may precede borders, and when it does many forms of hybridization and re-stitching occur across the boundary. Border culture, however, is very difficult to define as is culture in its own right. Efforts to reconstruct the initial thinking about border culture have led us back to the emergence of geographical and anthropological conceptualizations of territory. Herein, are found seeds of several modern and post-modern ideas about how cultures emerge and connect. Understanding border culture entails relating the international forces operating within nations with transnational forces produced by the presence of one nation within another to capture both the material and imagined qualities of hybridization and differentiation in the borderlands. Symbolic power resonates in contemporary explorations of culture and borders in anthropology and geography. The cultural turn liberated the concept of border culture from its anthropogeographical anchoring at the intersection of classical geopolitics, emergent geography, and incipient anthropology, and this cultural turn refreshed the conceptualization of culture at borders with a revitalized exploration of identity and belonging in borderlands, a re-assessment of affinity across boundaries and an extensive rethinking of imagination in the borderlands.

The cultural imagination and production at borders and in the borderlands links with the meaning of land and life in the borderlands to secure life in the cross-border region, sustain life in the border zone, and often enrich life in the borderlands and beyond. This security, sustainability, and enrichment are of vital importance with the re-emergence of border walls, fences, and barriers worldwide. Indeed, the cultural imaginary of borderlands "third nations" has often been centred by the wall that would divide them. Yet, there are also problems with the materialization of borders in borderlands of transition that result in polarization of places and spaces, and often result in the juxtaposition of secured and non-secured spaces and the uncertainties caused by these dialectics. Finally, we are left with a cultural heritage of borders that is problematical at best, and potentially devastating for future generations if the border dialectic is not addressed and mediated by the imaginaries and constructions that offer to secure, sustain, and enrich life at the border and in the borderlands.

Our goal, ultimately, is to understand more about the interplay of borderlands cultural imaginaries and materializations at the places and in the spaces where nation-states meet and interact. There is an imperative to approach this goal with social scientific conceptualizations as well as sensitivities gained from the humanities. Mark Salter argues that "the trope of the suture better captures the dual world-creating functions of the border", and that the critical border theories of Agamben, Walker, and Galli may help us to understand "the role of borders in the creation of both sovereign states and the system of sovereign states" (Salter 2012, 734). This concept of suture (or/) also conveys an evocative notion of knitting together the inside and the outside, and it signifies and empowers the role of the / in our cybernetic world, both as a separation and an integration agent (Comte and Levrat 2006, Wille et al. 2021). Will borders, like the suture (/), eventually become an extensive and bewildering array of binary cues linked to bar codes intelligible only to computers? And, do borders simply create a cacophony of notes in their intersection with cultural constructions? Or, does the interplay create melodies, songs, and perhaps symphonies of interaction to interpret? A recent fictional account about living and coping with the new security border in the Pacific Northwest in North America uses the metaphor of *Border Songs* to capture the essence of borderlands culture in transition (Lynch 2008). The language and structure of border songs may be elusive and difficult to understand, but they constitute a metonym so that we can all comprehend and appreciate the music.

References

Agnew, John. 1994. "The territorial trap: The geographical assumptions of international relations theory." *Review of International Political Economy* 1, (1): 53–80.

Aiken, Stuart C. 1991. "Person-environmental theories in contemporary perceptual and behavioral geography 1: Personality, attitudinal and spatial choice theories." *Progress in Human Geography* 15, (2): 179–193.

Alimia, Sanaa. 2019. "Performing the Afghanistan-Pakistan border through refugee ID cards." *Geopolitics* 24, (2): 391–425.

Alvarez, Robert R. 1995. "The Mexican-US border: The making of an anthropology of borderlands." *Annual Review of Anthropology* 24: 447–470.

Alvarez Perez, Marcela, and Mark T. Berger. 2009. "Bordering on the ridiculous: MexAmerica and the new regionalism." *Alternatives: Global, Local, Political* 34, (1): 1–16.

Amilhat Szary, Anne-Laure. 2012. "Walls and border art: The politics of art display." *Journal of Borderlands Studies* 27, (2): 213–228.

Amilhat Szary, Anne-Laure. 2015. Boundaries and borders. In John Agnew, Virginie Mamadouh, Anna J. Secor and Joanne Sharp, eds. *The Wiley companion to political geography*. New York: Wiley, 11–25.

Amilhat Szary, Anne-Laure. 2020. *Géopolitique Des Frontières. Découper La Terre, Imposer Une Vision Du Monde*. Paris: Le Cavalier Bleu.

Amilhat Szary, Anne-Laure, and Frédéric Giraut. 2015. *Borderities: The Politics of Contemporary Mobile Borders*. New York: Palgrave Macmillan.

Amoore, Louise, and Alexandra Hall. 2010. "Border theatre: On the arts of security and resistance." *Cultural Geography* 17: 299–319.

Ancel, Jacques. 1938. *Géographie des frontières*. Paris: Gallimard.

Anzaldúa, Gloria. 1987. *Borderlands/La Frontera: The New Mestiza*. San Francisco: Aunt Lute.

Appadurai, Arjun. 1996. *Modernity at Large: Cultural Dimensions of Globalization*. Minneapolis: University of Minnesota Press.

Artibise, Alan F. J.2005. "Cascadian adventures: Shared visions, strategic alliances, and imagined barriers in a transborder region." In Heather N. Nicol, and Ian Townsend-Gault, eds. *Holding the Line: Borders in a Global World*. Vancouver: UBC Press, 238–267.

Ashcroft, Bill. 2001. *On Post-colonial Futures: Transformation of a Colonial Culture*. London: Continuum.

Ashcroft, Bill, Gareth Williams, and Helen Tiffin. 2013. *Post-colonial Studies: The Key Concepts*. London: Routledge.

Atlantic Cities. 2013. "Can architects do for borders what they've done for embassies?" http://m.theatlanticcities.com/design/2013/06/.

Barth, Fredrik. 1969. *Ethnic Groups and Boundaries: The Social Organization of Culture Difference*. Oslo: Universitetsforlag.

Bal, Mieke. 1999. "Introduction." In Mieke Bal, and Bryan Gonzales, eds. *The Practice of Cultural Analysis: Exposing Interdisciplinary Interpretation*. Stanford: Stanford University Press, 1–15.

Bal, Mieke. 2012. *Double Exposures: The Practice of Cultural Analysis.* New York: Routledge.
Balibar, Etienne. 2002. *Politics and the Other Scene.* London: Verso.
Balibar, Etienne. 2003. *We, the People of Europe: Reflections on Transnational Citizenship.* Princeton: Princeton University Press.
Bann, Stephen. 1999. "The veils of time: On the historical dimension in cultural analysis." In Mieke Bal, and Bryan Gonzales, eds. *The Practice of Cultural Analysis: Exposing Interdisciplinary Interpretation.* Stanford: Stanford University Press, 122–136.
Barnes, Trevor. 2020. "David Lowenthal on geography and its past." *Landscape Research.* 47, (4): 452–463.
Berlowitz, Jo-Anne. 2003. "Border art since 1965." In Michael Dear, and Gustavo Leclerc, eds. *The Postborder City: Cultural Spaces of Baja Alta California.* New York: Routledge, 143–182.
Bhabbha, Homi. 1994. *The Location of Culture.* New York: Routledge.
Billinge, Mark. 1977. "In search of negativism: Phenomenology and historical geography." *Journal of Historical Geography* 3, (1): 55–67.
Birringer, Johannes H. 2000. *Performance on the Edge: Transformations of Culture.* New York: Continuum.
Boas, Franz. 1932. "The aims of anthropological research." *Science* 76, (1983): 605–613.
Boas, Franz, ed. 1938. *General Anthropology.* Boston: Heath.
Boas, Franz. 1940. *Race, Language and Culture.* New York: Macmillan.
Bonnemaison, Joël, and Luc Cambrézy. 1996. "Le lien territorial entre frontières et identités." *Géographie et Cultures* 20: 7–18.
Bowd, Gavin. 2012. *Un géographe francais et la Roumanie. Emmanuel de Martonne (1873–1955).* Paris: L'Harmattan.
Brah, Avtar, and Annie Coombes, eds. 2000. *Hybridity and its Discontents.* London: Routledge.
Bromberger, Christian, and Alain Morel. 2001. *Limites floues, frontières vives: des variations culturelles en France et en Europe.* Paris: Editions de la Maison des Sciences de l'Homme.
Brambilla, Chiara. 2014. "Shifting Italy/Libya borderscapes at the interface of EU/Africa borderland: A 'genealogical' outlook from the colonial era to post-colonial scenarios." *ACME: An International Journal for Critical Geographies* 13, (2): 220–245.
Brambilla, Chiara. 2015. "Exploring the critical potential of the borderscapes concept." *Geopolitics* 20, (1): 14–34.
Brambilla, Chiara, and Reece Jones. 2019. "Rethinking borders, violence, and conflict: From sovereign power to borderscapes as sites of struggles." *Environment and Planning D: Society and Space* 38, (2): 287–30.
Brambilla, Chiara, Jussi Laine, James W. Scott, and Gianlucca Bocchi, eds. 2015. *Borderscaping: Imaginations and Practices of Border Making.* Farnham: Ashgate.
Brown, Wendy. 2010. *Walled States: Waning Sovereignty.* New York: Zone Books.
Brunet-Jailly, Emmanuel. 2005. "Theorizing borders: An interdisciplinary perspective." *Geopolitics* 10: 633–649.
Buchanan, Allen, and Margaret Moore, eds. 2003. *States, Nations, Borders: The Ethics of Making Boundaries.* Cambridge: Cambridge University Press.
Cafarella, Scott, Joel Konrad, and Rebecca Sciarra. 2021. "Heritage borders and bordering heritage: A bio-cultural planning approach for managing trans-border cultural landscapes." In Victor Konrad, and Melissa Kelly, eds. *Borders, Culture, and Globalization: A Canadian Perspective.* Ottawa: University of Ottawa Press, 293–318.
Cahnman, Werner J.1944. "The concept of *raum* and the theory of regionalism." *American Sociological Review* 9, (5): 455–462.

Cathey, Libby. 2021. "After 20 years, US ground troops leave Afghanistan, but American left behind." *ABC News*. 30 August, 2021. 19:51. https://www.Abcnews.go.com/Politics/us-ground-troops-leave-afghanistan-20-years-americans/story?id=79728572.

Chang, Bo Won. 2010. "The power of geographic boundaries: Cultural, political, and economic border effects in a unitary nation." Graduate Thesis 11344, Iowa State University.

Chaturvedi, Sanjay. 2005. "Rajoja, representaatioita ja vastarintaa jälkikolonialistisessa Sri Lankassa." (Between Belonging(s) and Bounding(s): Representation and resistance in Postcolonial Sri Lanka). *Terra: The Journal of the Geographical Society of Finland* 117, (3): 202–210.

Childs, Peter, and Patrick Williams. 2014 [1997]. *An Introduction to Post-colonial Theory*. London: Routledge.

Chishti, Maliha. 2014. "Post-conflict Afghanistan: A post-colonial critique." PhD Dissertation, University of Toronto.

Cohen, Saul B.2003. *Geopolitics of the World System*. Lanham: Rowman and Littlefield.

Cole, Douglas. 1999. *Franz Boas: The Early Years, 1859–1906*. Seattle: University of Washington Press.

Comte, Henri, and Nicolas Levrat, eds. 2006. *Aux coutures de l'Europe: Défis et enjeux juridiques de la coopération transfrontalière*. Paris: L'Harmattan.

Darian-Smith, Eve. 1996. "Postcolonialism: A brief introduction." *Social and Legal Studies* 5, (3): 291–299.

Dear, Michael. 2013. *Why Walls Won't Work: Repairing the US-Mexico Divide*. New York: Oxford.

Dear, Michael, Jim Ketchum, Sarah Luria, and Doug Richardson, eds. 2011. *GeoHumanities: Art, History, Text at the Edge of Place*. New York: Routledge.

Dell'Agnese, Elena. 2005. "The US-Mexico border in North American movies: A political geography perspective." *Geopolitics* 10, (2): 204–221.

Dell'Agnese, Elena. 2016. "What (political) geography ought to be." *Semestrale di studie ricerche di geografia* 1: 109–121.

Derin, Fred. 2014. "Au-delà du nationalisme méthodologique : l'interculturel sans essentialisme." *Raisons politiques* 54, (2): 121–132.

Dijkink, Gertjan. 1998. "Geopolitical codes and popular representations." *Geojournal* 46, (4): 293–299.

Dittmer, Jason, and Nicholas Gray. 2010. "Popular geopolitics 2.0: Towards new methodologies of the everyday." *Geography Compass* 4, (11): 1664–1677.

Donnan, Hastings, and Thomas M. Wilson. 1999. *Borders: Frontiers of Identity, Nation and State*. Oxford: Berg.

Dupre, Louis. 1999. "Cultural variety and metaphysical unity." In Mieke Bal, and Bryan Gonzales, eds. *The Practice of Cultural Analysis: Exposing interdisciplinary interpretation*. Stanford: Stanford University Press, 255–267.

Elden, Stuart. 2013. *The Birth of Territory*. Chicago: The University of Chicago Press.

Erickson, Frederick. 1997. "Culture in society and in educational practice." In James A. Banks, and C. A. McGee Banks, eds. *Multicultural Education: Issues and Perspectives*. Boston: Allyn and Bacon, 32–60.

Español, Alicia, Giuseppina Marsico, and Luca Tateo. 2019. "Maintaining borders: From border guards to diplomats." *Human Affairs* 28, (4): 443–460.

Fabian, Johannes. 1999. "Culture and critique." In Mieke Bal, and Bryan Gonzales, eds. *The Practice of Cultural Analysis: Exposing Interdisciplinary Interpretation*. Stanford: Stanford University Press, 235–254.

Falke, Simon. 2012. "Peace on the Fence? Israel's Security culture and the separation Fence to the West Bank." *Journal of Borderlands Studies* 27, (2): 229–237.

Fall, Juliet. 2007. "Lost geographers: Power games and the circulation of ideas within Anglophone political geographies." *Progress in Human Geography* 31, (2): 195–216.
Fall, Juliet. 2012. "Reading Claude Raffestin: Pathways for a critical biography." *Environment and Planning D: Society and Space* 30, (1): 173–189.
Fall, Juliet, and Stephane Rosière. 2008. "On the limits of dialogue between francophone and anglophone political geography." Guest editorial. *Political Geography* 27: 713–716.
Faure, Alain. 1997. "Politiques de coopération et pratiques culturelles. Les intérêts en jeu sur l'espace franco-genevois." In Guy Saez, Jean-Philippe Leresche, and Michel Bassand, eds. *Gouvernance Métropolitaine et Transfrontalière: Action Publique Territoriale.* Paris: L'Harmattan, 73–82.
Featherstone, Simon. 2005. *Post-colonial Cultures.* Edinburgh: Edinburgh University Press.
Foucault, Michel. 1972. *The Archaeology of Knowledge and the Discourse of Language.* New York: Pantheon.
Foucault, Michel. 1980. *Power/Knowledge: Selected Interviews and Other Writings.* New York: Pantheon.
Foucault, Michel. 1994 [1970]. *The Order of Things: An Archaeology of the Human Sciences.* New York: Random House.
Foucault, Michel. 1994. "Technologies of the self." In Paul Rabinow, ed. *Essential Works of Foucault, 1954–1984. Volume 1 Ethics, Subjectivity and Truth.* New York: New Press, 223–251.
Foucher, Michel. 1984. "Les géographes et les frontières." *Hérodote* 33–34: 117–130.
Foucher, Michel. 1986. *L'invention des frontières.* Paris: Fondation pour les Etudes de Défense Nationale.
Foucher, Michel. 1991. *Fronts et frontières: Un tour du monde géopolitique.* Paris: Fayard.
Foucher, Michel. 2007. *L'obsession des frontières.* Paris: Perrin.
Fein, Seth. 2003. "Culture across borders in the Americas." *History Compass* 1, (NA025): 1–6.
Fox, Claire F.1999. *The Fence and the River: Culture and Politics at the U.S.-Mexico Border.* Minneapolis: University of Minnesota Press.
Francis, Mark. 2007. *Herbert Spencer and the Invention of Modern Life.* Newcastle: Acumen.
Geertz, Clifford. 1973. *The Interpretation of Cultures.* New York: Basic Books.
Gold, John Robert. 1980. *An Introduction to Behavioural Geography.* New York: Oxford University Press.
Golledge, Reginald G., Lawrence A. Brown, and Frank Williamson. 1972. "Behavioural approaches in geography: An overview." *Australian Geographer* 12, (1): 59–79.
Golledge, Reginald G., and Robert J. Stimson. 1987. *Analytical Behavioural Geography.* New York: Routledge Kegan and Paul.
Gómez-Peña, Guillermo. 1986. "Border culture: A process of negotiation toward Utopia." *The Broken Line/La Linea Quebrada, a Border Arts Publication* 1: 1–16.
Gómez-Peña, Guillermo. 1987. "Border culture and deterritorialization." *The Broken Line/La Linea Quebrada, a Border Arts Publication* 2: 1–10.
Goodenough, Ward. 1981. *Culture, Language and Society.* Menlo Park: Benjamin/Cummings.
Gottmann, Jean. 1952. *La politique des Etats et leur géographie.* Paris: Armand Colin.
Gottmann, Jean. 1973. *The Significance of Territory.* Charlottesville: University of Virginia Press.
Gottmann, Jean. 1980. *Centre and Periphery: Spatial Variation in Politics.* Beverley Hills: Sage.

Gray, Tim S. 1996. *The Political Philosophy of Herbert Spencer.* Aldershot: Avebury.

Gregory, Derek. 2004. *The Colonial Present: Afghanistan, Palestine, Iraq.* Malden: Blackwell.

Grimson, Alejandro. 1999. *Fronteras, naciones e identitades. La periferia como centro.* Buenos Aires: Ciccus/La Crujía.

Grison, Laurent. 2002. *Figures fertiles: essai sur les figures géographiques dans l'art occidental.* Nimes: J. Chambon.

Groc, Ian. 2011. "Salish sea change." *Canadian Geographic.* June. http://www.canadiangeographic.ca/magazine/jun11/.

Gupta, Akhil, and James Ferguson. 1992. "Beyond culture: Space, identity and the politics of difference." *Cultural Anthropology* 7, (1): 6–23.

Gupta, Akhil, and James Ferguson. 1997. *Culture, Power, Place: Explorations in Critical Anthropology.* Durham: Duke University Press.

Hallair, Gaelle. 2007. "Le géographe Emmanuel de Martonne et l'Europe centrale." Paris: PRODIG.

Haushofer, Karl. 1938. *Zeitschrift Fur Geopolitik.* Berlin: Vowinckel.

Hawley, John C., ed. 1996. *Writing the Nation: Self and Country in the Post-colonial Imagination.* Amsterdam: Rodopi.

Held, David, Anthony McGrew, David Goldblatt, and Jonathan Perratin, eds. 1994. *Global Transformations; Politics, Economics and Culture.* Stanford: Stanford University Press.

Helleiner, Jane. 2016. *Borderline Canadianness: Border Crossings and Everyday Nationalism in Niagara.* Toronto: University of Toronto Press.

Heyman, Josiah M. 2012. "Culture theory and the US-Mexico border." In Thomas M. Wilson, and Hastings Donnan, eds. *A Companion to Border Studies.* New York: Wiley, 48–65.

Hoskins, William George. 1955. *The Making of the English Landscape.* London: Hodder and Stoughton.

Howell, Colin, and Daryl Leeworthy. 2010. "Borderlands and frontiers in the writing of sport history: Confronting the metropolitan fallacy." In Stephen W. Pope, and John Nauright, eds. *The Routledge Companion to Sport History.* London: Routledge, 71–84.

IMTC. 2009. *International Mobility and Trade Corridor Resource Manual.* Bellingham: Whatcom Council of Governments.

Inskeep, Steve. 2021. "Scenes from the Afghanistan-Pakistan border." *National Public Radio (NPR).* September 10, 2021. https://www.npr.org>2021/09/10>scenes-from-the-afghanistan-pakistan-border.

Isby, David. 2011. *Afghanistan.* New York: Simon and Schuster.

Jameson, Frederic. 2009. *The Cultural Turn: Selected Writings on the Postmodern, 1983–1998.* New York: Verso.

Jazeel, Tariq. 2019. *Post-colonialism.* London: Routledge.

Johnson, David E., and Scott Michaelsen. 1997. "Border secrets: An introduction." In Scott Michaelsen, and David E. Johnson, eds. *Border Theory.* Minneapolis: University of Minnesota Press, 1–39.

Kennan, George F. 1991. *Measures Short of War.* Washington: National Defense University Press.

Kjellen, Rudolf. [1917]. 2010. *Der Staat als Lebensform.* Leipzig: Kessinger Publishing.

Klauser, Francisco R. 2012. "Thinking through territoriality: Introducing Claude Raffestin to anglophone sociospatial theory." *Environment and Planning D: Society and Space* 30, (1): 106–120.

Konrad, Victor. 2012. "Conflating imagination, identity and affinity in the social construction of borderlands culture between Canada and the United States." *American Review of Canadian Studies* 42, (4): 530–548.

Konrad, Victor. 2014. "Borders, bordered lands and borderlands: Geographical states of insecurity between Canada and the United States and the impacts of security primacy." In Elisabeth Vallet, ed. *Borders, Fences and Walls: State of Insecurity?* Aldershot: Ashgate, 85–104.

Konrad, Victor. 2015. "Toward a theory of borders in motion." *Journal of Borderlands Studies* 30, (1): 1–17.

Konrad, Victor. 2020. "Belongingness and borders." In J. W. Scott, ed. *A Research Agenda for Border Studies*. Oxford: Edward Elgar, 107–126.

Konrad, Victor. 2021. "New directions at the post-globalization border." *Journal of Borderlands Studies* 36, (5): 713–726.

Konrad, Victor, and Emmanuel Brunet-Jailly. 2019. "Approaching borders, creating borderland spaces, and exploring the evolving borders between Canada and the United States." *The Canadian Geographer / Le Géographe canadien* 63, (1): 4–10.

Konrad, Victor, and Michael Chaney. 1982. "The Madawaska Twin Barn of Maine's St. John Valley." *Journal of Cultural Geography* 4: 64–75.

Konrad, Victor, and John Everitt. 2011. "Borders and 'belongers': Transnational identities, border security, and cross-border socio-economic integration in the United States borderlands with Canada and the British Virgin Islands." *Comparative American Studies* 9, (4): 288–308.

Konrad, Victor, and Melissa Kelly, eds. 2021. *Borders, Culture, and Globalization: A Canadian Perspective*. Ottawa: University of Ottawa Press.

Konrad, Victor, and Heather N. Nicol. 2008. *Beyond Walls: Re-Inventing the Canada-United States Borderlands*. Aldershot: Ashgate.

Konrad, Victor, and Heather N. Nicol. 2011. "Border culture, the boundary between Canada and the United States of America, and the advancement of borderlands theory." *Geopolitics* 16: 70–90.

Kraidy, Marwan. 2005. *Hybridity: Or the Cultural Logic of Globalization*. Philadelphia: Temple University Press.

Kramsch, Oliver. 2002. "Reimagining the scalar topologies of cross-border governance: Eu (ro) regions of the post-colonial present." *Space and Polity* 6, (2): 169–196.

Kramsch, Olivier. 2010. "Regulating European borders: A cultural perspective." In Noralv Veggeland, ed. *Innovative Regulatory Approaches: Coping with Scandinavian and European Policies*. New York: Nova Science Publishers.

Krige, John, ed. 2019. *How Knowledge Moves: Writing the Transnational History of Science and Technology*. Chicago: University of Chicago Press.

Kroeber, Alfred L.1944. *Configurations of Cultural Growth*. Berkeley: University of California Press.

La Cecla, Franco. 2002. *Le malentendu*. Paris: Ballard.

Laine, Jussi et al. 2017. "Final report of the EUBORDERSCAPES project." Karelian Institute, University of Eastern Finland.

Leresche, Jean-Philippe, and Guy Saez. 1997. "Identités territoriales et régimes politiques de la frontière." *Pôle Sud*: 27–47.

Lévinas, Emmanuel. 1986. "Détermination philosophique de l'idée de culture." *Philosophie et Culture: Actes du XVIle congrès mondial philosophie* 1: 73–82.

Lewis, Herbert S. 2001. "The passion of Franz Boas." *American Anthropologist* 103, (2): 447–467.

Livon, Thomas. 2003. "Franz Boas and the discovery of culture." Senior Honors Thesis, Amherst College.

Lowenthal, David. 1961. "Geography, experience and imagination: Towards a geographical epistemology." *Annals, Association of American Geographers* 51, (3): 241–260.

Lowenthal, David. 1991. "British national identity and the English landscape." *Rural History* 2, (2): 205–230.

Lowenthal, David. 2000. "European identity: An emerging concept." *Australian Journal of Politics and History* 46, (3): 314–321.

Lugo, Alejandro. 1997. "Reflections on border theory, culture, and the nation." In David E. Johnson, and Scott Michaelsen, eds. *Border Theory*. Minneapolis: University of Minnesota Press, 43–67.

Lynch, Jim. 2008. *Border Songs*. New York: Knopf.

Mackinder, Halford. 1904. "The geographical pivot of history." *Geographical Journal* 23, (2): 421–444.

Mackinder, Halford. 1919. *Democratic Ideals and Reality: A Study in the Politics of Reconstruction*. New York: Simon and Schuster.

Maley, William. 2009. *The Afghanistan Wars*. New York: Macmillan.

Marié, Solène. 2020. "At the centre of the edge: The development of cross-border cities between Brazil and Uruguay and France and Germany." PhD dissertation, Universidade de Brasília and Université de Paris 8.

Marsico, Giuseppina. 2011. "The 'non-cuttable' space in between: Context, boundaries and their natural fluidity." *Integrative Psychological and Behavioural Science* 45, (2): 185–193.

Marsico, Giuseppina. 2016. "The borderland." *Culture and Psychology* 22, (2): 206–215.

Marsico, Giuseppina, and Achille C. Varzi. 2016. "Psychological and social borders: Regulating relationships." In Jaan Valsiner, Giuseppina Marisco, Nandita Chaudhary, Tatsuya Sato, and Virginia Dazzani, eds. *Psychology as a Science of Human Being: The Yokohama Manifesto, Annals of Theoretical Psychology*, Vol. 13. Geneva: Springer, 327–335.

Martínez, Oscar. 1994. *Border People: Life and Society in the U.S.-Mexico Borderlands*. Tucson: University of Arizona Press.

Mayer, Evelyn P.2014. *Narrating North American Borderlands. Thomas King, Howard F. Mosher, and Jim Lynch*. Mainzer Studien zur Amerikanistik. Band 64. Frankfurt: Peter Lang.

Meier, Daniel. 2020. "In-between spaces in the Levant: Conceptual reflections." *Mediterranean Politics* 6: 1–16.

Meinig, Donald W. 1970. "The Mormon culture region: Strategies and patterns of geography of the American West, 1847–1964." *Annals, Association of American Geographers* 60, (3): 428–446.

Michaelsen, Scott, and David E. Johnson. 1997. *Border Theory: The Limits of Cultural Politics*. Minneapolis: University of Minnesota Press.

Mignolo, Walter D. 2000. *Local Histories/Global Designs: Coloniality, Subaltern Knowledges, and Border Thinking*. Princeton: Princeton University Press.

Minghi, Julian. 1963. "Boundary studies in political geography." *Annals, Association of American Geographers* 53, (3): 407–428.

Mitchell, Don. 2000. *Cultural Geography: A Critical Introduction*. Oxford: Blackwell.

Mortenson, Greg, and David Oliver Relin. 2006. *Three Cups of Tea: One Man's Mission to Fight Terrorism and Build Nations–One School at a Time*. New York: Penguin.

Mountz, Alison. 2011. "The enforcement archipelago: Detention, haunting, and asylum on islands." *Political Geography* 30, (3): 118–128.

Muscarà, Luca. 2020. "The great swindle of nationalist sovereigntism: On territory, psychology, and communication technologies." In Sami Moisio, Natalie Koch, Andrew E. G. Jonas, Christpher Lizotte, and Juho Luukkonen, eds. *Handbook on the Changing Geographies of the State: New Spaces of Geopolitics*. Cheltenham: Edward Elgar, 96–106.

Muscarà, Luca. 2022. "Transatlantic landscapes: Gottmann and the roots of Lowenthal's intellectual heritage." *Landscape Research* 47, (4): 464–476.

Nail, Thomas. 2016. *Theory of the Border*. New York: Oxford University Press.

Nasser, Riad. 2019. "Identity beyond borders: National identity and the post-colonial alternative." *Social Semiotics* 29, (2): 145–171.

Nerland, Monika. 2010. "Transnational discourses of knowledge and learning in professional work: Examples from computer engineering." *Studies of Philosophy and Education* 29, (2): 183–195.

Newman, David, and Anssi Paasi. 1998. "Fences and neighbours in the postmodern world: Boundary narratives in political geography." *Progress in Human Geography* 22, (2): 186–207.

Norchi, Charles H. 2010. "Culture and law on the durand line." In William Ascher, and John M. Heffron, eds. *Cultural Change and Persistence: New Perspectives on Development*. New York: Palgrave-Macmillan, 202–232.

Paasi, Anssi. 1996. *Territories, Boundaries and Consciousness: The Changing Geographies of the Finnish-Russian Border*. New York: Wiley.

Paasi, Anssi. 1998. "Boundaries as social processes: Territoriality in the world of flows." *Geopolitics* 3, (1): 69–88.

Paasi, Anssi. 1999. "Boundaries as social practice and discourse: The Finnish-Russian border." *Regional Studies* 33: 669–680.

Paasi, Anssi. 2005. "Generations and the development of border studies." *Geopolitics* 10, (4): 663–671.

Peña, Sergio. 2021. "From territoriality to borderscapes: The conceptualization of space in border studies." *Geopolitics*. https://doi.org/10.1080/14650045.2021.1973437.

Perrin, Thomas. 2010a. *Culture et eurorégions. Enjeux institutionnels de l'action culturelle eurorégionale*. Grenoble: Institut d'Etudes Politiques de Grenoble.

Perrin, Thomas. 2010b. "Inter-territoriality as a new trend in cultural policy? The case of Euroregions." *Cultural Trends* 19: 125–139.

Perrin, Thomas. 2011. "Identité et culture aux frontières. L'action culturelle eurorégionale, entre identité 'patrimoniale' et identité créative." In O. Jane, and Q. Sole, eds. *Observar les fronteres, veure el món*. Catarroja: Afers, 19–34.

Pestre, Elise. 2021. "Geopolitical borders and psychic borders: Is a dialogue possible? Toward a geoclinical practice centered on the subject of migrants." *The Psychoanalytic Quarterly* 90, (3): 337–372.

Popescu, Gabriel. 2011. *Bordering and Ordering the Twenty-First Century: Understanding Borders*. Lanham: Rowman and Littlefield.

Prescott, James R. V. 1965. *Border Landscape: The Geography of Frontiers and Boundaries*. Chicago: Aldine.

Prokkola, Eeva-Kaisa. 2009. "Unfixing borderlands identity: Border performances and narratives in the construction of self." *Journal of Borderlands Studies* 24, (3): 21–38.

Ptak, Thomas, Jussi P. Laine, Zhiding Hu, Yuli Liu, Victor Konrad and Martin van der Velde. 2022. "Understanding borders through dynamic processes: capturing relational

motion from south-west China's radiation centre." *Territory, Politics, Governance* 10, (2): 200–218.
Rael, Ronald. 2017. *Borderwall as Architecture: A Manifesto for the US-Mexico Boundary.* Oakland: University of California Press.
Raffestin, Claude. 1974. "Eléments pour une problématique des régions frontalières." *L'Espace géographique* 1: 12–18.
Raffestin, Claude. 1977. "Paysage et territorialié." *Cahiers de Géographie du Québec* 21, (53–54): 123–134.
Raffestin, Claude. 1980. *Pour une géographie du pouvoir.* Paris: Litec.
Raffestin, Claude. 1986. "Eléments pour une théorie de la frontière." *Diogene* 132: 18.
Raffestin, Claude. 2012. "Space, territory, and territoriality." *Environment and Planning D: Society and Space* 30, (1): 121–141.
Rajaram, Prem Kumar, and Carl Grundy-Warr. 2008. *Borderscapes: Hidden Geographies and Politics at Territory's Edge.* Minneapolis: University of Minnesota Press.
Rancière, Jacques. 2015. *Dissensus: On Politics and Aesthetics.* New York: Bloomsbury.
Ratzel, Friedrich. 1940. *Erdenmacht und Voelkerschicksal.* Stuttgart: Engelhorn.
Raza, Syed Sami, and Michael J. Shapiro. 2019. "Introduction: Politics on Border - Critical reflections on the Pakistan-Afghanistan borderlands." *Geopolitics* 24, (2): 277–283.
Ristoleinen, Mari. 2014. "Zooming in - Zooming Out: Politics of Photographic Aesthetics across Finnish-Soviet Borders in the 1930s." *Nordlit* 31: 109–131.
Roberts, Gillian, and David Stirrup. 2013. *Parallel Encounters: Culture at the Canada-US Border.* Waterloo: WLU Press.
Rodney, Lee. 2017. *Looking Beyond the Borderlines: North America's Frontier Imagination.* New York: Routledge.
Rogoff, Irit. 2000. *Terra Infirma: Geography's Visual Culture.* London: Routledge.
Rosaldo, Renato. 1989. *Culture and Truth: Renewing the Anthropologist's Search for Meaning.* Boston: Beacon Press.
Rosière, Stephane, and Reece Jones. 2012. "Teichopolitics: Re-considering globalisation through the role of walls and fences." *Geopolitics* 17, (1): 217–234.
Rumford, Chris. 2011. "Seeing like a border." *Political Geography* 30, (2): 67–68.
Sack, Robert David. 1986. *Human Territoriality: Its Theory and History.* Cambridge: Cambridge University Press.
Sadowski-Smith, Claudia. ed. 2002. *Globalization on the Line; Culture, Capital and Citizenship at U.S. Borders.* New York: Palgrave.
Saleebey, Dennis. 1994. "Culture, theory and narrative." *Social Work* 39, (4): 351–359.
Salter, Mark B. 2012. "Theory of the / : The suture and critical border studies." *Geopolitics* 17, (4): 734–755.
Saldívar, Jose David. 1997. *Border Matters: Remapping American Culture Studies.* Berkeley: University of California Press.
Saldívar, Ramón. 2006. *The Borderlands of Culture: Americo Paredes and the Transnational Imaginary.* Durham: Duke University Press.
Schetter, Conrad. 2013. "The Durand line: The Afghan-Pakistani border region between Pashtunistan, Tribalistan and Talibanistan." *Internationales Asienforum* 44, (1–2): 47–70.
Schiller, Nina Glick, Linda Basch, and Cristina Blanc-Szanton. 1992. "Towards a definition of transnationalism." *Annals of the New York Academy of Sciences* 645: ix–xiv.
Schimanski, Johan, and Stephen Wolfe. 2007. *Border Poetics De-Limited.* Hannover: Wehrhahn.
Schimanski, Johan, and Stephen Wolfe. 2017. *Border Aesthetics: Concepts and Intersections.* Oxford: Berghahn.

Scott, James W. 1998. "Planning cooperation and transboundary regionalism: Implementing policies for European border regions in the German-Polish context." *Environment and Planning C: Government and Policy* 16, (5): 605–624.
Shimoni, Baruch. 2006. "Cultural borders, hybridization, and a sense of boundaries in Thailand, Mexico and Israel." *Journal of Anthropological Research* 62, (2): 217–234.
Simmel, Georg. 1968. *The Conflict in Modern Culture.* New York: Teachers College Press.
Slater, David. 1998. "Post-colonial questions for global times." *Review of International Political Economy* 5, (4): 647–678.
Smith, Barry. 1996. "Mereotopology: A theory of parts and boundaries." *Data Knowledge and Engineering* 20, (3): 287–303.
Sparke, Matthew. 2002. "Between post-colonialism and cross-border regionalism." *Space and Polity* 6, (2): 203–213.
Spencer, Christopher, and Mark Blades. 1986. "Pattern and process: A review essay on the relationship between behavioural geography and environmental psychology." *Progress in Human Geography* 10, (2): 229–248.
Spykman, Nicholas. 1938. "Geography and foreign policy." *American Political Science Review* 32, (1): 28–50.
Spykman, Nicholas. 1942. *America's Strategy in World Politics.* New York: Harcourt.
Stocking, George W.1974. *The Shaping of American Anthropology, 1883–1911: A Franz Boas Reader.* New York: Basic Books.
Sundberg, Juanita. 2008. "'Trash-talk' and the production of quotidian geopolitical boundaries in the USA-Mexico borderlands." *Social and Cultural Geography* 9: 871–890.
Tuan, Yi-Fu. 1979. *Landscapes of Fear.* New York: Pantheon Books.
Tunander, Ola. 2005. "Swedish geopolitics: From Rudolf Kjellen to a Swedish 'Dual State'." *Geopolitics* 10: 546–566.
Urry, John. 2007. *Mobilities.* Cambridge: Polity.
Valenzuela Arce, J. M. 1998. *Nuestros piensos: Culturas populares en la frontera Mexico-Estados Unidos.* Mexico: Dirección General de Culturas Populares-CONACULTA.
Valsiner, Jaan. 2014. *An Invitation to Cultural Psychology.* London: Sage.
Vandervalk, Sandra. 2017. "Line dancing." M.A. Thesis, Anthropology, Carleton University.
Vandervalk, Sandra. 2021. "Passing through and living here: Body and self in-between and on the edge in the borderlands region of Stanstead, Quebec and Derby Line, Vermont." In Victor Konrad, and Mellisa Kelly, eds. *Borders, Culture, and Globalization: A Canadian Perspective.* Ottawa: University of Ottawa Press, 163–186.
Van der Velde, Martin R. 1997. "So many regions, so many borders: A behavioural approach in the analysis of border effects." Conference at the 37th European Congress of the Regional Science Association, Radboud University Repository, Nijmegen.
Van Houtum, Henk. 2000. "III European perspectives on borderlands: An overview of European geographical research on borders and border regions." *Journal of Borderlands Studies* 15, (1): 56–83.
Van Houtum, Henk, Oliver Kramsch, and Wolfgang Zierhofer, eds. 2005. *B/Ordering Space.* Aldershot: Ashgate.
Vidal de la Blache, Paul. 1896. *Annales de Géographie.* Paris: Armand Colin.
Vidar Holm, Helga, Sissel Laegreid, and Torgeir Skorgen. 2011. *The Borders of Europe: Hegemony, Aesthetics and Border Poetics.* Aarhus: Aarhus University Press.
Vila, Pablo, ed. 2003. *Ethnography at the Border.* Minneapolis: University of Minnesota Press.
Villa, Raul Homero. 2000. *Barrio-Logos: Space and Place in Urban Chicano literature and Culture.* Austin: University of Texas Press.
Wandji, Dieunedort. 2019. "Rethinking the time and space of resilience beyond the West: An example of the post-colonial border." *Resilience* 7, (3): 288–303.

Wasko, Janet, and M. Erickson. 2008. *Cross-border Cultural Production: Economic Runaway or Globalization?*Amherst: Cambria Press.
Wastl-Walter, Doris, Barbara J. Morehouse, and Vera Pavlakovich-Kochi, eds. 2004. *Challenged Borderlands: Transcending Political and Cultural Boundaries.* Aldershot: Ashgate.
Weigert, Hans Werner. 1942. "Haushofer and the pacific." *Foreign Affairs* 20, (4): 332–342.
Wille, Christian, Astrid M. Fellner, and Eva Nossem, eds. 2021. *Bordertexture: A Complexity Approach to Cultural Border Studies.* Bielefeld: Transcript Verlag.
Wilson, Helen F. 2017. "On geography and encounter: Bodies, borders, and difference." *Progress in Human Geography* 41, (4): 451–471.
Wilson, Thomas M., and Hastings Donnan. 1998. *Border Identities: Nation and State at International Frontiers.* Cambridge: University of Cambridge Press.
Wright, John K. 1947. "Terrae incognitae: The place of the imagination in geography." *Annals, Association of American Geographers* 37, (1): 1–15.
WildFilmsIndia. 2014. *India-Pakistan Wagah borderceremony.* https://youtu.be/godCysdSEYY.
Yuval-Davis, Nira, Georgie Weymus, and Kathryn Cassidy. 2019. *Bordering.* Cambridge: Polity.
Zelinsky, Wilbur. 1959. "Walls and fences." *Landscape* 8, (3): 14–20.
Zhurzhenko, Tatiana. 2010. *Borderlands into Bordered Lands: Geopolitics of Identity in Post-soviet Ukraine.* Stuttgart: IbidemVerlag.

3

BORDER IMAGINARIES AND CULTURAL PRODUCTION

Imagination is both a process of thinking and the production of an idea.
An imaginary is supposed, insubstantial, or, even, unreal.
Border imaginaries may be unrealized manifestations of culture.
Yet, border imaginaries perform ostensibly powerful thoughts and ideas about borders, borderlands, and bordering.
These imaginaries may be produced as images and framed thought, and expressed as cultural production of the border.

The border itself is an imaginary that has often become a reality, and then the "real" or imagined border is open to re-imagination. The border is an evolving idea, and this idea is created and re-created in part by imagination. Perhaps the most compelling contemporary example of the border as an imaginary is former president Donald Trump's notion of the dysfunctional U.S.–Mexico border. His imaginary of the border underscored what he deemed the need for a bigger, better, and "beautiful" wall (Wright 2019). Creating and re-creating a social imaginary of border is a human approach to framing power, and this manifestation of power is the essence of the border. Border imaginaries portend the special relationship between human beings, their cultures, and the limitations of their power.

In this chapter, we explore border imaginaries of people and the cultural production linked to these imaginaries. Our path begins with a consideration of how imagination is associated with the construction and establishment of border imaginaries. Once we define our terms, the exploration continues with an illustration of how imaginaries of the border and at the border manifest in the metropolitan area of Detroit and Windsor. From there, we proceed to introduce how imagining the border works through an assessment of kinds of border imaginaries—life securing, life sustaining, life enriching—and through consideration of

DOI: 10.4324/9781003301486-3

imagining the border as symbolic, mythological, legendary, and traditional. We consider notions of thresholds, hybridity, transition, parallelism, parallax, and paradox in the "spatial grammar" (Widdis 2015) or "alphabet" (Amilhat Szary 2020) in what may be described as a lexicon of borders and borderlands. Also, we examine mapping and technologies associated with border imaginaries, and how these somehow dominate the production of border culture. Then, we shift to imagining and performing new kinds of borders of the body, and imagining the border in transnationalism and globalization, and, now, in post-globalization, the re-engagement of, and with, borders. These shifts are contextualized in the post-humanistic re-ordering of borders within emerging ecologies of the Anthropocene (Dalby 2020a and b, Amilhat Szary 2014) and the re-assertion of border walls (Vallet 2014). Also considered are natural overflows of borders such as invasive species and resulting sanitary borders. The chapter concludes with a discussion of how border imaginaries are essentialized and materialized, that is, how people move from border imaginaries to borders and back again in their continual production and reproduction of border culture.

3.1 Imagination and the establishment of border imaginaries

Imagination has long been situated as a form of environmental adjustment and autistic thinking (Morgan 1931). It is considered "necessary to enable us to recognize things in the world that are familiar". Imagination is "also necessary if we are to see the world as significant of something unfamiliar, if we are ever to treat the objects of perception as symbolizing, or suggesting things other than ourselves" (Warnock 1976, 9–10). Imagination, then, engages the "transliminal mind" (Rugg 1963) to differentiate the "for-itself" of existence from the "in-itself" of the world of being (Sartre 2012 [1936]). Simply put, imagination is the "mental representation of something" (Gendler 2011).

The imaginary is the "unceasing and essentially undetermined creation of figures/forms/images, on the basis of which alone there can ever be a question of 'something'. What we call 'reality' and 'rationality' are its works" (Castoriadis 1997, 3). These manifestations of imagination combine as social imagination (Taylor 2004) and as human imagination and consciousness as the basis for existentialism (Sartre 2004 [1960]). Border making is in itself an essential component of the imaginary of the state (Debardieux 2019), and this border making is shared and/or repudiated in varying degrees by people living in the states or moving through them.

Border imaginaries constitute an increasingly more extensive component in the literature of border studies, and, particularly, the scholarship focused on how borders work in globalization. Research on border imaginaries is central to the understanding of border culture. Also, it links border culture research to the broader goals of critical border studies and the articulation of political cultures of the border (Parker and Vaughan-Williams 2009, 2012). In the quest for alternative border imaginaries in a mobile and transnational world (Vaughan-Williams 2009), diverse and broadened "imaginations and practices of border making" (Brambilla et al. 2015) emerge and evolve to portray, guide, and validate the plural and multidimensional "borderscapes" in globalization.

Border imaginaries are spatial, social, and, inherently cultural. Spatial imaginaries research in geography, including work by Derek Gregory (1995, 2010) on the geographical imagination more generally, and by Bernard Debardieux (2019) more specifically on imagining borders, is developing a corpus of thought, where, according to Josh Watkins (2015), the field of study was characteristically lacking in conceptualization and verification. Yet, as Watkins (2015) explains, there is an extensive literature on imaginaries of places, idealized spaces, and spatial transformations. Four competing conceptions of spatial imaginaries are semiotic orders, worldviews, representational discourse, and performative discourses. Performative discourses are most promising, according to Watkins (2015), because they clarify the association between spatial imaginaries and material practices. Social imaginaries of space are "instituting" in connecting a collective symbolic universe to its institutions, and "constitutive" in connecting individuals and collectives to spaces and spatial practices that identify them (Debardieux 2019, Van Lanen 2019). Whereas Bernard Debardieux's (2019) social imaginaries are focused on the spatialities of state imaginary, national imaginary, and post-national imaginary, the author also reflects on spatial state imaginaries in a globalizing world. Herein is evident a springboard to consideration of border imaginaries, which in our estimation are made more visible and potentially viable in globalization.

In globalization, powerful imaginaries of the border position and code a complex, varied, and plural bordering between peoples (Schimanski and Wolfe 2017, Rodney 2017). Accordingly, the Canada–U.S. border, like all borders, is increasingly everywhere yet nowhere as bordering becomes more complex and universal, detached from the border, and linked to globalization tendencies (Konrad and Brunet-Jailly 2019). An overview of border imaginaries between Canada and the U.S. reveals a broadly based set of imaginaries including a sense of the border as "managed" (Konrad 2020a). Within this border imaginary are a series of subsidiary imaginaries or perceived realities of border governance: control of the border assures control of the territory; borders are most effectively governed by federal authorities; distance from the border calibrates with the reduction of border governance; differentiation of security and non-security spaces and places; complication of governance resulting from the interaction of multiple agencies and the rapid introduction of technologies and new procedures; and the spectre of militarization as the unifying governing principle, particularly on the U.S. side of the border. Beyond these imaginaries of the culture of border governance are other prevailing border imaginaries. These include an embodied imagination of a biopolitical border which is bordering people everywhere. Also, there is the imaginary of the reinvented border, driven by U.S. interests over Canadian interests as an unbalanced border. Another imaginary is the view that multiculturalism stops at the border, and that multicultural Canada faces a unicultural border with the U.S. Consequently, the Canada–U.S. border is imagined as an inadequate and unfair border. Yet, in 2021, with the border largely closed to discretionary travel during the pandemic, many of these imaginaries have become subdued or sublimated as Canadians acknowledge and even celebrate their bordered distance from the U.S. Now, we focus our discussion on border place and locale in order to reveal more about how border imaginaries and cultural production operate.

3.1.1 Detroit, U.S./Windsor, Canada

Detroit is the largest city located directly on the border between the U.S. and Canada. It faces Windsor, Ontario, across the Detroit River. Residents of Windsor see Detroit's skyline, and, similarly, residents of Detroit can see the lower profile of the much smaller city of Windsor. Broader details of urban form and function are apparent, but a great deal of everyday life is open to the imagination.

With Detroit and Windsor as an example, we explore the ways in which people imagine and objectify the border. In an essay entitled "Sight and site on the line: The cultural imaginary of borderlands in North America", Lee Rodney (2021) introduces the cultural imaginary of borderlands through the role of art and media projects in resuscitating borderlands in the Detroit–Windsor area. In recent decades, the promise and celebration of the borderlands in the 1990s was replaced by the era of the official borderline. However, as borders have become more relational and mobile virtual interfaces, these borders have become actualized through embodied behaviours and concrete objects. Rodney illustrates how bodily metaphors of the border as a wound and the boundary as a cultural skin materialize as abjected sites in cultural imagination. These are sites of "dissensus", provoked by aesthetic engagement as opposed to consensus (Rancière 2015), and they make us question authority and the exclusionary paradigms of Western aesthetics. The sites are at once relational, conditional, and diverse, and they make us want to see the border even more. Accordingly, Rodney shows us projects of crossing, mapping, re-imagining, performing, and documenting the line that offer alternative imaginaries and understanding of space and identity along new "social trails" across the border.

Michael Darroch (2021) explores the imagining of nighttime Detroit in a richly illustrated essay about how, in illumination and in darkness, iconic features in Detroit's skyline produce moods and atmospheres that affect Windsor. As Darroch indicates, cultural experiences of night and day are not typically theorized in borderlands, and so this study offers a unique insight. Nighttime cultural life is expressed as an intense local experience that rounds out the rhythms of the border city as they are imagined and practised. Although Detroit glows over Windsor to both enchant and revile across the border, the boundary and/as the river enables Windsor to be an "intimate onlooker", perceiving, imagining, and participating in nighttime Detroit. The border between darkness and light is diffused and recast as Detroit's electrified images cross the border and are processed in Windsor.

FIGURE 3.1 Night Scene, Windsor, Ontario, Canada. Detroit in the Distance ca. 1930. Post Card and Greeting Co. Ltd. University of Windsor, Leddy Library, Mike Skreptak Collection, Black Binder 3. http://swoda.uwindsor.ca/node/1738. Courtesy of the Southwestern Ontario Digital Archive, Leddy Library, University of Windsor, and Michael Darroch, York University.

Symbolic objects of cultural significance, the "beaming" Penobscot Building for example (Figure 3.1), become central in this cross-border engagement. Darroch illustrates how the Penobscot Building, and other iconic structures in nighttime Detroit, are vividly imaginable but perhaps always just beyond reach.

Another focus on the border in this region, and more broadly, is a retrospective on the *Border Cultures* series at the Art Gallery of Windsor, 2013–2015 (Konrad 2021, Mitra 2021). The *Border Cultures* series is one of the most extensive border exhibitions curated in the past 30 years and focused on the Canada–U.S. border. The study (Mitra 2021, Konrad 2021) includes a synopsis of the exhibitions drawn from the published catalogue *Border Cultures* (Mitra 2015) and a "conversation" between the curator, Srimoyee Mitra, and Lee Rodney, Michael Darroch, and Victor Konrad, about the exhibitions, and Mitra's assessment of the meaning and impact of the works. Launched in 2013, the *Border Cultures* series of exhibitions were developed to deepen our understanding of what it means to be a border city in the twenty-first century. "This three-part exhibition was conceptualized as a research platform, bringing together regional, national, and international artists to examine the complex and shifting notions of national boundaries" (Mitra 2015). The works of the artists offered in the exhibitions collectively and consecutively mark a sparking of imaginaries and the production of culture at and about the border.

Collectively, these studies and other research focused on border imaginaries and production of border culture at Detroit/Windsor illustrate several important insights about border imaginaries, and link these insights to aspects of cultural production at the border. First, there is both competition and convergence of border imaginaries for both "Windsorites" and "Detroiters". Imaginaries of the border separate and coalesce in spaces at and near the boundary. Some imaginaries prevail either to predominate above others, or last significantly over time. An example is the prevalence of the imaginary of the border as a Canadian shield against crime emerging from Detroit. Another imaginary is that although Detroit and Windsor are distinctive, they continue to be symbiotic, particularly in their economic interaction. Furthermore, the imaginary of resilience in the borderlands of Windsor/Detroit is one of the most sustainable notions held on both sides of the border despite "boom and bust" cycles in the manufacturing economy and hollowing out of the inner cities. As Lee Rodney (2021) illustrates in various celebrations of the borderline, even the enhancement of the security line in recent decades has not diminished the integrative grip of the embodied border.

3.1.2 Border imaginaries: Life securing, sustaining, enriching

Border imaginaries link with a vast array of cultural meaning of landscape, aesthetics, identities, belonging, settlement, community, migration, work, play, stories, and other forms of border experience. Some of these imaginaries are life securing. They are the perceptions of the necessities for survival in the borderlands and they include views on whom to align with, where to cross the border, how to behave in border crossing, and, generally, how to compromise in-between states. In the Detroit–Windsor borderlands, the automobile industry prevails on both sides of the border, engages a substantial proportion of the work force, and forges the vision of a "working" border conduit, and corporeal connections. The border becomes embodied and personalized. The border becomes part of life, and necessary for life. Life securing imaginaries are not necessarily the imaginaries of the state but rather grassroots, borderland approaches.

Some imaginaries, then, may be deemed life sustaining for they are aligned with everyday facilitation of life in the borderlands. Everyday border engagement and living with borders is at the very core of border experience (Jones and Johnson 2016). Border life is vernacular and commonplace, even routine. Crossing practices are based on imaginaries and calculations of what works best, what is convenient, and what is sustainable. Identity markers and symbols in the border landscape sustain the imaginaries. The border becomes home, and this home is familiarized through imaginative and creative assignments of self, family, community, and even state in the border space. When the order or placement of these assignments in the imaginary of border space changes, sustainability of the border imaginary is challenged or even altered.

Other imaginaries are life enriching and reflect the mutual engagement and linkage of creative people and agencies across borders. In the case of the Detroit/Windsor border, the life enriching imaginaries are evident in the creative works of local artists. Dylan Miner and the Broken City Lab art collective, based in Windsor, have arranged "playful and poetic strategies, ideas and experiments to subvert the growing distance between the neighbouring cities" and activated "personal and collective stories and experiences living in Windsor and living through the changing infrastructure of the borders. They staged actions, hosted discussion and hang-out sessions to create a foundation upon which a renewed relationship between the cities could be imagined (and enacted)" (Mitra 2015, 32). For the *Border Cultures* exhibition, Broken City Lab created two large-scale aluminium pendants that when placed together formed a heart. One half-heart was installed on a streetlight in Windsor; the other half-heart was installed on a streetlight in Detroit (Figure 3.2). When viewed together the text reads "Together Forever, Never Apart"; when viewed separately the text reads "Together Never" and "Forever Apart". Acrylic replicas of the half hearts were placed in the Art Gallery of Windsor (Mitra 2015, 32–33).

(a) (b)

FIGURE 3.2 (a and b) Together/Never Forever/Apart (Broken City Lab) "Together Forever / Never Apart" (2013) uses the icon of childhood friendship lockets to comment on the complex and often disconnected relationship that Windsor and Detroit have with one another. Laser cut and etched in mirrored acrylic, one half of the broken locket was installed on Pellisier Street in Windsor, Ontario, while the second half was installed on Gratiot Avenue in Detroit, Michigan. The work was also included in the Art Gallery of Windsor's exhibition Border Cultures: Part One (homes, land). Photos reproduced with permission of Justin Langlois and Broken City Lab. http://www.brokencitylab.org/#togetherforever

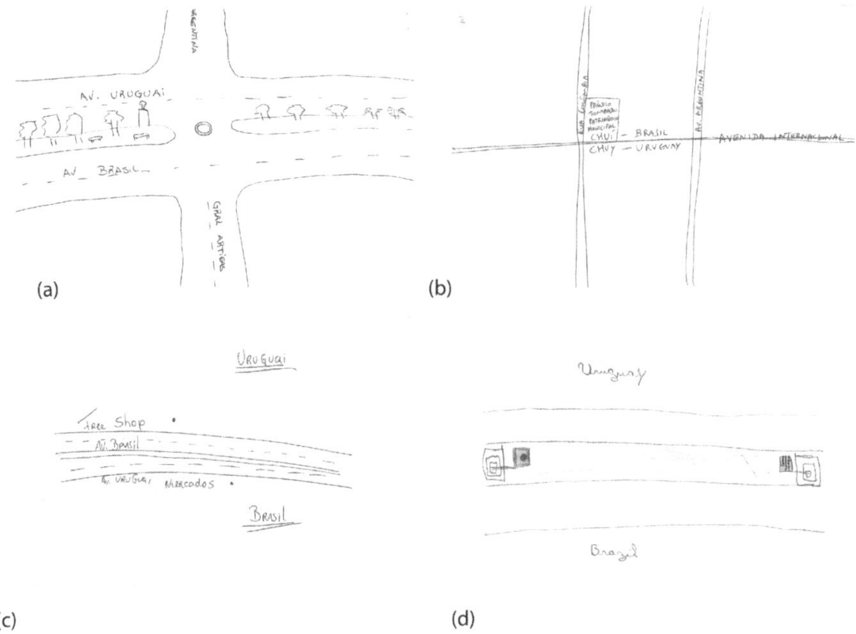

FIGURE 3.3 (a,b,c,d) Mental Maps of Inhabitants in the Bi-National Space of Chuí, Brazil, and Chuy, Uruguay. Source: Gianlluca Simi. 2018. Between the Line: The semiotics of everyday life in the Brazil/Uruguay borderlands. PhD University of Nottingham. Images reproduced with permission from the author.

The border imaginaries that are life securing, life sustaining, and life enriching are not necessarily mutually exclusive. These imaginaries may be intertwined as illustrated in a case study of living the line along the border of Uruguay and Brazil. In this context, people are living "in" the line between the twin border towns of Chuí (Brazil) and Chuy (Uruguay). In such configurations of open borders, the line is endowed with a thickness that makes it possible for local inhabitants to live "between" the two realms of national sovereignties assigned to this place from distant capitals (Simi 2018). The mental maps of inhabitants from both Chuí, Brazil, and Chuy, Uruguay, confirm the thickness and habitability of the border line. Uruguay and Brazil are placed "beyond" and "outside" of the border life zone (Figures 3.3a,b,c,d).

3.2 Imagining the border: Mythologies, legends, cultural traditions

Jacques Derrida (2011) remarked on the complicated being of life on border lines. In addition to everyday experience with multiple realities of being, borderline life is formed and informed by mythologies, legends, and cultural traditions. These sources of information about the border serve to form imaginaries and create a symbolical dimension of the border. Among the foremost of borderline mythologies, *White Mythologies* (Young 2004 [1990]) establish the colonial order of things including border imaginaries. These white mythologies protract Eurocentrism and make "the 'Third World' an unassimilable excess, surplus to the narrative of the West" (Young 2004, 1). Cross-border mythologies may originate in vague and unsubstantiated ideas of origin, destination, and trajectory (Lieto 2015). Drawing from Roland Barthes (1973 [1957]), we may understand how the border proclaims an endowment of significance rather than fact, and that the fact of the border is actually a token for something else (Huppatz 2011).

In classical Greek times, the border was personified by three gods.

> The couple Hestia/Hermes gives a classical account of the complexity of the limits: Hestia goddess of the hearths, spokeswoman of a sedentary world, the one who "makes [of] the domestic space, that she roots in the deepest, an inside, fixed, delimited, immobile, a center which confers to the family group, by assuring its spatial base, permanence in the time, singularity on the surface of the ground, security in front of the outside." (Vernant, 2004, personal translation) Is she really opposed to Hermes, god protector of roads and crossroads, tutelary figure of the legitimate motives (traders) or not (thieves), as of the orators, but also charged to lead the souls in their descent to the underworld?
>
> *(Amilhat Szary 2020)*

In this ancient tension, we can read two elements that persist in the meaning of contemporary frontiers: we must therefore consider them not only as artifacts intended to protect the sedentary within their territorialized settlements, but also as non-linear markers of space, essential to the mobile part of our activities (Hermes figurines were placed in gymnasiums as well as in libraries, a place where spirits travel). We must also keep in mind the influence on the boundaries of human existences of a third deity, Dionysus, "that 'outside' of the Greek Pantheon" (Barbaud, 2012, 156). Hybrid par excellence (his gestation initiated in the belly of his mother, Semele, continued in the thigh of Zeus, his father), wandering, he "crosses the countries, transgresses the customs, arrives foreigner from the confines of the world", "blurs the limits of the sexes and the balance of the masculine and the feminine, in the city, as the rational order of the language" (Amilhat Szary 2020).

Six intertwined and prismatic facets of border culture process are revealed in this classical account and more broadly in the literature related to borders and culture. These facets are symbols, thresholds, altered states, spatiality, power, and diversity. Each of these facets are associated with a well-developed set of ideas about borders, particularly in the geographical literature, but our aim in the following brief discussion is to list and define the concepts as they relate to the imagination of border culture. All of the concepts are treated in greater depth in the following chapters of the book.

3.2.1 Symbols of the border

The border is predominantly a symbolic form, and like other semiotic devices it serves to convey and perform the meaning of the border and the process of bordering in an array of mutant to blatant, ephemeral to permanent, and suggestive to demonstrative ways. Furthermore, the symbol of the border may become reified in legend and folklore. In North America, for example, border stories of the Texas–Mexico border embellish the symbolic differentiation of two "nations" that were once a Hispanic continuity (Paredes 1993). On the northern border, from Maine and the Maritimes to Washington and British Columbia, wherever forests prevailed, woodsmens' crafts, songs, tall tales, and other lore combined to knit a tradition across the boundary in a time when labour mobility and cross-border fluidity were important (Ives 1978). Some of these legends, Paul Bunyan's massive stature and heroic exploits (Dorson 2013), for example, served to establish the "woods" as a lasting imaginary of connective borderlands between the U.S. and Canada. In Ireland, where the border between Northern Ireland and the Republic of Ireland is most apparent and emphatic as a symbol of cultural division, migratory legends about the supernatural symbolize another important border to cross in the Irish experience (Almqvist 1991).

For most of us, recognized symbols of the border are generally road signs, national symbols like flags, and of course border crossing ports-of-entry where crossing is sanctioned. Along vast unpopulated stretches of the border, permanent stone or concrete markers declare the boundary at regular intervals, whereas in populated areas barriers are constructed to identify and enforce the boundary. This convention is worldwide and it is being bolstered in the twenty-first century by a return to walls as a response to bordering against terrorism and unwanted migrants (Rosière and Jones 2011, Vallet 2014). Yet, marking the boundary of the state is also reliant on symbolic differentiation at the border. How did this imaginary originate? The idea of the modern border is contemporary with the occidental division between nature and culture, and that as such, the first imaginary projected onto the border is that of division (Amilhat Szary 2014). This is the origin of the false yet prevailing and durable idea of the natural border. Subsequent imaginaries of the border shift to cooperation and panic and offer a broadly based chronology to help us understand and situate the border imaginaries discussed in this chapter. Natural features—rivers, highlands, lakes, deserts, and more—have always been convenient and significant in this regard to offer formidable border imaginaries, but the "supernatural" is even more powerful to symbolize the border. Niagara Falls, a prominent symbol of the border between Canada and the U.S. is often touted as "supernatural" (McGreevy 2009). On the southern border, "retablos" or votive paintings ensconce border legends of Mexican migrants to validate "miracles on the border" (Durand and Massey 1995). Visions, beliefs, and more, including fictions, create and sustain the imaginaries at the boundaries of the U.S. (Sadowski-Smith 2008).

Symbolic differentiation at the border is an extensive topic and requires comparative analysis in a global context in order to grasp the variation in border semiotics worldwide. This is beyond the scope of this study and it is not the focus of this chapter. Rather, our aim in exploring the nature of imaginaries of the border is to identify components and characteristics of these imaginaries: thresholds, altered states (parallelism, paradox, parallax, hybridity), spatiality, power, and diversity (gender, race, ethnicity).

3.2.2 Thresholds

Arnold Van Gennep, a Belgian scholar writing in France during the early twentieth century, envisioned the now famous concept of "rites of passage" (Van Gennep 2019 [1909]). For Van Gennep, the stages were intuitive (Hockey 2002), and he saw that life consisted of a series of transitions: separation from the old role, a liminal period between roles, and the assumption of a new role. Also, he viewed territorial passage as one form of the rites of passage. This allows us to intuit that the second or liminal stage is the "border" or perhaps more accurately borderland component where border imaginaries are tested and validated as the mobile border evolves (Fourny 2013). Moreover, as a model of both social transition and territorial passage, the rites of passage denote a threshold to crossing over a space—social or geographical—where imagination is evaluated. This threshold may be at the borderline but more likely it encompasses a more expansive space between the old and the new, the territory left behind and the territory gained. Michaela D. Walsh (2014) records performances of border crossing from Mexico as thresholds and transnational sites of belonging among the Hrahnu Indigenous people. A study from Australia illustrates crossing the threshold between white women and Chinese hawkers in the colonial white imaginary (Bagnall 2002). Imaginaries of the border may vary as continuous to discontinuous across the stages and the spaces, but invariably they are impacted by thresholds of the border and the borderlands.

3.2.3 Altered states: Parallelism, paradox, parallax, hybridity

A "spatial grammar" is welcome at this point in order to clarify the altered states that manifest in the border imaginary. Randy Widdis (2015) provides a syntax of flows, corridors, gateways, hubs, and networks to help envision and analyze the ongoing evolution of borderlands spaces. Notions of parallelism and parallax are useful to situate those imaginaries of the border that manifest as altered states as they meet the borderline. One may envision border imaginaries from one side and the other of the boundary, border imaginaries that are distinctive and essentially parallel. The borderline may operate to create a paradox at the border. However, if a border imaginary permeates the borderline and crosses the boundary it may be altered in its substance by the parallax of the borderline.

Although the altered states of parallelism, paradox, and parallax are useful theoretical concepts, and are evident in the way some border imaginaries interact with the borderline, a more common reaction is hybridization. Baruch Shimoni (2006) has documented hybridization in cultural border crossing in Thailand, Mexico, and Israel. His research confirms hybridization along cultural borders in globalization, as well as an orientation of people towards their cultural borders, and a sense of boundaries that emerges at the approach to these cultural borders. The cultural border between peoples may then have greater impact on border imaginaries than the actual borderline. Hybridization is significant in comprehending border imaginaries but it is even more evident in the production of border culture as manifested in the borderlands, and discussed in Chapter 4 and Chapter 5 of this book.

3.2.4 Spatiality

Awareness and acknowledgement of spatiality and its impact on human spatiality has grown extensively in the social sciences and the humanities during the past 50 years (Tally 2012). Among the prominent geographers who have argued for greater recognition of the spatiality of social life, David Harvey (2005, 2009 [1973]) and Edward Soja (1985, 1989) have offered theoretical perspectives to inform understanding of how borders are impacted by spatial processes of dispossession, accumulation, and transformation. More specifically, David Harvey's (1981) notion of the "spatial fix" offers understanding of the partitioning of the world into spatial entities that are bordered. Moreover, the ossification of space resulting from this partitioning helps us to understand the rigid border imaginaries that result from this process. Edward Soja's (1999) concept of "third space" enlarges the border space aperture to provide a spatial context for borderlands imaginaries and advances the spatiality of border imaginaries and discourses from dialectics to "trialectics", thus engaging borderlands space. Other aspects of spatiality inform our understanding of border imaginaries. These include extra-territoriality which engages with spaces beyond borders and includes them within the imaginary of sovereign space (Hudson 1998). Furthermore, studies of globalization have emphasized the spatial impacts of flows and networks in a world where all places and particularly cities have altered human spatial relations. Manuel Castells' (2011 [1996], 2015) contributions on the *Rise of the Network Society* and the concepts of "spaces of flows" and "spaces of places" enable border imaginaries.

Inspired by these ideas and insights, studies of border imaginaries have pursued a fuller understanding of spatiality. Josh Watkins (2017) has noted border externalization and extraterritorial subjugation in Australia's migration information campaigns. Krisztina Varró (2014) has identified multiple, intertwined spatial imaginaries of the Dutch–German–Belgian borderlands in her research on cross-border regional governance. A recent assessment of Brexit geographies and relational territorialities on the "Island of Ireland" reveals underlying spatial imaginaries and metageographies for cross-border cooperation, territoriality, and identity (Walsh 2020). In Kuwait, the spatial imaginary of the port city prevails substantially over the desert lands in this small borderland nation-state situated between Saudi Arabia and Iraq (Beaugrand 2018). Yet, most attention in the literature of border imaginaries appears to focus on the qualities that migrants aspire to in the borderland space (Mendez and Rodrieguez 2009). After all, spatial imaginaries of the border and the borderlands are based in aspiration and drawn from selected images that support the desire.

3.2.5 Power

Border imaginaries also need to be empowered. This empowerment may be institutionalized as in the case of the European Union where Europeanization and bordering associated with this process are well constructed and powerfully delivered as a set of transnational and "super-national" imaginaries (Burkner 2015). Empowerment may also be more subtle as in the case of *Envisioning Eden* (Salazar 2010). Mobilizing cross-border imaginaries in tourism is often accomplished by creating imaginaries based on the exotic and ideal, promoting the imaginaries relentlessly, engaging peer pressure, and branding the successful imaginaries. For individuals and groups, innumerable border crossings generate "ever thickening webs of interconnectivity". This powerful substantiation and validation of border crossings helps people to envision a wider world and globalization. It will be informative to consider the impact of the current pandemic on cross-border imaginaries, and to evaluate whether the imaginaries of the destinations and the border crossings associated with them will be the same as before the impact of the virus. Meanwhile, in a growing number of border contexts around the world, people are both metaphorically and literally *Up Against the Wall* (Casey and Watkins 2014) as they re-imagine borders simultaneously as barriers and conduits.

3.2.6 Diversity

Another aspect shaping border imaginaries is diversity. Ethnicity, race, age, language, and gender, among other factors of diversity, help to form the border imaginary. Language is a form of bordering, yet humans have the capacity to master several languages. Consequently, imaginaries and discourses of multilingualism are shaped by debate and consensus as in the case of Swedish in Finland (Hult and Pietikainen 2014). Emil Edenborg (2020) evaluates and compares the geopolitical imaginaries in Russia and in Sweden derived from narratives of migrants' sexual violence. Edenborg maps the ways in which gendered and racialized boundary constructs create conditions of possibility for bordering practices, including the delineation of national identity and Europeanness, and legitimizing stricter border regimes against migrants, particularly in Russia. In Hispaniola, racial bordering operates at various social levels but it has been particularly strident in utilizing the boundary between the Dominican Republic and Haiti to keep Haitians out (Milagros 2016). Yet, the Dominican racial imaginary and the border are at a crossroads, and a more complex national imaginary rejecting racism and xenophobia is beginning to emerge. Similarly, it appears evident that Latino cultural politics in the U.S.–Mexico borderlands is diversifying with feminist, racial, and ethnic imaginaries encompassed in migrant imaginaries of the border and borderlands (Camacho 2008).

3.3 Mapping and technologies in the creation of border imaginaries

In the digitalized spaces of the contemporary world, borders are now imagined and materialized through Internet providers. Although satellite capacity and coverage enables any part of the globe to be viewed with amazing resolution, the images are made available selectively, particularly in countries where ideologies of political and territorial control prohibit sharing the images with the public at large. Consider the case of Google Maps, generally the most accessible and widely available digital cartography. Google Maps may be available freely throughout Europe, the Americas, and elsewhere in the so-called free world, but the application is currently not available in China, Crimea, Cuba, Iran, Myanmar, North Korea, Sudan, and Syria. Most of these countries (or regions) are in conflict or isolation. The application is available in Russia although users are obliged to utilize hardware that allows government monitoring and access. Google Maps are not available in China for several reasons. Most apparent is the general ban on all Google products in China. Ostensibly, China offers its own digital mapping applications such as Baidu Maps and Gaode Maps but these are restricted and audited by the government so that images are offered selectively. "Maps" is available but again government vetted. Consequently, border research utilizing Google imagery may not be carried out in China although other applications may be used. The result is that the information will be filtered through the government lens, and border images will be restricted and edited. Accordingly, even universal, digitized images are political imaginaries, and inherently cultural. Most importantly, Google sells images to countries that the countries want to see, thus extending state imaginaries. In this regard, two neighbouring countries may receive access to two different maps of the same place (Graham and Zook 2013).

3.3.1 Natural borders

Numerous borders around the world are aligned with and likely emerged from the presence of natural features offering necessary and often convenient lines of demarcation (Paasi 2009, Sahlins 1990). This evident reality has helped to form cultural acceptance and acquiescence to natural borders (Konrad et al. 2020). Also, the natural border helps to shape the border imaginary of separation thus leading to socio-cultural and political confirmation of natural borders, and to questions and concerns about borders that do not appear to be natural. Yet, the prevalence of boundaries worldwide, that have been shaped by territorial accretion, colonialism, mathematical surveys, and negotiation, has shifted the modern and post-modern imaginary of the border to an abstract and linear notion. These imaginaries of the border compete in our minds as we engage with borders.

A foundational perspective may be gained from "Natures of borders: From historical to prospective epistemologies" (Amilhat Szary 2014). The essay acknowledges the radical disjunction between nature and human society, and the way humans have zoned nature, essentially imposing our border imagination on the natural domain. Three contexts are outlined in the bordering of the environment. First, based on the ingrained concept of the modern state, humans visualize nature as and at a dividing line. This form of territorialization attributes divisive functions to nature, and these divisions are "naturalized". Only recently have these notions been challenged by conceptualizations of, for example, the interconnectedness of forest root systems with "mother" trees (Simard 2021), and the interactive and extensive function of fungi and other aspects of the entangled "underland" (Sheldrake 2020, Macfarlane 2019). Second, then, nature has been theorized as integrative, and ecological theories also promote human and non-human relationships. Third, transnational environmental questions have re-positioned and challenged "natural" borders and borders in nature. The emergence of new threats associated with environmental change has caused concern and panic among humans, but these threats have also suggested new bordering possibilities as environments change. The methods and concepts for maintenance of nature have much in common with the governance of human populations, and our imaginaries of borders in nature and human society may in some instances coincide. Yet, the contemporary environmental crisis has extended both our understanding and our questioning of the "natures of borders".

Research in China's south-central borderlands reveals that whereas natural boundaries such as the Mekong, Red, and Salween Rivers, and the Himalayan cordillera form codified and accepted boundaries for the nation-state, border imaginaries, both historical and contemporary, move beyond these limits (Konrad and Hu 2021). James C. Scott (2009) has argued a thesis of state avoidance and articulated the "art of not being governed" in this region designated "Zomia". The emergence and evolution of borderlands in upland Southeast Asia has been slow and research in the region contributes to a fuller understanding of both state avoidance and frontier adaptation (Konrad 2019, 479). Freedom from the state hypothesis is a provocation to rethink ethnicity in this vast and remote terrain, to expand on the nomad–sedentary dialectic, and revisualize the complex relationships between centres and peripheries (Bourdier et al. 2015, 10–11). Historical cross-border interaction and river basin Indigenous territories have evolved into contemporary ethnic minority culture areas that transcend official state boundaries between China and Myanmar, Laos and Vietnam. Ethnic minorities imagine both an official state boundary to be avoided if possible, and local, unattended crossings to be frequented for day-to-day interaction across the border (Figure 3.4). In Kokang, situated between the Salween River in Myanmar and the boundary between China and Myanmar, the inhabitants are ethnically Han Chinese (Hu and Konrad 2018). The conflicts of the last decade between the Myanmar armed forces and the Kokang have disrupted the close relationship and interaction between Chinese and Kokang but the border imaginaries have become stronger. Since hostilities began, the Han Chinese who live in adjacent Yunnan Province imagine the border at its former and natural place—the Salween River. This view encompasses Kokang and enables acceptance of Kokang refugees in China despite strong anti-refugee laws and sentiment in China. The Kokang view themselves as part of China, and with the advent of hostilities the already

FIGURE 3.4 Informal Border Crossing between China and Myanmar near Yingjiang, North of Ruili, China. Photo by Victor Konrad.

informal and "unnatural" border between China and Kokang was crossed easily by refugees seeking asylum with friends, relatives, and business partners.

3.3.2 Landmarks

Border imaginaries are constructed around landmarks of natural, social, cultural, and political significance. In the case of Kokang, the Salween River and the height of land that forms the official China–Myanmar boundary are expansive landmarks (Hu and Konrad 2018). Within these contextual parameters, there are numerous other landmarks to situate the border within the cultural imagination. These include the dramatic bend of the Salween at the division of Kokang and Wa territories, and the border towns of Laugai in Kokang and Nansan in Yunnan. The landmarks have been critical for defining and defending Kokang territory since the Han Chinese settled in the region, and particularly since China relinquished Kokang to Burma by treaty during the nineteenth century. The landmarks help to sustain the border imaginary of Kokang and particularly an "autonomous" minority territory within Myanmar (Konrad 2020b).

Research on spatial landmarks in defining border imaginaries is extensive in the psychological and medical literature, but it remains an underdeveloped interest in border studies. It may prove useful to draw from the animal behaviour literature to explore how landmarks operate in different cultural contexts to help develop imaginaries of the border. The research in animal behaviour has shown that landmarks help to define territorial boundaries (Eason et al. 1999), establish territory (LaManna and Eason 2003), and partition territory (Mesterton-Gibbons and Adams 2003). Species, including humans, utilize landmarks in developing territorial behaviour. It would be revealing to understand more fully how humans then incorporate landmarks into their development of border imaginaries.

Landmarks have always been crucial for nomadic peoples in order to identify ecological limits to self-sustaining territory, as well as to confirm these limits to mark land and water use patterns, and to define the edges of nomadic space-time homelands. Some of these landmarks are imposing such as the Royal Kurgans in the Asian Steppes (Parzinger et al. 2016). These massifs served as landmarks to travellers and also as boundaries to communities of ancient nomads. Ancient Chorasmia (600 BC–AD 100) originated as a polity between semi-nomadic and sedentary areas of central Asia marked by a combination of landmark and established boundaries (Minardi 2015). Similarly, the Libyan Desert massifs of Gilf el-Kebir and Jebel el-'Uweinat, 120 kilometres apart in the extreme southwest of what is now Egypt, marked territories conceived and occupied from 8000–3500 BCE (Honore 2019). Rock art on the massifs documents migrations associated with these landmarks, and records the transition from hunter gatherers to herd keepers in these "symbolic territories". More recently, Bedouin nomads cognizant of an ecologically defined range for grazing have been excluded from portions of this range due to strict bordering measures along the Israeli–Egyptian boundary (Meier and Tsoar 1996).

These illustrations, and the innumerable instances of violence at state borders resulting from nomadic solidarity and non-status migrant resistance (Nail 2012), emphasize the collision of conceptions of nomadic, landmark-based guides to territoriality with the boundary contained idea of the nation-state. This collision raises concerns over basic human rights for nomadic peoples (Gilbert 2007, 2014) and it leads as well to efforts to map territories and create nomadic pathways through multiple literacy theory (Masny and Waterhouse 2011). "Nomadic territories and times", according to Saskia Sassen (2010, 237), have been re-invigorated as part of the transformation from modernity through an "unshackling of fundamental categories of social existence (time, subjectivity, territory, authority, rights)". Sasken continues that "we lack the language to capture the thousands of operations worming themselves into the established cages of these foundational elements". However, she acknowledges that this slippery part of transformation and "denationalization" may be captured through art where the constraints of language and the conceptional deficit will not suffice. An example provided by Saskia Sassen is described as "Our over-cantilevered bridge cannot cope with the warming waters below". It was an installation offered as part of the "Faith in Infrastructure" exhibition at the Serpentine Gallery, London, October 18, 2008 (Koob-Sassen 2008).

3.3.3 Sensing the border

Another topic worthy of greater thought and exploration is sensing the border. Here we engage border imaginaries and other human senses to expand our encounter with borders. In his highly original and seminal work on the geopolitics of sensing and knowing, Walter Mignolo (2011a and 2011b, 2012) primarily re-examines border thinking in a de-colonized context, particularly with regard to cosmopolitanism, yet he also calls for rethinking border imaginaries of the subaltern. In doing so, Mignolo engages with a broader range of senses and knowledge that has been suppressed by the colonial ego and the imaginaries of territory and borders by the colonizers who were invested substantially in territorial acquisition. Sensing the border then requires an approach and sources that are more democratic and inclusive of Indigenous and diverse origins.

In our contemporary world, sensing the border is approached in several ways. There is extensive work enabled by remote sensing technologies that allows accurate depictions of borders and borderlands from satellite imagery and other technological advances (Sabins 1987), and, more recently, remote sensing of place through satellite images as visual spatial imaginaries (Shim 2014). Also, there is the research emerging in cultural psychology on how borders are imagined (Marsico 2016). Although both of these directions in research require more attention by border studies specialists interested in understanding aspects of border imaginaries (Konrad 2013, 2020b), more immediate attention, in the context of this book, and its focus on border culture, needs to be accorded to how the border is sensed through the creative lens of artists.

A brief example will suffice. "Sensing the Border at Roxham Road" (Cressman 2019) is a virtual reality project by artist Michel Huneault produced by the National Film Board of Canada. The project depicts irregular immigrant border crossing attempts at Roxham Road port-of-entry on the Canada–U.S. border. Thirty-three photos convey 180 crossing attempts within a three-dimensional map. The individuals are in silhouette to protect identities but also to add to the impression of confusion at the border. The result is an ontological and epistemological indeterminacy that questions the representation of the border through visual and aural senses, and a sense of touch. Overall, the observer is struck by the fundamental opacity of the border for irregular immigrants attempting to cross the divide.

3.3.4 Boundary survey art

At this point, we turn our attention back in time to the art of conveying the borderline imposition in an indeterminate space for colonizers. The aim in this discussion is to document briefly how boundary survey work has created art, how this art visualizes and organizes the opacity of new and unfamiliar environments, and how this art enables and expands understanding of the creation of new border landmarks and perceptions associated with colonialization and nation building. Artists have contributed to the colonial tracing of borders throughout the world. Nineteenth century boundary surveys in North America were conducted by military and civilian engineers and cartographers who drew impressions of borderlands in addition to delineating the borderline. On occasion, the surveyors were accompanied by painters and photographers who depicted their impressions of borders. Border imaginaries of the boundary between the U.S. and Mexico are found in the artistic renderings accompanying the surveys (Bartlett et al. 1996). The artistic depictions of the border completed during the U.S.–Mexico boundary survey of the 1850s were presented to the U.S. Congress by Major William H. Emory in 1856 and published subsequently (Emory 2000). The 32 steel engravings and 32 drawings by Arthur Schott (surveyor) and John Weyss (artist) trace the border from the point where the boundary departs the Rio Grande River up to the point where it meets the 111th meridian. The art records the location of boundary markers (landmarks or monuments), but the art also provides details of extensive wilderness landscapes and particularly the arroyos and desert vegetation (Kelsey 2007, Rebert 2011).

On the northern border, the colonial boundary between the U.S. and British North America was surveyed during the early nineteenth century. Some gaps were filled in the east after Canadian Confederation in 1867, and the western and northwestern boundaries were surveyed during the second half of the nineteenth century and into the early twentieth century. Artistic rendering of the border was accomplished through paintings and prints, and then later with photographs. In the early nineteenth century, the detailed, competent, and colourful etchings and prints produced by Charles W. Bartlett, in his travels along the boundary and throughout the borderlands, provided an extensive documentation and insightful depiction of land and life in the "Canadas" (Bartlett and Miles 2001). The photographs recording the Northwest Boundary Survey of 1857–1862 convey the challenging terrain and immense Pacific coast forest wilderness (Eason 2015). With the initiation of aerial photography in the twentieth century, geographical vision was extended to encompass and combine the photograph and the map to define the limits of the state (Dyce 2013). More recently, numerous projects have aimed to capture land and life along the "longest undefended border in the world" including a display of poignant images of the new border by photographer Andreas Rutkauskas (Rutkauskas and McManus 2016), and the memorable documentation of border people and places in the bicentennial gift from Canada to the U.S. in 1976–*Between Friends/Entre Amis* (Canada 1976).

Beyond North America, boundary surveys have been accompanied by artistic representations of border imaginaries in contexts where borders were being established by colonial powers or re-defined by states. The literature is sparse on this contribution to our understanding of border imaginaries in most world regions. Kathleen Stewart Howe and Nitza Rosovsky (1997) document the "revelation" of the Holy Land in an exploration of Palestine and its boundaries. Research in China does not offer artistic representations associated with boundary surveys because the surveys were conducted by the military in the Communist era to confirm boundaries and the documentation is classified. In Europe, state boundaries have in large part been established for centuries, and the outgrowing boundary of the European Union follows the established boundaries of member nation-states. Boundary survey art in Africa and South America confirms that it exists but to a lesser extent.

3.3.5 Architecturalization of the border

Another form of the artistic rendition of the border imaginary may be found in the architecture of the border and border crossings. Sharon Zukin (1993) includes these constructs in her articulation of "landscapes of power". Considerable attention is currently focused on the wall constructions along the U.S.–Mexico border, on "Trump's" wall and preceding fences and barriers constructed by the U.S. to stem the flow of illegal migrants, drugs, and guns. Although this border architecture gained considerable notoriety during the Trump regime, the Berlin Wall was arguably even more notorious during the Cold War. Both of these walls, and many others around the globe including the wall dividing Israel and the West Bank, are not recognized as architectural achievements but rather as stark, functional barriers. Although the Great Wall of China (actually numerous walls built over centuries) served a similar purpose in the past, today it stands as an architectural marvel and achievement of its time.

Although walls are on the rise and in the news, these architectural constructions are often less demonstrative of border culture than the artistic renderings applied to them in protest by those who would have the walls dismantled. Some of the artists are internationally recognized like Banksy (Elsworth-Jones 2013), whereas legions of graffiti artists have also applied their visions to walls in Israel, the U.S., and Mexico, and elsewhere around the globe. Ronald Rael adds his contribution of participatory public pedagogy to question and resist the dominant narrative of the wall in his evocative installation "Teeter-Totter Wall" (Kaplan 2021). This prize-winning installation illustrates that the border wall is at once architecture and manifesto (Rael 2017). In the essay "Border wall as architecture", Rael suggests that the wall also be viewed as productive infrastructure, and proposes an array of retrofits and new projects—water treatment wall, solar wall, water and life safety wall, bike path and pedestrian wall—that builds on existing conditions and works to solve problems created by the barrier (Rael 2014). Moreover, the spaces adjacent to the walls have been incorporated into border landscapes that convey imaginaries of how the border was celebrated before the walls and may be celebrated despite the walls (Herzog 2001). In Tijuana, Mexico, adjacent to the border wall and falling to the Pacific beach is a community park where residents of Tijuana, and visitors, may approach the wall and look through the stanchions to the barren and patrolled strip of land on the U.S. side of the border. The park provides benches, varying vistas, parking, and a festive atmosphere. This park offers an architectural imaginary in contrast to the border wall.

Similarly, but several thousand kilometres up the Pacific coast on the border between Canada and the U.S., the Peace Arch International Park occupies the "international" space between the Canadian and U.S. ports-of-entry at White

FIGURE 3.5 Peace Arch Monument, White Rock, BC, Blaine, WA. Photo reproduced with permission from Laurie Trautman, Border Policy Research Institute.

Rock, BC, and Blaine, WA. The Peace Arch monument, a classical gateway edifice, is in the centre of the park surrounded by lawn and trees (Figure 3.5). Here, motorists leave their cars during long waits at the border to walk about. Others stop for picnics and to exercise their dogs. The space was designed as a place to rest, acknowledge the peaceful ambience, and celebrate the cooperation and friendship between the U.S. and Canada (Konrad and Nicol 2008). Most recently, during the COVID-19 pandemic in 2020–2021, the space allowed families from either side of the border to unite without officially leaving their countries because the Canada–U.S. border was closed to all but essential travel.

In Europe, architecturalization of the border has advanced to landscapes of effective design for the border. An original and comprehensive study by Mark Eker and Henk Van Houtum (2013) identifies, maps, and records in numerous ways the "border land" of the Netherlands. The book is an atlas, a set of insightful essays, a visual documentary, and a planning document for the design of the Dutch–German–Belgian borderlands. It is richly illustrated to the extent that the reader becomes familiar with the borderlands in a multi-sensory way, and offers a welcome model for future landscape architectural studies and manuals for border architectural design. Anna Grichting (Grichting and Zebos-Knos 2017) has also contributed substantially to understanding the social ecology of border landscapes in Europe and Asia. Among her works is a digital and dynamic atlas for collaborative planning of the evolving Green Line in Cyprus (Grichting 2015), and a study of the greening of the Red Zone or demilitarized zone of Korea (Grichting and Kim 2014).

Border architecture in the twenty-first century, however, largely aligns with an imaginary of the border focused on control and security. In airports the aim is to ensure mobility while establishing an overt and calculative architecture of affective control (Adey 2008). Forward-looking designers are experimenting with systems of multi-robot border patrolling that would make previous architectures of bordering redundant (Marino et al. 2013). The vision for the new Gordie Howe International Bridge between Windsor and Detroit will augment the existing Ambassador Bridge, built in the early twentieth century, with a state-of-the-art infrastructure complex constructed through a public–private partnership (Lesnau 2016). New border infrastructure projects like the Gordie Howe Bridge may benefit from current visions of territorial engagement as commons and breathing spaces (Flaherty 2019), but in order to accomplish this vision we will need to expand our border imaginaries beyond security primacy and the imperative to control space within established perimeters.

3.4 Performing the border: Renewable imaginaries

Human spatial behaviour acknowledges borders as external and territorial because, as John Agnew (1994) argues, nation-states are caught in a "territorial trap" in which we imagine states as fixed units of sovereign space, a distinct domestic and foreign polarity, and containers of societies. In a world of transnational flows and mobility, all of these assumptions are open to question and challenge and we need to imagine new kinds of borders beyond the line, and transition to engaging with both border landscapes and border aesthetics (Dell'Agnese and Amilhat Szary 2015). In the summer of 2020, with the border sustained emphatically between the U.S. and Canada due to COVID-19 restrictions, the Peace Arch Park became a meeting place for families and friends divided by the border. The "Summer of Love" and "Peace" was imagined in an in-between space where smiling Mounties and border officials mixed with happy beavers and dogs, all surrounding an iconic VW hippy bus (Figure 3.6). Yet, we need to acknowledge as well that many borders like the Mexico–U.S. border are "lines in the sand" that are aspired to (St. John 2012), reified in cinema (Dell'Agnese 2005), and memorialized in song (Madrid 2011). Nevertheless, beyond all these desires and emotional attachments to the line, there is also a spirit of faith, ritual, and resistance that transcends the U.S.–Mexico border (Hondagneau et al. 2004), and most other borders as well.

The following discussion offers a brief synopsis and insight into a substantial literature that explores the imaginaries of the border which form, guide, and renew our performance and materialization of the border. These bordering imaginaries contribute to the everyday construction of geographical visualizations and realizations like the Mediterranean neighbourhood (Scott et al. 2019). Some of

FIGURE 3.6 Summer of Love, 2020. Peace Arch Park. Photo reproduced by permission from Laurie Trautman, Border Policy Research Institute.

these new or revived imaginaries of the border extract the line and replace it with the body. The contemporary border places mobility at the service of security thereby finitely grading and risk scoring forms of movement such that the body is divided even within itself (Deleuze 1995). Yet, as Deleuze and Guattari (1992) would have it, this process is not without mediation, and the border is theorized as "becoming" in the de- and re-territorialization of the border (Woodward and Jones 2005, 237). Our conceptualization of these renewable imaginaries of the border is that they are creative and reflective of culture. We agree with Christina Giudice and Chiara Giubilano (2015) that "re-imaging the border" is viewing "border art as a space of critical imagination and creative resistance." Border art may also produce the opposite effect aligning this space in a post-politics of images (Amilhat Szary 2021). And, new and emerging imaginaries of the border inevitably result in conflicting imaginaries as in the case of the construction of African asylum seekers in the Israeli political discourse (Weisblum 2019).

3.4.1 From line to body: Bodylines and bodies on the line

The contemporary border places mobility at the service of security, finitely grading and risk scoring forms of movement such that the body is divided even within itself (Deleuze 1992). As a consequence, biometric borders govern mobilities (Amoore 2006), and people are taken apart through a form of digitized dissection at the border (Amoore and Hall 2009). The body is no longer important but its parts are because they may be traced, as for example through iris scans and other forms of codification and algorithmic re-calculation (Soto 2021, Virilio 2003). Paul Virilio (2003) surmises that this means identity will be replaced by traceability. Although border guards are seen as complicit in this dissection (and desecration) (Bigo 2014, Prokkola and Ridanpaa 2015), the ultimate responsibility lies with the faceless and un-personified state which evades accountability. This unsettling condition, the distillation of the border to checkpoints and bodies, gives rise to reaction, resistance, and often creativity (Jeganathan 2018). Our purpose is to focus on the cultural dimension of biopolitics rather than the more extensive considerations framing bodies on the line.

Achille Mbembe (2019) differentiates bodies from corpses in the final subjugation of life through the power of death. The ultimate expression of sovereignty is in the power to decide who may live and who must die, but most exercise of sovereignty at the border seeks to differentiate and subjugate bodies through bodylines of identity and traceability. Bodylines in border culture are evident in the discourse of border crossers (Fellner 2020). For example, a Mexican body as cultural representation and metaphor emerges from the immigration discourse of Mexican border crossers (Aguirre and Simmons 2008). Body parts like skin become rich metaphors for the cultural border between self and the world (Benthien 2004). Embodying representations of border crossings on the Mexico–U.S. border—cactus carvings and desert defecations—conjure imaginaries of Mexican border crossers as desecrators of protected space (Sundberg and Kaserman 2007). Even body counts on the Mexico–U.S. border would have us imagine the Mexican "body-politic" at the border materialized not as becoming, but rather as receding (Soto 2021). Technologies for audializing migrant bodies (Weitzel 2018) and encoding bodies into the European digital border (Kuster and Tsianos 2016) de-materialize and abstract the body as liquefied in a mobile border context.

3.4.2 Imagining new kinds of human borders in transnationalism and globalization

We imagine new kinds of borders of transnationalism and globalization in this mobility regime (Shamir 2005), yet people are caught lagging in between or thwarted by borders in motion (Konrad 2015, Nail 2016). Whereas border control has aimed to enhance security by focusing on the body rather than the border in this mobile border regime, it has instead enhanced (in)securitization practices of border control (Bigo 2014). The biometric border may be devised to measure the body but is tied to social, political, and cultural imaginaries (Whyte 2020).

The anthropology and geography of globalization and transnationalism conveys deterritorialized identities of communities in a world of increased movement and flows (Kearney 1995). These deterritorialized identities function like previous, territorialized, imagined communities (Anderson 1983), and these imagined communities re-imagine intercultural communication and connection across borders (Sorells 2010). History, power, and social justice are all re-interpreted in new imaginaries of community in transnational space as illustrated in Dana Diminescu's (2012) *e-Diasporas Atlas*. Becoming citizens is re-imagined (El-Haj 2009). For example, the transnational imagination of Chinese leaving China, informed by foreign media, creates new imaginaries of citizenship outside of China's constraints (Sun 2002). These imaginaries may be conditioned by an accessible transnational cinema (Higbee and Lim 2010). The cinema may also promote fascist imaginaries as evidenced in Hindi films of the India–Pakistan border (Banaji 2007). Yet, film festivals may provide alternative imaginaries of conflict as seen at the Sarajevo Film Festival (Deiana 2019). A classic example of the re-imagining of borders in transnationalism and globalization is the creation of the Department of Homeland Security in the U.S. After 9/11, security of U.S. borders required a complete overhaul of security risk, security procedures, and security structures, and a new imaginary of national security emerged (Mabee 2007). A more comprehensive treatment of border culture in transnationalism follows in the final chapter of this book.

3.4.3 Boundaries of race, ethnicity, gender, and religion

Sadly, imagining national security borders in the U.S. and elsewhere has become conjoined with recognizing only whiteness at a secure border (Jones 2016). Other colours are reflected at the border (Bebout 2016). Imagining boundaries of race, ethnicity, gender, and religion has produced an extensive literature in critical border studies. The edges of transnationalism and globalization are etched at national boundaries and borders between communities in racial, ethnic, gender, and religious imaginaries and manifestations (Yeoh et al. 2003). Racialized and gendered figures have become articulators of the border (Biemann 2002), whereas in the early modern imagination monsters guarded the borders of the "civilized" world (Byars and Broedel 2018, Schmoll 2020). Re-imagining borders in a crowded world, however, leaves little space for accommodation. In Malaysia, tightened Malay identity precludes Indonesian migrants (Spaan et al. 2002). Even Australia's insular imagination conflates beaches, borders, unwelcome boats, and foreign bodies (Perera 2009).

Imagining border spaces is mobilized and framed in a variety of ways. Cinematic explorations of race and gender unveil the border and Southern spaces (Mains 2004). Young Canadian Muslims visualize U.S. security and surveillance at the border as racialized management of identities (Nagra and Maurutto 2016). On the other hand, British Jazz easily crosses borders of race, nation, and class (Moore 2017). In the midst of the migration crisis, imagining Europe's borders has spawned commemorative art of migrant tragedies (Horsti 2016), and imagining the female refugee has constructed victims from visual images that prevail observers to "click to donate" (Johnson 2011).

3.4.4 Boundaries and profiling

The young Canadian Muslims seeking entry to the U.S. at border crossings in airports and by rail, road, or sea all claim that they have been profiled as a risk due to their religion and ethnicity (Nagra and Maurutto 2016). Augmented with former president Trump's Executive Order to restrict Muslim entry to the U.S., the practice of profiling lends a sharper edge to how the border is imagined as well as how the border is managed. Since the events of 9/11, profiling, although not acknowledged in Department of Homeland Security policy guidelines and statutes, has become even more commonplace, and an increasingly dominant technology of bordering (Shamir 2005). Although it is widely practised, the constitutionality of profiling illegal immigrants remains a matter of legal debate (Gallini and Young 2010). The practice is, however, well established and almost universal among border agents based on numerous anonymous interviews worldwide. Henk Van Houtum (2010) has referred to the practice as "human blacklisting" and a form of apartheid. A comprehensive analysis of profiling is offered in Leila M. Whitley's (2015) doctoral dissertation. In Europe, profiling is now practised at internal borders of the EU as well as at the Shengen boundary (Schwarz 2016).

3.4.5 Invisible boundaries

In a transnational world where traditional nation-state boundaries are augmented if not blurred by mobile borders among people, and divisions of faith, colour, wealth, class, and gender are more delineated and complex, some boundaries are recognized by only a selection of the population, and some boundaries are invisible. Borders that travel, and particularly the figured border, become less apparent and less visible (Ono 2012). Invisible boundaries may be less apparent but they are not necessarily less significant. For example, workers in the new information technology economy have engaged in a transformation of the economy but they have also crossed a definitive yet invisible boundary in human aptitude and work ethos concomitant with more visible boundaries of wealth and mobility (Walkerdine 2006). Yet, there is a "culture map" in global business based on invisible boundaries of communication style, feedback conventions, persuasion tendencies, leadership, decision models, trust traditions, handling disagreements, and time management. Furthermore, Erin Meyer (2014) has promoted the idea that national culture determines how people in a nation behave and develop behavioural stereotypes. These invisible boundaries matter because they underlie imagined institutions and power (Amilhat Szary and Giraut 2015, Ray 2017).

3.5 Border ecologies

Nature has been known to overflow and obliterate borders constructed by humans such as in former Mayan or Southeast Asian territories, and in other contexts globally. These natural regenerations may be viewed as sublime retribution for human lordship and excess, but they may also be imagined as subject matter for a horror tale in which strangler figs crush temples and palaces. Prevalent, however, are imaginaries of human obliteration of border ecologies. These imaginaries have generated a substantial and rapidly growing literature of the Anthropocene, and within this an expanding focus on borders in the Anthropocene (Dalby 2020a). Attention to imagining borders in the Anthropocene is the culmination of research on borders and environmental sustainability constructed on several pillars of research on borders and environment. These pillars are (1) cross-border ecologies including boundary waters, (2) borders and conservation, (3) eco-activism at borders, and (4) sanitary borders and invasive species. Also emerging from these foundations to complement research on the Anthropocene are new ecovisions that cross boundaries to help situate post-humanistic borders.

3.5.1 Anthropocene bordering

Although one may argue that we already find humanity well ensconced in the new era of the Anthropocene, beyond both the Quaternary in earth history and modernity in human experience, our framings of sustainability need to move beyond modernity (Maggs and Robinson 2016). Scientific framings of sustainability strain under Anthropocene realities. Similarly, bordering sustainability in the Anthropocene remains yoked in efforts to govern pollution, resources, wildlife, and other aspects of the environment by territorial jurisdiction (Dalby 2020b). Required is a rethinking of bordering practices that govern environmental matters, and re-imagining the relationships of territory to ecological function. Dalby (2020b) offers three reasons for this recalibration: increased national system instability, new conditions of non-stationarity, and inadequacy of stable base line assumptions for dealing with rapid change across boundaries. Boundaries are not where they used to be. Both ecological boundaries and human territorial borders are mobile, and perhaps even more mobile in globalization (Amilhat Szary 2014, Amilhat Szary and Giraut 2015). Global warming is altering ecological borders, particularly in polar regions where rapidly changing extent and depth of sea ice are reconfiguring natural boundaries and engaging geopolitical shifts to capture newly accessible resources (Steinberg et al. 2015). Furthermore, sea levels are rising due to melting sea ice and glaciers, thus impacting territorial boundaries of island and coastal nations.

Within this massive global shifting of ecological and human territorial boundaries, and the conflict of territorial imaginaries associated with it, border imaginaries will need to change. Currently linked to ossified territorial limits, border imaginaries will need to accommodate border motion in the conditions of instability, non-stationarity, and established base lines, as identified above. Also, border imaginaries will need to loosen territorial bonds, national identity confines, security framings, and socio-political constraints to enable visions of ecological responsibility to prevail over the self-interests of geopolitical cultures (Tuathail 2005). Simon Dalby (2019) offers a perspective on how Canadian geopolitical culture needs to shift in its engagement with climate change and sustainability. Encountering the Anthropocene requires not only new directions in green political thinking (Biermann and Lovbrand 2019) but in green geopolitical thinking as well.

One approach that builds from the bottom up and shows promise for more extensive territorial engagement is permaculture. Permaculture is an approach to land management adopting arrangements observed in flourishing ecosystems. It builds on successful relations of humans, non-humans, and the natural environment. Permaculture may provide imaginaries of the Anthropocene embracing advanced technical design practice, holistic life philosophy, and intersectional social movement (Roux-Rosier et al. 2018). What would borders look like in such multilayered ecosystems? Clearly, this is a question worthy of immediate attention and considerable thought beyond the aim of this brief introduction to bordering in the Anthropocene.

3.5.2 Ecologies across borders

As a prelude and perhaps a transition to imaginaries of sustainable Anthropocene ecologies, some ecological visions have crossed boundaries to engage frontiers in foreign environmental contexts. Traditionally, these have been artificially maintained arboretums or gardens that convey ideas and ecological orders in museum contexts, particularly in hostile and intemperate environments. English gardens are replicated in British Empire outposts around the globe. Similarly, French imperial landscape designs and ecologies have accompanied French settlers to the corners of the earth. The colonial outpost of Louisbourg situated on Cape Breton Island in Nova Scotia, Canada, has been reconstructed from its eighteenth-century ruins, complete with gardens in the classical French design and ecology (O'Neill 1983, Johnston 2001). Several centuries later, as the Anthropocene crystallizes into ecological imaginary and materiality, these gardens provide historical-geographical context and continuity as well as evidence of discontinuity of ecologies in alien environments. A visit to Louisbourg confirms the artificial nature of the gardens protected in an eighteenth-century fortress replica surrounded by an encroaching scrub spruce forest. If geopolitical cultures do not evolve, ecologies may not resonate with borders resulting in dystopic geographies. Accordingly, it is instructive to explore the ecologies that have crossed borders to understand the processes involved, and to visualize the imaginaries across borders.

In nearby Halifax, Nova Scotia, Lhotsampa refugees from Bhutan grow vegetables adapted from their homeland in the Glen community garden provided by the city (Hinton and Schnurr 2021). As we exemplified in the introduction to this book, the garden is culturally appropriate and environmentally adaptable. The garden contributes to traditional diets, a feeling of being at home, solidifying gardener identities, and building and strengthening social capital. Also, it is a healthy adaptation that offers a transition of Lhotsampa community to Nova

Scotia. In the words of Kavita, one of the respondents interviewed, "I think of my garden here as the same as my three acres in Bhutan." In this instance, Lhotsampa ecological imaginaries have worked across boundaries to recreate home, community, and culture in the process of transferring ecologies.

Borders in the contemporary, postcolonial world characteristically divide ecologies. In North America, borders between Mexico and the U.S. and between Canada and the U.S. divide deserts, prairies, woodlands, drainage basins, and water bodies. Even natural borders like the Rio Grande or St. Lawrence Rivers are the centre or core of ecological regions rather than boundaries between ecologies. In order to ensure sustainability of border environment, cooperation has been fashioned in a context of ecological space, primarily within the framework of watersheds or drainage basins. On the U.S. border with Mexico, transboundary ecosystem management was imagined within watersheds once the recognition emerged that scarce water resources required coordinated management across the international boundary and state boundaries (Ganster 2000, Hoffman 2006). Given the regional variation that compounds and largely parallels the major watershed delineations along the Mexico–U.S. border, the imaginaries of border ecologies align with these regions (Brown 2020, 325). In the Canada–U.S. border context the pattern is very much the same although aspects of sustainability across the border extend beyond water and clean air to engage forest and grassland ecosystems in horizontal and in vertical (mountain) environments (Konrad and Nicol 2008, 217–255).

During the late twentieth century, as free trade regimes flourished in North America, imaginaries of continental management of the environment led to the establishment of the Commission for Environmental Cooperation (CEC), formed by a side agreement of the North American Free Trade Agreement (NAFTA) (Coronado 2020). At once a model for trilateral cooperation in environmental affairs, an institution, and a vision for ecological sustainability, the CEC has prevailed through undulating political ideologies and visions of environmental protection and stewardship in Mexico, the U.S., and Canada. Success has been measured in ecologically significant aspirations and accomplishments such as Monarch butterfly rehabilitation, although deforestation and Monarch habitat remains in danger. Success is also measured in meeting practical if smaller scale domestic and international objectives in conserving, protecting, and enhancing the environment. Subdued during the Trump administration, the CEC vision has been reactivated by the instalment of Joe Biden as the 46th president of the U.S., and his immediate re-engagement with the Paris Accord.

Imaginaries of border ecologies extend beyond environmental sustainability to infuse ecological ideology into social and political domains. The films *Maquilapolis* and *Sleep Dealer* explore the confluence of ecology, labour, race, and gender along the Mexico–U.S. border, and illustrate the naturalization of ecological devastation (Orihuela and Hageman 2011). Moreover, Lawrence Herzog (2003) extends the ecological framework to identify seven ecologies of the border in global Tijuana: global factory zones, transnational consumer spaces, global tourism districts, post-NAFTA neighbourhoods, transnational community places, spaces of conflict, and invented connections. Border landscapes are social ecologies in which societies engage differentially and consistently with border place and environment (Grichting and Zebich-Knos 2017, Sadowski-Smith 2013).

Border ecologies like other ecologies are changing and dynamic. In a richly illustrated book documenting border ecologies in Hong Kong, Joshua Bolchover and Peter Hasdell (2016) record the gradual alteration and then final elimination of the border ecological zone originally established to buffer Hong Kong from China. The authors conclude that by 2050 there will be no vestige of the zone as Shenzen and Hong Kong merge. Elsewhere in China, similar rapid development of urban areas and resource development such as hydro-electric projects along the international border threaten ecological sustainability. In Yunnan Province, China's foremost "powershed", upland forest and riparian ecosystems along the border are being dissected by utility and transportation corridors that have emerged in less than a decade to alter the landscape and environment of the borderlands (Ptak and Konrad 2021).

3.5.3 Borders to conserve nature and attack nature

Borders also help to conserve nature in parks and protected areas. National, state, provincial, and international parks, reserves, and refuges at the border between Canada and the U.S. actually help guard nature on the line at various scales. Although the boundary slices across habitat, migratory routes, watersheds, and ecological zones like the Frontenac biosphere extending across the New York State–Ontario boundary between the Canadian Shield and the Adirondacks, ecological designations protect some of these areas.

> To some extent these natural areas have been sutured at the border as national and provincial/state parks, wilderness areas, and reserves and refuges of many types meet along the boundary. A prominent example is the linkage of Glacier and Waterton Lakes National Parks along the Rocky Mountain front in Montana and Alberta. These National Parks align some interpretive programs, link visitor transportation, and celebrate a joint Science and History Day. Yet, parks and reserves at the border also serve to buffer the line between countries, states and provinces and communities, and establish an official government presence on the frontier.
>
> *(Konrad and Nicol 2008, 219)*

As Maano Ramutsindela (2007) argues, transfrontier conservation in Africa is at the confluence of capital, politics, and nature. In an assessment of African peace parks at borders, Ramutsindela (2017, 112) concludes that peace park creation shows that while the state limits its authority over the edge space, it holds on to the space and its border citizens. Peace parks are transformed into resource frontiers by multiple forces including but not limited to environmental concerns. These resource frontiers enable a racialized dual land tenure system that strengthens rights of (white) landowners while it marginalizes communal (Black) land users. Whereas peace parks derive power and recognition from their articulation of a broader ecological imaginary of conservation and environmental agendas, their internal power is tied to prevailing property regimes and the business model of transnational operation. Mozambique has extended state power through enhanced articulation of sovereignty in multiscalar interactions in the Great Limpopo Transfrontier Park (Lunstrum 2013). In the Park, "land grabs" and "green grabs" have displaced more than 7000 people from the border park (Lunstrum 2016). Nature at borders is not only about natural imaginings but in fact embraces a complex and multiscalar intertwining of conservation and power relations (Amilhat Szary 2014).

3.5.4 Eco-activism at the border: The eco-frontier as conflict zone

Ecologies imagined under stress and attack from human action characteristically mobilize eco-activism at sites of incursion. Here radical activists express their commitment for the wild in ritual demonstrations and forms of resistance (Pike 2017). Various forms and levels of environmentality mobilize ecological rationalities and power to create and sustain protected areas. Networks are formed across distance and the extent of influence of activists. Strategies of the wider conservation lobby align the local with the global (Ramutsindela et al. 2020). Activism is the catalyst for linking the mental, social, and environmental ecologies (Guatteri 1992) and activism is also the force integrating social ecology and eco-art (Burmur et al. 2013). For example, in Ecuador's upland communities of ex-patriots from North America and Europe, wall art and billboards support eco-activism and policies of sustainability. Transnational protest and global activism necessarily take eco-activism across borders but do not necessarily focus on the border (Bennett 2005).

National imaginaries of hydrocarbon development and production in Ecuador and Bolivia are bordered among those who support the extraction economy as national policy and those who would limit development and protect endangered ecologies of nature and Indigenous peoples (Perreau and Valdivia 2010). "Eco-governmentality" envisions environmental governance that is engaged with ecological principles and mindful of Indigenous rights across boundaries (Valdivia 2015, Lu et al. 2016). Yet, these border places remain marginalized spaces where extractivism prevails. As Lucile Medina (2013) illustrates, Central American borders are complex cross-border interfaces. Whereas an ecological context may prevail across boundaries of El Salvador, Honduras, and Nicaragua, borders block nature allowing it to be attacked and challenged at the border (Medina-Nicolas 2007). In Ecuador's Galapagos Islands, borders between the Galapagos National Park and inhabited areas are envisioned as incommensurable spaces of natural (protected) and human (productive) space (Valdivia et al. 2014).

Nature at the border, according to Sylvain Guyot (2011), may be theorized as green gerrymandering and conceptualized as eco-frontier. Encompassed in the eco-frontier are virtual and mental imaginaries of natural spaces of eco-conquest (Westernized representation of nature), and geographical processes to understand green dynamics of territorial appropriation and conquest. Generations of imperial, geopolitical, and global eco-frontiers co-exist but also grate against each other resulting in disparate imaginaries and ultimately eco-activism. The politics of eco-frontiers emerges when environmentality meets borderities (Guyot 2015). Nature itself may not be more poignant at the border, but duelling imaginaries of nature may be enacted there for enhanced exposure. In the wilderness of Lapland and boreal Quebec, imaginaries of bounded "Nordic Indigenous natures" are activated by Sami and Cree to legitimate Indigenous involvement and management of the resources and nature of "Laponia" and "Assinica" (Maraud and Guyot 2016).

3.5.5 Sanitary borders and invasive species

As we complete this book the world is combating the greatest cross-border microbial invasion and pandemic in a century. COVID-19 crossed borders rapidly in a mobile world resulting in a global pandemic that re-ignited global nationalism (Bieber 2020) and re-delineated borders. Human bodies exposed to the coronavirus now have one additional component to decide admissibility at the border (Tedeschi 2020). Migrants in the "stay at home" world of the pandemic face both greater chance of contracting the virus and greater chance of being stopped at borders (Guadagno 2020). In the European Union, the border response to the pandemic has varied among European nations but invariably the tendency has been to engage and tighten border restrictions to impact migrants and residents in variable ways (Goniewicz et al. 2020). The pandemic has been almost beyond the imaginary, by February of 2022, killing almost six million people worldwide, with over 900,000 dead in the U.S. alone.

Whereas national and certainly human borders have had a limited impact on the spread of the pandemic, borders have been used as sanitary barriers throughout the world. Quarantine—a form of sanitary bordering—is utilized routinely by Australia for phytosanitary and sanitary incursion management, thus establishing an imaginary of the Island Nation as an entomological control space (Maynard et al. 2004). This no rules barred approach, and the vision that has emerged from it, has helped Australia to contain COVID-19 more effectively (Moloney and Moloney 2020), at least during initial waves of the pandemic. The experience of Canada and the U.S. in combating Mad Cow Disease at the turn of the twentieth century was not as successful. Two infected cows rapidly spread the disease through herds on both sides of the long border resulting in massive exterminations to contain the disease, and extensive economic impacts in both countries (O'Neill 2005). The lessons learned from the mad cow and SARS epidemics helped to condition a rapid Canada–U.S. border closure almost immediately after the pandemic was declared by the World Health Organization in March 2020.

Differential sanitary regulations also work in other domains such as wildlife management. Due to the fact that EU policies and regulations for sanitary disposal of carcasses are interpreted and applied differentially in Spain and Portugal, vultures halt at an invisible border (confirmed by GPS) on the Iberian Peninsula corresponding with the border between the two countries (Arrondo et al. 2018). In other parts of the world, sanitary borders also align with national boundaries due to laws and traditions (Weiner and Rogers 2002). Examples include the rice laws in Japan that protect agriculture and vested interests on the premise of sanitary concerns and efforts to maintain genetic purity (Davis and Oh 2007, Horiuchi and Saito 2010). Similarly, the purity law or "reinheitsgebot" assures that German beer remains brewed with pure ingredients, but also protects German brewing interests at home and abroad (Van Tongeren 2011). This policy, like the designation of Cassis or Champagne in France, has been assaulted by the levelling regulatory efforts of the EU.

The imaginary of invasion prevails in many of the sanitary borderings worldwide. These concerns for biosecurity extend beyond the nativism debate of spatializing and ethnicizing the right to belong, with very destructive consequences possible (Fall 2013). An invasive species is "one that arrives (often without human assistance) in a habitat it had not previously occupied, then establishes a population and spreads autonomously" (Simberloff 2010, 131). Many species, however, have been introduced in colonial times and well before and after then. It is as if humans accelerated and advanced life's tendency to wander. In a climate-changed world, mobile species and species mobility are likely to increase as climate conditions change (Fall 2014), and ecosystems become mobile both in spatial and ecological dimensions.

We conclude this brief discussion of invasive species and imagined border ecologies with an emphatic example drawn from popular fiction. Carl Hiaasen is a satirist and master of the eco-mystery genre, who writes about Florida and the ambition, greed, vanity, and disappointment of his characters who collide with the environment and fragile ecosystems of the "Sunshine State". In his latest novel *Squeeze Me* (2020) Hiaasen portrays how unleashed nature, in the form of invasive Burmese Pythons (up to 20 feet long), find their way from the nurturing everglades across multiple borders to exclusive Palm Beach. Here, one large specimen consumes a diminutive socialite, a mystery unfolds (uncoils), and the story finally resolves in and around the presidential resort. Although the story is fiction, the ecological implications are real and stark, and the reader is left with surreal yet very probable imaginaries of unfolding ecological mayhem.

3.5.6 New ecovisions across new boundaries and panic at the border

In order to envision contemporary, dynamic ecologies in a rapidly changing and warming environment new boundaries may need to be imagined and acknowledged. Coastline reconfigurations, polar sea ice disintegration, Amazonian rainforest removal, and numerous other changes in ecologies redraw environmental boundaries and impact human boundaries—political, social, and cultural. Efforts to imagine and predict the ecological impacts of human and natural processes may be useful in ecosystem management and sustainability. An example is found in the conceptualization of the Crown of the Continent, the 10,000-foot isoline that contains the heights extending from the southwestern U.S., across two borders with Canada into Alaska (Pedynowski 2003). In this zone, looking and working across state boundaries enables assessments like consistent snow pack recording for water resource management and global warming prediction. Wildlife management gains from the definition of transboundary linkages of species such as wolves and bears, and the construction of conservation corridors to enable their migrations and protect their habitat and survival (Prato and Fagre 2010).

New ecovisions are also unsettling for humans and their polities. This causes panic at the border (Amilhat Szary 2014). Whereas greater attention associated with panic at the border has been focused on the boundary issue of refugees and asylum seekers (Agnew 2019), border panic also manifests in pandemics—our current COVID-19 pandemic and the AIDS crisis of the 1980s and 1990s (Bayramoglu 2021). Panic is instilled by intrusion, and the perceived intruders are constructed as the alien to be vilified and halted at the border. The panic is exacerbated by the realization, although not necessarily the acknowledgement, that borders are fragile constructs. For Turks caught in a panic over AIDS, "the movement of sexually and racially 'other' bodies across borders was seen as a threat to the fragile construed border between 'Turkishness' and 'foreignness'" (Bayramoglu 2021, 1589). Border panic extends into the human performance of place as it positions and aligns, and lays bare the imaginaries of the border place (Hill 2006).

3.6 The post-humanistic border

Borders have become central in social and political transformation of the world and human affairs. Borders have spread through the widening and multiplication of bordering practices to the extent that understanding borders is as much about socio-cultural practices and discourses as about territorial lines and political institutions. Furthermore, anthropogenic approaches suggest that non-human agents are given motion by human agency, and that these non-human actors must be identified and acknowledged as well in our theorization of borders and borderings. We need to imagine and understand the non-human agencies and the linkages between human and non-human agencies (Dalby 2020a). The premise and the perception need to shift to the understanding that humans are not in control of everything, and that ultimately border culture needs to be viewed through a wider and integrative ecological lens.

If we return to our prevailing example of the COVID-19 pandemic, we certainly may acknowledge the agency of the virus. This virus has occasioned an immediate change in human movement, re-organization of state borders, and social, economic, and cultural bordering. Although the virus has led to the human immobility and other changes in motion surrounding borders, human agencies are responsible for the bordering processes such as lockdowns and selective border crossings. The pandemic response is viewed as a growing *border orientation* globally (Kenwick and Simmons 2020).

This example, and the recent research on borders in motion (Konrad 2015, Nail 2016) and post-human ecologies (Braidotti and Bignall 2019) assert the importance of understanding the anthropogenic and post-humanistic conceptualization of borders. The post-humanistic border appears to be moving between territorial ambiguity and human belongingness (Konrad 2021). Although borders are set in motion when they are established, the motion has achieved thresholds of resonance and dissonance in globalization that extend beyond the power and grasp of the state and its inhabitants. Borders in motion have created anxiety among people (Almond 2016), and generated confusion and complexity in border governance and institutions. Moreover, borders in motion are conceptualized as asynchronous with the architecture and process of the state system, even though their expanded and enhanced motion may be seen as human efforts to extend the viability of borders in globalization. The post-humanistic border is emerging between territorial ambiguity arising from de-territorialization and re-territorialization, as well as forces beyond human control, and the imaginaries of borders influenced by anxiety, panic, and imperatives of human belongingness. This mobile border is in part situated by human agency and in part unleashed by post-human forces unlocked in the process of globalization (Konrad 2021).

3.7 Border culture production: Essentialization and materialization of border imaginaries

Cultural production emerges from some border imaginaries. Many border imaginaries are idealized but not manifested realizations and productions. Culture is on the move and cultural productions of bordering are everywhere, and they remain particularly concentrated in borderlands. And, as established in recent theoretical and empirical studies, interactions among cultural components are complex and multidimensional rather than binary (Mayer 2014, Rodney 2017). In a sense, culture is being decolonized with expanding transnationalism, but when this happens border culture may produce both representations of hybridity and forms derived from contestation. It appears that borders undergoing decolonization and other significant changes encourage more cultural production than more stable borders. Consequently, it is probable that extensive cultural production at borders conveys expanded cultural meaning in transnationalism and globalization.

Border essentialization and materialization occur in the process of moving from border imaginaries to borders and back again. Borders are imbued with substance. This substance may be essentialized in that the border becomes intrinsic, the main thing, wholly consuming and needed or required. Similarly, borders are substantiated in prevailing material constructs. These materializations may be powerful to the extent that they conjure up new imaginaries and enhanced impressions of the border.

Chiara Brambilla (2009) comments on the paradoxical structures between essentialization, which limits or funnels the border imaginary in an intrinsic way, and creativity which expands the border imaginary, allows multiple expressions and meanings, and liberates the imaginary. Essentialization of the border imaginary then limits theorization of the border (Vila 2003). Consequently, discrete identity categories in border conflict and post-conflict societies such as Cyprus, Northern Ireland, and Israel are not conducive to amelioration and require de-essentialization (Bekerman et al. 2009). Even Jewish–Palestinian encounter groups in dialogue may not be able to advance beyond essentialization discourses and may indeed become sites of essentialization (Helman 2002). Films like Spike Lee's *Jungle Fever* and Octavia Butler's *Kindred* de-essentialize interracial representations through "Black" and "white" border crossings (Paulin 1997). Perhaps one of the most egregious examples of essentialist border rhetoric originates in Donald Trump's creation of racial identities and other dangerous liminalities at the Mexico–U.S. border (Heuman and Gonzalez 2018).

The border wall, particularly in its more recent and extensive materializations, leads to re-imagining the U.S.–Mexico border (Casey and Watkins 2014). Picket fences have been re-materialized as concrete barriers and steel walls with successive waves of new imaginaries (McGuire 2013). Crossing materializations that are novel and extensive, like the imposing, new checkpoints along the Chinese border with Vietnam, Laos, and Myanmar (Hu and Konrad 2021), and "the road" or Albanian–Greek cross-border motorway (Dalakoglou 2010) establish new images of cross-border control and mobility. At the Sino-Kazakh boundary, the Khorgos crossing, by virtue of its location on the Belt and Road thoroughfare across Eurasia, has materialized as a quixotic crossing expressing soft power, security, and suspect loyalties, as well as emphasizing the role of the crossing in furthering the Belt and Road imaginary (Grant 2020). In Nepal, facing the fence with China involves production and performance of a Himalayan border in extreme conditions and extensive spaces yet in global focus (Murton 2019). Materialization of the border in the landscape and the social lives of border people in Eurasia now places a "border fence in the backyard" (Troscenko 2016).

The problem with a wall—imagined, virtual, or manifested—is that it materializes as a lot to leave behind when it is no longer functional and its purpose has waned.

References

Abu El-Haj, Thea Renda. 2009. "Becoming citizens in an era of globalization and transnational migration: Re-imagining citizenship as critical practice." *Theory into Practice* 48, (4): 274–282.

Adey, Peter. 2008. "Airports, mobility and the calculative architecture of affective control." *Geoforum* 39, (1): 438–451.

Agnew, John. 1994. "The territorial trap: The geographical assumptions of international relations theory." *Review of International Political Economy* 1, (1): 53–80.

Agnew, John. 2019. "The asymmetric border: The United States place in the world and the refugee panic of 2018." *Geographical Review* 109, (4): 507–526.

Aguirre, Adalberto, and Jennifer K. Simmons. 2008. "Mexican border crossers: The Mexican body in immigration discourse." *Social Justice* 35, (4): 99–106.

Almond, Brenda. 2016. "Border anxiety: Culture, identity and belonging." *Philosophy* 91, (4): 463–481.

Almqvist, Bo. 1991. "Crossing the border: A sampler of Irish migratory legends about the supernatural." *Bealoideas* 59, 209–278.

Amilhat Szary, Anne-Laure. 2014. "Natures of borders: From historical to prospective epistemologies." In Maano Ramutsindela, ed. *Cartographies of Nature: How Nature Conservation Animates Borders*. Cambridge: Cambridge Scholars Press, 31–54.

Amilhat Szary, Anne-Laure. 2020. *Géopolitique Des Frontières. Découper La Terre, Imposer Une Vision Du Monde*. Paris: Le Cavalier Bleu.

Amilhat Szary, Anne-Laure. 2021. "Borders: The topos of/for a post-politics of images?" In Johan Schimanski, and Jopi Nyman, eds. *Border Images, Border Narratives: The Political Aesthetics of Boundaries and Crossings*. Manchester: Manchester University Press, 151–167.

Amilhat Szary, Anne-Laure and Frederic Giraut. 2015. *Borderities: The Politics of Contemporary Mobile Borders*. London: Palgrave Macmillan.

Amoore, Louise. 2006. "Biometric borders: Governing mobilities in the war on terror." *Political Geography* 25, (3): 336–351.

Amoore, Louise, and Alexander Hall. 2009. "Taking people apart: Digitized dissection and the body at the border." *Environment and Planning D: Society and Space* 27, (3): 444–464.

Anderson, Benedict. 1983. *Imagined Communities: Reflections on the Origin and Spread of Nationalism*. London: Verso.

Arrondo, Eneko, Marcos Moleon, Amara Cortes-Avizcanade, Jose Jimenez, Pedro Beja, Jose A. Sanchez-Zapata, and Jose A. Donazar. 2018. "Invisible barriers: Differential sanitary regulations constrain vulture movements across country borders." *Biological Conservation* 219: 46–52.

Bagnall, Kate. 2002. "Across the threshold: White women and Chinese hawkers in the white colonial imaginary." *Hecate* 28, (2): 9.

Banaji, Shakuntala. 2007. "Fascist imaginaries and clandestine critiques: Young Hindi film viewers respond to violence, xenophobia and love in cross-border romances." In Muhaskshi Bharat, and Nirmal Kumar, eds. *Filming the Line of Control: The Indo-Pak Relationship Through the Cinematic Lens*. Oxford: Routledge, 1–25.

Barbaud, Thierry. 2012. "Transgression et Fondation : Quelques Limites Antiques." In Anne-Laure Amilhat Szary, Ed., *Frontières, Penser à La Limite*, L'Archicube 13. Paris: Ecole Normale Supérieure: 154–163.

Barthes, Roland. 1973 [1957]. *Mythologies*. London: Paladin.

Bartlett, Charles W., and Richard Miles. 2001. *A Printmaker in Paradise: The Art and Life of Charles W. Bartlett: With a Catalogue Raisonee of Etchings and Color Woodblock Prints*. Honolulu: Art Media Resources.

Bartlett, John Russell, Henry Cheever Pratt, and Seth Eastman. 1996. *Drawing the Borderline: Artist-explorers of the U.S.-Mexico Boundary Survey*. Albuquerque: University of New Mexico Press.

Bayramoglu, Yener. 2021. "Border panic over the pandemic: Mediated anxieties about the AIDS crisis in Turkey." *Ethnic and Racial Studies* 44, (9): 1589–1606.

Beaugrand, Claire. 2018. "Borders and spatial imaginaries in the Kuwaiti identity." *Geopolitics* 23, (3): 544–564.

Bebout, Lee. 2016. *Whiteness on the Border: Mapping the U.S. Racial Imagination in Brown and White*. New York: NYU Press.

Bekerman, Zvi, Michalinos Zembylas, and Claire McGlynn. 2009. "Working toward the de-essentialization of identity categories in conflict and postconflict societies: Israel, Cyprus, and Northern Ireland." *Comparative Education Review* 53, (2): 213–234.

Bennett, W. Lance. 2005. "Social movements beyond borders: Understanding two eras of transnational activism." In Donatella Della Porta, and Sidney Tarrow, eds. *Transnational Protest and Global Activism*. New York: Rowman and Littlefield, 213–226.

Benthien, Claudia. 2004. *Skin: On the Cultural Border between Self and World*. Montreal: McGill-Queen's University Press.

Bieber, Florian. 2020. "Global nationalism in the times of the COVID-19 pandemic." *Nationalities Papers*, 1–13. Cambridge: Cambridge University Press.

Biemann, Ursula. 2002. "Performing the border." In Claudia Sadowski-Smith, ed. *Globalization on the Line*. New York: Palgrave Macmillan, 99–118.

Biermann, Frank, and Eva Lovbrand. 2019. "Encountering the anthropocene: Setting the scene." In F. Biermann, and E. Lovbrand, eds. *Anthropocene Encounters: New Directions in Green Political Thinking*. Cambridge: Cambridge University Press. 1–22.

Bigo, Didier. 2014. "The (in)securitization practices of the three universes of EU border control: Military/navy-border guards/police-data base analysts." *Security Dialogue* 45, (3): 209–225.

Bolchover, Joshua, and Peter Hasdell. 2016. *Border Ecologies: Hong Kong's Mainland Frontier*. Basel: Birkhauser.

Bourdier, Frederic, Maxime Boutry, Jacques Ivanoff, and Oliver Ferrari. 2015. *From Padi States to Commercial States: Reflections on Identity and Social Construction of Space in the Borderlands of Cambodia, Vietnam, Thailand and Myanmar*. Amsterdam: Amsterdam University Press.

Braidotti, Rosi, and Simone Bignall. 2019. *Posthuman Ecologies: Complexity and process after Deleuze*. London: Rowman and Littlefield.

Brambilla, Chiara. 2009. "Borders: Paradoxical structures between essentialization and creativity." *World Futures* 65, (8): 582–588.

Brambilla, Chiara, Jussi Laine, James W. Scott, and Gianluca Bocchi. 2015. *Borderscaping: Imaginations and Practices of Border Making*. Farnham: Ashgate.

Brown, Christopher. 2020. "Comparative examination of binational watershed research in North America." In Guadalupe Correa-Cabrera, and Victor Konrad, eds. *North American Borders in Comparative Perspective*. Tucson: University of Arizona Press, 323–360.

Burkner, Hans-Joachim. 2015. "Beyond constructivism: Europeanization and bordering under the imprint of power and imaginaries." In C. Brambilla, J. Laine, J. W. Scott, and G. Bocchi, eds. *Borderscaping: Imaginations and Practices of Border Making*. Farnham: Ashgate, 27–40.

Burmur, Christoph, Roberto Nigro, and Gerald Raunig. 2013. "Post-media activism, social ecology and eco-art." *Third Text* 27, (1): 10–16.

Byars, Jana, and Hans Peter Broedel. 2018. *Monsters and Borders in the Early Modern Imagination*. New York: Routledge.

Camacho, Alicia Schmidt. 2008. *Migrant Imaginaries: Latino Cultural Politics in the U.S.-Mexico Borderlands*. New York: NYU Press.

Canada, NFB (National Film Board of Canada). 1976. *Between Friends / Entre Amis.* Toronto: McClelland and Stewart.

Casey, Edward S., and Mary Watkins. 2014. *Up Against the Wall: Re-imagining the U.S.-Mexico Border.* Austin: University of Texas Press.

Castells, Manuel. 2011 [1996]. *The Rise of the Network Society.* Chichester: John Wiley and Sons.

Castells, Manuel. 2015. "Space of flows, space of places: Materials for a theory of urbanism in the information age." In Richard T. LeGates and Frederic Stout, eds. *The City Reader.* London: Routledge. 240–241

Castoriadis, Cornelius. 1997. *The Imaginary Institution of Society.* Cambridge: MIT Press.

Coronado, Irasema. 2020. "A model for trilateral collaboration. The commission for environmental cooperation: Whither the CEC?" In Guadalupe Correa-Cabrera, and Victor Konrad, eds. *North American Borders in Comparative Perspective.* Tucson: University of Arizona Press, 361–378.

Cressman, Gwendolyne. 2019. "Sensing the border at Roxham road." *Intermédialités: histoire et théorie des arts, des lettres, et des techniques/Intermediality: History and Theory of the Arts, Literature and Technologies* 34 (fall 2019).

Dalakoglou, Dimitris. 2010. "The road: An ethnography of the Albanian-Greek cross-border motorway." *American Ethnologist* 37, (1): 132–149.

Dalby, Simon. 2019. "Canadian political culture: Climate change and sustainability." *The Canadian Geographer/Le Géographe canadien* 63, (1): 100–111.

Dalby, Simon. 2020a. *Anthropocene Geopolitics: Globalization, Security, Sustainability.* Ottawa: University of Ottawa Press.

Dalby, Simon. 2020b. "Bordering sustainability in the anthropocene." *Territory, Politics, Governance* 8, (2): 144–160.

Darroch, Michael. 2021. "Imagining night-time Detroit." In Victor Konrad, and Melissa Kelly, eds. *Borders, Culture, Globalization: A Canadian Perspective.* Ottawa: University of Ottawa Press, 61–84.

Davis, Christina, and Jennifer Oh. 2007. "Repeal of the rice laws in Japan: The role of international pressure to overcome vested interests." *Comparative Politics* 40, (1): 21–40.

Debardieux, Bernard. 2019. *Social Imaginaries of Space: Concepts and Cases.* Cheltenham: Edward Elgar.

Deiana, Maria-Adriana. 2019. "Re-thinking border politics at the Sarejo film festival: Alternative imaginaries of conflict transformation and cross-border encounters." *Geopolitics* 24, (3): 670–690.

Deleuze, Gilles. 1992. "Postscript on the Societies of Control." In Imre Szeman and Timothy Kaposy, eds. *Cultural Theory: An Anthology.* Malden: Wiley, 139–153.

Deleuze, Gilles. 1995. *Negotiations: 1972–1990.* New York: Columbia University Press.

Dell'Agnese, Elena. 2005. "The U.S.-Mexico border in American movies: A political geography perspective." *Geopolitics* 10, (2): 204–221.

Dell'Agnese, Elena, and Anne-Laure Amilhat Szary. 2015. "Borderscapes: From border landscapes to border aesthetics." *Geopolitics* 20, (1): 4–13.

Derrida, Jacques, and Tom Conley. 2011. "Living on border lines." *Parages.* [1986 Paris: Galilee]. Stanford: Stanford University Press, 103–191.

Diminescu, Dana. 2012. *E-Diasporas Atlas.* Paris: Editions de la Maison des Sciences de l'Homme.

Dorson, Richard. 2013. *Folklore and Fakelore: Essays Toward a Discipline of Folk Studies.* Cambridge: Harvard University Press.

Durand, Jorge, and Douglas S. Massey. 1995. *Miracles on the Borders: Retablos of Mexican Migrants to the United States.* Tucson: University of Arizona Press.

Dyce, Matt. 2013. "Canada between the photograph and the map: Aerial photography, geographical vision and the state." *Journal of Historical Geography* 39: 69–84.

Eason, James A. 2015. "When narrative fails: Context and physical evidence as means of understanding the Northwest boundary survey photographs of 1857–1862." *Journal of Contemporary Archival Studies* 2, (2): 2.

Eason, Perri K., Cobbs, Gary A., and Kristin G. Trinca. 1999. "The use of landmarks to define territorial boundaries." *Animal Behaviour* 58, (1): 85–91.

Edenborg, Emil. 2020. "Saving women and bordering Europe: Narratives of "migrants' sexual violence" and geopolitical imaginaries in Russia and Sweden." *Geopolitics* 25, (3): 780–801.

Eker, Mark, and Henk Van Houtum. 2013. *Grens Land/Border Land: Atlas, Essays and Design: History and Future of the Border Landscape*. Nijmegen: Blauwdruk.

Elsworth-Jones, Will. 2013. *Banksy: The Man Behind the Wall*. London: St. Martin's Press.

Emory, Deborah Carley. 2000. "Running the line: Men, maps, science, and art of the United States and Mexico boundary survey, 1849–1856." *New Mexico Historical Review* 75, (2): 221.

Fall, Juliet. 2013. "Beyond the nativism debate." In Andrew Dobson, Kezia Barker, and Sarah L. Taylor, eds. *Biosecurity: The Sociopolitics of Invasive Species and Infectious Diseases*. Oxford: Routledge, 167–181.

Fall, Juliet. 2014. "Governing mobile species in a climate-changed world." In Johannes Stripple, and Harriet Bulkeley, eds. *Governing the Climate: New Approaches to Rationality, Power and Politics*. Cambridge: Cambridge University Press, 160–174.

Fellner, Astrid M. 2020. "Counter-mapping corporeal borderlands: Border imaginaries in the Americas." In Florian Weber, Christian Wille, Beate Caesar, and Julian Hollstegge, eds. *Geographien der Grenzen*. Wiesbaden: Springer, 287–300.

Flaherty, George F. 2019. "Border architecture: Territories, commons, and breathing spaces." In Swati Chattopadayay, and Jeremy White, eds. *Routledge Companion to Critical Approaches to Contemporary Architecture*. New York: Routledge, 175–186.

Fourny, Marie-Christine. 2013. "The border as liminal space: A proposal for analyzing the emergence of a concept of the mobile border in the context of the Alps." *Journal of Alpine Research/Revue de géographie alpine* 101, (2).

Gallini, Brian R., and Elizabeth L. Young. 2010. "Car stops, borders and profiling: The hunt for undocumented (illegal) immigrants in border towns." *Nebraska Law Review* 89: 709–737.

Ganster, Paul. 2000. *The U.S.-Mexican Border Environment: A Roadmap to a Sustainable 2020*. San Diego: San Diego University Press.

Gendler, Tamar. 2011. "Imagination." In Edward N. Zalta ed. *Stanford Encyclopedia of Philosophy*. Stanford: Stanford University Press.

Gilbert, Jeremie.2007. "Nomadic territories: A human rights approach to nomadic peoples' land rights." *Human Rights Law Review* 7, (4): 681–716.

Gilbert, Jeremie. 2014. *Nomadic People and Human Rights*. New York: Routledge.

Giudice, Christina, and Chiara Giubilano. 2015. "Re-imagining the border: Border art as a space of critical imagination and creative resistance." *Geopolitics* 20, (1): 79–94.

Goniewicz, Krzysztof, Amir Khorram-Manesh, Atila J. Hertelendy, Mariusz Goniewicz, Katarzyna Naylor, and Frederick M. Burke. 2020. "Current response and management decisions of the European Union to the COVID-19 outbreak: A review." *Sustainability* 12, (9): 3835.

Graham, Mark, and Matthew Zook. 2013. "Augmented realities and uneven geographies: Exploring the geolinguistic contours of the web." *Environment and Planning A* 45, (1): 77–99.

Grant, Andrew. 2020. "Crossing Khorgos: Soft power, security, and suspect loyalties at the Sino-Kazakh boundary." *Political Geography* 76: 102070.
Gregory, Derek. 1995. "Imaginative geographies." *Progress in Human Geography* 19, (4): 447–485.
Gregory, Derek. 2010. "Seeing red: Baghdad and the event-ful city." *Political Geography* 29, (5): 266–279.
Grichting, Anna. 2015. "Boundaryscapes: A digital and dynamic atlas for collaborative planning of the Cyprus Green Line." *Territorio* 9: 108–116.
Grichting, Anna, and Kwi Gon Kim. 2014. "The Korea DMZ: From a red zone to a deeper shade of green." In Keith Tidball, and Marianne Krasny, eds. *Greening the Red Zone*. Dordrecht: Springer, 197–201.
Grichting, Anna, and Michele Zebich-Knos. 2017. *The Social Ecology of Border Landscapes*. London: Anthem Press.
Guadagno, Lorenzo. 2020. *Migrants and the COVID-19 Pandemic: An Initial Analysis*. Geneva: International Organization for Migration.
Guattari, Felix. 1992. *Chaosmose*. Paris: Galilée.
Guyot, Sylvain. 2011. "The eco-frontier paradigm: Rethinking the links between space, nature and politics." *Geopolitics* 16, (3): 675–706.
Guyot, Sylvain. 2015. "The politics of eco-frontiers: When environmentality meets borderities." In Anne-Laure Amilhat Szary, and Frederic Giraut, eds. *Borderities: The Politics of Contemporary Mobile Borders*. London: Palgrave Macmillan, 68–84.
Harvey, David. 1981. "The spatial fix – Hegel, von Thunen, and Marx." *Antipode* 13, (3): 1–12.
Harvey, David. 2005. *The New Imperialism*. Oxford: Oxford University Press.
Harvey, David. 2009 [1973]. *Social Justice and the City*. Athens: University of Georgia Press.
Helman, Sara. 2002. "Monologic results of dialogue: Jewish-Palestinian encounter groups as sites of essentialization." *Identities* 9, (3): 327–354.
Herzog, Lawrence A. 2001. *From Aztec to High Tech: Architecture and Landscape Across the Mexico-U.S. Border*. Baltimore: Johns Hopkins University Press.
Herzog, Lawrence A. 2003. "Global Tijuana: The seven ecologies of the border." In Michael Dear, and Guastavo Leclerc, eds. *Postborder City*. New York: Routledge.119–142
Heumann, Amy N., and Alberto Gonzalez. 2018. "Trump's essentialist border rhetoric: Racial, identities and dangerous liminalities." *Journal of Intercultural Communications Research* 47, (4): 326–342.
Hiaasen, Carl. 2020. *Squeeze Me*. New York: Knopf.
Higbee, Will, and Song Hwee Lim. 2010. "Concepts of transnational cinema: Towards a critical transnationalism in film studies." *Transnational Cinemas* 1, (1): 7–21.
Hill, Leslie. 2006. "Border panic: Introduction." In Leslie Hill, and Helen Paris, eds. *Performance and Place*. Basingstoke: Palgrave Macmillan, 149–154.
Hinton, Lucy, and Matthew A. Schnurr. 2021. "Newcomers and a sense of belonging: Community gardening as integration." In Victor Konrad, and Randy W. Widdis, eds. *Borders, Bordering and Borderlands in Atlantic Canada*. Victoria: Borders in Globalization e-book, 102–118.
Hockey, Jenny. 2002. "The importance of being intuitive: Arnold Gennep's *The Rites of Passage*." *Mortality* 7, (2): 210–217.
Hoffman, Kelly Ann. 2006. *The U.S.-Mexican Border Environment: Transboundary Ecosystem Management*. San Diego: San Diego University Press.
Hondagneau, Pierrette, Genelle Guadinez, Hector Lara, and Billie C. Ortiz. 2004. "There's a spirit that transcends the border: Faith, ritual and post-national protest at the Mexico-U.S. border." *Sociological Perspectives* 47, (2): 133–159.

Honore, Emmanuelle. 2019. "Prehistoric landmarks, contrasted territories: Rock art of the Libyan Desert massifs, Egypt." *Quaternary International* 503: 264–272.

Horiuchi, Yusaku, and Jun Saito. 2010. "Cultivating rice and votes: The institutional origins of agricultural protectionism in Japan." *Journal of East Asian Studies* 10, (3): 425–452.

Horsti, Karina. 2016. "Imagining Europe's borders: Commemorative art of migrant tragedies." In L. Mannik, ed. *Migration by Boat: Discourses of Trauma, Exclusion, Survival.* Oxford: Berghahn, 83–100.

Howe, Kathleen Stewart, and Nitza Rosovsky. 1997. *Revealing the Holyland: The Photographic Exploration of Palestine.* Berkeley: University of California Press.

Hu, Zhiding, and Victor Konrad. 2018. "In the space between exception and integration: The Kokang borderlands on the periphery of China and Myanmar." *Geopolitics* 23, (1): 147–179.

Hudson, Alan. 1998. "Beyond the borders: Globilization, sovereignty and extra-territoriality." *Geopolitics* 3, (1): 89–105.

Hult, Francis M., and Sari Pietikainen. 2014. "Shaping discourses of multilingualism through a language ideological debate: The case of Swedish in Finland." *Journal of Language and Politics* 13, (1): 1–20.

Huppatz, Daniel J. 2011. "Roland Barthes, mythologies." *Design and Culture* 3, (1): 85–100.

Ives, Edward. 1978. *Joe Scott: The Woodsman Songmaker.* Urbana: University of Illinois Press.

Jeganathan, Pradeez. 2018. "Border, checkpoints, bodies." In *Routledge Handbook of Asia's Borderlands.* London: Routledge.

Johnson, Heather L. 2011. "Click to donate: Visual images, constructing victims and imagining the female refugee." *Third World Quarterly* 32, (6): 1015–1037.

Johnston, Andrew John Bayly. 2001. *Control and Order in French Colonial Louisbourg, 1713–1758.* Lansing: Michigan State University Press.

Jones, Reece. 2016. *Violent Borders: Refugees and the right to move.* New York: Verso.

Jones, Reece, and Corey Johnson. 2016. *Placing the Border in Everyday Life.* New York: Routledge.

Kaplan, Heather G. 2021. "Border tuner and teeter-totter wall: Two works of participatory public pedagogy." *Visual Inquiry* 10, (1): 31–48.

Kearney, Michael. 1995. "The local and the global: The anthropology of globalization and transnationalism." *Annual Review of Anthropology* 24, (1): 547–565.

Kelsey, Robin. 2007. *Archive Style: Photographs and Illustrations for US Surveys, 1850–1890.* Berkeley: University of California Press.

Kenwick, Michael R., and Beth A. Simmons. 2020. "Pandemic response as border politics." *International Organization* 74.S1: E36–E5823.

Konrad, Victor. 2013. "Continental East-West and global North-South? Re-imagining (B)orders in globalization." *International Studies* 50, (1–2): 16–34.

Konrad, Victor. 2015. "Toward a theory of borders in motion." *Journal of Borderlands Studies* 30, (1): 1–17.

Konrad, Victor. 2019. "State avoidance and frontier adaptation: Engaging the borderlands of Southeast Asia." *Journal of Borderlands Studies* 34, (3): 479–482.

Konrad, Victor. 2020a. "Reimagining the border between Canada and the United States." In Guadalupe Correa-Cabrera, and Victor Konrad, eds. *North American Borders in Comparative Perspective.* Tucson: University of Arizona Press, 72–97.

Konrad, Victor. 2020b. "Belongingness and borders." In James W. Scott, ed. *A Research Agenda for Border Studies.* Oxford: Edward Elgar, 109–128.

Konrad, Victor. 2021. "The post-humanistic border: Moving between territorial ambiguity and human belongingness." Paper presented at AAG, 2021, Seattle.

Konrad, Victor, and Emmanuel Brunet-Jailly. 2019. "Approaching borders, creating borderland spaces, and exploring the evolving borders between Canada and the United States." *The Canadian Geographer/Le Géographe canadien* 63, (1): 4–10.

Konrad, Victor, and Zhiding Hu. 2021. "Expanded border imaginaries and aligned border narratives: Ethnic minorities and localities in China's border encounters with Myanmar, Laos and Vietnam." In Johan Schimanski, and Jopi Nyman, eds. *Border Images, Border Narratives: The Political Aesthetics of Boundaries and Crossings.* Manchester: Manchester University Press, 127–147.

Konrad, Victor, Laine, Jussi P., Liikanen, Ilkka, Scott, James W., and Randy Widdis. 2020. "The language of borders." In Stanley D. Brunn and Roland Kehrein, eds. *Handbook of the Changing World Language Map.* New York: Springer, 2175–2191.

Konrad, Victor, and Heather Nicol. 2008. *Beyond Walls: Re-inventing the Canada-United States Borderlands.* Aldershot: Ashgate.

Koob-Sassen, Hilary. 2008. "Serpentine gallery manifesto marathon, 'faith in infrastructure'." Serpentine Gallery, London, October 18, 2008. www.TheErrorists.com.

Kuster, Brigitta, and Yassiliss Tsianos. 2016. "How to liquefy a body on the move: Eurodac and the making of the European digital border." In Raphael Bossong and Helena Carrapico, eds. *EU Borders in Shifting Internal Security.* New York: Springer, 45–63.

LaManna, Justin R., and Perri K. Eason. 2003. "Effects of landmarks on territorial establishment." *Animal Behaviour* 65, (3): 471–478.

Lesnau, Jessica R. 2016. "While we're going, we'll need roads: Building the bridge of the future: Public-private partnerships for future border infrastructural development." *Texas A&M Law Review* 4: 261.

Lieto, Laura. 2015. "Cross-border mythologies: The problem with traveling planning ideas." *Planning Theory* 14, (2): 115–129.

Lu, Flora, Gabriela Valdivia, and Nestor L. Silva. 2016. *Oil, Revolution and Indigenous Citizenship in Ecuadorian Amazonia.*New York: Springer.

Lunstrum, Elizabeth. 2013. "Articulated sovereignty: Extending Mozambican state power through the Great Limpopo Transfrontier Park." *Political Geography* 36: 1–11.

Lunstrum, Elizabeth. 2016. "Green grabs, land grabs, and the spatiality of displacement: Eviction from Mozambique's Limpopo National Park." *Area* 48, (2): 142–152.

McGreevy, Patrick. 2009. *Imagining Niagara: The Meaning and Making of Niagara Falls.* Amherst: University of Massachusetts Press.

McGuire, Randall H. 2013. "Steel walls and picket fences: Rematerializing the U.S.-Mexican border in ambos Nogales." *American Anthropologist* 115, (3): 466–480.

Mabee, Bryan. 2007. "Re-imagining the borders of U.S. security after 9/11: Securitization, risk, and the creation of the department of homeland security." *Globalizations* 4, (3): 385–397.

Macfarlane, Robert. 2019. *Underland: A Deep Time Journey.* London: Penguin.

Madrid, Alejandro L. 2011. *Transnational Encounters: Music and Performance at the U.S.-Mexico Border.* Oxford: Oxford University Press.

Maggs, David, and John Robinson. 2016. "Recalibrating the anthropocene: Sustainability in an imaginary world." *Environmental Philosophy* 13, (2): 175–194.

Mains, Susan P. 2004. "Imagining the border and Southern spaces: Cinematic explorations of race and gender." *Geojournal* 59, (4): 253–264.

Maraud, Simon, and Sylvain Guyot. 2016. "Mobilization of imaginaries to build Nordic Indigenous natures." *Polar Geography* 39, (3): 196–216.

Marino, Alessandro, Lynne E. Parker, Gianluea Antonelli, and Fabrizio Caccavale. 2013. "A decentralized architecture for multi-robot systems based on null-space-behavioural control with application to multi-robot border patrolling." *Journal of Intelligent and Robotic Systems* 71, (3–4): 423–444.

Marsico, Giuseppina. 2016. "The borderland." *Culture and Psychology* 22, (2): 206–215.

Masny, Diana, and Monica Waterhouse. 2011. "Mapping territories and creating nomadic pathways with multiple literacy theory." *Journal of Curriculum Theorizing* 27, (3). 287–307

Mayer, Evelyn P. 2014. *Narrating North American Borderlands: Thomas King, Howard F. Mosher and Jim Lynch*. Mainz: Peter Lang.

Maynard, Glynn V., Graeme Hamilton, and Judy F. Grimshaw. 2004. "Quarantine – Phytosanitary, sanitary and incursion management: An Australian entomological perspective." *Australian Journal of Entomology* 43, (3): 318–328.

Mbembe, Achille. 2019. *Necro-Politics*. Durham: Duke University Press.

Medina-Nicolas, Lucile. 2007. "Central American borders as the core of the regional integration process." *Geopolitics* 12, (1): 78–108.

Medina-Nicolas, Lucile. 2013. "A complex cross-border interface. The case of the Gulf of Fonseca: El Salvador, Honduras and Nicaragua." *Limina R* (online) 11, (2): 54–69.

Meier, Avinoam, and Haim Tsoar. 1996. "International borders and range ecology: The case of Bedouin transborder grazing." *Human Ecology* 24, (1): 39–64.

Mendez, Eloy, and Isabel Rodrieguez. 2009. "Imaginaries and migration." *Journal of the Southwest* 51, (4): 477–490.

Mesterton-Gibbons, Michael, and Eldrige S. Adams. 2003. "Landmarks in territory partitioning: A strategically stable convention?" *The American Naturalist* 161, (5): 685–697.

Meyer, Erin. 2014. *The Culture Map: Breaking Through the Invisible Boundaries of Global Business*. New York: Public Affairs Press.

Mignolo, Walter D. 2011a. "Border thinking, decolonial cosmopolitanism and dialogues among civilizations." In Maria Rovisco and Magdalena Nowicka, eds. *The Ashgate Research Companion to Cosmopolitanism*. Farnham: Ashgate, 329–348.

Mignolo, Walter D. 2011b. "Geopolitics of sensing and knowing: On (de)coloniality, border thinking and epistemic disobedience." *Postcolonial Studies* 14, (3): 273–283.

Mignolo, Walter D. 2012. *Local Histories/Global Designs: Coloniality, Subaltern Knowledge and Border Thinking*. Princeton: Princeton University Press.

Milagros, Ricourt. 2016. *The Dominican Racial Imaginary: Surveying the Landscape of Race and Nation in Hispaniola*. New Brunswick: Rutgers University Press.

Minardi, Michele. 2015. *Ancient Chorasmia: A polity between the semi-nomadic and sedentary cultural areas of Central Asia: Cultural interactions and local developments from the sixth century BC to the first century AD*. Leuven: Peeters.

Mitra, Srimoyee. 2015. *Border Cultures*. London: Black Dog Publishing.

Mitra, Srimoyee. 2021. "*Border Cultures*: A Retrospective. Part 2. *Border Cultures*: The Exhibitions." In Victor Konrad and Melissa Kelly, eds. *Borders, Culture, and Globalization: A Canadian Perspective*. Ottawa: University of Ottawa Press, 115–128.

Moloney, Kim, and Susan Moloney. 2020. "Australian quarantine policy: From centralization to coordination with mid-pandemic COVID-19 shifts." *Public Administration Review* 80, (4): 671–682.

Moore, Hilary. 2017. *Inside British Jazz: Crossing Borders of Race, Nation and Class*. London: Routledge.

Morgan, John J. B. 1931. "Imagination." In John J. B. Morgan, ed.*Child Psychology*. New York: Richard R. Smith, 215–244.

Murton, Galen. 2019. "Facing the fence: The production and performance of a Himalayan border in global contexts." *Political Geography* 72: 31–42.

Nagra, Baljit, and Paula Maurutto. 2016. "Crossing borders and managing racialized identities: Experiences of security and surveillance among young Canadian Muslims." *Canadian Journal of Sociology* 41, (2): 165–194.

Nail, Thomas. 2012. "Violence at the borders: Nomadic solidarity and non-status migrant resistance." *Radical Philosophy Review* 15, (1): 241–257.

Nail, Thomas. 2016. *Theory of the Border*. Oxford: Oxford University Press.

O'Neill, Anne. 1983. "The gardens of 18th century Louisbourg." *The Journal of Garden History* 3, (3): 176–178.

O'Neill, Kate. 2005. "How two cows make a crisis: U.S.-Canada trade relations and mad cow disease." *American Review of Canadian Studies* 35, (2): 295–319.

Ono, Kent A. 2012. "Borders that travel: Matters of the figural border." In Karma R. Chavez, Julia R. Johnson, and Kent A. Ono, eds. *Border Rhetorics: Citizenship and Identity on the U.S. Mexico Frontier*. Montgomery: University of Alabama Press, 19–32.

Orihuela, Sharada Balachandran, and Andrew Carl Hageman. 2011. "The virtual realities of U.S.-Mexico border ecologies in *Maquilapolis* and *Sleep Dealer*." *Environmental Communication* 5, (2): 166–186.

Paasi, Anssi. 2009. "Political boundaries." *International Encyclopedia of Human Geography* 8: 217–227.

Paredes, Am. 1993. *Folklore and Culture on the Texas-Mexican Border*. Austin: University of Texas Press.

Parker, Noel, and Nick Vaughan-Williams. 2009. "Lines in the sand? Towards an agenda for critical border studies." *Geopolitics* 14, (3): 582–587.

Parker, Noel, and Nick Vaughan-Williams. 2012. "Critical border studies: Broadening and deepening the 'lines in the sand' agenda." *Geopolitics* 17, (4): 727–733.

Parzinger, Herman, Anton Gass, and Jorg Fassbinder. 2016. "The latest geo-archaeological and geophysical studies at the foot of Royal Kurgans." *Science First Hand* 1: 74–89.

Paulin, Diana R. 1997. "De-essentializing interracial representations: Black and White border-crossings in Spike Lee's *Jungle Fever* and Octavia Butler's *Kindred*." *Cultural Critique* 36: 165–193.

Pedynowski, Dena. 2003. "Prospects for ecosystem management in the crown of the continent ecosystem, Canada-United States: Survey and recommendations." *Conservation Biology* 17, (5): 1261–1269.

Perera, Suvendrini. 2009. *Australia and the Insular Imagination: Beaches, Borders, Boats and Bodies*. New York: Springer.

Perreau, Tom, and Gabriela Valdivia. 2010. "Hydrocarbons, popular protest and national imaginaries: Ecuador and Bolivia in comparative context." *Geoforum* 41, (5): 689–699.

Pike, Sarah M. 2017. *For the Wild: Ritual and Commitment in Radical Eco-Activism*. Berkeley: University of California Press.

Prato, Tony, and Daniel P. Fagre. 2010. "Sustainable management of the crown of the continent ecosystem." *The George Wright Forum* 27, (1): 77–93.

Prokkola, Eva-Kaisa, and Juha Ridanpaa. 2015. "Border guarding and the politics of the body: An examination of the Finnish border guard service." *Gender, Place and Culture* 22, (10): 1374–1390.

Ptak, Thomas, and Victor Konrad. 2021. "'Crossing the river by feeling the stones': How borders, energy development, and ongoing experimentation shape the dynamic transformation of Yunnan Province." *Journal of Borderlands Studies* 36, (5): 765–790.

Rael, Ronald. 2014. "Border wall as architecture." In E. Vallet, ed. *Borders, Fences, Walls: State of Insecurity?* Farnham: Ashgate, 267–278.

Rael, Ronald. 2017. *Borderwall as Architecture: A Manifesto for the US-Mexico Boundary.* Berkeley: University of California Press.

Ramutsindela, Maano. 2007. "Transfrontier conservation in Africa: At the confluence of capital, politics and nature." *CAB International.* Wallingford.

Ramutsindela, Maano. 2017. "Greening Africa's borderlands: The symbiotic politics of land and borders in peace parks." *Political Geography* 100, (56): 106–113.

Ramutsindela, Maano, Sylvain Guyot, Sebastien Boillat, Frederic Giraut, and Patrick Bottazzi. 2020. "The geopolitics of protected areas." *Geopolitics* 25, (1): 240–266.

Rancière, Jacques. 2015. *Dissensus: On Politics and Aesthetics.* London: Bloomsbury.

Ray, Tim. 2017. "Why invisible boundaries matter: Imagined institutions and power." *Prometheus* 35, (4): 305–323.

Rebert, Paula. 2011. "A civilian surveyor on the United States-Mexico boundary: The case of Arthur Schott." *Proceedings of the American Philosophical Society* 155, (4): 433–462.

Rodney, Lee. 2017. *Looking Beyond the Borderlines: North America's Frontier Imagination.* New York: Routledge.

Rodney, Lee. 2021. "Sight and site on the line: The cultural imaginary of borderlands in North America." In Victor Konrad, and Melissa Kelly, eds. *Borders, Culture, and Globalization: A Canadian Perspective.* Ottawa: University of Ottawa Press, 39–60.

Rosière, Stephane, and Reece Jones. 2011. "Teichopolitics: Reconsidering globalization through the role of walls and fences." *Geopolitics* 17, (1): 217–234.

Roux-Rosier, Anahid, Ricardo Azambuja, and Gazi Islam. 2018. "Alternative visions: Permaculture as imaginaries of the anthropocene." *Organization* 25, (4): 550–572.

Rugg, Harold. 1963. *Imagination.* New York: Harper and Row.

Rutkauskas, Andreas, and Karla McManus. 2016. "Border lines and crossing points: A response to Andreas Rutkauskas' photographs of the Canadian-U.S. border." *Imaginations: Journal of Cross-Cultural Image Studies* 7, (1): 142–151.

Sabins, Floyd F. 1987. *Remote Sensing – Principles and Interpretation.* New York: W.H. Freeman.

Sadowski-Smith, Claudia. 2008. *Border Fictions: Globalization, Empire and Writing at the Boundaries of the United States.* Charlottesville: University of Virginia Press.

Sadowski-Smith, Claudia. 2013. "U.S. border ecologies, environmental criticism, and transnational American studies." In Joni Adamson, and Kimberly N. Ruffin, eds. *American Studies, Ecocriticism, and Citizenship.* New York: Routledge, 164–177.

Sahlins, Peter. 1990. Natural frontiers revisited: France's boundaries since the Seventeenth century. *American Historical Review* 95, (5): 1423–1451.

Salazar, Noel B. 2010. *Envisioning Eden: Mobilizing Imaginaries in Tourism and Beyond.* Oxford: Berghahn.

Sartre, Jean-Paul. 2004 [1960]. *The Imaginary: A Phenomenological Psychology of the Imagination.* London: Routledge.

Sartre, Jean-Paul. 2012 [1936]. *The Imagination.* New York: Routledge.

Sassen, Saskia. 2010. "Nomadic Territories and Lines." In James Elkins, Zhivka Valiavicharska and Alice Kim, eds. *Art and Globalization.* University Park, PA: Penn State University Press, 237–240.

Schimanski, Johan, and Stephen F. Wolfe. 2017. *Border Aesthetics: Concepts and Intersections.* Oxford: Berghahn.

Schmoll, Camille. 2020. *Les damnées de la mer. Femmes et frontières en Méditerranée.* Paris: La Découverte.

Schwarz, Inga. 2016. "Racializing freedom of movement in Europe: Experiences of racial profiling at European borders and beyond." *Movements. Journal for Critical Migration and Border Regime Studies* 2, (1).

Scott, James C. 2009. *The Art of not Being Governed: An Anarchist History of Upland Southeast Asia*. New Haven: Yale University Press.

Scott, James W., Filippo Celata, and Raffaella Coletti. 2019. "Bordering imaginaries and the everyday construction of the Mediterranean neighbourhood: Introduction to the special issue." *European Urban and Regional Studies* 26, (1): 3–8.

Shamir, Ronen. 2005. Without borders? Notes on globalization as mobility regime. *Sociological Theory* 23, (2): 197–217.

Sheldrake, Merlin. 2020. *Entangled Life: How Fungi Make Our Worlds Change Our Minds and Shape Our Futures*. New York: Random House.

Shim, David. 2014. "Remote sensing place: Satellite images as visual spatial imaginaries." *Geoforum* 51: 152–160.

Shimoni, Baruch. 2006. "Cultural borders, hybridization, and a sense of boundaries in Thailand, Mexico, and Israel." *Journal of Anthropological Research* 62, (2): 217–234.

Simard, Suzanne. 2021. *Finding the Mother Tree: Uncovering the Wisdom and Intelligence of the Forest*. London: Penguin.

Simberloff, Daniel. 2010. "Invasive species." In Navjot S. Sodhi, and Paul R. Ehrlich, eds. *Conservation Biology for All*. New York: Oxford University Press, 131–152.

Simi, Gianluca. 2018. "Between the line: The semiotics of everyday life in the Brazil/Uruguay border lands." PhD dissertation, Nottingham University.

Soja, Edward W. 1985. "The spatiality of social life: Towards a transformative re-theorisation." In Derek Gregory, and John Urry, eds. *Social Relations and Spatial Structures*. London: Palgrave, 90–127.

Soja, Edward W. 1989. *Postmodern Geographies: The Reassertion of Space in Critical Social Theory*. New York: Verso.

Soja, Edward W. 1999. "Thirdspace: Journeys to Los Angeles and other real and imagined places." *The Canadian Geographer* 43, (2): 209–212.

Sorells, Kanthryn. 2010. "Re-imagining intercultural communication in the context of globalization." In Thomas K. Nakayama, and Rona Tamiko Halualani, eds. *The Handbook of Critical Intercultural Communication*. Oxford: John Wiley and Sons, 171–189.

Soto, Gabriela. 2021. "Absent and present: Biopolitics and the materiality of body counts on the Mexico-U.S. border." *Journal of Material Culture* 26, (1): 43–63.

Spaan, Ernst, Van Naerssen, Ton, and Gerard Kohl. 2002. "Re-imagining borders: Malay identity and Indonesian migrants in Malaysia." *Tijdschrift vooreconomische en sociale gegraphie* 93, (2): 160–172.

St. John, Rachel. 2012. *Line in the Sand: A History of the U.S.-Mexico Border*. Princeton: Princeton University Press.

Steinberg, Philip E., Jeremy Tasch, Hannes Gerhard, Adam Keul, and Elizabeth A. Nyman. 2015. *Contesting the Arctic: Politics and Imaginaries in the Circumpolar North*. London: Bloomsbury.

Sun, Wanning. 2002. *Leaving China: Media, Migration, and Transnational Imagination*. New York: Rowman and Littlefield.

Sundberg, Juanita, and Bonnie Kaserman. 2007. "Cactus carvings and desert defections: Embodying representations of border crossings in protected areas on the Mexico-U.S. border." *Environment and Planning D: Society and Space* 25, (4): 727–744.

Tally, Robert, Jr. 2012. *Spatiality*. London: Routledge.

Taylor, Charles. 2004. *Modern Social Imaginaries*. Durham: Duke University Press.

Tedeschi, Miriam. 2020. "The body and the law across borders during the COVID-19 pandemic." *Dialogues in Human Geography* 10, (2): 178–181.

Troscenko, Elina. 2016. "With a border fence in the backyard: Materialization of the border in the landscape and the social lives of border people." In T. Beinga, and H. Toje, eds. *Eurasian Borderlands*. New York: Palgrave Macmillan, 87–106.

Tuathail, Gearoid O. 2005. "The frustrations of geopolitics and the pleasures of war: Behind enemy lines and America's geopolitical culture." *Geopolitics* 10, (2): 356–377.

Valdivia, Gabriela. 2015. "Eco-governmentality." In Tom Perreault, Gavin Bridge, and James McCarthy, eds. *The Routledge Handbook of Political Ecology*. New York: Routledge, 467–480.

Valdivia, Gabriela, Wendy Wolford, and Flora Lu. 2014. "Border crossings: New geographies of protection and production in the Galapagos Islands." *Annals, Association of American Geographers* 104, (3): 686–701.

Vallet, Elizabeth. 2014. *Borders, Fences and Walls: State of Insecurity?* Farnham: Ashgate.

Van Gennep, Arnold. 2019 [1909]. *The Rites of Passage*. Chicago: University of Chicago Press.

Van Houtum, Henk. 2010. "Human Blacklisting: The global apartheid of the EU's external border regime." *Environment and Planning D: Society and Space* 28, (6): 957–976.

Van Lanen, Sander. 2019. "Social imaginaries of space: Concepts and cases." *Tijdschrift voor Economische en Sociale Geografie* 111, (4): 686–687.

Van Tongeren, F. 2011. "Standards and international trade integration: A historical review of the German 'Reinheitsgebot'." In J. F. M. Swinnen, ed. *The Economics of Beer*. Oxford: Oxford University Press, 51–61.

Varró, Krisztina. 2014. "Spatial imaginaries of the Dutch-German-Belgian borderlands: A multidimensional analysis of cross-border regional governance." *International Journal of Urban and Regional Research* 38, (6): 2235–2255.

Vaughan-Williams, Nick. 2009. *Border Politics: The Limits of Sovereign Power*. Edinburgh: Edinburgh University Press.

Vernant, Jean-Pierre. 2004. *La traversée des frontières*. La Librairie du XXIe siècle. Paris: Le Seuil.

Vila, Pablo. 2003. "The limits of American border theory." In Pablo Vila, ed. *Ethnography at the Border*. Minneapolis: University of Minnesota Press, 306–342.

Virilio, Paul. 2003. *Unknown Quantity*. London, New York & Paris: Thames & Hudson; Fondation Cartier pour l'art contemporain.

Walkerdine, Valerie. 2006. "Workers in the new economy: Transformation as border crossing." *Ethos* 34, (1): 10–41.

Walsh, Cormac. 2020. "Brexit geographies: Spatial imaginaries and relational territorialities on the Island of Ireland." *Irish Geography* 52, (2): 137–152.

Walsh, Michaela D. 2014. *Partiendo La Madre: Borders, Thresholds, and Performance of Crossing among the Hnahnu*. PhD dissertation, San Diego: University of California.

Warnock, Mary. 1976. *Imagination*. Berkeley: University of California Press.

Watkins, Josh. 2015. "Spatial imaginary research in geography: Synergies, tensions, and new directions." *Geography Compass* 9, (9): 508–522.

Watkins, Josh. 2017. "Australia's irregular migration information campaigns: Border externalization, spatial imaginaries, and extraterritorial subjugation." *Territory, Politics, Governance* 5, (3): 282–303.

Weiner, Jonathan B., and Michael D. Rogers. 2002. "Comparing precaution in the United States and Europe." *Journal of Risk Research* 5, (4): 317–349.

Weisblum, Sharon. 2019. "Conflicting imaginaries of the border: The construction of African asylum seekers in the Israeli political discourse." *Journal of Borderlands Studies* 34, (5): 699–715.

Weitzel, Michelle D. 2018. "Audializing migrant bodies: Sound and security at the border." *Security Dialogue* 49, (6): 421–437.

Whitley, Leila M. 2015. "More than a line: Borders as embodied sites." PhD dissertation, Goldsmiths, University of London.

Whyte, Zachary. 2020. "Automation, biocrats, and imaginaries in biometric border worlds: A commentary." *Ethnos* 87, (2): 338–346

Widdis, Randy. 2015. "A spatial grammar of migration in the Canadian-American borderlands at the turn of the 20th century." In Benjamin Bryce, and Alexander Freund, eds. *Entangling Migration History: Borderlands and Transnationalism in the United States and Canada*. Gainesville: University Press of Florida, 47–76.

Woodward, Keith, and John Paul Jones III. 2005. "On the border with Deleuze and Guatteri." In Henk Van Houtum, Olivier Kramsch, and Wolfgang Zierhofer, eds. *B/ordering Space*. Aldershot: Ashgate, 235–248.

Wright, Melissa. 2019. "Border thinking, borderland diversity, and Trump's wall." *Annals, Association of American Geographers* 109, (2): 511–519.

Yeoh, Brenda, Willis, Katie D., and S. M. Aduhl Khader Fakhri. 2003. "Introduction: Transnationalism and its edges." *Ethnic and Racial Studies* 26, (2): 207–217.

Young, Robert. 2004 [1990]. *White Mythologies: Writing History and the West*. New York: Routledge.

Zukin, Sharon. 1993. *Landscapes of Power: From Detroit to Disneyworld*. Berkeley: University of California Press.

4

NATIONAL NARRATIVES AND COUNTER-NARRATIVES AT THE BORDER

Our stories of the border tell us who and where we are.
National narratives feed on the edges of territory.
We believe borders are somewhere between what we are told and what we know.
Borders create belongers; belonging creates borders.
Even transnational citizens are bordered.

Introduction: The Wagah border crossing, and the construction of national narratives and counter-narratives at the border

Every evening at the Wagah crossing, on the border between India and Pakistan, elite troops from both countries perform the border. The occasion is ostensibly the daily ritual of retiring the national flags, but the performance has expanded substantially with entire platoons of troops participating from each side, exaggerated march step competitions, and steely eyed stares of confrontation. The soldiers are dressed in their best uniforms, with additional flourishes of colour and design. There are national anthems blaring. Every step and action is elaborately choreographed. Appreciative crowds watching from bleacher seats on each side of the boundary cheer on their finest. Then the flags are down, the ceremony is over, and the performance ends—for another day.

The Wagah border-crossing ceremony has become a bulwark of border culture in both India and Pakistan, but it is now much more than a symbolic performance of Pakistani and Indian nationalism. Wagah has become an international tourist destination. Google offers more than a quarter of a million results on where to stay and what to see, and, of course thousands of posted videos on YouTube show highlights of lowering the flag and the "beating the retreat" ritual.

DOI: 10.4324/9781003301486-4

The village of Wagah is located 600 metres west of the border in Pakistan. Attari is its counterpart in India. Both settlements are on the road between Amritsar in India and Lahore in Pakistan. The border crossing is in a major corridor between the nations, yet the symbolic significance of the border crossing eclipses its economic and strategic importance. Here, India and Pakistan may perform the border to lower the temperature of border disputes and confrontations at other places along the border. Engaging tourists as audience, both national and international, further defuses the tension of the border and practices of bordering between Pakistan and India (Figure 4.1).

Yet, the border-crossing performance at Wagah is also reflective of the national narratives and counter-narratives constructed at the border. According to Neelima Jeychandran (2016), the Wagah lowering of flags ceremony remains to a certain degree a spectre of war although it is also emerging as a spectacle of peace. This symbolic confrontation, deemed as the Wagah "syndrome" of territorially rooted violence in South Asia by Willem Van Schendel (2007), and an exemplar of extreme othering in the case of India and Pakistan by Sanjay Chaturvedi (2002), has evolved through ritualization, and pluralisation of the enactment through social media and public theatre (Goeury 2008). More recently, with a growing tourist audience, and new practices in the ceremony to designate a border that is partially permeable, and a border space that has been transformed, "the border is an arena that reveals a certain porousness and fragility in the nation" (Parciak 2018, 744).

In this chapter, we engage with national narratives and counter-narratives at the border. Our overall aim is to unravel how national and official cultures of the

FIGURE 4.1 Wagah Border-Crossing Performance: Retiring the Flags in Unison. Photo courtesy of Dhananjay Tripathi.

border evolve and are challenged and change. Nationalist literatures praise border consolidation and many edifices and institutions celebrate and commemorate these official border cultures. We educate our children using maps and documentaries of the border, and we point to monuments to confirm the borders as territorial containers of the nation. As Anssi Paasi (1996) established in his seminal research on the Finnish–Russian border, identity construction is a key process in defining the border and identifying border culture. From identity construction the chapter proceeds to consider the security efforts of nation-states, and how these measures relate to othering practices and the development of anti-migration narratives. We consider counter-cultures of border control and resistance and the cultural expressions that convey the activism and political confrontation at the border. The idea and expression of citizenship is examined with respect to narratives of singular and multiple identities, and how identities have been transformed in globalization through migration and exile across borders. Finally, we explore how national narratives are exported. We examine border cultures of colonial and postcolonial experiences. Considerations of imperial distribution of Western border culture are evaluated against other world views from oriental, transnational, global, and now post-globalization frameworks. Why and how do the national narratives continue to prevail?

4.1 Building borderlands culture

A lingering notion is that borders are fundamentally sites of fortification between different peoples. Fortification requires construction of ideas as well as structures to confirm authority and affirm control. The idea of the border is as firmly rooted in human societies as the idea of territory, and the two social constructs are linked in the conceptualization of the nation-state (Elden 2013). Before the Treaty of Westphalia (1648) and legalization of borders as the defining limits of national authority, fortified borders and borderlands were viewed as demarcations between civilized and barbaric peoples (Henning 2005). Boundaries within civilization were lines of agreement and coalition, spaces of linkage, arrangements of lineage and fealty, and commitments to align. Nation-states reified the differences and the commonalities along border lines, but in many instances agreements did not endure and borders were not respected as conflicts emerged and realignments ensued.

Processes of imperialism and colonialism, among others related to extension of the state, added new dimensions of spatial control and authority and altered visions of borders between nations. Not only were political spaces defined within borders, but borders were considered as movable markers on a vast continental and then global playing field. According to Charles S. Maier (2016), the political space once contained within borders was now unleashed as international and then transnational conceptions and constructions of political space emerged. With the advent of globalization a further shift has occurred in how borders operate in political, social, economic, and cultural space, but our understanding of these dynamic relationships remains incomplete. Yet, we can acknowledge that borders are in the process of becoming, caught between territoriality and a-territoriality, beyond national containers but serving nation-states, and still very much components of political space in a post-globalization world.

In Europe, where the nature of borders has changed substantially in the past fifty years, a multiscalar complex of borders has emerged with varying degrees of cross-border cooperation and symbolism evident throughout the European Union and its neighbours (Scott 2012, Laine 2016). Borders have evolved from fortification to humanitarianization, and even the fortified Schengen border facilitates movement and humanitarian governance of the political space (Walters 2011). Borders also serve to expedite information flows and articulate transnational networks (Shields 2014). However, new state borders in the world do not reflect the multiscalar, humanitarian, and transnational evolution of borders. New state borders, according to David B. Carter and Hein E. Goemans (2011), are rarely "new" but rather they emulate previous administrative boundaries as safe and consistent borders. Furthermore, the syllogisms that strong borders make secure nations, and that borders conferred and confirmed by history are a national legacy and trust (Fravel 2008), prevail in a global template of nation-state borders. This template frames cultural expressions of nationalist literature and art to praise and celebrate border consolidation and the establishment of official border cultures, their monuments, and their walls.

4.1.1 National(ist) border literature and borderlands literature

Johan Schimanski (2015) reveals how border aesthetics work to sustain *cultural distancing* in the Norwegian–Russian borderscape. Political *resistance* is articulated in performative acts of borderscaping in the novels of John Fowles and Kjartan Flogstad to develop forms of distance and distancing that in a sense create the border and certainly emphasize the border's geopolitical significance. In adjacent Finland, *fear* is invested in border narratives. The fear of Russia is based on personal experiences and narrated memories, and this fear is a component in social and cultural construction of the border (Lauren 2012). These postures—fear, resistance, cultural distancing—are linked and expressed in narratives of the border. Finland's borders are narrated as well by stories of national origins and perseverance, none more pervasive and reflective of national ideology than the "Kalevala" (Wilson 1975). The Kalevala speaks to cultural and political independence and the liberation of Finnish tribes beyond the borders imposed by neighbouring colonial powers. Finland had been incorporated into Russia in 1809, and the border between Sweden and Russia was situated at the Tornio River in the middle of the culturally coherent Finnish-speaking region. Swedish novelist Mikael Niemi situates his story *Popular Music [from] Vittula* in Pajala along this border, thus creating a literary place centred in a borderland to stage local, regional, and national narratives of Finnish culture (Ridanpaa 2011). In Finland, literature and nation-building are inseparably intertwined, and the national culture project has prevailed as the differentiation of "us" and "them" (Pollari et al. 2015). However, as Tuulikki Kurki (2013) explains, the Karelian borderlands astride the Russian–Finnish boundary have evolved from a Soviet locality to a multi-voiced borderland in the literature of the region. Finnish women fall in love with Russian men, and all manner of border crossings are now evident.

When we shift our attention to border and borderlands literature in North America, the dimensions of the topic broaden significantly, in part because of the expanded geography, but more so because colonialism and revolution impacted nation-building, and frontier experience migrated differentially across the continent. Claudia Sadowski-Smith (2008) draws a context for border fictions and writing at the boundaries of the U.S., and she places this context between empire and globalization. Populating this vast history, geography, and imaginary, are diverse spaces of border fictions that feature Chicana/o writing of the U.S.–Mexico borderlands, American literature and lore that buttresses the U.S.–Mexico border construct, Asian and other immigrant border-crossing stories, Indigenous negation and manipulation, British, French and Canadian border literatures aimed at substantiating the vast Canada–U.S. border and verifying Canada, and the contemporary stories of transnationalism and border crossing in a post-9/11 North America. A review of this extensive literature is itself the subject of at least one book, and likely a series of topical and regional works. In the following brief discussion, our aim is to situate the nationalist border and borderlands literature in the border culture framework to illustrate how stories of the border work to delineate and confirm the border or to establish cross-border connections, or both.

North America's border fictions, according to Sadowski-Smith (2008, 2), assert that "a particular [border] place is as much affected by human projection and representation as people and communities are affected by landscapes". Border fiction draws on the imagination to depict the alternatives that invariably emerge at borders: the border as barrier, differentiator, conduit, filter, resource, and link, prominent among them. The increasingly transnational nature of borders affects those who live and travel in the borderlands. Border fictions express a range of narratives of the border. Among these are the porosity and vulnerability of the border and life associated with it, border places as sites of narrative construction, borders as metaphors, and the fact of the borderlands. Borderlands literature,

> like the border itself, is socially constructed, mainly by people who reside close to the border and live with its effects of coincident separation and linkage, the constant change and motion surrounding the line, the meshed or delineated identities that emerge, and the innovative and exemplary production and expression of imagination and creativity focused on the border.
>
> *(Konrad and Kelly 2021, 8)*

We focus on the literature of the Canada–U.S. borderlands at this point because we are both familiar with this border culture context and it offers significant insights. Gillian Roberts and David Stirrup (2013, 1) convey what they term the "prismatic" quality of the Canada–U.S. border "through which and at which broader questions of political, economic, and cultural relations within the Americas come into focus". The border has cultural implications for it serves as a protective barrier for Canada to be defined against "Americanization". The border is

> a site of policing bodies and identities marked by racialization, gender, and sexuality; a threat to Indigenous sovereignties; a dividing line between welfare state and the epitome of capitalism; a zone where state-funded culture meant to be "good for us" stands guard against imported popular culture; a contact zone where reading and viewing practices might be inflected with national significance; and what appears to be a sharp contrast to the militarized U.S.–Mexico border, even while agreements such as NAFTA locate Canada increasingly in relation to Mexico in particular and the Americas more generally.
>
> *(Roberts and Stirrup 2013, 1–2)*

This "discursive terrain" serves effectively to examine the Canada–U.S. border with regard to its function and relation to cultural texts (Roberts and Stirrup 2013, 3). In *Discrepant Parallels: Cultural Implications of the Canada–U.S. Border* (2015) and *Reading between the Borderlines: Cultural Production and Consumption Across the 49th Parallel* (2018), Gillian Roberts (with other contributors in the second volume) explores literature, as well as film, music, and other cultural media as ideals and realities of cultural work at the border. Roberts and Stirrup and their colleagues in the Culture and the Canada–U.S. Border (CCUSB) collective are recent substantial contributors to documenting and analyzing culture at the border. Their research follows a substantial focus on establishing Canadian literature and culture studies as distinctive in North America, and then orients towards the border to examine the edges of this culture and its interplay with American culture.

> The border is actually borders, and the metonym of the Canada–U.S. border as Canada in Canadian culture, has diffused as a meme through the Internet. We have moved from rediscovering and reimagining the border, to encountering borders beyond the line, and, now, to evaluating the perseverance of border culture in the face of overwhelming challenges from pandemics and populist/neo-nationalist intransigencies [nationalism exacerbates the narrative of the exclusionary nation-state]. Paradoxically, this is what enlivens and rejuvenates border culture; it needs to be in motion, ever-changing, on a live edge.
>
> *(Konrad and Kelly 2021, 14)*

In a vibrant book about the challenges of life on the edge, author Jim Lynch situates his novel *Border Songs* (2010) in the borderlands of Washington State and British Columbia. The protagonist Brandon Vanderkool is a six-foot-eight, tongue-tied, dyslexic, and awkward U.S. Border Patrol agent responsible for monitoring thirty miles of essentially invisible border following a boundary ditch. In this portrait of humour, tenderness, and charm of life at the border, *Border Songs* reveals the idea of borders as places, and constructs between people and the natural and human worlds. Borders are set between past and future ways of life. A perceptive awareness and sense of place is created about this small piece of the extensive Canada–U.S. border. Collectively, the ideas, images, experiences, and places in *Border Songs* convey a lyrical sense of the border where neighbours in different countries may reside together culturally, legally and spiritually, if not ideologically.

4.1.2 The cultures of border and borderlands consolidation

Ideology works to consolidate borders and also to consolidate across boundaries, thus constructing or adding to cultures of the border or borderlands. In Africa, some colonial legacy borders are consolidated with violence, displacement, and smuggling (Neto 2017, Bennafla 2002). Alejandro Lugo (2008) conveys at once the consolidated border between Mexico and the U.S. and the integration in the borderlands. In his book *Fragmented Lives, Assembled Parts*, he illustrates the intertwined "culture, capitalism and conquest" evident at the border and in the borderlands. Consolidation in the U.S. Department of Homeland Security, assembling border and transportation security agencies after the events of 9/11, has led to consolidation of the security culture of the border. Meanwhile, the process of "colonia" settlement establishment and expansion on the U.S. side of the border has extended consolidation of a Latino/a culture in the borderlands (Donelson and Esparza 2016).

Another illustration of the extension of cross-border culture is found in the banking industry (Buch and DeLong 2004). Evident in this context are the merged banking institutions across the Canada–U.S. border in which large Canadian chartered banks, among the largest financial institutions in North America, have acquired banks in the U.S. side of the borderlands, as well as financial institutions throughout the U.S., and particularly in the southeast and in California where Canadian "snowbirds" and ex-patriots congregate. These forms of banking acquisitions and expansion are also a feature of the financial industry in the European Union (Hernando et al. 2009).

Around the European Union, the external boundary of the EU is consolidated through crises such as the Crimean annexation by Russia and the massive in-migration of refugees after 2015 (Campesi 2018). The current war between Russia and the Ukraine is at once consolidating the external boundary of the EU, and also potentially shifting the stance of neutrality of states like Sweden and Finland, to a consideration of NATO membership to further strengthen solidarity in the face of Russian aggression. Inside the EU, Euroregions are envisioned as "soft spaces" between consolidation and transformation (Tell 2017), although the 2015 geopolitical crisis has hardened some of these internal borders thus suggesting that European bordering regimes remain in the state of becoming. We focus on the external border of the EU and the FRONTEX border as a detailed illustration of an official border culture.

4.1.3 FRONTEX and other official border security cultures

FRONTEX, the European external borders agency, was established in 2004. According to Andrew Neal (2009), the agency was less a product of securitizing links between terrorism, security, migration, and borders in response to the events of 9/11, but more due to the failure of the EU to achieve these aims. However, FRONTEX did develop an EU border strategy of integrated EU and globally connected response to security threats, integrated border management, and a global approach to migration (Carrera 2007). This multifaceted approach both looked into borders and looked out towards a global policing of migration. Borderwork needed to be conceptualized as beyond the inside/outside dichotomy (Vaughan-Williams 2008), and as Etienne Balibar (2002) had established, borders of Europe were vacillating but also changing and multiplying rather than simply disappearing as a result of the Maastricht Treaty.

Infused into this situation, FRONTEX emerged as an institution based on securitization practices and operational cooperation at external borders of the EU (Leonard 2010). Rational choice, social responsibility, and historical precedent were all intertwined and institutionalized (Ekelund 2014). During the last decade, so-called "humanitarian" politics of border policy emerged, and developed as a discourse legitimizing migration control (Pallister-Wilkins 2015, Horsti 2012). These justifications established modes of humanitarian governance of care with control as good practice, and security, technocracy, and humanitarianism became intertwined in border control practice. A convergence of humanitarianism, human rights, and security emerged to define FRONTEX and the European Union's border policy (Perkowski 2018). Ruben Zaiotti (2011) views the early development of the institution as a culture of border control. Max Janzon (2014) suggests that border security culture in Finland and in Europe more generally is a convergence of bordering practices: "east bordering" (response to Russia), social bordering (FRONTEX), and spatial bordering (networked border security). FRONTEX also develops a professional culture notably through the implementation of Borderguard Day (Figure 4.2).

Official border security cultures are evident globally although many have gained credence, stature, expanded relevance and attention in the wake of international terrorism at the turn of the century. These cultures develop through everyday practices of security actors and they are sustained by institutionalization of these practices (Cote-Boucher et al. 2014). Along the U.S.–Mexico border in south Texas, the U.S. Border Patrol is viewed by some as the first line of defence

FIGURE 4.2 The FRONTEX Border, Luhamaa, Estonia, and Shumilkina, Russia. Every vehicle is checked. Photo by Victor Konrad.

against the chaos brought about through illegal migration into the U.S. (Maril 2006). Another perspective, based on the assessment of legitimization narratives of the Border Patrol, suggests that narratives of criminality are linked with narratives of morality and even empathy (Vega 2018). The core vision of the first line of defence has established a culture of militarism in the Border Patrol that is often seemingly out of place when espoused by agents along the borders with Mexico, and particularly with Canada. Accordingly, in Border Patrol culture in the U.S., and in other border agency cultures, crises of identity occur and may be addressed by either hardening the resolve or engaging with change.

4.1.4 Peace parks and monuments at the border conserve the status quo

The border between Canada and the U.S. boasts numerous instances of commemoration of peace and friendship between the countries (Kuenker 2011). In the Niagara frontier, the Peace Bridge (1927) links Fort Erie, Ontario, and Buffalo, New York, in a region where early nineteenth century conflict between Great Britain and the fledgling U.S. dotted the landscape with numerous monuments to battles and fallen heroes. The Ambassador Bridge connects Detroit and Windsor in the busiest corridor between the two countries. Glacier and Waterton national parks, in the U.S. and Canada, respectively, are joined as an international peace park established in 1932. Also inaugurated in

1932, the International Peace Garden was located on the 49th parallel between Manitoba and North Dakota (Thomsen 1996). More than a decade earlier, in 1921, the Peace Arch or Peace Portal marked the cross-boundary connection between the U.S. and Canada on the Pacific coast. All of these monuments have persevered, and now, a century later, they are being renovated and in some instances re-evaluated. Subsequent to the events of 9/11, and enhanced security implementation at the border, the International Peace Garden became less accessible and the border was viewed as a barrier to tourism (Timothy and Tosun 2003). Peace Arch Park on the Pacific coast (Figure 3.4 previous chapter), however, provided a sanctuary and meeting place for American/Canadian couples and families who were restricted access across the border during the current pandemic. Yet, the fundamental and persistent purpose of these peace parks and monuments is to acknowledge that the border between Canada and the U.S. works to establish territorial integrity and national sovereignty while celebrating sustained cooperation. But, the fate of the Friendship Park at the far western end of the Mexico–U.S. border is very different than when it was established. Now the park area is under surveillance and scrutiny, with severely restricted hours of access (Tocilovac 2016).

Peace parks and monuments have been established at borders in many parts of the world, partly in response to the early example of collaborative efforts along the Canada–U.S. border. Currently, peace park initiatives are most advanced in Africa as discussed in the previous chapter (peaceparks.org 2021). Proposals abound for more peace parks in regions where conservation and conflict resolution concerns intersect (Marton-Lefevre 2007). These include a peace park in the Balkans, a snow leopard peace park in the Himalayas, and peace parks on the Amazon basin perimeter. Another initiative, that is well advanced, is a peace park in the Korean demilitarized zone (Mjelde et al. 2017). Also in Asia, a plan has been advanced for a marine peace park in the South China Sea (Geopolitical Monitor 2021). All of these initiatives, both realized and projected, convey the integration of conservation, security, and counter-insurgency in designated areas (Duffy 2016). Also evident is that peace parks require more and not less state control over frontier zones (Duffy 2001), and this situation generates a border culture that is destabilized by dislocation of inhabitants and state scrutiny, while conservation zones become places for poaching and the slaughter of animals (Dailymaverick 2022).

4.1.5 Teaching the wall and educating across the divide

Borders not only are socially constructed but they are learned. National narratives and counter-narratives are taught through an array of pedagogies at the border. These include signs with instructions and information regarding the border process, but also extend to multiple media displays of national narratives. In southern China, at crossings to Myanmar, Laos, and Vietnam, billboard-size video screens run constant messages of cross-border friendship, yet proclaim power over the border in neo-imperialistic trade initiatives, anti-drug campaigns, and central government achievements (Konrad and Hu 2021). Signs at the border between Bolivia and Chile state "El mar nos pertenece por derecho, recuperarlo es deber"—the sea is ours by right, it's a duty to get it back. An objective of extending border culture is to convey the understanding of a border regime and to educate compliance with the regime. Established examples include the Iron Curtain between east and west Europe, and particularly the Berlin Wall between East and West Berlin. Alternatively, questioning and changing the border regime is a strategy to educate across the divide. This strategy was utilized extensively by countries throughout Eastern Europe during the late Soviet era. Ultimately, in response to the resistance, the Berlin Wall was all removed except for a small section to commemorate the resistance and removal. The remnant is accompanied by an exhibition and interpretation centre. Germany has moved from teaching the wall to educating across the divide.

With the rise of walls and barriers throughout the world (Rosière and Jones 2012, Vallet 2014), more and more countries are at once faced with teaching the wall and coping with resistance to barrier constructs. Christine Leuenberger and Izhak Schnell (2020) illustrate *The Politics of Maps* in their analysis of cartographic constructions of the Israel/Palestine divide. The separation wall has emerged as a "canvas of resistance" on the one hand and a materialization of occupation on the other hand (Heneini and Basaree 2018). Although the wall is a posting site for all manner of markings and illustrations, some, like graffiti, are largely constructions of political discourse (Hanauer 2011), whereas other works are elevated art of resistance that teach lessons of the impact of separation (Parry 2011). Moreover, Palestinian children impacted by the separation wall have expressed their approaches to negotiating the wall, and drawing from the discourses and representations on it (Shalhoub-Kevorkian 2006). These discourses and representations resonate in the online communications of Palestinian students (Hart 2007).

Another example of children learning and coping with a barrier is found in Lampedusa, a small Italian island landfall in the Mediterranean between Tunisia and Sicily. In her essay "Negotiating in/visibilities beyond the spectacularization of Mediterranean frontiers", Chiara Brambilla (2021) explores young people's public visibility, alternative forms of political subjectivity, and revolutionary geographical imaginations. In her text, Brambilla explores the complex relationship between border regimes and regimes of visibility and invisibility related to the void of the humanitarian border. Narratives and images of borderscapes and Mediterranean migrations are despectacularized through performative methods of documentary film, exhibitions, and other learning approaches engaging school children in Tunisia and Lampedusa. In one instance, they create a world map of migrants' clothes. The aim is to instil a fluid and relational understanding of the space of political becoming, and a refusal to ingrain choices of the Italian and Tunisian, and global, narratives.

4.2 National identity construction, territorialization, and border culture in space and time

National identity and national boundaries have become intertwined to the degree that, when we speak about nation-states, we assume that they contain the territory of the state within an established boundary. John Agnew (1994) has designated these assumptions—states are fixed units of sovereign space, a domestic–foreign polarity, and states as containers of societies—as the territorial trap. The essential or fixed territory of states has been taken for granted, and we have anointed the state as territorial much as life on earth is terrestrial. Yet, territory is being constantly unbundled and re-aggregated, particularly in globalization. With this privileged territorial conception of the state, territories have been fixed and reified into set units of sovereign space. The conception has obscured interaction between processes operating at different scales. Ultimately, we consider the territorial state as formative and a container of society, and we equate society with national identity.

This argument, that the assumptions of fixation, polarity, and containment have led us to a territorial trap, may also offer the opportunity to question whether perhaps we may recreate the boundaries of life in a different way. Gilles Deleuze has urged a path away from the practical through the world of desire, to think differently and recreate ourselves, destroy common sense about what we are, and to be open to become (Colebrook 2020). This central Deleuzian question of "how might one live?" allows us to consider recreating the boundaries of life through literature and art (May 2005). "The territory is not the map" because we are continually coding and decoding space (Janz 2002, 1), and framing the earth between chaos, territory, and art (Grosz 2008). The borders in our world are socially constructed to appear rational and practical because we have imagined borders to work that way. We have constructed and narrated nations, states, territories, and identities. Yet, our encounters with borders reveal a more complex and intriguing situation where addressing border culture advances our capacity to think about and understand borders.

In the following brief discussion, we explore national identity construction in space and time, and particularly at the edge of territory. We argue that border culture is an integral component of national identity construction even though the territorial focus of national identity construction is within the national territory and its internal landmarks. Our initial purpose is to demystify and simplify understanding of the processes of national identity construction and the territorial contexts of these processes. The aim is to glean the basic components that articulate the relationships among territory, border culture, and national identity. Although there has been recent attention to these issues, a great deal of the research takes us back to the 1990s.

4.2.1 Basics of identity, territory, and border relationships

Guntrum Herb and David Kaplan (1999) suggest the concept of nested identities to clarify the relationship between nationalism, territory, and scale. In an introductory essay entitled "National identity and territory" Herb and Kaplan (1999, 10–19) establish some basic understandings. Bounded space or territory is a crucial element in the tension between power and identity. Territory offers power, and power over territory instils identity. Only territory provides the tangible evidence of a state's existence. A nation needs territory to establish its own state. At this point, the relationships between nation, identity, and territory become more ill defined. The nature of national territory is not as evident because states and nations may not be synonymous. Identity may coincide with ethnicity within a defined territory but this is not always the case. Self-determination is not an inevitable process. Also, the distinction between civic and ethnic nations is blurred. Nevertheless, nation and state are often viewed as synonyms and this leads to confusion between nationalisms of ethnicity, statism, and ideology (patriotism). Three models of the nation emerge. In the first, the nation evolves stronger loyalty from members than other communities in either an organic or artificial construction. The second model suggests that the nation shares an idyllic and often primordial past. Finally, the nation has a goal or destiny. Identity theory is rooted in self-determination, the maintenance of national identity, and the struggle to sustain cohesion through conflict if necessary (Schwartz et al. 2011). Accordingly, "strategies of remembrance" are mobilized through the rhetorical dimension of national identity construction (Bruner 2002).

This is where boundaries come into the picture. Nations, and certainly states and nation-states, build spatial identities (Brown 2001). Prasenjit Duara (1996, 168) explains how "a master narrative of descent privileges certain identity forming principles and hardens existing communal boundaries". Although boundary creation is always in flux and becoming, territory comes to define the group rather than the other way around. Territory imbues national spirit. All national anthems make reference to special qualities of their natural environment (Lowenthal 1994). Special qualities of the environment at the edges of territory receive special attention in anthems and other narratives of the nation and its identity. Ultimately, the struggle against outsiders who seek to destroy the nation transforms the territory into holy ground. The current resistance and conviction by the people of Ukraine, in the face of unprovoked Russian aggression, is a compelling and evocative illustration of this point.

4.2.2 Territorialization of identity

In 1996, Anssi Paasi published *Territories, Boundaries and Consciousness: The Changing Geographies of the Finnish–Russian Border.* This classic work in border studies established that borders are socially constructed as visible territorial identities and national identities are limited by boundaries, to maintain identities is to sustain boundaries, and to sustain boundaries is to construct inclusion and exclusion of social collectives. Boundaries are envisioned as social processes within a world of flows (Paasi 1998). National identity is constructed through extensive and complicated identity discourse and conveyed through boundary narratives (Paasi 1997, 2001, 2003, Newman and Paasi 1998).

During the decades since the publication of *Territories, Boundaries and Consciousness,* there has been substantial attention to the discursive construction of national identities (Wodak 2009), and more specifically identity construction at borders and in borderlands (Prokkola 2009). Several themes are apparent in this literature: constructing in-betweenness, reinforcing walls, recognizing border identifications, and moving beyond borders.

"In-between-ness" is a plural identity in a space between other identities. Karin Smeekens (2010) explains how Estonia has managed to develop a distinct identity on the border between Russia and Europe by reinforcing its linguistic distinctiveness, independence, technological innovation, and cultural heritage. Chiara Brambilla (2007) illustrates how the "plurivocality" of the Kwanyama people on the Angola–Namibia border emerges through a discursive construction of borders and identity to border identity. Indeed, along the Benin–Nigeria border, residents engaged in extensive cross-border exchange articulate that "we are the border" (Flynn 1997). In the Middle East, Hizbullah's identity construction emerges and flourishes in between (Alagha 2012). Similarly, border crossing is integral to identity construction of Polish migrants in Belfast (Kempny 2010). In order to construct in-betweenness, and to occupy "a place between places", language facility is necessary to build and sustain identity (Llamas 2007).

Language may also help to maintain a border and to reinforce walls between people. Combined with other components such as fear, myth, rhetoric, and exaggeration, "mental walls" at the border strengthen local identities and confirm national identities (Izotov 2012). Identity combines with religion and modernity to defend the border of Georgia with Russia (Pelkmans 2006). Mental walls combine with and reinforce state constructed regulations, procedures, and materialized barriers to maintain sovereignty at the border (Jones et al. 2017). Overall, these are efforts of border reconstruction and reinforcement (Wonders 2007).

Language and "autochthonous belonging" are prominent identifiers at the border. Ethnic groups' identity is a construct, and this construct is not a way of pushing the people who belong to these groups out of the polity. Ethnicity factors are prominent identifiers at the border. At India's borders ethnicity is refigured to enlarge "states of difference" (Middleton 2013). Among the additional narratives utilized in *Border Identification* (Vila 2005) are religion, gender, and class. Age is also an identifier among urban youth in their construction of culture and border identity (Bejarano 2007). Border identification often emerges by constructing the border from below as in the case of the Congolese–Rwandan state boundary (Doevenspeck 2011). People on both sides of the border make sense of their border world by identifying with narratives of economic interaction, othering, border control, and institutionalization. They become border people with border ways and affectations that may be documented most effectively through photographic and interview documentation to reveal characteristics and memories of border life (Vila 2013, Meinhof and Galasinski 2000).

Identities are constructed beyond borders by minorities within a nation-state and by transnational populations in host countries. Corey Johnson and Amanda Coleman (2012) refer to the internal other in exploring the relationship between regional exclusion and the construction of national identity. The Rohingya in Myanmar are a case in point (Ware and Laoutides 2018). Minorities construct national identities within a host nation-state, and they may reconstruct their national identity as they move to an adjacent nation-state, even if their origins as an ethnic group are in the adjacent state (Kleiner-Liebau 2009). Linked transnational and national identities may be constructed by developing new homeland territories in foreign lands subsequent to forced relocations or volunteer migrations as illustrated by Kazakhstan's Germans and Koreans (Diener 2006). In some instances national identity is stimulated through diaspora as in the case of Sikh nationalism in various countries around the world (Shani 2002). Korean women immigrants in the U.S. construct transnational identities through privileging their home experience (Park 2007). Identity construction and reconstruction in a transnational context is an extensive and complex topic that requires greater understanding of how identity is impacted by forces of globalization. The proximity of identity and language may be very violent because it imposes the constant re-affirmation, something that Derrida calls "differance" with an "a" (Amilhat Szary 2013).

4.2.3 Border heritage: The Past is a Foreign Country

David Lowenthal, a renowned cultural geographer and leading scholar in heritage studies, published one of his earliest articles on the futile but bitterly contested Aroostook War along the northeastern boundary between Canada (then part of Great Britain) and the U.S. (Lowenthal 1951). Although some of his more recent works engage with the boundaries of nationalism in England (Lowenthal 1991), the geographical implications of national anthems (Lowenthal 2006), and the bordered exceptionalism of Newfoundland in Canada (Lowenthal 2017), Lowenthal is recognized for his work on exploring the borders between the past and the present. Both *The Past is a Foreign Country* (1985) and *The Past is a Foreign Country Revisited* (2015) are acclaimed works in the expanding field of heritage studies. These books also provide substantial insights into how the past is bordered from the present, and how the past is viewed as distant and foreign. Heritage landscapes are often bordered in space to reveal them as explicitly distinct. Although identity may be reaffirmed and validated by the past, the past may also reveal threats and evils that do not square with the present. Consequently, there are risks of crossing the temporal border including disappointment, an inability to cope, difficulty in returning to the present, and endangering the temporal fabric that we envision and construct. According to Lowenthal (1975), people want the past, and they express this desire through nostalgia, which leads to repossessing the past and revisiting it through explanation, exaggeration, aggrandizement, and the search for a golden age. Yet, memory is incomplete for understanding the past, so we reconstruct the past to conform to our expectations, alter the evidence, and invent the past (Lowenthal 1998).

One of the most substantial temporal borders envisioned by human beings is the boundary or distinction between *ancients* and *moderns*. Within these constructed eras, more temporal boundaries segment and reify the past into conceivable periods such as the Renaissance and the Classical. We engineer bridges in time like the Enlightenment based on the presumed decay of nature and the hallowed effects of printing and science. On the one hand, people exhibit distaste for age because we believe in the organic analogy and we are averse to age in humans. Similarly, we decry decay of the world and its features and reject age and wear in artifacts. We proclaim and celebrate the superiority of youthful nations, thus engraving borders. On the other hand, people feel that old things should look old, and that decay demonstrates and secures antiquity. Those who value the aesthetics of decay value the beauty of patina, and the ideas of the sublime, transience, evanescence, accretion of experience, and temporal awareness (Lowenthal 1985, 74–182).

Knowing the past is based on experience and belief, and also largely on memory. Memory may be personal or it may be collective. It may be confirmable. There are many types of memory. Some are conscious and others are unconscious. Some memories are historical facts that we learn, and others are social conventions that we emulate. Recall may be episodic or instrumental, guided by conventions. Then there is reverie or unconstrained memory. These types of memory are intertwined in our lives. Often there is heightened recollection, and eventually memory wanes, and with disease it disappears. We forget. We revise. "Remembering the past is crucial for our sense of identity: … to know what we were confirms who we are" (Lowenthal 1985, 197). This is true for both personal and collective memory. Yet, the sense of personal continuity was rare before the nineteenth century, and then in the twentieth century memory became diffused (see also Ricoeur 2004). "The frequency with which we update and reinterpret our memory weakens coherent temporal identity" (Lowenthal 1985, 199). This weakening of temporal identities, when associated with the other shifts in globalization, helps to explain the decoupling of national identities and personal identities. Also, the weakening of temporal identities suggests that border identities have emerged more pervasive and consistent because anchors of both time and space have been loosened in globalization.

French historian Pierre Nora offers another perspective on how memory creates national identity (Nora and Kritzman 1996). By cataloguing memory places, Nora and his colleagues establish a poly-referential inventory to sketch the nation and the national identity. This inventory also contains conflict spaces and symbolic divisions at the edges of the nation and within France that reconfigure its relationship to the past.

> The creation of "realms of memory" is the result of modern society's inability to live within real memory; the consecration of a "realm of memory"

> takes place because real environments of memory have disappeared. The projection of a "realm of memory" is, therefore, the sign of memory's disappearance and society's need to represent what ostensibly no longer exists.
>
> *(Nora and Kritzman 1996, xii)*

In this representation of the past, borders may gain or lose significance, but ultimately borders gain historical credence in national narratives. The border crossing between China and Burma (now Myanmar), used by troops from China and its allies during WWII, is now a place where Chinese and foreign visitors are photographed (Figure 4.3).

In an essay published shortly before his death, David Lowenthal (2018, 32) acknowledged that "heritage has always been fractious and divisive … an elusive property of competitive groups … that functions as *casus belli* because it is an exemplary tribal bond". The role of heritage in sustaining and questioning borders, and in both constructing and challenging borderlands, remains an area of research that requires attention in border studies. The emerging field of critical heritage studies is meshing theory and approaches in both heritage and border studies to engage with issues in the politics of border heritage (Lois 2019). Among recent studies are the examination of scalar politics of border heritage in the EU's northern and southern border areas (Prokkola and Lois 2016), tourist lodging and spatial relations in European and North American cultural heritage

FIGURE 4.3 Wanding: China–Burma WWII Border Memorial Bridge Tourists, 2015. Photo by Victor Konrad.

borderlands (Timothy and Gelbman 2015), a critical assessment of world heritage sites on the Thai–Cambodian border (Meskell 2020), and a model for linking natural and cultural heritage in the Niagara region along the Canada–U.S. border (Cafarella et al. 2021).

The intersection of temporal and spatial borders has been acknowledged by border scholars, most recently in this engagement with critical heritage studies. Although there is substantial potential for more research in this area, border scholars also need to expand their understanding of the intersection of temporal and spatial borders without privileging either border studies or historical approaches. The work of Randy Widdis is exemplary in this regard because he employs historical geography approaches aligned with border theory to expand understanding of both spatial and temporal bordering processes. In a recent essay, "On globalization, borders, and borderlands: A historical geographical perspective" he states "Under current dialectical conditions of globalization and increased demands for security, borders are no longer just symbols of sovereignty and national histories; they are evolving into new forms and as such are taking on new functions" (Widdis 2019a, 573). Most of Widdis' scholarship focuses on enlarging understanding of the intersection of temporal and spatial borders, and how these borders have been crossed between Canada and the U.S. This scholarship contextualizes border culture, and in many instances offers temporal continuities and temporal boundaries of border culture. Among the contributions to this work are articles on railways in Canada–U.S. borderlands (2019b), nineteenth century maritime trade in the Great Lakes (2011), greater New England as a cultural borderland (2017), and borderland interaction in the Great Plains (1997). The western interior region of North America has inspired many of Widdis' theoretical insights on the intersection of temporal and spatial borders (Widdis 2015). Whereas few border scholars in the U.S. who focus on the U.S.–Canada border have embraced this degree of engagement with the theory of temporal and spatial border intersection, some have advanced the understanding of how the U.S. has looked northward over time and differentiated its national experience from Canada. Prominent among these scholars are Seymour Martin Lipset (2013 [1990], 1996), who compared American and Canadian nationalisms, and defined American exceptionalism, and Wilbur Zelinsky (2017), whose most recent work examines the shifting symbolic foundations of American nationalism.

4.2.4 *Altering border heritage in globalization:* The Past is a Foreign Country Revisited

In the second edition of his book, *The Past is a Foreign Country Revisited*, David Lowenthal (2015) reaffirms that the past is the prime source of personal and collective identity, and this past, in its vast range of relics and reminders, evokes rivalry and a "politics of the past" (Gathercole and Lowenthal 2004). "Resurgent conflicts over history, memory, and heritage pervade every facet of public culture, making the foreign country of the past ever more our domesticated own" (Lowenthal 2015, i).

> The past in the Internet age has become more intimate yet more remote, readily found but rapidly forgotten. Its range today is stupendous, embracing not just human but the terrestrial and even the cosmic saga. And it is seen and touched and smelled as well as heard and read about. Traumatic recollection and emphatic re-enactment demote traditional history. A clear-cut chronicle certified by experts has become a fragmented congeries of contested relics, remnants and reminiscences.
>
> *(Lowenthal 2015, i)*

The shift in border heritage has become demonstrable as more and stronger borders have emerged in the post-9/11 era. As borders thicken with enhanced security, border landmarks from the past either become more prominent or get in the way of walls and sensors. Restoration of monuments is hampered and visitation is restricted. More important, if not as readily apparent, are the impacts of security on traditional pathways across borders and throughout borderlands. In the Pacific coast border region of Canada and the U.S., settlers of Dutch origin in the borderlands established a strong cross-border network of farming communities with well-established traditions of agricultural exchange, worship, intermarriage, and historical/cultural reconstructions (Konrad 2010). Twenty-first-century impacts of security and recently the COVID-19 pandemic have impacted social interaction across the border thus limiting cross-border worship and marriage. Also, the historical and cultural landscape and structures, once a substantial draw for tourists from across the border, have substantially fewer visitors.

Chiara Brambilla (2015) reveals how a multilevel complexity of social and political practices and cultural productions emerges at the nexus of border and migration in the Mediterranean. Diffused and stratified borders beyond the nation-state emerge through

> dis-locations and re-locations, which initiate a complex interaction between processes and practices of border *externalization* and *internalization* (Fassin 2011). This means that one should critically investigate the complex relationships between the hardening and policing of external political and territorial borders (which are related to the exercise of modern state sovereignty) and the production of boundaries as internal social categorizations (which are related to the politics of identity). Embracing this viewpoint, a novel epistemological gaze on borders is outlined, which could be defined as "double". By *seeing double* it is possible to be aware of geographical and territorial borders, as well as ethnic, social and cultural boundaries, while also considering their visible and hidden interactions.
>
> *(Brambilla 2015, 112)*

FIGURE 4.4 LampedusaInFestival. Banner: "Little festival about communities, migration, struggles, sustainable tourism and sea stories". Photo by permission of Chiara Brambilla, University of Bergamo.

We would add that this double gaze is also capable of telescoping back in time, not in a teleological sense but through snapshots back in time as related to memories and artifacts.

Brambilla engages a "multidimensional choreography" (van Houtum 2009) of borders to explore the LampedusaInFestival as a counter-hegemonic Euro/African borderscape (Figure 4.4). The festival, organized by the Askavusa (barefoot) collective on the Mediterranean island of Lampedusa is at once a film festival, and a festival of visual arts, music, and narratives that express claims of resistance against the hegemonic regime of borders in the Mediterranean. The festival plays a role in the cultural politics of globalization in the region by using aesthetic practice to promote change. "What emerges is the role of the Festival in the process of 'politicization of the aesthetics' that is described by Rancière (2010) as a necessary act to critically rethink the contemporary world of transnational flows" (Brambilla 2015, 115). Furthermore, during the 2013 festival, the island's historical archives screened documentaries of Lampedusa from 1943 to 1968, from 1980 to 1990, and from 2007 to 2012, thus opening the aperture to the island's history. Parallel to this heritage is the "excavation" of the migrants' memories facilitated by the Archives of Migrants' Memories. Yet, both aspects of Lampedusa heritage become intertwined in an intersection of border culture in place.

4.3 Securitization and cultures of border conflict

Nations and nation-states secure their history and their territory through the establishment of geopolitical cultures. For example, Gearoid O Tuathail

(2005, 356) considers the film *Behind Enemy Lines* as a cultural and commercial product and an illustration of American geopolitical culture and dramatization of re-masculinization, moral ambiguity, and post-9/11 American militarism. American geopolitical culture is portrayed as impatient with multilateral diplomacy but focused on unilateral action and morally righteous violence. Similarly, geopolitical cultures have been articulated in other national contexts such as Russia (O'Loughlin et al. 2005). Alternatively, Canadian geopolitical culture has emerged as aligned with issues of climate change and sustainability (Dalby 2019).

Border cultures of securitization emerge to substantiate and protect national territory as defined by the "national" group in power. These geopolitical cultures are formed by forces of fear of difference and of nativism. Anti-migration narratives heighten insecurities in the national group and the construction of walls responds to the state of insecurity (Vallet 2014, Rosière 2020).The outcome is a powerful border culture of securitization that prevails by dominating the media discourse and defining the new norms of what a border is, and what it should be doing to filter in those who are admissible to the nation and the nation-state, and filter out those who are now considered and defined as illegal. Border security culture is by its very nature restrictive. A central objective of border security culture is to secure citizenship by narrowing the definition of who is admissible and governing the rules of admissibility. Again, media are appropriated to convey the projected problem of illegal migration and convince the nation that secured citizenship is necessary and worth fighting for, particularly at the border. Accordingly, borders have become a media focus in television programmes and in the cinema, thus expanding the border culture of securitization and conveying the urgency for risk assessment and management at the border.

4.3.1 *Anti-migration narratives within the context of de-bordering*

Anti-migration narratives are epitomized in the political rhetoric of hegemonic powers. In contrast to the beckoning and embellished narratives of previous centuries, in which colonial narratives espoused new and open land for the taking, contemporary migration narratives appear negative and threatening in a movement of reversal of the colonial standpoint. These anti-migration narratives are relied on by political actors as a unifying topic and an effective story to galvanize anti-migration public support (Sahin-Mencutek 2020). Anti-migration narratives function to structure ideology, to structure knowledge, draw boundaries between "us" and "them", shape public opinion, produce exclusionary policies, and legitimize actions. Yet, in the same instance, the narratives also provide some understanding of migrants, and their experiences and identities. Anti-migration narratives are entangled with narratives of identity, citizenship, and politics (as well as with narratives of the border) (Pickering 2006), moving it towards a fixed and almost deterministic reading of cultural politics.

Substantial diversity is evident in the characteristics, distinctiveness, meaning, and actors constructing migration narratives. Our aim in this brief discussion is to identify some commonalities in how anti-migration narratives engage with borders, and how they fit within the broader realm of migration narratives through a culturalist perspective. In this regard the narratives are first and foremost geopolitical boundary narratives (Jones 2009). The narratives speak to systemic global politics and align with shifts in these politics (Akanle 2018). The politics are most commonly associated with race, religion, Indigeneity, and territory in terms of excluding binaries. But in the case of the narratives surrounding the India–Bangladesh border fence, the narratives are also about alternatives or possibilities such as different political positions at the national level and in the borderland, and several borderlands narratives reflecting divergent political positions in the borderlands (McDuie-Ra 2014). Similarly, Yunnanese Chinese migrants to Burma (Myanmar) tell stories of opportunity in the face of discrimination at the border and Burmese anti-migrant narratives (Chang 2014). Narratives of Iranian women from the diaspora link politics and poetics in crossing borders, and illustrate the intersectionality of class and migration in their efforts to counter anti-migrant narratives (Dossa 2004, Fathi 2017). A trans-locational class emerges in migration to impact place-making, performance, gendering, belonging, and racialization. In Africa, the anti-migration narratives are associated with other narratives within a migration turn in African cultural production featuring films and stories set at the margins (Iheka 2018). Forgotten diasporas of Lusophone and Indian migrants are resurrected, and narratives of return are added to dispel the notion of exclusive exodus. Consistent themes, fugitivity for example, not only prevail in African migration narratives but in African American women's migration narratives (Moody 2018). In the final analysis, the anti-migration narrative usually prevails to gain more traction and adherence. Maureen Duffy (2019) illustrates how anti-migration narratives have the power to "wag the dog"; that is, feigning crisis in U.S. anti-migration narratives actually creates crisis.

4.3.2 Constructing walls and border culture

When narratives create crisis, the constructions of metaphorical walls and then actual barriers, fences and walls are not far behind. The following discussion is less about the types of walls and their configuration, and the geopolitics of border walls, and more about how these constructions constitute border culture. When we recognize border walls as both symbol and reality, it becomes possible to envision the other dialectical components emerging from the divide, and their implications. The arbitrary splitting of borderland languages and cultures becomes self-evident and a form of historical amnesia of the other side takes effect as we are lulled into a new rhythm at the border (Stavans 2010). The U.S.–Mexico border wall, for example, is narrated in a lifeless and desolate setting when in fact it is actually a dynamic and diverse context that is verdant with viable communities and rich cross-border cultural histories (Dorsey and Díaz-Barriga 2010). The imaginary of desolation reinforces calls for militarization. Miguel Díaz-Barriga and Margaret E. Dorsey (2020) see the wall as *Fencing in Democracy* and creating a culture of necro-citizenship enacted by consolidating the normalization of the state of exception. The wall becomes a signal of surrender, a panorama of despair, and a monument to defeat for some borderlanders, and others outside the borderlands. The wall perpetrates the politics of bisection in a very visible and visceral way. This effect is apparent at the broader scale of the Mexico–U.S. border and even more apparent at the scale of communities along the border. In the twentieth century, Ambos (combined) Nogales prevailed along the border between Arizona and Sonora, divided only by a picket fence—a line between neighbours (McGuire 2013). In the mid-1990s this fence was replaced by the first steel wall, and in 2011 by the second, bigger steel wall. Currently, Nogales is divided, no longer Ambos in name, but all efforts to limit the agency of border crossers have actually resulted in a heightened agency of crossers to become more determined and effective in working around the wall. Rather than dividing border culture the wall has become a component of the border culture, as it has in most border cities and towns (Beylier and Fortune 2022).

The border wall is at the centre of a vortex in which the border transforms, from embedding the myth of the frontier to a construction on the explicit line (Grandin 2019). The wall is, following Michel Foucault, an assembly of multiple and contradictory strategies of intertwined types of power: sovereign exclusion of the illegal, disciplinary detention of surveilled life, and bio-political circulation of migratory life (Nail 2013). These coexisting strategies of power also radiate through highly technological connections to the wall in sensors and drones (Nieto-Gomez 2014). They link as well to other "imperial designs" of the U.S. as recalled from Iraq and even Vietnam. Victoria Hatten (2016) relates how portable helicopter landing mats used in the Vietnam War have "re-surfaced" along the U.S.–Mexico border wall. In a sense, Trump's border wall, and the fencing projects preceding it back into the mid-1990s, are at once rhetorical devices used as ceremonial purification of external societies, and the symbolic objects to represent purification (Stewart 2019). The culture of the border wall encompasses and displays this extensive polysemy of the separation barrier with its dogma, myth, and defence conveyed in aesthetics on the wall and in border spaces (Ganivet 2019a).

> The border as a wall proposes an archaic static apparatus of rejection of the other-foreigner contrasting with the image of a globalized world where only economic and technological interests seem to flow. These walls crystallize a malaise that can be elucidated through art. By capturing the historical iconography, we understand the values that shape the current geopolitical wall.
>
> *(Ganivet 2019b)*

4.3.3 Border security culture

According to border security analysts, border security culture is what border security accumulates as, and sums up to, in terms of references and routines, thus creating a specific imaginary. Border security culture is the collective assemblage of cybersecurity, disaster resilience, reliability of security organizations, and national intelligence responding to an expanding culture of fear and lack of trust (Siedschlag and Jerkovic 2018). In the U.S., Department of Homeland Security (DHS) culture has been formative during the early twenty-first century, and according to some observers (Phelps et al. 2018), DHS has only recently been enabled to enforce the letter of the law and honour its social contract as the result of the restoration of effective sovereignty in the U.S. This view aligns Homeland Security culture and civic culture in the U.S. although this alignment is by no means evident.

Realizing border security culture is then ephemeral and perhaps even merely hypothetical. In his doctoral dissertation, Max Janzon (2014) explores the realization of border security culture in Finland, and by extension, in Europe. Janzon uses a constructivist approach for developing his explanation of how shared ideas and assumptions of border security professionals define a socially constructed spatial strategy, and frame a social meta-practice of border security culture to confirm border-related social practices, meanings, and patterns. Practices of East-borderness, Schengenization, integration, and cooperation constitute and confirm the Finnish border strategy and its sedimentation into a specific culture: "Rooted in convincing border strategy, the practices of east bordering, social bordering, and spatial bordering inhere in and constitute an influential bordering culture, and thereby Finnish (and European) border security culture is realized" (Janzon 2014, abstract).

Other research on border security culture affirms that key actors, and the discourses that they initiate, speak for the burgeoning European border security industry (Baird 2017a). Hubs of prevailing discourse develop around social control and surveillance to convey consistent elements of the border security culture. In Europe and in North America, multi-sited border security fairs have become mechanisms for constructing and communicating the rapidly evolving specialized knowledge that constitutes the integrative fabric of border security culture (Baird 2017b). Border security culture extends into the general public through the emergence of border-oriented militias, and into Indigenous populations living at the border determined to protect sacred land (Schaeffer 2022).

4.3.4 Border cultures of risk assessment and management

A culture of border risk assessment and management is forming in which risk analysis among security specialists is merging with border management practice. In Europe, FRONTEX's risk analysis procedures offer a base to align European border control regimes (Horii 2016). The common application of risk analysis within the risk-based governance of European border control has resulted in harmonization at the regional scale (Paul 2017). The acceptance and integration of risk analysis is due in part to the bridging of the two "cultures" of risk analysis–the quantitative and the qualitative (Jasonoff 1993), and also the acceptance that living and working on the border integrates knowledge, risk, and transdisciplinarity (Horlick-Jones and Sime 2004). Risk analysis has become a field within security studies (Petersen 2012) and a component in defining a culture of border risk assessment and management that includes collaborative border management in aspects of security ranging from customs to migration controls (Doyle 2010). In this field, what is meant by culture is the structured effort to optimize border security around the key rationales of neoliberalized border governance: internationalization, competitiveness, risk prevention, and the functioning of society (Prokkola 2013).

4.3.5 Border wars television and movies

In order to extend and interpret border security culture, and to engage with the politics surrounding borders, narratives of the border have been produced in film and television. Reece Jones (2014) focuses on the National Geographic Channel series *The Border* as an illustration of how "border wars" have become a popular consumer item on cable television. He employs critical discourse analysis to document the prevailing language of conflict and militarism that epitomizes this new front in the wars against things "un-American" and threatening to the U.S. The "border wars" are becoming naturalized (Dorr et al. 2014). *Border Wars* (Barry 2011) have become American wars with multiple media—books, television, film, Internet blogs—all aligning to convey the message of the border under siege. The following is a brief discussion of an extensive topic covered in most journals featuring border studies. A new journal in the field, published by the University of Victoria, Canada—*Borders in Globalization Review*—features film reviews and commentaries in every issue.

Although media and performance along the border are parts of a well-established tradition, some borders have enjoyed more star appeal, and these borders have been consistent subjects of cinema and television interest for the spectacle that they offer (Birringer 1998). Perhaps the most consistent and popular border portrayed in cinema and on television is the U.S.–Mexico border (Dell'Agnese 2005, Iglesias Prieto 2003, Staudt 2014). A long line of Westerns has been created by Hollywood along this border with violence and vengeance as mainstays (Fojas 2009, 2011). Also, more recently, the border has moved from providing context and setting for the production, to acting as leading character (Dell'Agnese 2005). In Finland, "watching the other" has become a national pastime with representations of Russia and Estonia prominent on Finnish national television (Nemeth 2015). Furthermore, border policy is held to account and criticized in border cinema in most border contexts, and particularly where recent migration crises—Europe, Southern Asia, Australia, Africa, the Americas—have caused massive dislocations and hardship (Beckham 2005, Bennett and Tyler 2007). Borders, between races, genders, and classes, and other bordered realities, are connectedly addressed in cinema and television (Bennett and Tyler 2007).

Each border region, and the numerous themes and genres, all deserve detailed discussion and analysis because film and television portrayals are extensive and rich illustrations of border culture. This is worthy of a separate volume and some of the relevant books have been noted above. However, we choose to conclude this brief preview with a focus on one film that has garnered substantial attention and critical acclaim. *Frozen River* is set at Akwesasne on islands in the St. Lawrence River at the Canada–U.S. boundary, and the junction of New York State and the provinces of Ontario and Quebec (for a detailed discussion and map of Akwesasne as borderland see Chapter 5). Courtney Hunt's film is about inter-American discourses, heterotopias, and translocal communities (Raussert 2011). The film relates a story of illegal border crossing and immigrant smuggling across the frozen yet dangerous river/border at the intersections of territory and culture. *Frozen River* revisits the Hollywood border film yet it re-calibrates the territorial border imaginary with the icy materiality of the border. As Klaus Dodds (2013) explains, the complex space of alienation, containment, dispossession, and incorporation that constitutes the border at Akwesasne helps us to theorize more effectively where and how sovereignty and dispossession are performed. The border is an active agent and topography is an accomplice as the protagonists muddle through the borderlands at the geographical and economic margin of the U.S., only to discover that dispossession and redemption are intertwined in the border crossing. Throughout the film, earthly forces and processes, the geopolitical, the geo-physical, and the bio-political, are foregrounded as interferences and interfaces of the border, where sovereign power is enacted, resisted, and ignored. *Frozen River* is acclaimed as one of the films on the "new frontiers for post-Western cinema" (Gonzalez 2015).

4.3.6 Securing citizenship

Citizenship is a contract between the individual and the state, in which the person commits to supporting and upholding the state in return for the protection, security, and rights afforded by the state. A central component in creating and sustaining border security culture is the standardization of citizenship. Standardization of citizenship enables clarification and securitization of citizenship. Yet, there are many instances where citizenship is questioned, confronted, activated, and contested at borders and in borderlands, and this complicates and thwarts securing citizenship (Schwiertz and Schwenken 2020, Díaz-Barriga and Dorsey 2020, Mudimbe 1995, Kirchoff 2020, Schilliger 2020, Staeheli 2011). This is an important matter, and so it is treated very briefly at this point in the book to offer a link to a broader consideration of citizenship and border culture addressed in the next section of this chapter. In contemporary Colombia, citizens concerned with assuring security have been less inclined to claim citizenship rights (Rojas 2009). In formative republican Turkey, the shift from "subjecthood" to citizenship saw rights and duties of citizenship evolve slowly and incompletely (Bilgin and Ince 2015). Peter Nyers (2004) relates how the enhanced securitization after 9/11 has created new and constrained forms of citizenship, despite the universal premise that citizenship and its rights are inherited property, and that intergenerational transfers of both property and citizenship are the rule (Shachar and Hirschl 2007). In the twenty-first century, the promise of citizenship, and the model of citizens' rights developed in the previous century, have been shaken if not unravelled by events like 9/11, global scale migrations, and a fundamental reconfiguration of the concept of citizenship in its own right.

4.4 Citizenship, multiple identities, migration, exile

Don Mitchell (2005) has forwarded a so-called SUV (sport utility vehicle) model of citizenship in which the individual emerges predominant. This is a conceptualization of citizenship based on radical individualism, extreme libertarianism, and transformed property relations. The new model of citizenship emphasizes the right to be left alone, not only on private property, but also in public space. This new conceptualization of citizenship, confirmed and re-bordered by legal decisions in the U.S., is at odds with cosmopolitan association and citizenship ideals espoused by political theorists and a large component of the American population. Yet, the new model appears to describe the ideas of citizenship emulated by a significant and vocal component of the American citizenry. Among these adherents are the Trumpists who stormed the U.S. Capitol on January 6, 2021, claiming rights and powers in line with their emerging, narrow view of citizenship.

Citizenship matters because it confirms membership in a society and affirms belonging to the society. Citizenship spells out the rights of the citizen, and it establishes the right to have rights in return for participation, both explicit and required—paying taxes and in some cases military conscription—and more generally recommended and urged—voting and community service (Bellamy 2008). Citizenship is increasingly a mobile and malleable component in the fluid relationship in globalization among state, territory, and identity (Laine and Casaglia 2017). Citizenship rules are not always static and consistent; they change to enfranchise genders and minorities and exclude others (Lister 2012). The nature of citizenship helps to define national culture, and national culture impacts the nature of citizenship (Stevenson 2001).

Citizenship comes into question during elections and when the state provides benefits, but usually these citizens' rights are established and documented. At the border, however, the person must provide proof of citizenship to enter another state, and often to leave the state of residence and citizenship. Matthew Sparke (2006) has designated the contemporary border as a neoliberal nexus of economy, security, and the bio-politics of citizenship. Proof of citizenship must now be unequivocal and machine readable. Mark B. Salter (2008) envisions the border as a space in which sovereignty and citizenship are performed both by the individual seeking to pass, and the sovereign that makes the rules. Decisions at the border impact and alienate all travellers through an embedded confessionary complex, and according to the "Agambenian" view of the border, this results in making the state border a permanent state of exception, and enhancing the importance of bio-politics. An alternative interpretation is that there is no state of exception but rather the revelation of how the rule is not followed elsewhere. In the following discussion, we explore how citizenship narratives manifest at borders, and how they relate to belonging in the construction of border culture. We assess dual and multiple citizenships as both assets and liabilities, and evaluate the relationship between transnationalism and citizenship, and the viability and possibility of non-state approaches to citizenship.

4.4.1 Citizenship narratives and borders

In the North American literary imagination, citizenship is being reconfigured as national identity is reformed through external influences and internal debates about who has rights, and what these rights are (Tan 2015). North American citizenship is in transition as Canadians, and Americans, in particular, are negotiating Canadian-ness and American-ness. Currently, these negotiations are less about the relationship between being American and Canadian, and more about revising the constituent components of American and Canadian citizenship. In re-narrativizing the national, the border matters more as a container and barrier than as a conduit, yet in Canada, citizenship has not regressed to a former, more elemental form but rather a more delineated discursive construction of "citizen/Self" and "non-citizen/Other" (Nobe-Ghelani 2017). In the U.S. and in Canada, citizenship groups have become more atomized and characterized as wilful citizens, precarious citizens (unhomed, displaced, unhinged), queer citizens, diasporic citizens, and Indigenous citizens, many living or staying in contested spaces, some with their citizenship deferred (Tan 2015).

In Europe, citizenship and borders exhibit a different dynamic relationship in which both borders and citizenship are becoming something different than what they were before the establishment of the European Union. Whereas borders have shifted from the national to the supra-national, citizenship has become at once transnational, sub-national, and decisively national, and growing. Citizenship narratives are layered and scaled, and often paradoxical as they pursue different political and aesthetic strategies (Schimanski and Nyman 2021). The political aesthetics of boundaries and crossings are articulated in the border narratives and images as paradoxes within emerging spheres that enable crossings of citizenship lines, cross-border citizenship, multiple citizenships, national spaces, state territories, private to public contexts, and plural cultural domains.

Whereas the impacts of shifts in citizenship narratives related to borders are evident on a global scale, these shifts appear to exhibit different characteristics in other world regions, although this observation requires research and documentation, particularly in the global south. Some insights are available from research in

Africa. Citizenship in Africa is increasingly contested with violent confrontations evident in many African nation-states (Dorman 2014). Contemporary political tensions are increasingly shaped and refracted by exclusionary narratives of who is and who is not included in the body politic. Although these tensions have roots in colonial and pre-colonial practices, norms, and laws, they are not just based on birthplace or ethnicity. Rather, control of labour and fertility have an impact on citizenship as gendered understandings, migrations, liberalization, and evolving political institutions shape belonging and narratives of citizenship. Christianity and sexuality also exhibit strong and critical intersections with citizenship (Van Klinken and Obdare 2018). In contemporary Southern Africa, xenophobia continues to impact citizenship through defining insiders from outsiders (Nyamnjoh 2006). Although countries like Zambia, Botswana, and Zimbabwe continue to cling to exclusionary narratives of citizenship, cross-border forces produce narratives of citizenship based less on the right of territory or descent and more on the sense of citizenship as a privilege to be earned (Dorman 2014).

On the other side of the world's southern hemisphere, Australia has developed a strongly racialized construction of citizenship. Kate Coddington (2019) describes a slow, violent, and deprived life of "alien citizens" who are bordered and excluded from belonging in Australia by state restrictions and barriers to full employment. Both refused asylum seekers, and the mainly aboriginal welfare recipients of the Northern Territory, are provided subsistence financial support through a cashless debit card. This cashless technology undermines the provision of care for these populations with precarious citizenship status, and it implies one additional reminder that they are bordered from belonging.

4.4.2 Belonging and belongingness

In order to comprehend how belonging engages with borders, citizenship, and territory, we must venture beyond assessments of state-based belonging (Migdal 2004) to access the theory of relations of part to whole, and of part to part within the whole. This theory of mereotopology derives from both classical and modern philosophical and logical studies and is applied, as it relates to border culture, in cultural psychology. Research in cultural psychology and philosophy supports a science of human liminal constructions, and explores the constant border-crossing in the space of human development (Marsico and Varzi 2016, 327). In border studies, a focus on mereotopology helps us "understand the basis of individual and social becoming that leads to belonging in territory, and the role of borders in the process of defining both territory and belongingness" (Konrad 2020, 110). This approach builds a foundation for linking belonging with territory and belonging with citizenship.

> If we accept the premise that borders make space intelligible, while they also disrupt and modify space at or near the border, it follows that humans will either adjust to these circumstances, in varying degrees, or they will

> not. Belonging in bordered space is then either expressed as belonging in one side of the space, belonging on either side, or belonging in various degrees on both sides of the border. So far, this characterization aligns with mereotopological constants and findings of cultural psychology wherein all of these states of belonging at the border may be theorized. The shared, split or attenuated belonging may then be articulated as plural, and expressed as well as a variety of transitional, liminal, alternating, marginal, ambiguous and hybrid forms. Each of these articulations needs to be evaluated with regard to its role in constituting belongingness at the border, and any possible linkages and relationships require examination.
>
> *(Konrad 2020, 112–113)*

Liminal space often creates unsettling understandings of home, homeland, and belonging in the in-between space, and associates this with places of isolation, fear, and exile (Anzaldúa 1987). Belonging at the border may then extend to the limits of belonging at all, creating new spaces of belonging (Bhattacharya and Payne 2016). These new spaces of belonging range from a hyphenated sense of belongingness to a sense of marginality to rootedness and knowing the border. It is also possible to have alternating narratives of identity and belonging at the border (Minesashvili 2016). The resulting ambiguity generates both liberation and transgression at the border (Hudson 2012), and it may also create feelings of actually belonging in an in-between space.

Globalization has altered the power relations at borders by modifying the dialectical relation between their fixed institutional nature and the constantly changing and fluid processes of bordering within and between societies (Newman 2003). In addition, globalization has extended transnational space and expanded the significance of belongingness in this space. New modes of belongingness and the border have both emerged as sites of belonging in a shifting transnational context. Processes like racialization have confined belongingness of Canadian women of colour (Chapra and Chatterjee 2009). Alternatively, Filipino seafarers have evolved distinct forms of belongingness ashore and abroad, and expanded their overall sense of belongingness (Acejo 2012). "On ship, they work within a hierarchy of inter-cultural relationships and occupational seafaring culture to sustain advanced inclusion. On land, they value social and economic status and community affiliations that allow them to remain integrated ashore" (Konrad 2020, 113–114). This two-poled sense of belonging is found in many contexts although there is also evidence that transnational social space is being "stitched" across borders to enable belongingness in distinct yet connected sites. Although belongingness has evolved in globalization, the fundamental link between border and belonging remains articulated in space on one side of the border or the other, or the shifting space in between. "Belongingness in globalization may be more plural, transitional, ambiguous and hybridized, but it remains anchored as always by home and group affiliation" (Konrad 2020, 114).

In a recent contribution to the *Research Agenda for Border Studies* (Scott 2020), Victor Konrad (2020) employs four case studies of belongingness and borders to illustrate aspects of theory and research potential. One of these case studies—the Basque Country—is recounted in this brief discussion to convey the complex relationship between borders, territory, and belongingness. Basques have perceived and constructed borders around "Euskadi" in addition to the provincial boundary drawn by Spain around the Basque Autonomous Territory. The borders evolve through the process of belonging and Basque "common togetherness" and "changing landscape of identities" (Bray 2004). The state of belongingness engages connectivities to places, environments, groups, ideologies, and beliefs. Belongingness is transitional, ambiguous, and marginal as well, depending on who and where they are. These dimensions of belongingness construct "living boundaries" that enable Basques to identify at once as a political, social, ethnic, and popular culture, and also embrace EU goals of cooperation and integration on both sides of the border (Bray 2004).

The Basque Country exhibits compounded belongingness with confluence of landscapes, "languagescapes", "culturescapes" (Appadurai 1996), and other representations of "borderscapes" (Brambilla 2015). As "cultural attributes all align or overlap each other, belongingness is asserted and sustained through association with plural and hierarchical attributes of bounded and defined Basque culture" (Konrad 2020, 121). Language is primary for defining Basque belongingness, and "speaking Basque is being Basque" (Douglas and Zulaika 2007, 402). The division of Basque space into seven provinces aligns with traditional livelihoods and also displays cultural continuities of national history, literary universe, gastronomy, political resistance, and economic transformation (Woodsworth 2008). Also important contributors to belongingness are symbolic places that engage the common togetherness and display deep culture, as well as historical and politically charged places of radical nationalism. Prominent among these are Gernika/Guernica (Spanish), portrayed by Picasso as a symbol of resistance and national identity. The Guggenheim Art Museum in Bilbao is viewed by the Basque political elite as indigenous to the Basque Country, and more broadly as a contested site of particularistic radicalism and even an expression of "McGuggenization" or global imperialism (Figure 4.5) (McNeill 2000). Nevertheless, Bilbao is viewed, both by residents and outsiders, as a city which encompasses national and global belonging, and, indeed, becomes a "crucible" for the negotiation of global belonging (Van Houtum and Lagendijk 2001). The Basque sense of international, transnational, and global is then extensive, multiscalar, and malleable because it is firmly rooted in belongingness that is well developed yet constantly becoming.

4.4.3 From narratives of dual citizenship as an asset, to experiences of multiple citizenship as a problem

Although the Basques may view themselves as well-defined citizens of Euskadi, and more loosely defined citizens of Spain and the European Union, their alignment with multiple citizenship is not evenly articulated and codified. The

FIGURE 4.5 Guggenheim Museum, Bilbao, Euskadi/España. Photo by permission of Aili Kurtis and Victor Konrad.

narratives of citizenship are intertwined. In many instances, "major minorities" claim multiple citizenships yet, as in the case of the Berber, Tuareg, and Tebu peoples of Libya, the multiple narratives of citizenship based on language and border control are actually still trumped by Libyan citizenship (Kohl 2014). Dual citizenship and multiple citizenships are, however, claimed by many people around the world and substantiated by their state governments with certification and passports. Many of these dual and multiple citizenships are the result of migration from one state to another, and the additional concurrence of both or more states that the migrant may hold multiple citizenships, and not need to give up a citizenship in order to gain others. For more than four decades, this has been the case between the U.S. and Canada. Dual and multiple citizenship policies vary around the world, and this discussion is not focused on this variation but rather on how narratives of multiple citizenship relate to border culture.

Narratives of multiple citizenships centre the margin and these multiple citizenships offer resistance to a dominating national citizenship. Southeast Asian borderlands are homelands for distinct ethnicities who often occupy autonomous territories at the edge of states in the region (Horstmann and Wadley 2006). Distinct language and culture and well-defined territorial limits are aligned with narratives of multiple citizenship to enable the ethnic groups to function across borders and sustain livelihoods in their state of residence. Kokang, an ethnically

Han Chinese people in Myanmar, have exercised their claim to roots in China after recent turmoil in Myanmar caused many Kokang to flee across the border and seek asylum (Hu and Konrad 2018). Similar to the Kokang, residents of the boundary region between Nepal and the Tibetan Autonomous Region of China view themselves as border citizens (Shneiderman 2013). Also in the Himalayan region, people in the former border enclaves of Bangladesh and India employ acts of belonging to make a choice of citizenship, although, in reality this choice may not be open to all (Ferdoush 2019).

In Canada, narratives of dual and multiple citizenships exhibit a range of situations that extend from positive assets of citizenship plurality to situations where narratives describe alienation and discrimination. Before 9/11 dual Canadian and American citizens enjoyed the assets of mobility across the border and a tax treaty between the countries. After 9/11 dual citizens were required to verify their citizenship to officials of both countries. Taxation became more complex and verifiable in the twenty-first century, and hundreds of thousands of dual citizens resident in Canada, who had come to Canada as children but never worked and lived in the U.S., discovered that they should have filed U.S. tax returns. Now they were at risk of being detained for tax evasion if they were identified during a casual border crossing. Narratives of border-crossing difficulties related to citizenship are often exaggerated by media and Internet accounts, and, consequently, these narratives have had an impact on developing a more toxic border culture, one that alienates, overwhelms, and sometimes destroys other border cultures.

Other difficulties face Indigenous peoples in Canada. Although treaty rights allow crossing the Canada–U.S. border with official Indigenous identification only, this identification may not be used to travel to other countries. The Iroquois (Haudenosaunee) Nationals Lacrosse Team, composed of Haudenosaunee resident in Canada, crossed the Canada–U.S. border but was stopped from flying from New York to the United Kingdom to compete in the world championship (Weigand and Howell 2021). The story is well known and recounted in various media. At Akwesasne, on the border between the U.S. and Canada, Mohawk residents of the reserve situated on islands in the St. Lawrence River, need to verify citizenship as they move between "official" state jurisdictions, all on their "national territory", on a daily, routine basis (Rouvière 2019). On Kahnawake, a Mohawk reserve near Montreal and the U.S.–Canada border but "contained" in Canada, the Mohawk establish narratives of self, home, and nation to confirm their Indigenous citizenship and identity within Quebec and Canada (Simpson 2004). In Ottawa-Gatineau, on the border between Quebec and Ontario, immigrants to Canada (re)produce a form of dual Canadian citizenship with decidedly different policy and practices in French and English (Veronis 2013).

4.4.4 Transnationalism and citizenship

Whereas narratives of dual and multiple citizenships convey a step towards transnationalism, narratives of transnational citizenship express liminality and in-betweenness enabled by being undocumented and excluded (Torres and Wicks-Asbun 2014). Among "Latinx" youth, this form of border thinking is decolonizing citizenship through communal, relational, and humanizing processes, negotiating race and politics of integration, and developing transnational belongings (Dyrness and Sepulveda III 2020). Arab-American youth, alienated from their legacy citizenship and not accepted as "rightfully American", imagine a form of post-nationalism where designated citizenship is less significant (El-Haj 2009). A hazy and under-defined border culture becomes evident. In Anthony Mann's *Border Incident*, Mexican migrant workers smuggled into the U.S. experience a dislocation and disenfranchisement characterized as "noir citizenship", "a condition of statelessness or non-existence that sheds light on the psychological contours of *film noir*" (Auerbach 2008, 102).

Narratives of transnational citizenship are fluid and changing. Aiwha Ong (1999) has remarked that this citizenship is overall flexible, and that cultural logics of transnationality dominate through regimes of state, family, and economy to shape and direct border crossings. With Brexit on the horizon, applications for Republic of Ireland citizenship increased and an all island identity was envisioned. Irish citizenship and national identity found itself in a shifting space (Wood and Gilmartin 2018). Julie Cupples and Kevin Glynn (2013) explore how cultural citizenship conveyed in the TV drama *ER* helps to mediate narrative tropes of Africa by complicating, contesting, and disrupting them. Drawing from episodes in conflict zones in the Democratic Republic of Congo and Darfur in Sudan, the research addresses "key aspects of the cultural politics of post-development and postcolonialism in ways that challenge familiar Western media tropes of the 'troubled continent' and destabilize the wider knowledges that sustain them" (Cupples and Glynn 2013, 1003). In this way a renewed cultural citizenship is formed.

4.4.5 Non-state approaches

Transnationalism is both anchored in states and transcendent beyond the state, thus complicating the role of the border, and extending the reach of border culture. The anthropology of citizenship shows limits of normativities embedded in state, non-governmental organizations, and donors discourses (Lazar 2013). In postcolonial contexts, citizens decide citizenship to a greater degree, and citizenship is based on everyday experiences in social, cultural, and historical contexts (Robins et al. 2008). The geographies of these everyday experiences occupy spaces beyond the state (Dickinson et al. 2008), and enlarge border culture in contested spaces of citizenship at borders, and in camps and in urban encounters (Maestri and Hughes 2017). Here, marginalized political subjects claim rights in and through space in different and often ambiguous ways including contestation and solidarity. Citizenship is evolving as transnational lived citizenship (Kallio and Mitchell 2016), yet, citizenship framings, both in and beyond the nation-state, are being de-centred from the "good citizen" as migrants and stationary people encounter and counter citizenship norms (de Koning et al. 2015).

These changes are evident in Europe, as the EU builds institutions of a non-state, expands citizenship practice, promotes continual change in policymaking and public participation, and, yet, attempts to forge European citizenship (Wiener 2018). This effort towards EU citizenship may be a step in the direction of global citizenship, based in global learning, appreciation, and responsibility (Laugran and Birk 2016), but the care about the future of the entire human race, and the universal communication community inherent in cosmopolitan citizenship (Linklater 1998), are not yet evident. Consequently, non-state approaches to citizenship remain unfulfilled, and enlarged cosmopolitan border culture remains in a state of becoming and apprehension.

4.5 Counter-cultures at the border

The border between Mexico and the U.S. has come to epitomize the act of counter-culture wherein border culture is formed in resistance to the mainstream and seeks alternatives. These alternatives in the cultural imaginary and the production of culture are sought on both sides of the border and expressed at the line and in the borderlands. Their significance, however, often transcends the contextual border to speak to issues of global significance and transnational impact. Counter-cultures are evident in the juxtaposition of national cultures, that is, in this case, the dominant cultures in the U.S. and Mexico. Mexican culture is itself a counter-culture in the Southwestern U.S. (Vzlez-lba-cz 1996). "Whiteness" on the border has mapped the U.S. racial imagination, and established counter-cultures of "white and brown" (Bebout 2016). According to Harris Feinsod (2017), the poetry of the Americas has shifted from good neighbours to counter-cultures.

Counter-cultures are formed as well in the resistance of alternative cultures within the dominant national cultures. Hipsters and jipitecas, for example, are literary counter-cultures on both sides of the Mexico–U.S. border (Adams 2004). Yet, these counter-cultures also transcend these borderlands to emerge as global expressions. Similarly, techno and new age have emerged as transnational counter-cultures (D'Andrea 2007). Places along the border and of the border, Tijuana for example, are expressed as the global border with "Tijuanologies", a cross-border playlist, La Cancion de Tijuana (the song of Tijuana), and dreams of border transcendence (Kun and Montezemolo 2012). Among counter-cultures at the border are Indigenous peoples whose border crossings manifest as cultural inversions (Davidson et al. 2003). These cultural inversions, particularly the infusion of comedy into otherwise tragic border crossings, described by Indigenous writer Thomas King in his novels, enable the author to reveal "the deliberate eradication of some borders and pointed maintenance of others, 'takes back' a form and a theory, which potentially allows for co-option, and engages in a performance that offers a marked potential for strategic cultural resistance" (Davidson et al. 2003, 74). The Mexico–U.S. border is also a post-humanistic and post-humanitarian border where people, places, and things in the environment have new meanings and impacts for border culture (Squires 2015).

The following discussion addresses three themes of counter-culture at the border. The first theme is border cultures of resistance, or what George McKay (1996) terms "senseless acts of beauty". The discussion then moves to border activism, although the focus will remain on activism in the context of border culture. Finally, we discuss political art as border culture.

4.5.1 Cultures of resistance at the border

Increasingly precise security at the border is questioned by the arts because security is not certain, definitely not decided, and certainly not final. The contemporary landscape of border security has conditions and limits, and the arts of both security and resistance play out in a kind of border theatre (Amoore and Hall 2010). William Walters (2006) has characterized these acts and arts of resistance as games with and without frontiers in which resistance is "imagineered". Our referent border, between the U.S. and Mexico, offers additional evidence to understand the nature of resistance at the border and how this resistance constructs border culture. The resistance at the U.S.–Mexico border is not only in direct response to power and domination, but rather, according to Howard Campbell and Josiah Heyman (2007, 3), resistance is "slantwise", that is actions that are obliquely or only indirectly related to power relations. Also, resistance is shaped by community struggles related to social variables like gender and violence (Tellez 2008). Furthermore, border rootedness and familiarity develop strategies of transformative resistance among youth to overcome violence and invasive inspection at the U.S.–Mexico border (Bejarano 2010). In Europe, reactions to post-2015 border hardening occasioned by the influx of migration have resulted in a spectrum of resistance to acceptance from Euroregions (Svensson 2020). Resistance may be direct and strong with regard to the impacts of border hardening on cross-border traffic, yet more diffuse with regard to human rights discourses.

4.5.2 Border activism and border culture

Resistance may develop a border culture of opposition and contradiction without strident activism and violence. Activism, however, gains attention and often garners support or countervailing resistance. Some border places, Ciudad Juarez for example, have become localities of violence and activism at the border, and part of the everyday life on the border (Staudt 2009). Christina Fernandez-Bessa (2019, 156) offers a theoretical typology of border activism. The "collective efforts by ordinary people to modify, mitigate or even dismantle a border regime" include migrant struggles, de facto citizen struggles, border protests, and institutional border activism. Social justice objectives are linked to and aligned with activism (Naples 2010). In El Salvador, cross-border activism has had an integrative impact, and "doing transnationalism" engages and connects activists (Miller 2011). Border-crossing repertoires of contention in Palestine activism have elevated to a global justice context (Morrison 2020). More often border solidarities manifest strongly at the scale of the site in contention as illustrated in migrant activism at the migrant camps in Calais, France, at the mouth of the access "Chunnel" to the United Kingdom (Rygiel 2011). Henk Van Houtum (2010) decries the human blacklisting that he labels the "global apartheid of the EU's external border regime", and he highlights the concerned response that has led to the establishment of "No Border Camps" by activists in solidarity with migrants in their camps at and near borders. Yet, this measure of solidarity among activists and migrants is also under siege, and it has resulted in a "crimmigration" of activism and protest against border controls in Spain (Lopez-Sala and Barbero 2019).

Psychologist Kathryn L. Norsworthy (2017) calls for embracing the complexities of international border crossings by pursuing an assessment of the mindful activism evident in first person narratives (testimonio) of experiences with oppression, violence, resilience, and empowerment. She and her colleagues have employed the decolonized praxis of mindful activism in Thailand and Burma (Myanmar). A similar approach has been employed to explore the activism and solidarity among the Kokang refugees along the border between Myanmar and China (Hu and Konrad 2018). This border region has experienced an upsurge of activism not only because of resistance to China's hydropower development, but also because, for the past decade, Myanmar's regimes have been in transition, thus empowering activists (Simpson 2013).

Community activism at the border is enabled by institutions and frameworks for public participation. In Windsor, Ontario, Canada, the impact of community activism has steered the siting of the new bridge between Detroit and Windsor (Sutcliffe 2008). Another type of community activism is illustrated in the networks of transnational queer activism in Europe where migration mobilizes and facilitates cross-border LGBTQ+ activism (Ayoub and Bauman 2019). Nativist activism among border watch groups in southern Arizona also exhibits a day-to-day kind of community activism (FidanElcioglu 2015). On the other hand, humanitarian activists on the U.S.–Mexico border wield geospatial technologies in challenging border securitization by remapping the border to facilitate migration (Walsh 2013).

Overall, activism unsettles the border culture and impacts governance of border regimes and institutions (Gill 2016). Cross-border ties are shifted and sometimes impacted in unpredictable ways as people take sides and become activists for a position. Even kin-states, where historic "national" ties are evident, as in the case of many European countries, show unexpected outcomes or a "boomerang effect" when activism is demonstrative on one side of the border and not the other (Liebich 2019). Kin minorities may find themselves effectively divided by a border that has always connected them.

4.5.3 Political art as border culture

Although border art is addressed in numerous ways throughout this book, there are aspects of border political art that relate specifically to activism and counterculture. Christina Aushana (2012) analyzes "artscapes" as forms of resistance and cultural production along the U.S.–Mexico border. She identifies four distinct periods of border art and activism: art activism in the 1960s and 1970s linked to the Chicano Art Movement; Guillermo Gómez-Peña and the Border Art Workshop/ Taller de Arte Fronterizo of the 1980s and 1990s; Ruben Ortiz-Torres and the activism of the early 2000s; and, Ricardo Dominguez and the Transborder Immigrant Tool. Political and artistic practice are intertwined in the context of the border as political art becomes border culture. In essence this transmutation may be interpreted in a broader context as a component of the "border as method" (Mezzadra and Neilson 2013). This nexus has seen considerable attention by scholars and curators, and it has become a focus for young scholars. Two recent dissertations address artistic activism at the border. Julio Hanson (2020) evaluates the power of artistic activism and illustrates how mobilization of the Internet has expanded influence and impact to challenge injustice. He identifies the most common causes as togetherness, consciousness, communication of feelings, action, raising finances and resources, and escapism. Mira Seyal (2020) examines how art activists engaged with the Mexico–U.S. border play a prominent role in articulating and amplifying stories of rightsholders, and embedding these stories in the public consciousness. The border is characterized as a vital twenty-first century reason for the promotion of democracy.

A challenge remains in differentiating the performance of activism in the borderlands. If we simply place the activism of Anzaldúa, Gómez-Peña, and other like-minded activists in one group, and the Minutemen and their cohort in another, we continue to perpetuate the border and barrier to greater understanding of the art (Lemus 2006, Amilhat Szary 2021). One approach to overcome this problem inherent to border art is to dislocate artistic and curatorial practices (Potzsch 2015). This helps us to articulate the opposition and defamiliarize established frames for perception and cognition. The current focus on the art of the migrant allows us to visualize the art as a migrant, and to see an art of transformation in motion (Nail 2020). Yet, we cannot lose sight of the purpose of effective border art. Border art is a "creative process successful in debunking the invisibility of the control apparatus that de-humanizes people at the border, and does so in an unequal manner" (Amilhat Szary 2020, 24). Border art occupies a unique, stimulating, and exemplary space of critical imagination and creative resistance (Giudice and Giubilaro 2015).

4.6 Border cultures of empire: Narratives and counter-narratives

Re-reading Deborah Root's book *Cannibal Culture: Art, Appropriation, and the Commodification of Difference* (2018 [1996]) reminds us how conquest and appropriation of culture has re-bordered the world, and created new forms and representations by expanding on established, borrowed, and exotic imaginaries. According to Root, art engages the politics of display to produce spectacle and extend entitlement. Fragments and tropes of the alluring foreign represent the cultural difference achieved through conquest and assured through appropriation. Culture is authenticated, integrated, deterritorialized, and encoded. Sometimes only the spirit is appropriated in colonial representation and landscape. Art is like taxidermy and leads to warehouses of treasures in which orientalist dreams mix with occidentalist realities, all delineating wild spaces from colonized places.

The masked multidimensionality of borders that creates art and is art, originates in the move beyond first space, the move beyond the nation-state as nationalities conquer, absorb, or contain other nationalities. Moving beyond first space is a fundamental shift from the known to the unknown and imagined, and with this move come efforts to sustain the national trajectory—to normalize and naturalize the national culture in alien space. These efforts are sustained with force and assured with domination. The imagination of us and them becomes the articulated and codified differentiation between nations. The basic binary is established and then multiplied as new world territorialization and bordering ensues in the process of colonization. In this process, new borders are established constantly as movement of the imperial culture meets and crosses cultures *in situ*. Reminiscent of a cloud shadow crossing the landscape, the process of colonization deprives the light and shades the space. Border binaries are extended but spaces in between also emerge through processes of hybridization and integration. Border cultures of exchange develop and in some instances replace border cultures of differentiation. The rise of postnational, postcolonial, and transnational border cultures signals the movement into third space, a space, according to Edward Soja (1996), where people and nations deconstruct the binary logic.

4.6.1 Moving beyond and expanding first space: From nation-state to empire

In her book, *Cultures of Empire* (2000), Catherine Hall differentiates "thinking the empire" from "thinking the postcolonial" to show how gender, race, and citizenship have created others "at home" as well as "away". She enlarges our understanding of the creation of the subaltern and its relationship to the colonial, and how the British Empire developed the belief that not just any "body" can become a citizen whereas "others" can become "subjects". Frontiers may be places of both encounter and transformation, and spaces of mobilities (Hingley 2018), yet throughout history people and nations have been differentiated at borders, and borders have been established and bolstered to separate nations and people. Imperial movements were and are built on the logic of the border to progressively assure that the colonizers could pass and that the colonized would be contained. The ordering and othering functions of borders were already well developed in imperial regimes, and these functions have continued to characterize borders (Van Houtum and van Naerssen 2002). The significance of borders has changed through eras of colonialism to transnationalism but basic functions have remained, including differentiation and control (O'Dowd 2002). Unfortunately, border function has been conflated with aspects of identity, nation, and the relationship between domestic and foreign. The U.S. identity as a nation insulated from violent intervention abroad appears as if a line may be drawn between domestic and foreign affairs (Kaplan 2005). This bordering of the domestic and the foreign is illusory and certainly impractical in globalization. Amy Kaplan (2005, 1–3) illustrates how U.S. imperialism in conflicts with Mexico, Spain, Cuba, and the Philippines defines the idea of nation as home inextricable from movements of empire. Americans continuously erected and unsettled the ever-shifting boundaries between the domestic and foreign, and the sense of home and abroad. Also, Americans cling to the logic that first space—the nation-state—is somehow sealed and protected by the border against backlash, despite the impacts of globalization and the extent and excess of American imperialism. Additionally, the border culture in expanded first space may be altered but not expunged.

4.6.2 New world territorializations and borderings: Extending binaries

The colonial world system and coloniality established epistemic differences between colonizer and colonized and among colonized entities (Mignolo 2012 [2000]). Border thinking characterized a colonial difference and created the subaltern through languages, literatures, and other knowledges. In this sense, binaries were extended and a second space was assured. North American colonization, initiated by the establishment of multiple second spaces by European imperial powers, was reduced by war and treaty in Europe to British, Spanish, and Russian colonies by the late eighteenth century. When the U.S. was born through revolution, it became a first space and soon expanded the American empire with conquests and acquisitions from second spaces held by Spain, Great Britain, and Russia. By the second half of the nineteenth century, Mexico, the U.S., and Canada had all emerged as first spaces, although only the U.S. could be characterized as an imperial power.

Claudia Sadowski-Smith (2008) relates the diverse spaces of border culture that emerged in North America as the result of centuries of shifting boundaries and colonial power dynamics. Overall regionalism and a diversity of land holding and land making epitomized the border cultures. Indigenous peoples were bordered and contained within the new nation-states in another extension of binaries. Instances of Indigenous alienation along the nation-state boundaries of Canada, the U.S., and Mexico resulted in complex spatialities where assimilation and exclusion operated coincidentally (Marak and Tuennerman 2013). North of the American empire, space was constructed by cultural technologies at the margins of settled territory (Berland 2009). South of the American empire, border culture was formed and sustained by prophecies and stories of the other and the in-between (Gómez-Peña 1996).

4.6.3 Into "third space": postnational, postcolonial, transnational border cultures

Edward Soja (1996) coined the term third space following the notion of "thirding" put forward by Foucault and Lefebvre to capture and convey a sense of deterritorialization of space inherent in globalization. In North America, borders evolved in globalization but maintained their state functions thus challenging border cultures to adapt (Ganster and Lorey 2004). American popular culture, steeped in sensation, flowed across continental, hemispheric, and global borders (Streesby 2002). Other aspects of border culture along U.S. boundaries have been contained in borderlands defined by security concerns and guarded by militias. Although third space is multiscalar, and more prominent in transnational popular culture, it remains unfulfilled and under populated in an increasingly segregated North America. Although localities along both the U.S.–Mexico border and the Canada–U.S. border sustain and innovate border culture, regional border cultures have become less evident and expressive, particularly along the U.S.–Mexico border. The wall dominates the border scene.

"Cosmopolitan Europe" has been characterized as between postnationality and postcoloniality, where the rights of non-citizens remain in question amid postnational articulations of EU membership and human rights (Zhang 2014). Also, as the EU has expanded, the Schengen border has changed in the trajectories of geopolitical border, national border, and bio-political border (Walters 2002). In each of these trajectories, cultures of border control have evolved (Zaiotti 2011). Citizenship at Europe's borders has changed as well as countries like Poland, Romania, and Bulgaria have altered citizenship laws akin to a postcolonial condition of the European polity (Rigo 2005). Accordingly, Europe is envisioned as replete with postcolonial spaces as well as postnational and transnational spaces (Teverson and Upstone 2011). The EU is seen as a gated community with a "two-faced" border and immigration regime (Van Houtum and Pijpers 2007), a regime that is both colonial and postnational (Hooper and Kramsch 2007).

The transnational element in third space remains constrained, particularly in the wake of securing Europe against migrations and the pandemic. Third space is evident in border contexts enabling China's economic and cultural expansion in Asia. It emerges in transnational initiatives such as South America's Mercosur and connective events such as the Arab Spring. Elsewhere, third space is atomized in space and time with seemingly unlinked expressions of transnational culture. An assessment of third space in the "Third World" would balance out understanding of the global transnational connective tissue beyond the obvious Internet and popular culture dimensions. There are some clues about how border culture mobilizes and extends transnationally in professional fields. Médecins Sans Frontières/Doctors without Borders (MSF) is a social imaginary that has created a humanitarian space (DeChaine 2002). The rhetoric of global community, a compelling humanitarian cause, volunteer professionals, and targeted philanthropy have all been mobilized effectively into a transnational movement

(Shamir 2005). MSF crosses borders, and operates in borderland settings, yet the organization negotiates working space with both national and postnational entities. The current COVID-19 pandemic, recent SARS and Ebola pandemics, and the naturalized pandemics like influenza and malaria have illustrated clearly that human health has no borders even though borders are invoked to combat crises (Vineis 2017). Yet, public health as a common good still eludes us because transnational gains remain undermined by national interests. The border remains as the site of "founding violence of the sovereign power", but borders, also envisioned as borderscapes—"sites of generative struggles where alternative subjectivities and agencies could be shaped", are potentially the spaces where the politics of fear may evolve into the politics of hope (Brambilla and Jones 2020).

References

Abu El-Hadj, Thea Renda Abu. 2009. "Imagining postnationalism: Arts, citizenship education and Arab-American youth." *Anthropology and Education Quarterly* 40, (1): 1–19.

Acejo, Iris. 2012. "Seafarers and transnationalism: Ways of belongingness ashore and abroad." *Journal of Intercultural Studies* 33, (1): 69–84.

Adams, Rachael. 2004. "Hipsters and Jipitecas: Literary countercultures on both sides of the border." *American Literary History* 16, (1): 58–84.

Agnew, John. 1994. "The territorial trap: The geographical assumptions of international relations theory." *Review of International Political Economy* 1, (1): 53–80.

Akanle, Olayinka. 2018. "International migration narratives: Systemic global politics, irregular and return migrations." *International Sociology* 33, (2): 161–170.

Alagha, Joseph. 2012. *Hizbullah's Identity Construction*. Amsterdam: University of Amsterdam Press.

Amilhat Szary, Anne-Laure. 2013. "Cultura de Fronteras." In Beatriz Nates Cruz, ed. *Fronteras*. Manizales, Colombia: Editorial Universitaria de Caldes, 43–60.

Amilhat Szary, Anne-Laure. 2020. "The risk of being a-political: Can 'border art' become a polity call?" *The Large Glass* 29/30: 18–25.

Amilhat Szary, Anne-Laure. 2021. "Borders: The topos of/for a post-politics of images?" In Johan Schimanski, and Jopi Nyman, eds. *Border Images, Border Narratives*. Manchester: Manchester University Press, 151–167.

Amoore, Louise, and Alexander Hall. 2010. "Border theatre: On the arts of security and resistance." *Cultural Geographies* 17, (3): 299–319.

Anzaldúa, Gloria. (1987). *Borderlands/La Frontera: The New Mestiza*. San Francisco: Aunt Lute Books.

Appadurai, Arjun. 1996. *Moderntity at Large: Cultural Dimensions of Globalization*. Minneapolis: University of Minnesota Press.

Auerbach, Jonathan. 2008. "Noir citizenship: Anthony Mann's *border incident*." *Cinema Journal* 47, (4): 102–120.

Aushana, Christina. 2012. "Transborder art activism and the U.S.-Mexico border: Analyzing 'artscapes' as forms of resistance and cultural production in the frame of globalization." *International Journal of Interdisciplinary Social Sciences* 6, (7): 127–141.

Ayoub, Phillip M., and Lauren Bauman. 2019. "Migration and queer mobilizations: How migration facilitates cross-border LGBTQ activism." *Journal of Ethnic and Migration Studies* 45, (15): 2758–2778.

Baird, Theodore. 2017a. "Knowledge of practice: A multi-sited event ethnography of border security fairs in Europe and North America." *Security Dialogue* 48, (3): 187–205.

Baird, Theodore. 2017b. "Who speaks for the European border security industry? A network analysis." *European Security* 26, (1): 37–58.

Balibar, Etienne. 2002. *Politics and the Other Scene*. London: Verso.

Barry, Tom. 2011. *Border Wars*. Cambridge: MIT Press.

Bebout, Lee. 2016. *Whiteness on the Border: Mapping the U.S. Racial Imagination in Brown and White*. New York: NYU Press.

Beckham, Jack M. 2005. "Border policy/border cinema: Placing *touch of evil, the border,* and *traffic* in the American imagination." *Journal of Popular Film and Television* 33, (3): 130–141.

Bejarano, Cynthia L. 2007. *Que Onda? Urban Youth Culture and Border Identity*. Tucson: University of Arizona Press.

Bejarano, Cynthia L. 2010. "Border rootedness as transformative resistance: Youth overcoming violence and inspection in a U.S.-Mexico border region." *Children's Geographies* 8, (4): 391–399.

Bellamy, Richard. 2008. *Citizenship: A Very Short Introduction*. Oxford: Oxford University Press.

Bennafla, Karine. 2002. *Le commerce frontalier en Afrique Centrale*. Paris: Karthala.

Bennett, Bruce, and Imogen Tyler. 2007. "Screening unliveable lives: The cinema of borders." In K. Marciniak, A. Imre, and A. O'Healy eds. *Transnational Feminism in Film and Media*. New York: Palgrave-Macmillan, 21–36.

Berland, Jody. 2009. *North of Empire: Essays on the Cultural Technologies of Space*. Durham: Duke University Press.

Beylier, Pierre-Alexandre, and Clea Fortuné. 2022. "Cross-border mobility in Nogales since Trump's election." *Journal of Borderlands Studies* 37, (1): 187–208.

Bhattacharya, Kakali, and Rachel Payne. 2016. "Mixing mediums, mixing selves: Arts-based contemplative approaches to border crossings." *International Journal of Qualitative Studies in Education* 29, (9): 1100–1117.

Bilgin, Pinar, and Basak Ince. 2015. "Security and citizenship in the global south: In/security citizens in early republican Turkey (1923–1946)." *International Relations* 29, (4): 500–520.

Birringer, Johanes H. 1998. *Media and Performance: Along the Border*. Baltimore: Johns Hopkins University Press.

Brambilla, Chiara. 2007. "Borders and identities/border identities: The Angola-Namibia border and the plurivocality of the Kwanyama identity." *Journal of Borderlands Studies* 22, (2): 21–38.

Brambilla, Chiara. 2015. "Navigating the Euro/African border and migration nexus through the borderscapes lens: Insights from the Lampedusa in festival." In Chiara Brambilla, Jussi Laine, James W. Scott, and Gianluca Bocchi, eds. *Borderscaping: Imaginations and Practices of Border Making*. Farnham: Ashgate, 111–121.

Brambilla, Chiara. 2021. "Negotiating in/visibilities beyond the spectacularization of mediterranean frontiers: Young peoples' public visibility, alternative forms of political subjectivity and revolutionary geographical imaginations." In Johan Schimanski, and Jopi Nyman, eds. *Border Narratives, Border Images*. Manchester: Manchester University Press.83–104

Brambilla, Chiara, and Reece Jones. 2020. "Rethinking borders, violence, and conflict: From sovereign power to borderscapes as sites of struggles." *Environment and Planning D: Society and Space* 38, (2): 287–305.

Bray, Zoe. 2004. *Living Boundaries: Frontiers and Identity in the Basque Country*. Bern: Peter Lang.

Brown, Chris. 2001. "Borders and identity in international political theory." In Mathias Albert, Yosef Lapid, and David Jacobson, eds. *Identities, Borders, and Orders*. Minneapolis: University of Minnesota Press, 117–136.

Bruner, Michael L. 2002. *Strategies of Remembrance: The Rhetorical Dimension of National Identity Construction*. Columbia: University of South Carolina Press.

Buch, Claudia M., and Gayle DeLong. 2004. "Cross-border bank mergers: What lures the rare animal?" *Journal of Banking and Finance* 28, (9): 2077–2102.

Cafarella, Scott, Joel Konrad, and Rebecca Sciarra. 2021. "A biocultural planning approach for managing transborder cultural heritage landscapes." In Victor Konrad, and Melissa Kelly, eds. *Borders, Culture, and Globalization: A Canadian Perspective*. Ottawa: University of Ottawa Press, 293–317.

Campbell, Howard, and Josiah Heyman. 2007. "Slantwise: Beyond domination and resistance on the border." *Contemporary Ethnography* 36, (1): 3–30.

Campesi, Giuseppe. 2018. "Crisis, migration and the consolidation of the EU border control regime." *International Journal of Migration and Border Studies* 4, (3): 196–221.

Carrera, Sergio. 2007. "The EU border management strategy: Frontex and the challenges of irregular immigration in the Canary Islands." *CEPS*, #261.

Carter, Daniel B., and Hein E. Goemans. 2011. "The making of the territorial order: New borders and the emergence of interstate conflict." *International Organization* 65, (2): 275–309.

Chang, Wen-Chin. 2014. *Beyond Borders: Stories of Yunnanese Chinese Migrants of Burma*. Ithaca: Cornell University Press.

Chapra, Aisha, and Soma Chatterjee. 2009. "Talking race, talking colour: Racialized women, their home and belongingness in multicultural Canada." *Canadian Woman Studies* 27, (2/3): 14–20.

Chaturvedi, Sanjay. 2002. "Process of othering in the case of India and Pakistan." *Tijdschrift voor economische en sociale geografie* 93, (2): 149–159.

Coddington, Kate.2019 "The slow violence of life without cash: Border, state restrictions, and exclusion in the UK and Australia." *Geographical Review* 109, (4): 527–543.

Colebrook, Claire. 2020. *Understanding Deleuze*. New York: Routledge.

Cote-Boucher, Karine, Frederica Infantino, and Mark B. Salter. 2014. "Border security as practice: An agenda for research." *Security Dialogue* 45, (3): 195–208.

Cupples, Julie, and Kevin Glynn. 2013. "Postdevelopment television? Cultural citizenship and the mediation of Africa in contemporary TV drama." *Annals, Association of American Geographers* 103, (4): 1003–1021.

D'Andrea, Anthony. 2007. *Global Nomads: Techno and New Age as Transnational Counter Cultures in Ibiza and Goa*. London: Routledge.

Dailymaverick. 2022. "Beyond its exceptional beauty, Kruger National Park is on the ropes and hurting." https://www.dailymaverick.co.za/article/2022-01-25-beyond-its-exceptional-beauty-kruger-national-park-is-on-the-ropes-and-hurting/.

Dalby, Simon. 2019. "Canadian geopolitical culture: Climate change and sustainability." *The Canadian Geographer / Le Géographe Canadien* 63, (1): 100–111.

Davidson, Arnold E., Priscilla L. Walton, and Jennifer C.E. Andrews. 2003. *Border Crossings: Thomas King's Cultural Inversions*. Toronto: University of Toronto Press.

De Koning, Anouk, Rivke Jaffe, and Martijn Koster. 2015. "Citizenship agendas in and beyond the nation-state: (En)countering framings of the good citizen." *Citizenship Studies* 19, (2): 121–127.

DeChaine, Robert D. 2002. "Humanitarian space and the social imaginary: Médecins sans Frontières/Doctors without borders and the rhetoric of global community." *Journal of Communication Inquiry* 26, (4): 354–369.

Dell'Agnese, Elena. 2005. "The U.S.-Mexico border in American movies: A political geography perspective." *Geopolitics* 10, (2): 204–221.

Díaz-Barriga, Miguel, and Margaret E. Dorsey. 2020. *Fencing in Democracy: Border Walls, Necrocitizenship, and the Security State*. Durham: Duke University Press.

Dickinson, Jen, Max J. Andrucki, Emma Rawlins, Daniel Hale, and Victoria Cooke. 2008. "Introduction: Geographies of everyday citizenship." *ACME: An International Journal for Critical Geographies* 7, (2): 100–112.

Diener, Alexander. 2006. "Homeland as social construct: Territorialization among Kazakhstan's Germans and Koreans." *Nationalities Papers* 34, (2): 201–235.

Dodds, Klaus. 2013. "'I'm still not crossing that': Borders, dispossession, and sovereignty in Frozen River (2008)." *Geopolitics* 18, (3): 560–583.

Doevenspeck, Martin. 2011. "Constructing the border from below: Narratives from the Congolese-Rwandan state boundary." *Political Geography* 30, (3): 129–142.

Donelson, Angela J., and Adrian X. Esparza. 2016. *The Colonias Reader: Economy, Housing and Public Health in U.S.-Mexico Border Colonias*. Tucson: University of Arizona Press.

Dorman, Sara Rich. 2014. "Citizenship in Africa." In Engin F. Isin, and Peter Nyers, eds. *Routledge Handbook of Global Citizenship Studies*. New York: Routledge, 161–172.

Dorr, Noam, Elcioglu, Emine Fiden, and Lindsay Gaydos. 2014. "Welcome to the Border: *National Geographic's Border Wars* and the naturalization of border militarization." *Working USA* 17, (1): 45–60.

Dorsey, Margaret E., and Miguel Díaz-Barriga. 2010. "Beyond surveillance and moonscapes: An alternative imaginary of the U.S.-Mexico border wall." *Visual Anthropology Review* 26, (2) 128–135.

Dossa, Parin. 2004. *Politics and Poetics of Migration: Narratives of Iranian Women from the Diaspora*. Toronto: Canadian Scholars Press.

Douglas, William A., and Joseba Zulaika. 2007. *Basque Culture: Anthropological Perspectives*. Reno: Center for Basque Studies, University of Nevada.

Doyle, Tom. 2010. "Collaborative border management." *World Customs Journal* 4, (1): 15–21.

Duara, Prasenjit. 1996. *Rescuing History from the Nation: Questioning Narratives of Modern China*. Chicago: University of Chicago Press.

Duffy, Maureen. 2019. "'Wagging the dog': Feigning crisis in U.S. Anti-migration narratives to create crisis." *Rei-Revista Estudos Institucionais* 5, (2): 656–698.

Duffy, Rosaleen. 2001. "Peace parks: The paradox of globalization." *Geopolitics* 6, (2): 1–26.

Duffy, Rosaleen. 2016. "War, by conservation." *Geoforum* 69: 238–248.

Dyrness, Andrea, and Enrique Sepulveda III. 2020. *Border Thinking: Latinx Youth Decolonizing Citizenship*. Minneapolis: University of Minnesota Press.

Ekelund, Helena. 2014. "The establishment of FRONTEX: A new institutionalist approach." *Journal of European Integration* 36, (2): 99–116.

Elden, Stuart. 2013. *The Birth of Territory*. Chicago: University of Chicago Press.

Fassin, Didier. 2011. "Policing borders, producing boundaries: The governmentality of immigration in dark times." *Annual Review of Anthropology* 40: 213–226.

Fathi, Mastoureh. 2017. *Intersectionality, Class and Migration: Narratives of Iranian Women Migrants to the UK*. New York: Springer.

Feinsod, Harris. 2017. *The Poetry of the Americas: From Good Neighbours to Counter Cultures.* New York: Oxford.

Ferdoush, Md Azmeary. 2019. "Acts of belonging: The choice of citizenship in the former border enclaves of Bangladesh and India." *Political Geography* 70: 83–91.

Fernandez-Bessa, Christina. 2019. "A theoretical typology of border activism: From the streets to the council." *Theoretical Criminology* 23, (2): 156–174.

Fidan Elcioglu, Emine F. 2015. "Popular sovereignty on the border: Nativist activism among two border watch groups in southern Arizona." *Ethnography* 16, (4): 438–462.

Flynn, Donna K. 1997. "'We are the border': Identity, exchange, and the state along the Benin-Nigeria border." *American Ethnologist* 24, (2): 311–330.

Fojas, Camilla. 2009. *Border Bandits: Hollywood on the Southern Frontier.* Austin: University of Texas Press.

Fojas, Camilla. 2011. "Hollywood border cinema: Westerns with a vengeance." *Journal of Popular Film and Television* 39, (2): 93–101.

Fravel, M. Taylor. 2008. *Strong Borders, Secure Nation: Cooperation and Conflict in China's Territorial Disputes.* Princeton: Princeton University Press.

Ganivet, Elisa. 2019a. *Border Wall Aesthetics: Artworks in Border Spaces.* Bielefeld: Transcript Verlag.

Ganivet, Elisa. 2019b. "Some considerations on the aesthetics of the geopolitical wall." *Borders in Globalization Review* 1, (1): 115–122.

Ganster, Paul, and David E. Lorey, eds. 2004. *Borders and Border Politics in a Globalizing World.* New York: Rowman and Littlefield.

Gathercole, Peter, and David Lowenthal. 2004. *The Politics of the Past.* London: Routledge.

Geopolitical Monitor. 2021. "Marine peace park plan offers promise for South China sea." https:www.geopoliticalmonitor.com/marine-peace-park-plan-offers-promise-for-south-chaina-sea/. Accessed February 16, 2021.

Gill, Nick. 2016. *Nothing Personal? Geographies of Governing and Activism in the British Asylum System.* New York: John Wiley and Sons.

Giudice, Christina, and Chiara Giubilaro. 2015. "Re-imagining the border: Border art as a space of critical imagination and creative resistance." *Geopolitics* 20, (1): 79–94.

Goeury, David. 2008. "Wagah border: Mise en tourisme d'un ritual nationaliste a la frontière indo-pakistanaise." *Civilisations: Revue internationale d'anthropologie et de sciences humaines* 57: 139–154.

Gómez-Peña, Guillermo. 1996. *The New World Border: Prophecies, Poems, and Loqueras for the End of the Century.*San Francisco: City Lights Books.

Gonzalez, Jesus Angel. 2015. "New frontiers for post-Western cinema: *Frozen River, Sin Nombre, Winter's Bone.*" *Western American Literature* 50, (1): 51–76.

Grandin, Greg. 2019. *The End of the Myth: From the Frontier to the Border Wall in the Mind of America.* New York: Metropolitan Books.

Grosz, Elizabeth A. 2008. *Chaos, Territory, Art: Deleuze and the Framing of the Earth.* New York: Columbia University Press.

Hall, Catherine. 2000. *Cultures of Empire: Colonizers in Britain and the Empire in the Nineteenth and Twentieth Centuries: A Reader.* Manchester: Manchester University Press.

Hanauer, David Ian. 2011. "The discursive construction of the separation wall at Abu Dis: Graffiti as political discourse." *Journal of Language and Politics* 10, (3): 301–321.

Hanson, Julio. 2020. "The power of artistic activism." Theses and Dissertations 1141. https://digital commons.pepperdine.edu/etd/1141.

Hart, Doug. 2007. "Life behind the wall: Palestinian students online." *Social Education* 71, (1): 44–47.

Hatten, Victoria. 2016. "Imperial designs: Remembering Vietnam at the U.S.-Mexico border wall." *Memory Studies* 9, (1): 27–47.

Herb, Guntram H. 1999. "Under the map of Germany, nationalism and propaganda, 1918–1945." *Political Geography* 18, (6): 741–743.

Herb, Guntram H., and David H. Kaplan. 1999. *Nested Identities: Nationalism, Territory and Scale*. New York: Rowman and Littlefield.

Heneini, Faraj R.-A., and Ruzaika Omar Basaree. 2018. "The separation wall in the occupied Palestine as a canvas of resistance: A controversial issue." *Pertanika: Journal of Social Sciences and Humanities* 26, (3): 1371–1385.

Henning, Joachim. 2005. "Civilization versus barbarians? Fortification techniques and politics in Carolingian and Ottonian borderlands." In Fioren Carter, ed. *Borders, Barriers and Ethnogenesis: Frontiers in Late Antiquity and the Middle Ages*. Tournhout: Brepols Publishers, 23–34.

Hernando, Ignacio, Nieto, Maria J., and Larry D. Wall. 2009. "Determinants of domestic and cross-border banking acquisitions in the European Union." *Journal of Banking and Finance* 33, (6): 1022–1032.

Hingley, Richard. 2018. "Frontiers and probabilities: The frontiers of the Roman empire and Europe." *European Journal of Archaeology* 21, (1): 78–95.

Hooper, Barbara, and Olivier Kramsch. 2007. "Post-colonizing Europe: The geopolitics of globalization, empire and borders: Here and there, then and now." *Tijdschrift voor economische en sociale geografie* 98, (4): 526–534.

Horii, Satako. 2016. "The effect of Frontex's risk analysis on the European border controls." *European Politics and Society*17, (2): 242–258.

Horlick-Jones, Tom, and Jonathan Sime. 2004. "Living on the border: Knowledge, risk and transdisciplinarity." *Futures* 36, (4): 441–456.

Horsti, Karina. 2012. "Humanitarian discourse legitimizing migration control: FRONTEX public communication." In M. Messer, R. Schroeder, and R. Wodak, eds. *Migrations: Interdisciplinary Perspectives*. Vienna: Springer, 297–308.

Horstmann, Alexander, and Reed L. Wadley, eds. 2006. *Centering the Margin: Agency and Narrative in Southwest Asian Borderlands*. Oxford: Berghahn.

Hu, Zhiding, and Victor Konrad. 2018. "In the space between exception and integration: The Kokang borderlands on the periphery of China and Myanmar." *Geopolitics* 23, (1): 147–179.

Hudson, Kimberly D. 2012. "Bordering community: Reclaiming ambiguity as a transgressive landscape of knowledge." *Affilia* 27, (2): 167–179.

Iglesias Prieto, Norma. 2003. "Border representations: Border cinema and independent video." In Michael Dear, and Gustavo Leclerc, eds. *Postborder City: Cultural spaces of Bajalta California*. New York: Routledge, 183–213.

Iheka, Cajetan. 2018. *African Migration Narratives: Politics, Race, and Space*. Rochester: University Rochester Press.

Izotov, Alexander. 2012. "Mental walls and the border: Local identity construction in Sortavala." *Journal of Borderlands Studies* 27, (2): 167–183.

Janz, Bruce B. 2002. "The territory is not the map: Place, Deleuze, Guatteri, and African philosophy." *Philosophia Africana: Analysis of Philosophy and Issues in Africa and the Black Diaspora* 5, (1): 1–18.

Janzon, Max. 2014. "Realizing border security culture in Finland (and Europe)." Ph.D. Dissertation, University of Helsinki.

Jasonoff, Sheila. 1993. "Bridging the two cultures of risk analysis." *Risk Analysis* 13, (2): 123–129.

Jeychandran, Neelima. 2016. "Specter of war, spectacle of peace: The lowering of flags ceremony at the Wagah and Hussainiwala border outposts." In Gay Morris, and Jens Richard Giersdorf, eds. *Choreographies of 21st Century Wars*. Oxford: Oxford University Press. 181–202

Johnson, Corey, and Amanda Coleman. 2012. "The internal other: Exploring the dialectical relationship between regional exclusion and the construction of national identity." *Annals, Association of American Geographers* 102, (4): 863–880.

Jones, Reece. 2009. "Geopolitical boundary narratives, the global war on terror and border fencing in India." *Transactions of the Institute of British Geographers* 34, (3): 290–304.

Jones, Reece. 2014. "Border wars: Narratives and images of the U.S.-Mexico border on TV." In Reece Jones, and Corey Johnson, eds. *Placing the Border in Everyday Life*. Farnham: Ashgate. 185–204

Jones, Reece, Corey Johnson, Wendy Brown, Gabriel Popescu, Polly Pallister-Wilkins, Alison Mountz, and Emily Gilbert. 2017. "Interventions on the state of sovereignty at the border." *Political Geography* 59, (4): 1–10.

Kallio, Kirsi Pauliina, and Katharyne Mitchell. 2016. "Introduction to the special issue on transnational lived citizenship." *Global Networks* 16, (3): 259–267.

Kaplan, Amy. 2005. *The Anarchy of Empire in the Making of U.S. Culture*. Cambridge: Harvard University Press.

Kempny, Marta. 2010. *Polish Migrants in Belfast: Border Crossing and Identity Construction*. Cambridge: Cambridge Scholars Publishing.

Kirchoff, Maren. 2020. "Differential solidarity: Protests against deportations as structured contestations over citizenship." *Citizenship Studies* 24, (4): 568–586.

Kleiner-Liebau, Desiree. 2009. *Migration and the Construction of National Identity in Spain*. Madrid: Iberoamerica.

Kohl, Ines. 2014. "Libya's 'major minorities': Berber, Tuareg and Tebre: Multiple narratives of citizenship, language and border control." *Middle East Critique* 23, (4): 423–438.

Konrad, Victor. 2010. *"Breaking Points" but "No Broken Border": Stakeholders Evaluate Border Issues in the Pacific Northwest Region*. Border Policy Research Institute, Research report 10.

Konrad, Victor. 2020. "Belongingness and borders." In James W. Scott, ed. *A Research Agenda for Border Studies*. Cheltenham: Edward Elgar, 109–128.

Konrad, Victor, and Zhiding Hu. 2021. "Expanded border imaginaries and aligned border narratives: Ethnic minorities and localities in China's border encounters with Myanmar, Laos and Vietnam." In Johan Schimanski, and Jopi Nyman, eds. *Border Narratives, Border Images*. Manchester: University of Manchester Press, 127–147.

Konrad, Victor, and Melissa Kelly, eds. 2021. *Borders, Culture, and Globalization: A Canadian Perspective*. Ottawa: University of Ottawa Press.

Kuenker, Paul. 2011. "One hundred years of peace: Memory and rhetoric on the United States/Canadian border, 1920–1933." *Hemisphere: Visual Cultures of the Americas* 4, (1): 94–116.

Kun, Josh, and Fiamma Montezemolo, eds. 2012. *Tijuana Dreaming: Life and Art at the Global Border*. Durham: Duke University Press.

Kurki, Tuulikki. 2013. "From Soviet locality to multivoiced borderland: Literature and identity in the Finnish-Russian national borderlands region." *Regional Studies of Russia, Eastern Europe, and Central Asia* 2, (1): 95–112.

Laine, Jussi P. 2016. "The multiscalar production of borders." *Geopolitics* 21, (3): 465–482.

Laine, Jussi P., and Anna Casaglia. 2017. "Challenging borders: A critical perspective on the relationship between state, territory, citizenship and identity: Introduction." *Europa Regional* 24, (1/2): 3–8.

Laugran, Irene, and Tammy Birk. 2016. *Globalization and Global Citizenship: Interdisciplinary Approaches*. New York: Routledge.

Lauren, Kirsi. 2012. "Fear in border narratives: Perspectives of the Finnish-Russian border." *Folklore: Electronic Journal of Folklore* 52: 39–62.
Lazar, Sian. 2013. *The Anthropology of Citizenship: A Reader.* New York: Wiley and Sons.
Lemus, Alberto Hernandez. 2006. "Performance activism at the borderlands: Minutemen, Anzaldúa, Gómez-Peña." *Politica y Cultura* 26: 109–129.
Leonard, Sarah. 2010. "EU border security and migration into the European Union: FRONTEX and securitization through practices." *European Security* 19, (2): 231–254.
Leuenberger, Christine, and Izhak Schnell. 2020. *The Politics of Maps: Cartographic Constructions of Israel/Palestine.* Oxford: Oxford University Press.
Liebich, Alexander. 2019. "The 'boomerang effect' of kin-state activism: Cross-border ties and the securitization of kin minorities." *Journal of Borderlands Studies* 34, (5): 665–684.
Linklater, Andrew. 1998. "Cosmopolitan citizenship." *Citizenship Studies* 2, (1): 23–41.
Lipset, Seymour Martin. 1996. *American Exceptionalism: A Double-Edged Sword.* New York: Norton.
Lipset, Seymour Martin. 2013 [1991]. *Continental Divide: The Values and Institutions of Canada and the United States.* New York: Routledge.
Lister, Ruth. 2012. "Citizenship and gender." In Edwin Amenta, Kate Nash, and Alan Scott, eds. *The Wiley-Blackwell Companion to Political Sociology.* New York: Wiley, 372–382.
Llamas, Carmen. 2007. "'A place between places': Language and identities in a border town." *Language and Society* 36, (4): 579–604.
Lois, Maria. 2019. "The politics ofborder heritage." In Tuuli Lahdeamaki, Suzie Thomas, and Yujie Zhue, eds. *Politics of Scale: New Directions in Critical Heritage Studies.* Oxford: Berghahn, 81–94.
Lopez-Sala, Ana, and Iker Barbero. 2019. "Solidarity under Siege: The crimmigration of activism(s) and protest against border control in Spain." *European Journal of Criminology.* 18, (5): 678–694.
Lowenthal, David. 1951. "The Maine Press and the Aroostook war." *Canadian Historical Review* 32, (4): 315–336.
Lowenthal, David. 1975. "Past time, present place: Landscape and memory." *Geographical Review* 65, (1): 1–36.
Lowenthal, David. 1985. *The Past is a Foreign Country.* Cambridge: Cambridge University Press.
Lowenthal, David. 1991. "British national identity and the English landscape." *Rural History* 2, (2): 205–230.
Lowenthal, David. 1994. "Identity, heritage and history." In John R. Gillis ed., *Commemorations: The Politics of National Identity.* Princeton: Princeton University Press, 41–57.
Lowenthal, David. 1998. "Fabricating heritage." *History and Memory* 10, (1): 5–24.
Lowenthal, David. 2006. "From harmony of the speheres to national anthem: Reflections on musical heritage." *Geojournal* 65, (1–2): 3–15.
Lowenthal, David. 2015. *The Past is a Foreign Country—Revisited.* Cambridge: Cambridge University Press.
Lowenthal, David. 2017. "Canadian historical nonchalance and newfoundland exceptionalism." *Acadiensis* 46, (1): 152–162.
Lowenthal, David. 2018. "Stewarding disputed heritage: Private property, tribal legacy, national patrimony, global commons." In Aribal Arregui, Gesa Machenthun, and Stephanie Wodiankce, eds. *Decolonial Heritage: Natures, Cultures, and the Asymmetries of Memory.* New York: Waxman, 31–54.

Lugo, Alejandro. 2008. *Fragmented Lives, Assembled Parts: Culture, Capitalism and Conquest at the U.S.-Mexico Border.* Austin: University of Texas Press.
Lynch, Jim. 2010. *Border Songs.* New York: Knopf.
McDuie-Ra, Duncan. 2014. "The India-Bangladesh border fence: Narratives and political possibilities." *Journal of Borderlands Studies* 29, (1): 81–94.
McGuire, Randall H. 2013. "Steel walls and picket fences: Rematerializing the U.S.-Mexican border at Ambos Nogales." *American Anthropologist* 115, (3): 466–480.
McKay, George. 1996. *Senseless Acts of Beauty: Cultures of Resistance Since the Sixties.* London: Verso.
McNeill, Donald. 2000. "McGuggenisation? National identity and globalization in the Basque country." *Political Geography* 19, (4): 473–494.
Maestri, Gaja, and Sarah M. Hughes. 2017. "Contested spaces of citizenship: Camps, borders and urban encounters." *Citizenship Studies* 21, (6): 625–639.
Maier, Charles S. 2016. *Once Within Borders.* Cambridge: Harvard University Press.
Marak, Andrae M., and Laura Tuennerman. 2013. *At the Border of Empires: The Tohono O'odham, Gender, and Assimilation.* Tucson: University of Arizona Press.
Maril, Robert Lee. 2006. *Patrolling Chaos: The U.S. Border Patrol in Deep South Texas.* Austin: University of Texas Press.
Marsico, Giuseppina, and Achille C. Varzi. 2016. "Psychological and social borders: Regulating relationships." In J. Valsiner, G. Marsico, N. Chaudhary, T. Sato, and V. Dazzani, eds. *Psychology as a Science of Human Being: The Yokohama Manifesto, Annals of Theoretical Psychology 1.* Geneva: Springer, 327–335.
Marton-Lefevre, Julia. 2007. *Peace Parks: Conservation and Conflict Resolution.* Cambridge: MIT Press.
May, Todd. 2005. *Gilles Deleuze: An Introduction.* Cambridge: Cambridge University Press.
Meinhof, Ulrike H., and Dariusz Galasinski. 2000. "Photography, memory, and the construction of identities on the former East-West German border." *Discourse Studies* 2, (3): 323–353.
Meskell, Lynn. 2020. "World heritage and wikileaks: Territory, trade and temples on the Thai-Cambodian border." In Philippe Peycan, Shu-Li Wang, Hui Yew-Foong, and Michael Hsiao, eds. *Heritage as Aid and Diplomacy in Asia.* Singapore: ISEAS, 17–51.
Mezzadra, Sandro, and Brett Neilson. 2013. *Border as Method, or, the Multiplication of Labour.* Durham: Duke University Press.
Middleton, Townsend. 2013. "States of difference: Refiguring ethnicity and its 'crisis' at India's borders." *Political Geography* 35: 14–24.
Migdal, Joel S., ed. 2004. *Boundaries and Belonging.* Cambridge: Cambridge University Press.
Mignolo, Walter. 2012 [2000]. *Local Histories/Global Designs: Coloniality, Subaltern Knowledges, and Border Thinking.* Princeton: Princeton University Press.
Miller, Arpi. 2011. "Doing transnationalism: The integrative impact of salvadoran cross-border activism." *Journal of Ethnic and Migration Studies* 37, (1): 43–60.
Minesashvili, Salome. 2016. "Narrating identity: Belongingness and alterity in Georgia's foreign policy." In K. Kakchia, and A. Makkarov, eds. *Values and Identity as Sources of Foreign Policy in Armenia and Georgia.* Tbilisi: Universal, 11–33.
Mitchell, Don. 2005. "The S.U.V. model of citizenship: Floating bubbles, buffer zones, and the rise of the 'purely atomic' individual." *Political Geography* 24, (1): 77–100.

Mjelde, James W., Hyesun Kim, Tae-Kynn Kim, and Choong-Ki Lee. 2017. "Estimating willingness to pay for the development of a peace park using CVM: The case of the Korean demilitarized zone." *Geopolitics* 22, (1): 151–175.

Moody, Jocelyn K. 2018. "Fugitivity in African women's migration narratives." *Canadian Review of Comparative Literature / Revue Canadienne de Litterature Comparée* 45, (4): 636–638.

Morrison, Suzanne. 2020. "Border-crossing repertoires of contention: Palestine activism in a global justice context." *Globalizations* 19, (1): 17–33.

Mudimbe, Valentin Y. 1995. *Nations, Identities, Cultures*. Durham: Duke University Press.

Nail, Thomas. 2013. "The crossroads of power: Michel Foucault and the U.S.-Mexico border wall." *Foucault Studies* 15: 110–128.

Nail, Thomas. 2020. "What are the migrant arts?" *The Large Glass* 29/30: 5–9.

Naples, Nancy A. 2010. "Borderlands studies and border theory: Linking activism and scholarship for social justice." *Sociology Compass* 4, (7): 505–518.

Neal, Andrew. 2009. "Securitization and risk at the EU border: The origins of FRONTEX." *JCMS: Journal of Common Market Studies* 47, (2): 333–356.

Nemeth, Agnes. 2015. "Watching the other: Across the border representations of Russia and Estonia on Finnish national television." *Journal of Borderlands Studies* 30, (1): 37–52.

Neto, Pedro Figueiredo. 2017. "The consolidation of the Angola-Zambia border: Violence, forced displacement, smugglers and savimbi." *Journal of Borderlands Studies* 32, (3): 305–324.

Newman, David. 2003. "Borders and power: A theoretical framework." *Journal of Borderlands Studies* 18, (1): 13–25.

Newman, David, and Anssi Paasi. 1998. "Fences and neighbours in the postmodern world: Boundary narratives in political geography." *Progress in Human Geography* 22, (2): 186–207.

Nieto-Gomez, Rodrigo. 2014. "Walls, sensors and drones: Technology and surveillance on the U.S.-Mexico border." In Elisabeth Vallet, ed. *Border Fences and Walls: State of Insecurity?* Farnham: Ashgate, 191–210.

Nobe-Ghelani, Chizwru. 2017. "Border narratives in Canadian social work: Neoliberal nationalism in the discursive construction of 'citizen/self' and 'non-citizen/other'." *Transnational Social Review* 7, (2): 129–142.

Nora, Pierre, and Lawrence D. Kritzman. 1996 [1992]. *Realms of Memory: Conflicts and Divisions*. New York: Columbia University Press.

Norsworthy, Kathryn L. 2017. "Mindful activism: Embracing the complexities of international border crossings." *American Psychologist* 72, (9): 1035–1043.

Nyamnjoh, Francis B. 2006. *Insiders and Outsiders: Citizenship and Xenophobia in Contemporary Southern Africa*. London: Zed Books.

Nyers, Peter. 2004. "Introduction: What's left of citizenship?" *Citizenship Studies* 8, (3): 203–215.

O'Dowd, Liam. 2002. "The changing significance of European borders." *Regional and Federal Studies* 12, (4): 13–36.

O'Loughlin, John, Geroid O. Tuathail, and Vladimir Kolossov. 2005. "Russian geopolitical culture and public opinion: The mask of proteus revisited." *Transactions of the Institute of British Geographers* 30, (3): 322–335.

Ong, Aiwha. 1999. *Flexible Citizenship: The Cultural Logics of Transnationality*. Durham: Duke University Press.

Paasi, Anssi. 1996. *Territories, Boundaries and Consciousness: The Changing Geographies of the Finnish-Russian Border*. New York: Wiley-Blackwell.

Paasi, Anssi. 1997. "Geographical perspectives on Finnish national identity." *Geojournal* 43, (1): 41–50.

Paasi, Anssi. 1998. "Boundaries as social processes: Territoriality in the world of flows." *Geopolitics* 3, (1): 69–88.

Paasi, Anssi. 2001. "Europe as a social process and discourse: Considerations of place, boundaries, and identity." *European Urban and Regional Studies* 8, (1): 7–28.

Paasi, Anssi. 2003. "Region and place: Regional identity in question." *Progress in Human Geography* 27, (4): 475–485.

Pallister-Wilkins, Polly. 2015. "The humanitarian politics of European border policing: Frontex and border police in Evros." *International Political Sociology* 9, (1): 53–69.

Parciak, Ronie. 2018. "Borderline nationalism: Restructuring the Wagah-Attari 'retreat ceremony' and its media representations." *South Asia: Journal of South Asian Studies* 41, (4): 744–762.

Park, Keumjae. 2007. "Defending transnational identities without leaving home: Korean immigrant womens' cognitive border-crossing." *Sociological Forum* 22, (2): 200–218.

Parry, William. 2011. *Against the Wall: The Art of Resistance in Palestine*. Chicago: Chicago Review Press.

Paul, Regine. 2017. "Harmonization by risk analysis? Frontex and the risk-based governance of European border control." *Journal of European Integration* 39, (6): 441–456.

Pelkmans, Mathijs. 2006. *Defending the Border: Identity, Religion, Modernity in the Republic of Georgia*. Ithaca: Cornell University Press.

Perkowski, Nina. 2018. "Frontex and the convergence of humanitarianism, human rights and security." *Security Dialogue* 49, (6): 457–475.

Petersen, Karen Lund. 2012. "Risk analysis – A field within security studies?" *European Journal of International Relations* 18, (4): 693–717.

Phelps, James, Bozeman, J. Micahel, and Monica Koenigsberg. 2018. "Comprehending the polar shift in border security culture: Restoring effective sovereignty." In Alexander Siedschlag, and Andrea Jerkovic, eds. *Homeland Security Cultures*. London: Rowman and Littlefield, 79–102.

Pickering, Sharon. 2006. "Border narratives." In Sharon Pickering, and L. Weber, eds. *Borders, Mobility and Technologies of Control*. Dordrecht: Springer, 45–62.

Pollari, Mikko, Hanna-Leena Nissila, Kukka Melkas, Olli Loytty, Ralf Kauranen, and Heidi Gronstrand. 2015. "National, transnational and entangled literatures: Methodological considerations focusing on the case of Finland." In Ann-Sofie Lonngren, Heidi Gronstrand, Heede Dag, and Anne Heith, eds. *Rethinking National Literatures and the Literary Canon in Scandanavia*. Cambridge Scholars Publishing, 2–29.

Potzsch, Holger. 2015. "Art across borders: Dislocating artistic and curatorial practices in the Barents Euro-Arctic Region." *Journal of Borderlands Studies* 30, (1): 111–125.

Prokkola, Eeva-Kaisa. 2009. "Unfixing borderland identity: Border performances and narratives in the construction of self." *Journal of Borderlands Studies* 24, (3): 21–38.

Prokkola, Eeva-Kaisa. 2013. "Neoliberalizing border management in Finland and Schengen." *Antipode* 45, (5): 1318–1336.

Prokkola, Eeva-Kaisa, and Maria Lois. 2016. "Scalar politics of border heritage: An examination of the EU's Northern and Southern border areas." *Scandanavian Journal of Hospitality and Tourism* 16, (1): 14–35.

Rancière, Jacques. 2010. "The aesthetic heterotopia." *Philosophy Today* 54 (supplement): 15–25

Raussert, Wilfred. 2011. "Inter-American border discourse, heterotopia, and translocal communities in courtney hunt's film *Frozen River*." *Norteamerica* 6, (1): 15–33.

RIcœur, Paul. 2004. *Memory, History, Forgetting*. Chicago: University of Chicago Press.

Ridanpaa, Juha. 2011. "Pajala as a literary place: In the readings and footsteps of Mikael Niemi." *Journal of Tourism and Cultural Change* 9, (2): 103–117.

Rigo, Enrica. 2005. "Citizenship at Europe's borders: Some reflections on the post-colonial condition of Europe in the context of EU enlargement." *Citizenship Studies* 9, (1): 3–22.

Roberts, Gillian, and David Stirrup, eds. 2013. *Parallel Encounters: Culture at the Canada-U.S. Border*. Waterloo: Wilfrid Laurier University Press.

Roberts, Gillian. 2015. *Discrepant Parallels: Cultural Implications of the Canada-U.S. Border*. Montreal and Kingston: McGill-Queen's University Press.

Roberts, Gillian, ed. 2018. *Reading between the Borderlines: Cultural Production and Consumption Across the 49th Parallel*. Montreal and Kingston: McGill-Queen's University Press.

Robins, Steven, Andrea Cornwall, and Bettina Von Lieres. 2008. "Rethinking 'citizenship' in the postcolony." *Third World Quarterly* 29, (6): 1069–1086.

Rojas, Christina. 2009. "Securing the state and developing social insecurities: The securitization of citizenship in contemporary Colombia." *Third World Quarterly* 30, (1): 227–245.

Root, Deborah. 2018 [1996]. *Cannibal Culture: Art, Appropriation, and the Commodification of Difference*. New York: Routledge.

Rosière, Stephane. 2020. *Frontières de fer: Le cloisonnement du monde*. Paris: Syllepse.

Rosière, Stephane, and Reece Jones. 2012. "Teichopolitics: Re-considering globalization through the role of walls and fences." *Geopolitics* 17, (1): 217–234.

Rouvière, Laetitia. 2019. "Entre souveraineté indigène et sécurité nationale: Négocier la sécurité frontalière et la culture Mohawk à Akwesasne." *The Canadian Geographer/Le Géographe canadien* 63, (1): 57–68.

Rygiel, Kim. 2011. "Bordering solidarities: Migrant activism and the politics of movement and camps at Calais." *Citizenship Studies* 15, (1): 1–19.

Sadowski-Smith, Claudia. 2008. *Border Fictions: Globalization, Empire and Writing at the Boundaries of the United States*. University of Virginia Press.

Sahin-Mencutek, Zeynep. 2020. *Migration Narratives in Policy and Politics*. Ryerson Centre for Immigration and Settlement and CERC in Migration and Integration. Paper No. 17, 1–27.

Salter, Mark B. 2008. "When the exception becomes the rule: Borders, sovereignty, and citizenship." *Citizenship Studies* 12, (4): 365–380.

Schaeffer, Felicity Amaya. 2022. *Unsettled Borders: The Militarized Science of Surveillance on Sacred Indigenous Land*. Durham: Duke University Press

Schilliger, Sarah. 2020. "Challenging who counts as a citizen: The infrastructure of solidarity contesting racial profiling in Switzerland." *Citizenship Studies* 24, (4): 530–547.

Schimanski, Johan. 2015. "Border aesthetics and cultural distancing in the Norwegian-Russian borderscape." *Geopolitics* 20, (1): 35–55.

Schimanski, Johan, and Jopi Nyman, eds. 2021. *Border Images, Border Narratives*. Manchester: Manchester University Press.

Schwartz, Seth J., Luyckx, Koen, and Vivian L. Vignoles. 2011. *Handbook of Identity Theory and Research*. New York: Springer.

Schwiertz, Helge, and Helen Schwenken. 2020. "Mobilizing for safe passages and escape aid: Challenging the 'asylum paradox' between active and activist citizenship, humanitarianism and solidarity." *Citizenship Studies* 24, (4): 493–511.

Scott, James W. 2012. "European politics of borders, border symbolism and cross-border cooperation." In Thomas M. Wilson and Hastings Donnan, eds. *A Companion to Border Studies*, Oxford: Blackwell83–99.

Scott, James W., ed. 2020. *A Research Agenda for Border Studies.* Cheltenham: Edward Elgar.

Seyal, Mira. 2020. "Human rights and art activism: The U.S.-Mexico Border." PhD. Dissertation, Columbia University.

Shachar, Ayelet, and Ran Hirschl. 2007. "Citizenship as inherited property." *Political Theory* 35, (3): 253–287.

Shalhoub-Kevorkian, Nadera. 2006. "Negotiating the present, historicizing the future: Palestinian children speak about the Israeli separation wall." *American Behavioural Scientist* 49, (8): 1101–1124.

Shamir, Ronen. 2005. "Without borders? Notes on globalization as a mobility regime." *Sociological Theory* 23, (2): 197–217.

Shani, Giorgio. 2002. "The territorialization of identity: Sikh nationalism in the diaspora 1." *Studies in Ethnicity and Nationalism* 2, (1): 11–19.

Shields, Peter. 2014. "Borders as information flows and transnational networks." *Global Media and Communication* 10, (1): 3–33.

Shneiderman, Sara B. 2013. "Himalayan border citizens: Sovereignty and mobility in the Nepal-Tibetan autonomous region (TAR) of China border zone." *Political Geography* 25, (2): 151–180.

Siedschlag, Alexander, and Andrea Jerkovic, eds. 2018. *Homeland Security Cultures.* London: Rowman and Littlefield.

Simpson, Adam. 2013. "Challenging hydropower development in Myanmar (Burma): Cross-border activism under a regime in transition." *The Pacific Review* 26, (2): 129–152.

Simpson, Audra. 2004. "To the reserve and back again: Kahnawake Mohawk narratives of self, home and nation." PhD Dissertation, McGill University.

Smeekens, Karin. 2010. "In-between-ness: Identity construction at the border of two 'new empries'." M.A. Thesis, Radboud University.

Soja, Edward. 1996. *Thirdspace: Journeys to Los Angeles and Other Real-and-Imagined Places.* Malden: Blackwell.

Sparke, Matthew B. 2006. "A neoliberal nexus: Economy, security and the biopolitics of citizenship on the border." *Political Geography* 25, (2): 151–180.

Squires, Vicki. 2015. *Post/Humanitarian Border Politics between Mexico and the U.S.: People, Places, Things.* London: Palgrave Macmillan.

Staeheli, Lynn A. 2011. "Political geography: Where's citizenship?" *Progress in Human Geography* 35, (3): 393–400.

Staudt, Kathleen. 2009. *Violence and Activism at the Border: Gender, Fear, and Everyday Life in Ciudad Juarez.* Austin: University of Texas Press.

Staudt, Kathleen. 2014. "The border performed in films: Produced in both Mexico and the U.S. to 'Bring out the worst in a country'." *Journal of Borderlands Studies* 29, (4): 465–479.

Stavans, Ilan, ed. 2010. *Border Culture.* Santa Barbara: Greenwood.

Stevenson, Nick. 2001. "Culture and citizenship: An introduction." In Nick Stevenson, ed. *Culture and Citizenship.* London: Sage, 1–10.

Stewart, Lauren. 2019. "Trump's border wall rhetoric." Marshall University, COLA Research and Creativity Conference.

Streesby, Shelley. 2002. *American Sensations: Class, Empire, and the Production of Popular Culture.* Berkeley: University of California Press.

Sutcliffe, John B. 2008. "Public participation in local politics: The impact of community activism on the Windsor-Detroit border decision making process." *Canadian Journal of Urban Research* 17, (2): 57–83.

Svensson, Sara. 2020. "Resistance or acceptance? The voice of local cross-border organizations in times of re-bordering." *Journal of Borderlands Studies* 37, (3): 493–512.

Tan, Kathy-Ann. 2015. *Reconfiguring Citizenship and National Identity in the North American Literary Imagination*. Detroit: Wayne State University Press.

Tell, Stefan. 2017. "Euroregions as soft spaces: Between consolidation and transformation." *European Spatial Research and Policy* 24, (2): 93–110.

Tellez, Michelle. 2008. "Community of struggle: Gender, violence, and resistance on the U.S.-Mexico border." *Gender and Society* 22, (5): 545–567.

Teverson, Andrew, and Sara Upstone, eds. 2011. *Postcolonial Spaces: The Politics of Place in Contemporary Culture*. London: Palgrave Macmillan.

Thomsen, Charles. 1996. "Border vision: The international peace garden." *Manitoba History* 31: 36–41.

Timothy, Dallen J., and Cevat Tosun. 2003. "Tourists' perceptions of the Canada-U.S. border as a barrier to tourism at the international peace garden." *Tourism Management* 24, (4): 411–421.

Timothy, Dallen J., and Alon Gelbman. 2015. "Tourist lodging, spatial relations, and the cultural heritage of borderlands." *Journal of Heritage Tourism* 10, (2): 202–212.

Tocilovac, Marko. 2016. "Frontière symbolique et construction plurielle d'imaginaires : une étude de cas au Friendship Park (San Diego, Californie, Etats-Unis)." In Michelle Auzanneau, and Luca Greco, eds. *Dessiner les frontières*. Lyon: ENS.

Torres, Rebecca Maria, and Melissa Wicks-Asbun. 2014. "Undocumented students' narratives of luminal citizenship: High aspirations, exclusion, and "in-between" identities." *The Professional Geographer* 66, (2): 195–204.

Tuathail, Gearoid O. 2005. "The frustrations of geopolitics and the pleasures of war: *Behind enemy lines* and American geopolitical culture." *Geopolitics* 10, (2): 356–377.

Vallet, Elisabeth, ed. 2014. *Borders, Fences and Walls: State of Insecurity?* Farnham: Ashgate.

Van Houtum, Henk. 2009. "Mapping transversal borders: Towards achoreography of space." In B. Riccio, and C. Brambilla, eds. *Transnational Migration, Cosmopolitanism and Dis-located Borders*. Rimini: Guaraldi, 199–137.

Van Houtum, Henk, and Arnoud Lagendijk. 2001. "Contextualizing regional identity and imagination in the construction of polycentric urban regions: The cases of the Rhur area and the Basque country." *Urban Studies* 38, (4): 747–767.

Van Houtum, Henk, and Ton Van Naerssen. 2002. "Bordering, ordering and othering." *Tijdschrift voor economische en socialegeografie* 93, (2): 125–136.

Van Houtum, Henk, and Roos Pijpers. 2007. "The European Union as a gated community: The two-faced border and immigration regime of the EU." *Antipode* 39, (2): 291–309.

Van Houtum, Henk. 2010. "Human blacklisting: The global apartheid of the EU's external border regime. *Environment and Planning D: Society and Space* 28, (6): 957–976.

Van Klinken, Adriaan, and Ebenezer Obdare. 2018. "Christianity, sexuality and citizenship in Africa: Critical intersections." *Citizenship Studies* 22, (6): 557–568.

Van Schendel, Willem. 2007. "The Wagah syndrome: Territorial roots of contemporary violence in South Asia." In Amrita Basu, and Srirupa Roy, eds. *Violence and Democracy in India*. Amsterdam: Seagull Books, 36–82.

Vaughan-Williams, Nick. 2008. "Borderwork beyond inside/outside? Frontex, the citizen-detective and the war on terror." *Space and Polity* 12, (11): 63–79.

Vega, Irene I. 2018. "Empathy, morality and criminality: The legitimization narratives of U.S. Border patrol agents." *Journal of Ethnic and Migration Studies* 44, (15): 2544–2561.

Veronis, Luisa. 2013. "The border and immigrants in Ottawa-Gatineau: Governance practices and the (re)production of a dual Canadian citizenship." *Journal of Borderlands Studies* 28, (2): 257–271.

Vila, Pablo. 2005. *Border Identifications: Narratives of Religion, Gender, and Class on the U.S.-Mexico Border.* Austin: University of Texas Press.

Vila, Pablo. 2013. "The importance of photo-interviewing as a research method in the study of identity construction processes: An illustration from the U.S.-Mexico border." *Visual Anthropology* 26, (1): 51–68.

Vineis, Paolo. 2017. *Health Without Borders: Epidemics in the Era of Globalization.* New York: Springer.

Vélez-Ibáñez, Carlos G. 1996. *Border Visions: Mexican Cultures of the Southwest United States.* Tucson: University of Arizona Press.

Walsh, James. 2013. "Remapping the border: Geospatial technologies and border activism." *Environment and Planning D: Society and Space* 31, (6): 969–987.

Walters, William. 2002. "Mapping Schengenland: Denaturalizing the border." *Environment and Planning D: Society and Space* 20, (5): 561–580.

Walters, William. 2006. "No border: Games with(out) frontiers." *Social Justice* 33, (1): 21–39.

Walters, William. 2011. "Foucault and frontiers: Notes on the birth of the humanitarian border." In Ulrich Brodding, Susanne Krasmann, and Thomas Lemke, eds. *Governmentality: Current Issues and Future Challenges.* New York: Routledge, 138–164.

Ware, Anthony, and Costas Laoutides. 2018. *Myanmar's Rohingya Conflict.* Oxford: Oxford University Press.

Weigand, Heidi, and Colin Howell. 2021. "Sport, globalization, and the bordering process: The Iroquois nationals lacrosse team and the issue of contested national identities." In Victor Konrad, and Melissa Kelly, eds. *Borders, Culture and Globalization: A Canadian Perspective.* Ottawa: University of Ottawa Press, 277–292.

Widdis, Randy. 1997. "Borderland interaction in the international region of the great plains: An historic-geographical perspective." *Great Plains Research* 7, (Spring): 103–137.

Widdis, Randy. 2011. "'Across the boundary in a hundred torrents': The changing geography of marine trade within the Great Lakes borderland during the nineteenth and early twentieth centuries." *Annals, Association of American Geographers* 101, (2): 356–379.

Widdis, Randy. 2015. "Looking through the mirror: A historical geographical view of the Canadian-American borderlands." *Journal of Borderlands Studies* 30, (2): 175–188.

Widdis, Randy. 2017. "Greater New England as cultural borderland: A critical appraisal." *Acadiensis* 46, (1): 97–121.

Widdis, Randy. 2019a. "On globalization, borders, and borderlands: A historical geographical perspective." *The Canadian Geographer/LeGeographecanadien* 63, (4): 573–593.

Widdis, Randy. 2019b. "Railways and borderland spaces: The Canada-U.S. case." *The Canadian Geographer/Le Geographecanadien* 63, (1): 11–26.

Wiener, Antje. 2018. *European Citizenship Practice: Building Institutions of a Non-State.* London: Routledge.

Wilson, William A. 1975. "The 'Kalevala' and Finnish politics." *Journal of the Folklore Institute* 12, (2/3): 131–155.

Wodak, Ruth. 2009. *Discursive Construction of National Identity.* Edinburgh: Edinburgh University Press.

Wonders, Nancy A. 2007. "Globalization, border reconstruction projects, and transnational crime." *Social Justice* 34, (2): 33–46.

Wood, Patricia Burke, and Mary Gilmartin. 2018. "Irish enough: Changing narratives of citizenship and national identity in the context of Brexit." *Space and Polity* 22, (2): 224–237.

Woodsworth, Paddy. 2008. *The Basque Country: A Cultural History*. Oxford: Oxford University Press.

Zaiotti, Ruben. 2011. *Cultures of Border Control: Schengen and the Evolution of European Frontiers*. Chicago: University of Chicago Press.

Zelinsky, Wilbur. 2017. *Nation into State: The Shifting Symbolic Foundations of American Nationalism*. Raleigh: University of North Carolina Press.

Zhang, Chenchen. 2014. "Between postnationality and postcoloniality: Human rights and the right of non-citizens in a 'Cosmopolitan' Europe." In Nikita Dhawan, ed. *Decolonizing Enlightenment: Transnational Justice, Human Rights and Democracy in a Postcolonial World*. Berlin: Barbara Budrich, 243–259.

5

CULTURAL PRODUCTION AND BORDER CROSSINGS

Border culture is most evident at border crossings and in borderlands.
The border is a cultural production anchored in imaginaries.
Border culture may connect people, but it may also divide them.
Culture in the border zone may not be sustainable.
If you are different, you are the border.

Introduction: Borders activate culture

Cultural production *of* the border, and cultural production *at* the border may coincide and they definitely intertwine, but the process and the product of border culture need to be theorized discretely in order to understand and appreciate border culture production. Cultural productions at the border, border fences or walls, for example, are powerful activators and re-activators of other cultural production (Amilhat Szary 2012a). Material productions of cross-border space emerge from interactions and retroactions, and these productions are part of a broader range of encounters, networking, social relations, and political strategies (Durand 2015). The discursive spaces and physical places convey the material reality of cultural production at and of the border (Saldívar 1997). Bounding difference requires an acknowledgement of the "intersectionality" that accompanies and catalyzes the material production of gender, caste, class, and environment, for example, as seen in Nepal (Nightingale 2011). Cultural productions will be unequal (Collins 2009), variable and protracted (Schindel 2019), and repetitive (Faist 2014). As illustrated in the case of the Sino-Nepalese border, the cultural production and performance of the border relates to transborder social identification, in this case the Mustangi people who occupy the immediate borderlands (Murton 2019).

Accordingly, we initiate this extensive discussion of cultural production and border crossings by examining the role of ethnic and linguistic minorities

DOI: 10.4324/9781003301486-5

in situating and sustaining the borderlands. Our case studies are limited to a discussion of Yunnan's ethnic minorities and production of the border between China and Vietnam, Laos, and Myanmar, and the linguistic minorities and borderland sustainability in Karelia, overlapping Finland and Russia. The following section of the chapter portrays the border as a cultural project. We begin this lengthy component of the book with a focus on Europe, in which an assessment of European Union cultural and INTERREG projects provides the context for an immense and somewhat impenetrable literature, and this broader context is complemented by brief illustrations of European cross-border "radavism" (cycling) and Basque cultural identity. Next in this set of ten case studies are three illustrations of border culture from the Canada–U.S. border: Quebec borders and bordering culture; "line dancing" between Stanstead, Quebec, and Derby Line, Vermont; and the cultural policies and governance of borders at the Mohawk reserves of Akwesasne and St. Regis, astride the borders between Ontario, Quebec, and New York State, on the international boundary between the U.S. and Canada. Then, we move to far reaches of the globe with three case studies that explore the border as cultural project in South America, the Middle East, and the Korean Peninsula. Firstly, we examine distinction and affirmation of borderlands community, place, and space along the border between Chile and Peru. Next, we consider Turkey as situated in the middle and on the edge of border culture. Thirdly, we depict the Korean demilitarized zone (DMZ) as a cult of the border. The last of the ten case studies takes us back to the border between Windsor and Detroit, and elsewhere along the Canada–U.S. border to show how the border is curated as a cultural project.

At this juncture in the chapter, we shift the discussion to a consideration of impossible borders that reject crossings, even by culture. The Israeli–Palestinian border is our prime example, and this illustration serves as well to situate an assessment of boycott politics crossing borders and creating new borders. We then move the discussion from impossible borders to the immutable and irrevocable U.S.–Mexico border. We complete this section of the chapter with a focus on Indigenous art in border spaces of refusal.

Then the attention moves to walls, perhaps the most evident and emphatic representations of border culture. Our discussion of this global phenomenon is limited to the cultural production of border walls in China, and the more recent establishment of walls along the U.S. border with Mexico.

The final substantive section of the chapter is on "queering the line", that is taking the border to all kinds of limits. In this discussion we begin with queer borders and bordering, and focus on the queer politics of migration as an element in bio-politics at the border. Then, we consider technologies of movement and networks that have changed border cultures. A final consideration is with the culture produced among disabled and disadvantaged people at borders. We conclude the chapter with a contemporary assessment of COVID-19 and the reinforcement of border culture.

Underlying cultural production of the border, and innumerable, ongoing border crossings, are the narratives and imaginaries derived from previous border crossings. These narratives and imaginaries are inevitably impacted by top-down and bottom-up forces, and negotiated to produce medial forms. Victor Konrad and Zhiding Hu (2021) suggest this process may be identified as the *border discourse cycle*, the circulation and revision of written and visual discourse about a border in the public sphere. "Imaginaries and narratives merge, link, collude, and reinforce border discourse. Top-down narratives and imaginaries negotiate border space with bottom-up narratives and imaginaries. These, in turn, reinforce, modify, or adjust border crossing, bordering practices and borderscapes"—geopolitical and epistemic multidimensionality of the border enabling understanding of borders in globalization. "The border discourse cycle of repeated and revised processes may then manifest in a sequence of empowerment, contestation, borderation (border as catalyst for engaging border constituencies), and negotiation" (Konrad and Hu 2021, 132).

This concept of the border discourse cycle is rooted in different but aligned ideas of liminality (Turner 1969) and in/visibility (Arendt 2013 [1958]), both linked to fundamentals of transition in duality. The border discourse cycle acknowledges reshuffling and realignment of spatialities and temporalities in globalization (Sassen 2000). Unanchored from bounded territory (Agnew 1994), borders and borderlands are now recognized as spaces of exception by some authors, and located beyond nation-states rather than just between them (Gregory 2004, Agamben 2005). Borders are in motion (Urry 2012, Amilhat Szary and Giraut 2015, Konrad 2015, Nail 2016), and this mobility and fluidity enlarges spaces of exception and time-space constructs for the multiscalar production of borders (Laine 2016). Borderscapes (Rajaram and Grundy-Warr 2007, Brambilla 2015, Brambilla et al. 2015) are created by actors at various scales and in multiple spatial and temporal contexts. In this expanding "borderworld", dissensus vies with consensus to characterize the conceptualization and materialization of borders (Rancière 2015, Rodney 2017). With a growing participation of actors in borderlands and bordering, a broader range and complexity of cultural production of borders is evident (Schimanski and Wolfe 2010). Also, the aperture for expression of border aesthetics is enlarged, and the concomitant richness and complexity of cultural production of borders invites greater research and understanding (Schimanski 2015, Schimanski and Wolfe 2017).

5.1 Role of ethnic and linguistic minorities in situating and sustaining borderlands

In many parts of the world, ethnic minorities have been associated with borderlands since state borders were drawn between and through their territories. These ethnic minorities may be people who belong to an ethnic group that is a relatively small part of a greater state population. Also, an ethnic minority may be a group that has different national or cultural traditions from the main population. In Claude Levi-Strauss' (1952) structuralist view, ethnic minorities are a component of cultural diversity analogous to biological diversity, and that human diversity enhances cultural vitality. Fredrik Barth (1969, 10–11) characterizes the ethnic group as "largely biologically self-perpetuating". It "shares fundamental cultural values realized in overt unity in cultural forms, makes up a field of communication and interaction, and has a membership which identifies itself, and is identified by others, as constituting a category distinguishable from other categories of the same order". "Fredrik Barth views ethnic structures both in primordialist and constructivist terms. Primordialist, because ethnicities are persistent structures, despite transborder movement; and constructivist, because cultures' boundaries can be crossed, with an open-ended scenario" (Bahnev 2021, 1). Barth's (1969, 15) view of ethnic group boundaries is that they "canalize" social life, and that this in turn maintains the ethnic boundary.

These classical perspectives on ethnic minorities and ethnic group boundaries have been revised with critical perspectives, for example, on boundaries and minorities in Western Europe (De Marchi and Boileau 1982), and Black and Indigenous experiences in the Americas (Cornell 1992, Horacio 1993). Arjun Appadurai (1990) attributes disjuncture and difference in the global cultural economy to the tension between cultural homogenization and cultural heterogenization in globalization. These advances are acknowledged in Michaelson and Johnson *Border Theory* (1997). More recently, Sarah Radcliffe and Sallie Westwood (2005) offer new ways of thinking about the nation, nationalism, and national identities which draw on links between popular culture and Indigenous movements, issues of race and gender, and ideologies of national identity to re-theorize the policies of nationalism. This is a world of pluri-nations and ethnicized identities in an ever-changing struggle for democracy. Townsend Middleton (2013) accounts for these "states of difference" in the ethnicity refiguring and its crisis at India's borders. Yet, in some instances, for example, the land border along the Torne River between Sweden and Finland, linguistic, social, and ethnic differences among four distinct groups prevail over the state boundary, and cooperation is mobilized among the groups rather than across the state boundary (Lunden and Zalamans 2001).

For many ethnic minorities located at the state border, this borderland situation was not a positive choice, but rather a place of refuge from the state, where the state's quasi absence allowed them to maintain their "unorthodox" livelihoods (Scott 2009). For some ethnic minorities, borders help establish their identities and enable their livelihoods. Even closed borders do not halt cross-border interaction. Sanctioned borderlands of cross-border trade and migration renew and validate the role of ethnic minorities in cross-border engagement and interaction. Borderlands culture flourishes locally where it is nourished by sustainable tradition, confirmed identity and firm attachment to place and space. Both locality and ethnicity, then, help to create imaginaries of borders and borderlands, and to anchor the narratives associated with these imaginaries (Schimanski and Nyman 2021).

Making visible and giving voice through border imaginaries and narratives empowers minority and local constituencies as long as local and minority imaginaries and narratives do not eclipse the national discourse. Among the strategies to ensure that this incursion does not occur is the simple act of apportioning space. National border space is assigned, identified, and fortified, yet it is also often limited to national border crossings. Whereas national authority prevails along the entire boundary, it is exercised strategically at and near national crossings. This leaves ample border space for contestation, ameliorating trauma associated with bordering, the revitalization of visibility, and the expression of local and ethnic minority identity. Moderation of the national and the local, and particularly engagement of minority constituencies has evolved a "borderation" effect wherein the border is the catalyst for mediation and merging of multiscalar border narratives (Konrad and Hu 2021). "Borderation" is a process akin to, but more specific than, "borderity" (Amilhat Szary and Giraut 2015), the governmentality of territorial limits. This "borderation" works at multiple scales and also at the same scale where some ethnic minorities are joining with others to operate more effectively in border space. Diverse border space is then negotiable between and within scales. In this negotiable and diverse border space, border images and narratives help to ease a rapid borderlands transformation, and to make sense of border spaces that have changed substantially in the experience of people inhabiting them.

5.1.1 Yunnan's ethnic minorities and the production of the border between China and Vietnam, Laos, and Myanmar

In Yunnan Province and adjacent borderlands of Myanmar, Laos, and Vietnam, there is an alignment of national spaces with minority identity, and empowerment of both the local and the national, and making space for the global. For three decades, China has accelerated trade and interaction across its boundaries. The "Belt and Road" initiative (BRI) emphasizes that China's territorial vision has moved beyond the historical metaphor of the "wall" to define edges and limits, yet articulate borderlands creation that combines cross-border engagement with territorial integrity (Sidaway and Woon 2017). In these new borderlands, extensive infrastructure enhancement, economic development, cultural viability, and political positioning all play roles in re-scaling and re-articulation of border space, and shaping coexistent spaces of exception and integration (Hu and Konrad 2018).

The Belt and Road narrative of cross-border expansion, extension into foreign and challenging territory, engagement with non-Han peoples, economic and cultural growth, Chinese hegemony, and the narrative's revisions and renewals during the last decade, are all steeped in Silk Road history and tradition. In this way, the Sino-centric global vision links to an extensive and inclusive master narrative, which in turn is translated into local and regional borderlands imaginaries and narratives. These regional and local imaginaries and narratives may align with the national, or, more commonly, they may adjust imaginaries and narratives to express ethnic identity and local prerogative. The evolved imaginaries and narratives are used by government and media actors connected to the Chinese state, as well as provincial and local authorities, ethnic minorities, and other constituencies to negotiate border crossing and enable bordering (Lagerqvist 2013).

The first case study in this chapter explores how narratives and imaginaries of border crossings and processes contribute to border negotiation in the public sphere, and, particularly, how these aesthetic forms deliver a range of "top-down" and "bottom-up" discourses among national interests and a richly intertwined tapestry of minorities in this mountainous region. Notably, the "Tea Road" narrative speaks of ancient, well-worn trading routes for tea and other commodities originating in the heart of Yunnan and extending across the formidable Himalayan massif, and this narrative is used for geopolitical marketing purposes (see Figure 5.1). The "Tea Road" narrative, a derivative, parallel, and variant of the "Silk Road" narrative, has been co-opted by Yunnan Province to situate the southwestern region of China at the apex of time-honoured border crossing routes (Zhou 2012). Yet, the narrative also serves Chinese national interest, defining and substantiating the historical roots and legitimacy of the BRI. Furthermore, the narrative resonates globally because the story of Chinese "roads" beyond the famously isolated dynastic kingdom are legend. Also, the narrative works exceptionally well to infuse recognition and external connection into localized, high quality tea production by ethnic minorities in Yunnan.

FIGURE 5.1 The 'Tea Road' Cross-border Narrative is a derivative, parallel and variant of the `Silk Road' narrative to convey an ancient and well-worn trading route for commodities in the Himalayas. Yunnan Province in China has co-opted the narrative to situate the region as the apex of time-honoured trading routes, but it also resonates as a national narrative to substantiate China's Belt and Road initiative, and a global narrative of legendary `roads'. Photo reproduced by permission ofYuli Liu.

Ethnic minorities are more numerous and evident along the border between Yunnan Province, China, and Myanmar, Laos, and Vietnam than they are in the heartlands of these states. Characteristically, minority territories and cultural presence extend across the boundary throughout the region although strong national identities are also expressed at the border. Cross-border extent of ethnic minority territories is evident, particularly among Dai (Tai), Hmong (Miao, Zhuang), Shan, and Kachin (Lisu). Ethnic group names may differ across the border but most aspects of culture extend across the boundary. Even the Han Chinese majority in Yunnan is represented as a cross-border ethnic presence in Myanmar's Kokang "autonomous territory" (Hu and Konrad 2018). Our research has shown that "border people" have evolved specific roles that link with their location, cultural traditions, business interests, and ethnic identities. In the mountainous northwestern borderlands, Lisu are gatekeepers of mountain trails and passes. In the major gateway between Myanmar and China, Jingpo traders play a prominent role as intermediaries. Dai also operate in this region but they are more prominent as business leaders and agriculturalists in the upper Mekong region where Myanmar, Laos, and China converge. Where the Shan states meet Yunnan, Wa control cross-border trade, both legal and illicit, through small, isolated border crossings in the uplands. East of the Mekong valley, Hani tea traders occupy the borderlands. The Hmong in the eastern portion of the borderlands manage cross-border agricultural trade ranging from spices to water buffalo.

Our fieldwork (Konrad and Hu 2021) confirms the role of minorities is to anchor the border while facilitating "borderwork" or everyday and ordinary construction, shifting, and dismantling of borders (Rumford 2012). Due to the remote nature of the borderlands, far from Kunming and central Yunnan, and also far from the populated parts of Myanmar, Laos, and Vietnam, central governments in all of the countries depend on de-centralized border control. This control is assured to a degree by national military presence in borderlands but it depends also on ethnic minority participation in border security management. During the past decade, the approach used by central authorities in Myanmar has been to invest some ethnic minorities like the Kokang and Wa with limited autonomy to manage and control their territories, but this has led to conflicts between central and provincial (state) authorities, when authorities are not aligned, and more recently when regimes in Myanmar changed. During the past decade, along the land border with Southeast Asia, China has evolved an approach to engage ethnic minorities in localized border control, by compromising national control to enable traditional trade and interaction patterns. Upscale trade is facilitated through special trading zones at major crossings; local exchange is allowed with few restrictions except in the drug trade, which is controlled vigorously. The goals are to facilitate increasing cross-border flows and to manage the border more efficiently. The ethnic minority role is to link formal and informal borders, and to align opposing forces of mobility and Indigeneity.

Our research shows that ethnic minorities have evolved from border keepers to border managers throughout the borderlands. Armed border keepers in the Shan and Wa states, for example, have shifted from being stewards of the drug trade to a greater engagement in a combination of illicit and legal trade, while they develop economies of their territories and enhance well-being of local inhabitants. In some parts of the Myanmar–China borderlands, where hostilities linger between central government forces and Kachin and Kokang minorities, the fortified border allows rebels to hide in China. In major crossing corridors, however, labour migration, extensive trade, and growing collaboration prevail, all facilitated by ethnic minority linkages across the border.

In segmented territories extending across the border, ethnic minorities sustain cross-border linkages through family and traditional trade connections now sanctioned and encouraged by authorities (Wang et al. 2013). These linkages are accomplished in part through cross-border periodic markets in the Yunnan–Vietnam border area (Masaru and Badenoch 2013). In Ruili and surrounding Dehong County, Jingpo and Dai, in cooperation with Han, are active in operating the growing cross-border trade in hardwoods and jade. Some Dai peddlers in Dehong dress in traditional Thai clothing to de-stabilize their lower status position in Han-dominated society in the region (Siriphon 2007). Together, the minority and majority ethnic groups in the region are facilitating China's largest trade centre for natural resources, and products emerging from these valuable commodities (Bie et al. 2014). In some remote areas, Lisu territory for example, cross-border interaction is emerging more slowly, but this region may see considerably heightened trade in hardwoods as resources are depleted in areas closer to Ruili, and if endemic conflict between the central government and ethnic minorities in far northern Myanmar winds down. According to a Lisu headman in the village adjacent to Hou Qaio, normalization in adjoining Myanmar may result in accelerated cross-border interaction and greater manifestation of cross-border connections. The patterns are consistent. Cross-border connections, sustained even in times of closed borders, flourish when borders are loosened. Yet, more instructive than this predictable result are the patterns of collaboration among ethnic minorities, and between ethnic minorities and the Han majority as borders are opened. "Border strategies" of trade mobility among Dai (Tai Lue) on the China–Laos frontier rely on sustained connection and adherence with Han authority and approach as "part of a long-applied governing pattern of 'experimentation under hierarchy' on the Sino-Lao frontier" (Diana 2013, 25).

Borderlands are situated and sustained because ethnic minorities have been made visible and given voice through narratives acknowledged by others, and particularly by the national government. In Yunnan, governments at all levels respond to minority voices, and this empowers ethnic minorities. Border policy aligns national and minority interests and displays them together when they coincide, but separates them spatially when they do not, as illustrated in the adjacent formal and informal crossings evident all along the border. Minority symbols of cultural identity —dress, rituals, monuments—are both allowed in the borderlands space, and appropriated by the national government for display in the "national" space within the borderlands. This may be allowed in exchange for minority participation in trade and extraction of resources in the borderlands. Throughout the borderlands, and particularly at crossings where multiple narratives of territorial control are evident—Dalou, Ruili, Jinhong—the national government sanctions borderlands culture parks to celebrate and align minority identities with the national. In this way ethnic minorities are often forced to "know their place" politically as well as culturally.

Contestation may occur without necessarily eclipsing the national voice. The national voice prevails in the "reserved space" of national crossings. These national crossings have strict rules and conventions of behaviour that must be adhered to by all border crossers. Invariably, these rules are posted in several languages including English, and rules are enforced by the military. The crossings are formidable and messages of compliance are clear and reinforced by media presentations. Yet, there is extensive and precipitous localization that occurs just beyond the national crossing space. Everyone knows where to cross easily; contestation is the simple act of crossing elsewhere than at the national crossing.

The engagement of local and minority constituencies so that border and local and minority culture are aligned may be termed "borderation", and viewed as an example of becoming in the borderscape. The ethnic minority identifies with and utilizes the border as part of cultural expression, and this border identity and culture is branded in tourism and other economic ventures. Dai peoples in the upper Mekong valley exemplify this "borderation", and, due to their success in marketing their border identity, they have expanded their cultural entrepreneurship into other parts of the borderlands beyond their traditional homeland. Our research confirms that new Dai places and spaces have emerged in other culture areas, particularly where development opportunities exist.

Culturally diverse border space is evident in areas of rapid borderlands transformation, particularly in cross-border urban areas. Fences are typically a last resort to divide interests, people, and flows where change is too rapid and authority needs to be exercised, although during the recent COVID-19 pandemic, fences have been extended along the China–Myanmar border as a crossing control mechanism. The Ruili, China-Muse, Myanmar interface is an example of long-standing border fencing due to the concentrated efforts of both Chinese and Burmese to cross and trade illegally at this juncture between the two countries. More typically border space is negotiated and people know where to cross. Most local border crossing is informal until thresholds of employment, sale of higher order goods and services, and legality are crossed. Through negotiation and compromise, both local minority constituencies and national interests remain empowered during borderlands transformation.

5.1.2 Linguistic minorities and borderland sustainability in Karelia

The linguistic and cultural minority region of Karelia pre-dated encroachment of the Soviet border into Finland. The region, bounded by the White Sea and the large Lake Onega and Lake Ladoga on the north and east, and the Karelian Isthmus between Lake Ladoga and the Gulf of Finland in the south, also contains the Karelian borderland in Finland (Figures 5.2a and b). This borderland is constituted of North Karelia and South Karelia. In Russia, the geopolitical components are the populated Karelian Isthmus near St. Petersburg and centred on Vyborg in the south, north to the components of the Republic of Karelia: Ladoga Karelia, Olonets Karelia, and White Karelia. The Karelian language survives in rural areas in Russia's Republic of Karelia although Russian predominates and is the official language. In Finland, the Finnish language predominates although there are approximately 5,000 Karelian speakers. Approximately one million Finns, however, do trace their roots to Russian Karelia because of population relocation after Soviet expansion into the region after WWII. Previously, during the twentieth century, and for almost a millennium, the Karelian region was a borderland in contention between European powers in the Baltic region. Finnish–Russian Karelia, according to James W. Scott (2013), has most recently been re-constructed through "familiarity" to transcend national appropriations of Karelia, by Russia and Finland, into a "Eurovision" of a common regional space, wherein history is reframed as multifaceted regional ideas.

Whereas the familiarity is constructed of numerous, palpable aspects of common language and history, consistent landscapes, architecture, literature, and even food (Wells 2016), Karelia remains materialized largely as a landscape of contested and commemorated memory (Raivo 2004). Indeed, given the definitive nature of the Finnish–Russian border, and the reticence of many Finns to venture into Russian Karelia, memory plays an enlarged part in characterizing Karelia, particularly for Karelians throughout Finland (Armstrong 2004). Accordingly, Karelia portrays layers and sub-regional components of borderland identity within a sustained cultural and historical ambiguity (Scott 2013).

Among the scholars focused on research related to this borderland, many associated with the Karelian Institute of the University of Eastern Finland, Tuulikki Kurki (2013, 2014) draws attention to the multi-voiced nature of the borderland as expressed in its literature and representations of identity. In her recent research, Kurki (2018) has focused on the narratives of border crossing trauma as expressed in hyper-naturalist prose and surreal forms of narration. In "From heroism to grotesque: The invisibility of border-related trauma narratives in the Finnish–Russian borderlands", she argues:

> Until the late twentieth century, the writers [of Finnish language literature of border crossing in Karelia] mostly employed a documentary style of narrating and eye-witnessing narratives when writing about traumatic experiences ... The border crossers were seen as "heroic survivors", and there was no space for a discussion about their traumas. The traumas were not regarded as being particularly significant in the context of the prevailing national order. Similar features characterize the reception of these border-related trauma narratives in Russian Karelia until the end of the Soviet era. However, during the post-Soviet era, the writers have diverged from the documentary style of writing, and used various narrative strategies of

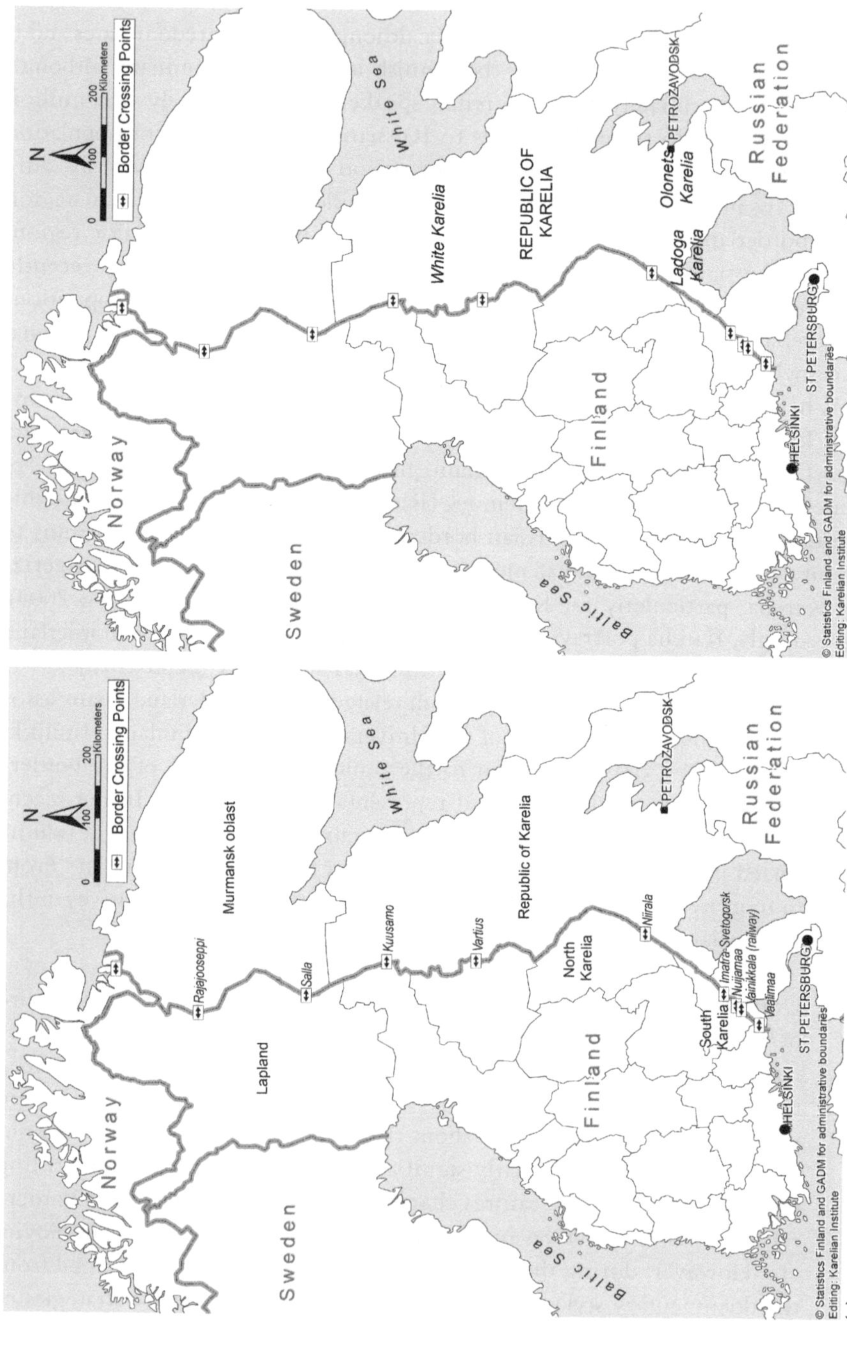

FIGURE 5.2 (a and b) The Karelian Borderland, Finland and Russia. Both maps produced by Matti Fritsch. Reproduced with permission of the

> fiction, such as hyper-naturalism and the grotesque, when addressing the traumatic events. With the narrative strategies of fiction, personal experiences, existing knowledge about historical traumatic events together with the narrators' inner reflections have become visible in ways that were not previously possible.
>
> *(Kurki 2021, 107)*

In this context, border narratives expand to encompass and address traumatic experiences that actually deal with border crossing, and being and becoming in the borderlands. Also in recent research, Tuulikki Kurki (2020) relates how the "unspeakable" aspects of trauma are articulated through everyday objects (for example, photographs, drawings, comics) in materialized narratives of border. Trauma is related to culture in as much as it generates multigenerational perspectives for families and individuals, and these perspectives shape and etch sharply their identity and culture.

5.2 Border as a cultural project

Border culture may then galvanize the resolve of isolated and localized social cohesion along the length of the border, and in this way, it accomplishes the border as a cultural project. The border becomes the catalyst for cultural production. The border is the culture, and the culture the border. Border and culture are intertwined in purpose and design in material culture and expressions of music, cinema, art, dance, literature, architecture, and more. The border affirms borderlands community, space, and place. Cultural production is dynamic as it addresses, records, confronts, alters, and ameliorates flows across the border and in the borderlands. Cultural policies of bordered states may be adjusted and integrated at the border. Culture mediates governance at borders. Overall, culture becomes apparent at the border because, at the boundary, culture is obliged to reveal itself.

In this section of the chapter, we explore a variety of projects that reveal the ingenuity and diversity of border culture in ten different contexts. Our approach is very far ranging in order to capture some of the richness of cultural production as it is formulated and displayed in projects originated by different groups and communities in border contexts around the world. This is not an exhaustive assemblage but rather a representation of distinctive border projects at various scales that reveal initiatives designed to ameliorate the engagement of cultural edges. Firstly we examine some official European Union projects of wide scope, and others at a more focused scale. Then, we shift to the Americas to examine Quebec's bordering project during the late twentieth century, and the affirmation of borderlands communities at the Chile–Peru border. The Middle East interface with Europe is another stop. Here, we examine the bordering project of Turkey to confront and adjust the cultural flows impacting its borders. Also, we compare how Basque identity is enabled and confronted in southwestern Europe.

In this illustration, and in the study focused on the Akwesasne Mohawk Nation at the Canada–U.S. border, we engage with cultural policies and governance. Another two examples are also drawn from the Canada–U.S. border: line dancing as a metaphor for the realization of border culture at Stanstead, Quebec, and Derby Line, Vermont, and the cultural acts of curating the border in Windsor and Detroit. Finally, we examine the cult of the border as it is revealed at the DMZ between North and South Korea.

5.2.1 The European Union cultural and INTERREG projects

According to Solène Marié, as stated in her recent doctoral dissertation "At the center of the edge: The development of cross-border cultural networks in border cities between Brazil and Uruguay and France and Germany" (2020),

> With regard to culture, [European Union] member-states did not immediately trust the European Union to get involved in these issues. Only in the 1992 Maastricht Treaty was an article included for the first time on the topic of the cultural competences of the Union. Even so, these remain very limited, complementary to the actions of member-states and strictly framed by the principle of solidarity. This reluctance is characteristic of the entire cultural sector to the exception of the audiovisual industry which, given its economic aspect and larger audience, was considered a priority sector for EU action from the late 1980s (Autissier 2006). Furthermore, cultural policies and the structuring of the cultural sector differ largely from one member-state to another and this complexifies the creation of unified policies and programmes at the EU level.
>
> The first large-scale EU programme geared towards the funding of cultural projects was launched in 1996 under the name of KALEIDOSCOPE. The "Culture 2000" programme followed, with a cycle of activity which ran from 2000 to 2006. It was thereafter maintained for another cycle of six years (2007–2013) under the name of "Culture". In the most recent cycle (2014–2020), the former Culture, MEDIA and MEDIA Mundus Programmes were fused and became the Creative Europe Programme.
>
> Culture 2000 focused on the development of a common cultural space for European population by promoting cooperation between artists, producers, cultural networks, public cultural institutions as well as other partners. It served to fund: specific projects related to the cultural field in Europe; activities included within structured cultural cooperation agreements; and special cultural events with a European or international dimension (Weber 2007).
>
> During the 2007–2013 period, lines of action remained similar and cultural professionals expressed disappointment. In terms of official discourse, culture is definitely presented as a priority, or even one of the four "pillars"

> of the organization. But in terms of real priorities, namely those which are budgeted, cultural cooperation has become peripheral. … the European Union and the Council of Europe … have been able to develop neither corresponding strategies nor programmes to respond to the expectations of the various cultural cooperation actors and to the building of Europe (Weber 2007).
>
> *(Marié 2020, 198–199,* our translation*)*

Solène Marié (2000, 199) continues her assessment with reference to a 2004 study conducted by Relais Culture Europe, which likens the EU cultural programmes to a cultural service rather than a programme of cultural subsidies. The commission operates a complicated budget file; it emphasizes project management over cultural content; artistic content is barely acknowledged; and funding appears contingent on management over artistic criteria (Autissier 2006).

Marié (2020, 200) continues:

> In its most recent form as the Creative Europe programme, this funding stream continues to generate criticism from cultural actors on a number of points. Firstly, the form of the project presented for funding remains more important than its contents: the most important issue is the creation of perennial management structures rather than the quality of the project. Secondly, programme aims and criteria are seen as complex: one participant complains about the necessity to "tweak" the project to match it with a programme objective and its specifics. Thirdly, there are entry barriers for applications as applicants are required to have existed for a minimum of two years, have significant financial reserves and cannot include a fee for the work generated by the application process into the project budget. Fourthly, the number of available programmes and unclear communication for the European Commission make it complex for often understaffed cultural organizations to navigate the funding opportunities: another participant says "We don't have an overall idea of the programmes and we don't have time to read them all."

Most structural EU funding for cultural projects originates from European Territorial Cooperation programmes such as INTERREG (Perrin 2013). "In this instance, cultural actions are managed within institutional structures which are specifically framed to correspond to EU funding specificities" (Marié 2020, 200). These projects are contained by and materialize within Euroregions, or cross-border cooperation initiatives (Perrin 2015). "In this context, cultural actions within Euroregions are used for differentiation, while including them within administrative set-ups which are unlikely to allow for future autonomy of the project outside the latter (Perrin 2013)" (Marié 2020, 200–203). INTERREG cultural projects also suffer from insufficient financial means, insufficient staffing, administrative complexity, cooperation with distinct national contexts, linguistic difficulties, understanding of institutional contexts, organization of the sector, and business models (Marié 2020, 204).

Among the numerous European Union initiatives aimed at European integration and Europeanization, the INTERREG projects of cross-border, transnational, and interregional cooperation were designed to strengthen economic and social cohesion throughout the EU (During et al. 2007).

> The aims concerning economic and social cohesion and a balanced and sustainable development of the European territory became increasingly dependent on cross-cultural understanding because of the enlargement in 2004. Special emphasis has therefore been placed on integrating remote regions and those which share external borders with candidate countries.
>
> *(During et al. 2007, 9)*

The framework for INTERREG III was divided into strands: (A) local development of social facilities, economy, and environment in cross-border cooperation; (B) spatial development strategies, linking cities and management of resources in transnational cooperation; and (C) development of networks and joint structures in interregional cooperation. "In the mid-term evaluations of INTERREG III, culture was mentioned as a major factor determining the success or failure of programs and projects" due to the complex task of ensuring cooperation between and among communities with "different language, mentality, perceptions, attitudes, habits, values, history and sometimes socio-economic systems" (During et al. 2007, 9). Furthermore, it was noted after the evaluation of INTERREG II (1996–2003), that there was "an insufficiently developed trans-European cooperation culture between public authorities, institutions, citizens and businesses" (During et al. 2007, 10). Also, "cultural variety" was deemed an issue by the European Commission, and this was addressed through the establishment of CULTPLAN in order to examine the relation between cultural variety and the practice of INTERREG. "The aim [of CULTPLAN] was to gain an understanding of the role of culture by looking at cultural mechanisms instead of labeling certain parts of Europe" (During et al. 2007, 10). Complex and interconnected questions of "Where does culture manifest itself? How does culture work? How does one recognize culture? How should cultural differences be dealt with? and How can we benefit from cultural variety?" aimed to reveal the "positive power of cross-cultural cooperation" (During et al. 2007, 11–12). Ultimately, many of these questions were reframed and focused on cross-border cooperation.

An immense literature has emerged from the INTERREG projects throughout Europe, and a significant number of these projects have addressed aspects of cultural cooperation and awareness, particularly at borders. Attention has been focused in many instances on studies in Eastern Europe and the Balkans, although all European regions are included. A recent book on *European Territorial Cooperation* (Medeiros 2018) provides an extensive overview, and the initial chapter by Bernhard Reitel, Birte Wassenberg and Jean Peyrony (2018) offers a 30-year summary of the experience of INTERREG in bridging European territories. Whereas the authors of this assessment document extensive territorial cooperation and integration according to economic indicators, social and humanitarian values are not as well developed across borders. Yet, there are numerous instances recorded in the literature where INTERREG projects have accomplished positive returns in cross-cultural and cross-border cooperation. In the Baltic Sea area, for example, cross-border cultural understanding has been achieved through creating related cross-border destinations and encouraging tourism within a regional framework (Nilsson et al. 2010). Enhancing cross-border cultural awareness and extending cross-border regionalization, at the Finnish–Swedish border, for example, also depends on local cooperation (Prokkola 2011). Although contemporary Europe continues to grapple with the problem of sustaining cultural variety, while attempting extensive efforts of cultural Europeanization, projects of local and regional cross-border cooperation display dividends of increased cultural awareness and understanding. Examples originating in European cycling and the Basque region briefly illustrate these cross-border cultural enhancements, before we turn our attention back to case studies from other parts of the world.

5.2.2 European radavists

An interesting example of the border as a cultural project is found in the "Grenzfahrungen" (borderline experiences) of "radavists" (cycling enthusiasts) who engage in a journey along the line of the former "Iron Curtain" (Radavist 2021). Groups of cyclists, often in club colours, follow the line as closely as possible to acquire the experience of touching in with a former border now removed, not to memorialize the border, but, instead, to sense what it may have been. Similar radavist adventures follow the national boundaries of Europe, now often more subdued in the landscape. Cycling the French–Spanish border through the Pyrenees adds the challenge of locating accessible roads near the border in the mountainous terrain. Overall, these radavist projects engage with borders that were and have been, borders where the cyclist does not need to dismount and confirm identity.

One prominent example of the implementation of cycling routes as tools for cross-border integration may be found in the Vennbahn cycling route which extends throughout the German–Belgian–Dutch–Luxembourgian borderlands. Here, cycling culture is meshed with cross-border cultural awareness building through the engagement of cyclists from all of these countries in a common enthusiasm (Stoffelen 2018). The common experience follows trails that connect across the borders such as green belts and abandoned rail lines (Stoffelen and Vanneste 2017). This establishment and re-establishment of cross-border "trails" offers a strong cultural sinew for cross-border cooperation. Additional cultural affirmation is provided through the heritage of cycling in and throughout this cross-border region (Stoffers 2012).

5.2.3 Basque identity

For the Basques of northern Spain and adjacent southwestern France, numerous borders have been produced to confront the international boundary that dissects their homeland and the nation-states that have tried to immerse their culture. Basque Country or "Euskadi" is a changing, multiply-bounded territory based on aspects of tradition, livelihood, political affiliation, and more, with bounded enclaves within the overall territory (Woodsworth 2008). Although there is a provincial boundary drawn by Spain around the Basque Autonomous Territory, the authorized border is less consequential than borders constructed by Basques themselves. For the Basques, borders evolve through the process of belonging. A state of belongingness outlines their territory as well as their "common togetherness" and "changing landscape of identities" (Bray 2004). Belongingness for the Basques involves multiple connectivities to places, environments, groups, ideologies, and beliefs, and all of these may be transitional, ambiguous, and marginal constructs of "living boundaries" that enable the Basques to identify at once as a political, social, ethnic, and popular culture, and embrace as well EU goals of cross-frontier cooperation and European integration (Bray 2004).

Compounded belongingness in the Basque Country emerges with the confluence of landscapes, "languagescapes", "culturescapes" (Appadurai 1996), and other representations of "borderscapes" (Brambilla 2015). As cultural attributes align or overlap each other, belongingness is asserted and sustained through association with plural and hierarchical attributes of bounded and defined Basque culture (Konrad 2020, 121). Language is the primary defining element, partly because of its uniqueness among European languages. Reinforcing linguistic space is a fiercely defended political space, in which, and for which, Basque nationalists have fought for their territory, and engaged in "terrorism" to this end. This political space is aligned with traditional upland livelihoods, coastal lifeways, industrial legacies, and deeply seated traditions to confirm Basque Country. Cultural solidarities and continuities are displayed and enacted in a "national" history, literary universe, gastronomy, political resistance, and economic transformation (Woodsworth 2008).

5.2.4 Quebec borders and bordering culture

Compounded belongingness as expressed by the Basques is revealed as well in other "national" projects such as the adjacent Catalans in Spain, and elsewhere in Europe as in Scotland. Michael Keating (1996, 65–106) also includes Quebec as an illustration of *Nations against the State*, wherein he explores the politics of nationalism and its implications for territorial redefinition. After October 30, 1995, when 49.4 percent of Quebec voters favoured separation from Canada, the question of secession was narrowly defeated, yet the debate about what could happen, and how secession could unfurl, continued with vigour (Young 1998). One central question related to where the borders of an independent Quebec would be situated (Reid 1997). Legal experts debated whether the principle of *uti possidetis* applied (Radan 1997). This principle of international law provides that states emerging from decolonization shall presumptively inherit the colonial administrative borders that they held at the time of independence (Ratner 1996). Quebec embraced the position but it was denied by the Supreme Court of Canada in a decision on August 20, 1998, mainly on the basis that Quebec is already an integral part of a decolonized state. Provincial borders could not become national borders (Radan 1998). Most Indigenous peoples in Quebec also opposed Quebec secession, and claimed that if Quebec could secede from Canada, they could secede from Quebec and establish their borders (Sanders 1995).

Although the debate on Quebec borders after secession still continues in some political and legal circles, the question of secession has drifted out of focus, and the construction of Quebec's "national" borders has become a project of cultural differentiation from other boundaries in Canada. Whereas most provincial boundaries in Canada are viewed as structural, Quebec's borders with both Ontario and the Atlantic provinces are envisioned additionally as cultural (Friedman 1996). In Quebec, as in Scotland, national identity and political culture are viewed by majorities of citizens as hierarchies of belonging with national affiliation articulated at several levels (Henderson 2007). Furthermore, as immigration adds to the diversity of the Quebec population, a form of "intercultural nationalism" is emerging, which, also aligned with globalization, is building a more "national" state in Quebec than in the past (Blad and Couton 2009). Northern Quebec, once predominantly Indigenous, is emerging as integral to the south through the agency of water, and hydro power development (Desbiens 2004). The Quebec national project and the construction of Quebec borders are both in a sustained state of becoming in order to ensure flexibility to adapt to changing conditions.

Quebec's borders with the U.S. states New York, Vermont, New Hampshire, and Maine are layered cultural constructions where Anglophones and Francophones, Canadians and Americans, Quebecers and New Englanders, isolated border communities, and Indigenous populations all retain identities and link with counterparts across a boundary that has only recently become securitized. Before the turning point of 9/11, and most recently the pandemic closure of the Canada–U.S. border to all but essential crossing, this border remained one of the most flexible and permeable border regions between Canada and the U.S. Descendants of nineteenth- and twentieth-century migrants from Quebec formed substantial components of the populations of the adjacent U.S. border states. After the Canada–U.S. trade agreement and North American Free Trade Agreement (NAFTA) were implemented, daily cross-border exchange, as illustrated in the Maine–Quebec woods industry linkages, produced a special borderlands character in the work zone of the cross-border region (Slowe 1991). This border culture of intertwined occupations and daily patterns also impacted people in a broader state-based border region in the U.S. and in the Quebec border regions of Monteregie, Estrie, and Chaudiere-Appalaches. Estrie, formerly known as the Eastern Townships, once contained a population that was largely

Anglophone with strong familial links to the adjacent states of New Hampshire and Vermont. The "Northeast Kingdom" (northeastern border region) remains a borderland with a cultural identity tied more closely to adjacent Quebec than to New England (Phaneuf 2013).

In recent research on the post-9/11 political culture in the U.S. states adjacent to Quebec, findings suggest that Congressional members from these states were well aware of border issues, and specifically issues related to Quebec, and that this awareness and knowledge was in sharp contrast to that exhibited by Congressional members from other U.S. States (Boucher et al. 2019). Another study focusing on the U.S. mid-term Congressional elections of 2014, shows that Quebec affects U.S. public debates in the adjacent borderland states, where being "right next door" to Quebec requires a crucial knowledge of Quebec's distinctive culture (Gagnon 2016). Quebec's cultural sovereignty and unique identity in North America remain relevant in North American integration (Gagne 2003).

In Quebec, the French language evolved in the province, borders culture into space as it borders Anglophone cultures out or restricts Anglophone enclaves in the province. Bordering is both enabled and constrained through language (Sowards 2019), and in many instances, as is the case in Quebec, the language bordering is differential, often incomplete, contested, and, ultimately, constantly evolving. Language policy aims to complete and stabilize re-bordering but codification of language and alignment of language and political boundaries is never complete (Baba and Dahl-Jorgensen 2013). Bordering culture, and particularly linguistic culture, in Spain has resulted in similar differential impacts as in Quebec and other contexts where bordering in language has been exercised (Moffette 2018).

Indigenous "hand talk" or sign language offers a fascinating counterpoint (Davis 2010). Although at first glance this form of communication may appear demeaning or prejudiced, Indigenous sign language reveals a spectrum of discourse from ceremonial to conversational forms, thus actually revealing a diversity, complexity, and adaptability of sign language. Yet, the capacity for exchanges between Indigenous and ex-European "speakers" is largely historical, whereas the capacity for communication among Indigenous people has been sustained in both ceremonial and conversational contexts.

5.2.5 "Line Dancing" at Stanstead, Quebec, and Derby Line, Vermont

At this juncture in the discussion, we change the scale to the community focus in order to engage with a set of cross-border places which are often cited and discussed when cross-border issues arise along the Canada–U.S. border. Stanstead, Quebec, and Derby Line, Vermont, are border places that epitomize *Life on the Line* (Farfan 2009). Here, border communities are not only linked across the border, but literally joined by the border as the line runs through properties, buildings, and people's lives. Whereas this situation was workable during the past, intensive securitization after 9/11 has caused substantial inconvenience and other costs. In order to reduce the transaction costs imposed by enhanced securitization, Todd Hataley and Scott J. Mason (2018) recommend engagement through the collective efficacy of common culture. In effect, this involves utilizing and building on the base of known and trusted border interactions and familiarities.

> The activity of line dancing is represented as a metaphor for how the border between Canada and the U.S. at Stanstead, Quebec and Derby Line, Vermont, is made real through human enactment, how creative human response transforms it, and at the same time, how identities are also shaped and changed by the collectively imagined border.
>
> *(Vandervalk 2020, 111)*

In the summer of 2015, Sandra Vandervalk began her fieldwork in the cross-border community by attending a line dancing class, ostensibly to connect with potential informants in the community. In her subsequent research, and building on the insights of Anne-Laure Amilhat Szary (2012b) on the geopolitical meaning of arts upsurge on the Canada–U.S. border, Vandervalk examined the impact of processes of securitization that created new ways of living in a perpetually in-between place. She illustrates how, through the metaphor of line dancing, borderlanders creatively respond to enhanced security restrictions on their mobility and actions in their border community. People work within a set of rules in line dancing, yet they create their individual body responses in the art form. Similarly, when "line dancing" at the border, people articulate individualized moves and actions to confront and align with the border (Vandervalk 2021).

> I would argue that while the project of increasing security at the border has undoubtedly increased the gulf between the two sides of the line, the border has always been central to existence, to the ways of being in the world of those who live in proximity to it. The border is a bizarre human production and enactment, and the borderlanders are participants in this enactment—they define its presence, they challenge and redefine the rules of engagement with it, and at the same time, it shapes their identities—as border people. The border is central to their life-world, its enactment is written into their bodies, and they willingly share it with those who truly understand its life-making and affirming capacities. As I found out over the course of my time in the region, new line-dancers are always welcome to the class.
>
> *(Vandervalk 2020, 113)*

5.2.6 Cultural policies and governance at borders: Akwesasne

Border culture is evident wherever boundaries separate or sort people and their goods, ideas, or other belongings. This is because different realization, knowing, and civility meet and negotiate at these edges, whether they are formal nation-state limits to territory, or lines between ethnicities, classes, or genders where othering is practiced. In these contexts, border culture is created, reinforced, challenged, removed, re-invented, enacted, and displayed in many forms. A compelling example where many of these currents meet may be found in Akwesasne, a Mohawk Indigenous reserve situated at the coincident borders of the U.S. and Canada, and the provinces of Ontario and Quebec, and state of New York (Figure 5.3). The reserves, Akwesasne in Canada and St. Regis in the U.S., are located in traditional Mohawk territory, yet the international boundary between Canada and the U.S. now dissects both the larger Mohawk culture area and the residual reserves. Furthermore, state and provincial jurisdictions, particularly for resource management and health care provision, among other sub-national authorities, also impact the Mohawk residents differentially, thus creating a confusing and costly array of barriers to movement and interaction within "Mohawk territory". The barriers have become accentuated subsequent to border security enhancements after the events of 9/11, but the Mohawk have pushed back and contested the expanded security and regulation at the international and sub-national boundaries. In response, Canada Border Services Agency (CBSA) recently moved its border inspection facility off the reserve to the

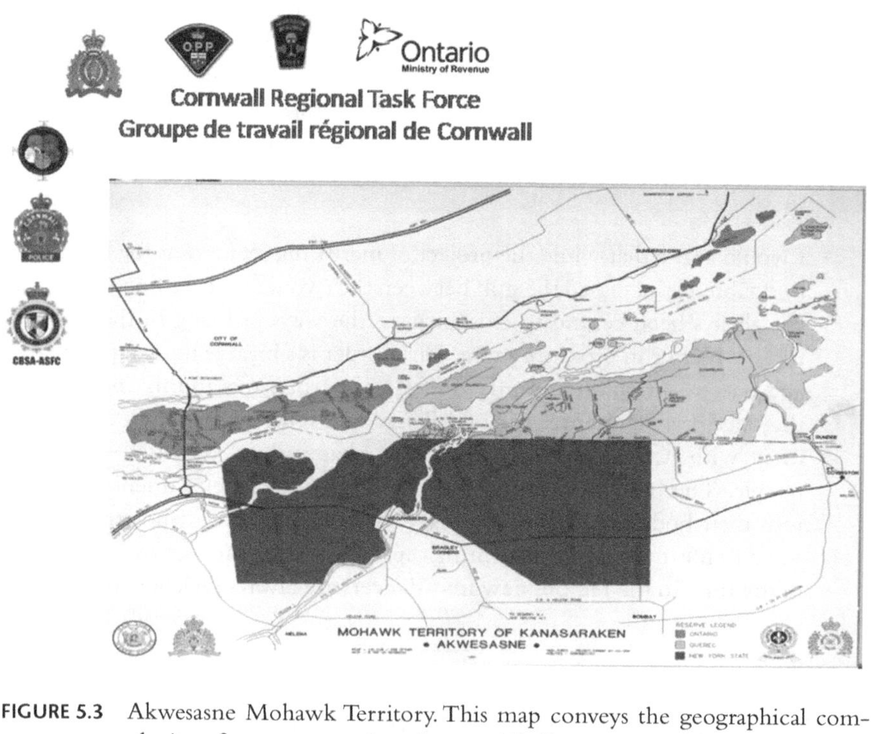

FIGURE 5.3 Akwesasne Mohawk Territory. This map conveys the geographical complexity of country, state/province and Indigenous jurisdictions. This complexity of jurisdictions compels security agency cooperation. The security agencies identified on the map have in some instances changed names and logos since the map was produced. Map reproduced courtesy of Media Relations, RCMP/GRC, Canada.

adjacent municipality of Cornwall. The U.S. facility is already just outside the St. Regis component of the Mohawk reserve. Yet, free movement within the reserve area remains hampered by CBSA requirements for Indigenous residents to report to CBSA after any crossing of the international boundary. Furthermore, sub-national jurisdiction barriers and practices in resource management, health care, licensing, education, and other facets of everyday life remain largely in place (Rouvière 2019).

In this setting, it is first instructive to differentiate culture at the border and border culture. Whereas culture at the border is evident in the Mohawk persistence as a coherent cultural entity astride the boundary between two more recently emergent, and decidedly more plural "cultural" presences—the U.S. and Canada—border culture is the expression of knowledge and realization that reveals in the imagination and production at the borders between peoples. In this regard, the Mohawk both reside at the border and "own the border" in their reserves, a fact that has now been acknowledged, albeit grudgingly, by the U.S. and Canadian border agencies with signs in English, French, and Mohawk at the ports of entry, and cultural sensitivity training for border agents. Mohawk expressions of border ownership range from a determination to move and sell goods like cigarettes throughout the reserves (thus depriving federal authorities of tax revenues) to dispersal of community facilities including churches, the lacrosse arena, community cultural centre, and essential emergency services on both sides of the border. Cross-border trips are frequent and routine in order to enable Mohawk participation in community culture as well as the day-to-day essentials of work, school, recreation, and worship. Although federal authorities aim to monitor these cross-border trips and enforce reporting requirements, Mohawk residents are increasingly resistant to the inconvenience. This is not the "romance of resistance" as is often portrayed as a cultural response for Indigenous peoples (Sparke 2008). Crossing is an essential component of the daily, weekly, monthly, and seasonal circulation pattern in Mohawk society. Crossing is actually expedited in the winter when ice roads enable more efficient linkages among portions of the reserves. As illustrated in the film *Frozen River*, these winter crossings also expand the potential for illicit movements of goods and people through the Mohawk borderlands (Dodds 2013). With the firm and drivable ice, the border is at once everywhere and nowhere. Mohawk culture now encompasses the border as well as traditional tenets of Mohawk society because the border permeates every aspect of living on the reserves. All border policies are cultural policies. Mohawk culture has become border culture.

5.2.7 Affirmation of borderlands community, place and space along the Chile–Peru border

In June, 2010, we participated in the Border Regions in Transition (BRIT) conference in the borderlands of Arica, Chile, and Tacna, Peru. Anne-Laure Amilhat Szary had researched her dissertation in this cross-border region, and established the networks to bring BRIT to this unique borderland place. We travelled throughout the cross-border region and ventured up to the high Andean plateau and the border with Bolivia. Arica and Tacna are outpost cities in the narrowed Atacama Desert between the imposing Andes and the equally dominant Pacific Ocean. Arica and Tacna are internationally recognized for their role in the nineteenth-century Pacific War to define the borders between Chile and Peru. Chile prevailed over Peru and Bolivia, and excluded access to the Pacific for Bolivia (Borchard 1922, Skuban 2007, Gonzalez Miranda 2009). The two small cities, and the adjacent region, today constitute an active border zone of exchange in an isolated region that is enclosed by imposing natural boundaries. The cities are not situated directly at the border but rather more than an hour's drive apart by automobile. Arica is located on a rare natural harbour on the linear coast, and guarded by a nineteenth-century fortress on the nearby coastal heights. Tacna is close to the coast but slightly inland in an oasis in Peru's expansive share of the Atacama Desert. In the past, the places were connected by a railway line which still operates mostly as a tourist train. Currently, the predominant link is the Pan-American Highway (Tapio Ladino and Gonzalez Gil 2014). The border is literally a "line in the sand" (Skuban 2007) punctuated only by a large and fortified border crossing facility (Figure 5.4).

FIGURE 5.4 Waiting at the Atacama Desert Border Crossing between Tacna, Peru, and Arica, Chile. Photo by Victor Konrad.

Haraldo Dilla Alfonso and Camilla Alvarez Torres (2018) characterize the border region as an assemblage of economic circuits that constitute a cross-border urban complex linking largely unusable space in between. Despite the sizeable interstitial distances, this is an intense border region; and because of the distances, particularly to other places in Peru and Chile, the region is limited largely to local arrangements and activities. There are literally millions of crossings annually in both directions although these are mainly tied to the "informal economy". The exchange is asymmetrical and favourable mainly to the Chilean city (Dilla Alfonso and Alvarez Torres 2019). Chileans access less expensive goods and services such as medical care in Tacna. Peruvians sell less expensive goods in trips to Arica. The asymmetries and the mobilities generated in these processes contribute to a strong sense of the border which further emphasizes differences between the Chilean and Peruvian places (Contreras et al. 2017). The cross-border space has been likened to a "hyper-frontier" due to its intensified and accelerated engagement and interaction, albeit in an isolated context (Guizardi et al. 2015). Michel Foucher (2000), however, reserves the concept of hyper-border for more politically active and contestable borderlines.

According to Alberto Diaz Araya (2003) a legacy of "Chilenización" in the cross-border region has contributed substantially to the asymmetry of the borderlands in addition to the more recent contributing factors of economic disparity, exchange rates, and differential mobility. In order to counteract this prevailing imaginary, and the discourses associated with it, and to establish a balanced border culture, several approaches have been forwarded to establish a positive and complementary "political psychology of border integration" (Gonzalez-Riesle 2015). One of the objectives is to establish a peace culture that moves beyond the ingrained legacy of the Pacific War and the protracted controversies, re-enactments in the landscape, historical recounting, and place branding that have enshrined the conflict in and as the cross-border region (Parodi Revoredo and Gonzalez Miranda 2014). Another objective is to develop a truly bi-national education strategy in the borderlands. A third objective is to strengthen cooperation in integrative policies and programmes. Recent improvements in the supply of cultural infrastructure in Tacna, particularly the construction and renovation of architectural components, have contributed substantially to provide spaces and venues for celebrating cross-border culture (Ale Mendoza 2018). It appears that the incipient efforts to move beyond the dualistic border cultures of Tacna and Arica, that we witnessed and debated with local academics and officials in our 2010 conference, have established some traction and led to a more integrated border culture in the Chile–Peru borderlands.

5.2.8 Turkey: In the middle and on the edge of border culture

Turkish culture addresses, records, confronts, alters, and ameliorates flows of ideas, values, identities, and beliefs that cross its borders on all of its frontiers. Turkey is at once in the middle of border culture—between east and west—and at the edges of European and Middle Eastern cultural regions. At these interfaces, identities are interrupted, and culture also expresses discrepancies between official culture and the real experiences of upheaval and disruption (Robins 1996). These distinctions are predicated on so-called civilizational difference, and articulated on the modern imaginary of nationalism as incorporated into the agenda of the modern Turkish state, legacy of the Ottoman Empire. European discourses produce a border mentality and a profound impasse in relations between Turkey and Europe (Robins 2003). The result is that cosmopolitan possibilities have been over-ridden in Turkish culture even though they pre-existed in the Ottoman Empire. Also, the result is that binary distinctions between Europe and Turkey have been frozen due to historically produced fictions of Europe and Turkey (Robins 2003). These observations by Kevin Robins raise many issues related to border culture at the margins of Turkey: How does border culture differ in the east and in the west (Varol and Soylemez 2019)? How does Turkish border culture mediate relations with, for example, Bulgaria and Russia, and not with Greece and Armenia (Grigoryan et al. 2019)? What can the situation of the stateless Kurds teach us about border culture? How has border culture been impacted with the massive waves of asylum seekers to Turkey from Middle Eastern conflicts? What is the role of border culture in intractable border conflicts such as the situation in Cyprus? All of these questions and more could consume discussion for the rest of this chapter, but we focus only on the last two questions.

The first question relates to the impact of asylum seekers on border culture. Although a new culture of migration based on Turkish–Syrian links and flows now predominates as both inflow in the south and potential outflow into the European Union, this pattern has been built on generations of migration flows between Turkey and Germany (Sirkeci and Cohen 2016). And, although border zones have been articulated as bio-political spaces, the suspension of rights and sovereign surveillance, and even death, have been long-time features of bio-politics at the border between Turkey and Europe (Topak 2014). Although for most migrants, the destination is Europe, they are obliged to wait as legal and political transformations of border control trickle down to their everyday lives in camps and other temporary settings (Strasser and Tibet 2020). Meanwhile, refugees from Syria engage with and attempt to adapt to Turkish language and culture through a combination of Turkish government programmes, the work of international agencies, and mainly their own efforts (Bicer 2017). Given the Islamic orientation of the government in Turkey, there is a focus on "religious culture and ethics" in the education of Syrian migrant children in Adana, Turkey (Kizilabdullah and Yuruk 2018). Overall, the migrants contribute to the enlargement of the "new Islamic popular culture" in Turkey by adding music, literature, and other art forms of "performance, politics, and piety" (Stokes 2014). Also, the migrants have contributed to the sustained, gendered nature of the public sphere already established in recent decades with the fashion for veiling in contemporary Turkey (Kilicbay and Binark 2002).

Next, we consider briefly the simultaneously evolving yet continuously unresolved border between North Cyprus and the Republic of Cyprus, between

Turkish Cypriots and formerly Greek Cypriots, between Greece and Turkey, and between the European Union and its "inner neighbour" North Cyprus. Anna Casaglia (2019), in a critical analysis of the EU enlargement in Cyprus, refers to the in/visibility of Turkish Cypriots, that is they are both in view and out of regard on the island. In her recent book, Casaglia (2020) paints a sensitive and detailed picture of life in the divided capital of Nicosia. She engages with the complex cultural and political geographies of the divided space, and addresses the interconnection of diverse agents operating at different scales. The conflicts, the partition, and the collective memory have contributed to a symbolism that has shifted from the geopolitical to the socio-political and socio-cultural sphere of interpretation. Renditions of border art in Nicosia reflect this. Also, inside the old Venetian walls of Nicosia, at a demilitarized checkpoint on the Greek Cypriot side of the city, symbols of Greek alignment prevail and underline the caption on the map in the photo which reads "I do not forget" (Figure 5.5). Nicosia has been interpreted as a culture of denial in "the shadows of no man's land" (Boedetje et al. 2007), where open borders may now be evident, yet minds remain closed (Sahin 2011). In an article titled "The glocal green line: The imperial cartopolitical puppeteering of Cyprus", Rodrigo Bueno-Lacy and Henk van Houtum (2019) urge us to delocalize the "green line" because, as they suggest, the problem is not between local sides but rather a succession of "imperial puppeteering"

FIGURE 5.5 A Demilitarized checkpoint in the Greek Cypriot Side of Nicosia inside the Old Venetian Walls. The caption on the map in the photo reads "I do not forget'. Note the Greek Cypriot flag symbols extending to the barrier. Photo reproduced by permission from Anna Casaglia, University of Trento.

introduced by Britain but sustained by Hellenic irredentism, Turkish nationalism, Cold War geopolitics, UN conflict resolution, and EU expansion. Their point is well developed, yet the continued intractability of the situation is in no small part sustained by local memory of conflicts, the transfer and redistribution of properties on both sides of the line, and the continued enmity of "Greek" and "Turkish" Cypriots both on the island and in places that they landed around the world. Recent efforts to humanize the green line, both in Nicosia, and along its entire extent, are promising signs that Cyprus may again become a positive place of cultural encounter (Rogge and Grunbart 2015, Konrad and Rouvière 2016).

5.2.9 The Korean DMZ and the cult of the border

Although the green line in Cyprus remains a zone with reminders of a conflict now almost fifty years old, with limited crossing points, the Korean DMZ sustains, after more than 60 years, a closed zone two and one half miles wide by one hundred and fifty-five miles long. Suk-Young Kim (2014) describes the DMZ as performing emotional citizenship: it separates ideologies and politics, yet it links past and prospective cultural continuity in an in-between space. The ambiguous yet politically divisive ontology of the DMZ makes it appealing to tourists, media, and artists (Kennedy 2016). It has become a place with zones of seeing that are artistic, touristic, and digital. Moreover, Beccy Kennedy (2016, 287) remarks, it is "difficult" for persons to see a place that is at a standstill. This reading offers a suggestion that the DMZ, one of the most dramatic spaces on the earth, a place where war and peace are one, actually has achieved a cult status, not because we may enter its space, but precisely because we are prevented from doing so. As Suk-Young Kim (2011, 381) states, both the DMZ and the DMZ Special Exhibition at the Korean War Memorial in Seoul are "staging the cartography of paradox", and recalling what was never experienced by most who view it. This perspective, "the transnational appeal of excess and otherness", has been dubbed "Asian extreme" in cult cinema (Hughes, J. 2017).

Yet, the Korean DMZ has achieved cult status for another reason as well. Even more than the green line in Cyprus, the DMZ has become a sanctuary for nature due to human exclusion from the space. In 1997, Ke Chung Kim's article in *Science* documented the preservation of biodiversity in the DMZ (Kim 1997). The situation has been characterized as "turning a diplomatic failure into an environmental success" where species of plants and animals, and unique ecosystems prevail (Brady 2008). One author has described the scene as the "exquisite corpses of nature and history" (Thomas 2009, 1). The forced preservation of rare species of plants and animals in an otherwise environmentally degraded Korean Peninsula has resulted in not only moral and environmental value of the DMZ space, but also economic value as tourists flock to look into the space (Lee and Mjelde 2007).

Perhaps the greatest value of the DMZ, in the estimation of tourists, is the emotional impact of the place and the space (Lee and Lee 2007). Perceived values

FIGURE 5.6 Korean Family Photo at the DMZ. Photo by Anne-Laure Amilhat Szary.

and satisfaction of visitors has promoted destination loyalty among tourists from South Korea and abroad (Kim and Thapa 2018). At the core of this war-related tourism are several motivations: opposition to the political regime in North Korea, knowledge and appreciation of the historical and cultural context, curiosity and adventure in a dangerous place, viewing the consequences of war, and, finally, and alternatively, nature-based tourism (Bigley et al. 2010). Among the attractions of the place is the "rogue infrastructure" of landmines (Kim 2016, 162). Visitors are drawn to the "volatile materiality of the mines, and the multiple natural, technological, and political entanglements with humans who exist alongside" (Kim 2016, 162–164). Furthermore, Korean families come to the DMZ to catch a glimpse of the land of their parents and grandparents, to engage with their ancestors, and unite symbolically with them (Figure 5.6). Although we are prevented from entering the DMZ, we may peer into it to see what war can do to a place, and how a culture of post-conflict emerges and verges into nature again.

5.2.10 Curating the border in Windsor–Detroit, and elsewhere along the Canada–U.S. border

In chapter three, we focused on the imaginaries of border culture in the Detroit–Windsor borderlands. In the following discussion the focus is on producing and curating the border in works of art and landscape inspired and created in the region. Then, we expand the discussion briefly to the Canada–U.S. border to offer some context. We begin with the impact of the works displayed at the Art Gallery of Windsor during the *Border Cultures* exhibitions (2013–2015). *Border Cultures* (Mitra 2015) has done the important cultural work of placing borders into perspective for the public, and the exhibitions provide a model for engaging cultural productions at and about the border between the U.S. and Canada. The exhibition is a challenge and a call for more attention by artists, curators, art galleries, and governments to the borders that both separate and join people. Moreover, *Border Cultures*, both the exhibitions and the book, establish a framework for extensive artistic reaction to a growing presence of borders and bordering. The framework addresses the border in everyday life as border and life unfold. The first part, as outlined in chapter three, focuses on homes and land, the second part on work and labour, and, finally, the third part on the immediacy of security and surveillance.

> Cultural production is essential to respond to borders of all kinds, and understanding this cultural production is fundamental to understanding borders. As the works featured in *Border Cultures* attest, cultural production at and about the border is linked to mobilities, agency, and citizenship. All of these human concerns and rights are now in question at the Canada–U.S. border and at borders around the globe. They are at the heart of geopolitics in a world that is changing rapidly. Cultural production at and about borders is a rich and resonant expression of how we view the border and how we deal with it. This cultural production must be understood to inform our various perspectives—security, sustainability, trade, migration, governance—surrounding borders.
>
> *(Konrad 2021, 111)*

The Border Bookmobile (2009–2013) was a component of the *Border Cultures* exhibition in 2013, where it served as a public reading room and archive at the Art Gallery of Windsor (Rodney 2021). The Border Bookmobile was created in response to the schism between local knowledge and national political narrative, and in dialogue with the concept of "insite art" (2005, Beecroft 1988). As a "transborder travelling archive, the Border Bookmobile aimed to contextualize the border cities of Windsor and Detroit within the shifting narratives of border regions in North America and other parts of the world in the aftermath of 9/11 and the 2008 economic crisis" (Rodney 2021, 44). Contained in a 1993 Chrysler minivan, the collection/exhibition also offered a place for visitors to share border impressions and stories. Although, official histories and narratives of Detroit and Windsor only tangentially reference the other place, the stories of long-time residents of both cities suggest more integrated and continuous interaction. The Border Bookmobile served to mitigate divergent narratives of national pride in Windsor and national shame in Detroit, explore the post-urban malaise in both cities, and provide a cross-border community archive. For three years before coming to rest at the *Border Cultures* exhibition, the Border Bookmobile travelled to locations throughout Windsor and Detroit as a social platform to animate and activate discussion on the past and the present in the cities, and the border policies that articulated the relationship (Rodney 2021, 44–48).

In 2018, Lee Rodney was the lead organizer of a group of artists, historians, and geographers in a mobile research-creation workshop named Buoyant Cartographies, designed to investigate the space of the Detroit River as a migratory route for wider transboundary understanding. The river was positioned as a connection rather than a division line, and the focus of attention was on shoreline locations at the river's edge. Rodney explains:

> Focusing our attention on this river border as a material site and geopolitical space enabled us to investigate alternate possibilities for sensing and envisioning the layered and conjoined histories of this fluid space. The Ojibwe name for this location is *waawiiatanongziibi*, or where the river bends, suggesting a radically different spatial imaginary than the divided space that has been established through colonial and national histories (Nahdee 2016). Experimental cartographies can thus help to develop alternate ways of experiencing such sites, an initial step toward decolonizing the spatial imaginary through a project of delinking. Our Buoyant Cartographies workshop focused on performative and intermedial investigations into spatial meanings and their construction through walking workshops conducted on the Detroit and Windsor shorelines, as well as on Peche Island, which sits in the middle of the Detroit River.
>
> *(Rodney 2021, 52–53)*

The Detroit River is engaged as the historic point of connection rather than division, and a transborder cultural geography of the Great Lakes counteracts the limited understanding of the borderlands staged through media that lock on crises of trade and migration. One of the goals of the workshop was to research, visit, and map the proposed, and contested, site of the Gordie Howe International Bridge between Sandwich, Ontario, and Delray, Michigan. Although the site is a rich location in Indigenous histories, it is currently a place of growing border complexes and industrial landscapes. Consequently, the Buoyant Cartographies workshop questioned relationships between landscape, territory, and power contributing to national narratives and prized and celebrated spaces, and, alternatively, revealed hidden and occluded histories. Buoyant Cartographies aims to complicate the role of the Great Lakes in forming part of the Canada–U.S. border. The "workshop located and marked critical insertion points in the mainstream narratives that mark public spaces along the Windsor and Detroit shorelines in official ways".

> As a form of 'research creation', Buoyant Cartographies took its lead from the spatial turn in the arts, through which new articulations of

> 'communities of sense' have been established to describe a fundamental shift in the way that we understand aesthetics and politics as mutually informing one another rather than as separated domains (Hinderliter et al. 2011).
>
> *(Rodney 2021, 56–57)*

The border between Canada and the U.S. has long inspired exhibitions of paintings, photographs, sculpture, and installations of art at or near border places, and particularly border crossings. In the nineteenth and twentieth centuries, caricatures conveyed the border in politics, trade, and everyday life (Nicol 2012, 2015). *Between Friends/Entre amis* (Canada, NFB 1976), Canada's gift to the U.S. on the occasion of the U.S. bicentennial, depicted local ties, cross-border linkages, cooperation, mutual interests, and intertwined identities at places all along the thousands of kilometres/miles of the boundary. The border was seen as both one, from sea to sea, and as regional components compartmentalized to make it palpable. Yet, the celebration of the border in *Between Friends/Entre amis* and Peter Max's brightly coloured illustrations at border crossings aimed at conveying consistency and unity along the line (Konrad 2021, 109).

Anne-Laure Amilhat Szary (2012a) notes that artists have worked consistently to capture the significance and convey the meaning of the border between Canada and the U.S. After the events of 9/11 and the emergence of the border as a more defined site of security and insecurity, artists in both countries took the pulse of the border and expressed the changes in the borderlands. Some of these artists and their work are featured in *Border Cultures*, and they are part of wide-ranging assessments of the consequences of re-bordering the continent. Most of the exhibitions and events, however, have tended to be associated with specific localities along the border, as in the case of the *Stanstead Project, or How to Cross the Border*, or with particular cultural groups, such as Indigenous peoples in *Border Zones* at the University of British Columbia Museum of Anthropology (Amilhat Szary 2012a). *Border Zones* also extends First Nations to interpret what the border means for Indigenous peoples in terms of differentiation and hybridity. The localized focus is desirable given the extensive, regional nature of the Canada–U.S. border, and the complexities addressing that broad range of issues that vary between regions and places along the border.

> Yet the border has itself grown to be a more formidable and common foe in the psyche of Canadians and borderland Americans, thus adding a similarity and sameness to border concerns across the continent and calling for artistic production to address these issues.
>
> *(Konrad 2021, 110)*

Art displays at borders and at politically sensitive places similar to borders affect the meaning of art works as well as the meaning of place (Amilhat Szary 2012b). "Border art is being strengthened by the harshening of border politics and this factual coincidence lays the ground for a geopolitical analysis of a renewed display of art" (Amilhat Szary 2012b, 219). This may be a new kind of art such as art that combines fusion and displacement and shatters the distorting mirrors of the "Western avant-garde" (Gómez-Peña 1991). For a growing number of border specialists, particularly those dealing with highly visible and sensitive border zones, the border art scene renews the debate on the display of art, it questions public and private modes of display in disputed places, and it contributes to the emergence of art geopolitics (Amilhat Szary 2012b, 222, Ganivet 2019).

Border studies specialists continue to question what and where cultural production contributes in our epistemology of the border. "Can cultural production be more than a side issue in border studies?" (Dell'Agnese and Amilhat Szary 2015, 4). Our position, quite emphatically and clearly, is that cultural production is more than a side issue or "soft" side of border studies because it frames and illuminates the political (Amilhat Szary 2012a).

> Yet, according to Lee Rodney and Srimoyee Mitra (Mitra 2015), although there are some important border artworks and projects, conversations specifically about the Canada–U.S. border in the contemporary art world are quite limited. So, even though visual arts on the Canada–U.S. border (Amilhat Szary 2012a), and elsewhere that people engage and cultural productions about the border (Schimanski and Wolfe 2017), has increasingly called attention to the border, there remains an immense potential and need to explore the Canada–U.S. border, and borders in Canada more generally, through art. Also, it is important to connect the insights on the Canada–U.S. border with those gained through such works as those, for example, appearing in the Way Past Kennedy Road Collective's exhibit *Sanctuary Inter/rupted*, which explores issues of internal bordering and unbelonging in Toronto (Fakhrashrafi et al. 2019). In these works, Black, Indigenous, and other racialized women artists raised issues of everyday deportability, the ways that illegalization is mapped on the body, and the consequent refusal to reaffirm the multicultural nation.
>
> *(Konrad 2021, 110–111)*

5.3 Impossible borders, troublesome borders, the rejection of crossings (even by culture), and the immutability and irrevocability of border culture

Some borders are not crossed. It is not that the borders are impermeable, but rather that social, political, and cultural differentiation aligned with these borders is so strong that surveillance detects the differences and security forces act accordingly to limit or eliminate engagement. Often, these impossible borders are acknowledged on both sides and those who should not cross simply do not cross. Characteristically, in a world of enhanced flows, these borders are securitized, whereas in previous eras, prohibitions may have been sufficient to ensure compliance. In the era of globalization and post-globalization, borders have become more complex and in motion (Amilhat Szary and Giraut 2015, Konrad 2015, Nail 2016), as well as multiscalar (Laine 2016) and polymorphic (Burridge et al. 2017), thus contributing and expanding barriers to crossing. In the following discussion we encounter impossible borders linked to cultural differentiation. Cultural borders may create mental barriers whereas crossing these cultural borders and associated mental borders may enhance creativity (Maddux and Galinsky 2009) as well as understanding and acceptance. Cultural borders may be associated with boycott politics. Another context is Indigenous art refusing to cross borders. In North America, the southern border of the U.S. is considered problematical, in part due to its cultural contrast with the border between the U.S. and Canada (Correa-Cabrera and Konrad 2020). The U.S.–Mexico border may not be impossible, but it vacillates between immutability and constant cultural flux. We begin with perhaps the most vivid example of an impossible border, the green line boundary between the Palestinian West Bank and Israel.

5.3.1 Israel/Palestine

David Newman has written extensively about borders, bordering, and territory, particularly as they relate to Israel–Palestine. *Territory and Borders* (Newman 2013) draws from his knowledge and understanding of the complex territorial issues. He has characterized a shift from national to post-national territorial identities in Israel–Palestine (Newman 2001), and focused on the role of borders in conflict resolution (Newman 2002, 2012). In a 2014 Border Regions in Transition (BRIT) conference hosted by Newman and his colleagues, participants were provided with the opportunity to visit sites along and on both sides of the security wall that now divides the West Bank from Israel. Insights into the complex border culture that has evolved in the Israeli–Palestinian conflict and its aftermath need to be visualized to comprehend more fully how culture and politics intertwine in this intensely bordered space.

An all-day (BRIT) field trip from Ben Gurion University in Beer-Sheva conveyed participants in sight of the wall to the north of the country, and the Sea of Galilee, where we turned in to the West Bank and traversed the territory in sight of Israeli settlement enclaves and Palestinian towns, before engaging in a privileged crossing at a highly securitized point along the boundary. This experience, as well as additional field trips into parts of Jerusalem and views of the surrounding territories and settlements left an indelible impression of a divide so extensive that a borderlands culture of sharing and interaction appeared to be impossible. Contributing to this impression is height, or perhaps more aptly put "altitude", in which Israeli neighbourhoods in Jerusalem are elevated and look down on Palestinian enclaves, and West Bank Israeli settlements perch on hilltops and "climb" up secure slopes (Levy 2008, Bille and Battaglia 2020). Also significant, delineation of territory extends to zones of differentiation and exclusion within the West Bank, to limit and control Palestinian movement and to enable Israeli movement. Overlapping is discouraged if not outright forbidden. Culture, in all its facets—language, dress, food, music, and certainly religion—is compartmentalized. Yet, the border is not a simple line of demarcation but rather a weaving, interrupted, and complex artifact (Fellner 2020). Furthermore, Israelis are not one cohesive monolith of culture and polity but rather a complex amalgam of beliefs, sects, ethnicities, and values. Similarly, Palestinians remain divided and stratified in numerous ways. Also, the border wall has become a repository of contestation surrounding the strict differentiation of cultural boundaries. The wall, and the spaces associated with it, display a wide array of images and narratives to convey not only concerns about and resistance to the security wall, but also visions of what could be (McDonald 2009). The wall is a pretext to what is invisiblized by it (Latte Abdallah and Parizot 2015).

In a recent consideration of the Israel–Palestine conflict and the contested histories surrounding the conflict, Neil Caplan (2019) weighs the intractable and tractable aspects of the conflict, and although no definitive resolution is promoted, the sense of promise is palpable, if only because hostilities have become more muted in recent years. Although the rhetorics of belonging in national narratives remain in Israel/Palestine (Bernard 2018), and the parallel discourses continue (Matthews 2011), there is also evidence that the borders are being re-approached (Sufian and Levine 2007) with a recognition that borders, and border walls, remain organic and open to revisioning. The intractable position that territory is the kernel of the nation (Yiftachel 2002), and that ethnocracy is the means to the realization of Israel (Yiftachel 1999), are now reviewed and debated (Dowty 2012). There appears to be an emerging realization that legal repression at the border (Ron 2000) and heightened levels of border anxiety, particularly among Palestinians (Long 2006), are not sustainable conditions, and that the so-called "road map" to conflict resolution may have been a "road map to nowhere" (Reinhart 2006). The paradox of "unbounded territoriality" in the Israel/Palestine context is that it has led to territorial control and settler colonialism (Hughes 2020).

Another paradox is that the wall of suppression has become the internationally viewed canvas of resistance (Parry 2011). Samud, meaning steadfastness or steadfast perseverance, has become the ideological theme and political strategy of Palestinians to resist oppression, and Samud has been conveyed through graffiti and murals on the separation wall as a "global message board" (Larkin 2014). In a sense, the globe has become "Palestinianized" and Samud has become the art of existence (Gould 2015), and this art has gone beyond resistance (Salih and Richter-Devroe 2014). The art has extended beyond the Palestinians to empower self-expression beyond Israel's walls and checkpoints in an effort to reclaim humanity (Ziadah 2012). In this way, the wall speaks through transnational networks in and beyond Palestine (Toenjes 2015), and the representations of conflict connect images of war, resistance, and identity in Palestinian art (Gandolfo 2010). Yet, architecture and art have also become weapons in the Israeli–Palestinian conflict (Delso 2018). A form of concrete punishment, or "concrete sealing" of Palestinian houses associated with persons targeted by the Israeli Defense Force, has become an effective weapon, and it achieves an extreme artistic and aesthetic result to reinforce pre-existing asymmetries of space and time relationships of Israeli and Palestinian populations (Weizman 2007). As Connie Gagliardi (2020) suggests in a recent article, the artistic expressions have become extreme, and "Palestine is not a drawing board" as is expressed with finality in the defacement of street art on the separation wall. Also, much happens on the walls within the refugee camps where graffiti relates the situation of the Palestinians (Lehec 2017, 2020).

5.3.2 Boycott politics cross borders and create new borders

Activism across borders for Palestinian justice has generated the Boycott, Divestment and Sanctions (BDS) movement aimed at ending the occupation of Arab lands, ending discrimination against Palestinians in Israel, and respecting the Palestinian right of return to occupied territory (Morrison 2015a). For example, the "We Divest" campaign targeted immense retirement funds like TIAA-CREF in the U.S. to divest holdings profiting from Israeli investment (Morrison 2015b). Although the boycott movement and associated divestment and sanctions aimed at territorial reinstatement and de-bordering, one impact is to create new borders with the BDS tools. Although these new borders may complicate and confuse boundaries, they do not reinstate territorial conditions without the participation of all parties/polities involved. David Newman (2016) comments that academic boycotts are not effective blanket boycotts of Israel, and that they fail except to draw media attention. On the other hand, Judith Butler (2015) contends that academic boycotts that focus on cultural and political institutions that fail to oppose the occupation of the West Bank do have an impact.

Boycotts of Israel are a recurrent effort that engages one constituency or another, but unlike the boycott of South Africa in the later years of apartheid, the boycotts have not achieved "true transnationality" (Van Bochove 2012). The Arab boycott of the 1990s actually transitioned from boycott to economic cooperation (Feiler 1998) and academic boycotts have been similarly limited (Newman 2008) although religious motivation develops a strong cultural element in boycott (Muhamad et al. 2019). As cross-border solidarity and lockdown expand in the academic boycott movement, and as advocates focus on more effectively defined rights of education and freedom of movement for Palestinians, and target the neoliberalization of the academy, and academic repression and censorship of the Palestinian question, the prospects for boycott success increase (Maira 2021). A chronology of art conveys how at one point it was possible to "cross the wall" through art, but then after 2006, and the boycotts, this was no longer possible (Amilhat Szary 2013). Key components of boycott politics, then, are clear definition of a leading, or at most a few, central issues, articulation of concerns to accomplish activism across borders, and political spirituality to motivate and sustain border crossing. As Luis D. León (2014) explains, "La Causa" of Cesar Chavez was transmuted into a religious movement where boycotting grapes won hearts and minds, but performing religion in the context of political theatre enabled border crossing in several contexts.

5.3.3 North American borders in comparative perspective: The troublesome U.S.–Mexico border

The border between Mexico and the U.S. has become increasingly troublesome, not because the border is impassable but because it is permeable and increasingly plural and confounding. Furthermore, as Guadalupe Correa-Cabrera and Victor Konrad (2020) illustrate, the Mexico–U.S. border also crystallizes American political division and draws media attention and focus from other borders in North America. An impossible border does not work, but a troublesome border may not work effectively. Indeed, it is hampered to the extent that extreme measures are invoked in an attempt to make it function. Again, as in Israel, and in increasing numbers of other contexts around the globe (Vallet 2014, Casey and Watkins 2014), walls are constructed as desperate measures to repair the border. Michael Dear (2013) assembles a compelling argument "why walls won't work" at the U.S.–Mexico divide. The walls do not address the underlying causes of a dysfunctional border. Scholars of the border and an increasingly diverse and extensive number of authors have grappled with the question of what is wrong with the U.S.–Mexico border. One major issue is that most of their works in English look at the border from the American side. Also, due to the complexity of the border, most approaches focus on one facet of the problem.

The following brief discussion offers an overview of the extent and dimensions of this troublesome border. Some solutions are implicit, but the purpose is to outline and characterize the culture of the border. Tony Payan (2016) envisions U.S. and Mexico in a collision of three "border wars": drugs, immigration, and homeland security. Although these border wars may be examined as distinct, they do comprise a triad of intertwined and irreconcilable problems. The informal economy of the drug trade has emerged as a primary contributor to the dysfunctional border (Staudt 1998). Numerous innovations made by the drug cartels based in Mexico have contributed to sustained drug smuggling across the border. Among these are a reliance on female drug smugglers (Campbell 2008) and the engagement of migrants to carry the illicit cargo into the U.S. (Slack 2019). The spectre of the "illegal alien" predominates at the border (Nevins and Nevins 2002), and no effort to reverse the notion of illegality has been successful (Chacon and Davis 2018). The result is that migrant life is devalued and migrant deaths have accumulated substantially at the border (Nevins 2007). Also, Latina/o inhabitants of the borderlands are questioned about their citizenship and rights in their homeland (Cisneros 2014). They proclaim "the border has crossed us" (Anzaldúa 1987, Cisneros 2014). The border has become a "hard line" articulating "life and death" (Ellingwood 2009), a "line in the sand" (St. John 2012) where fugitive landscapes accumulate (Truett 2008), and homeland security prevails and policing the border is the highest priority (Andreas 2012). The promise of NAFTA—open markets—was subverted by the rapid enhancement of closed borders (Andreas 1996). The "children of NAFTA", Mexican workers, found themselves working for Americans across the border in Mexico and gaining little from free trade (Bacon 2004). A "hyperborder" has been created at the southern edges of the U.S. (Romero 2008), and this border construct is imbued with kinetic forces (Nail 2016) that propel it into a dystopic space where illegality and insecurity prevail. Here, in the "shadow of the wall" a culture of violence rules (Heyman 2018).

5.3.4 Indigenous art in border spaces of refusal: Reconfiguring the impossible border

What do you do with an impossible border? Do you simply take it out? Do you change it to make it fit into your perspective on space and place? Indigenous people in North America have limited spaces in places that they were assigned in colonization. The limitations, either to alienation in remnant reserve lands, or restrictions to crossing boundaries constructed and enforced in postcolonial North America, are viewed or ignored as impossible borders by Indigenous people across the continent. The racial geographies have not been inherited but rather "Indian given" (Saldana-Portillo 2016) with the result that spaces and places are bordered by agency out of Indigenous control. Heidi Weigand and Colin Howell (2021) recount the story of how the Haudenosaune lacrosse team from Canada, bound for a tournament in the United Kingdom, was stopped in New York before flying to the UK, because, although their Indigenous identification (Haudenosaune Passport) was sufficient to allow passage between Canada and the U.S., the Haudenosaune Passport was not acceptable for access to the UK and back again into North America from Europe. For the Haudenosaune lacrosse team, the boundary around North America had become an impossible border. This is a graphic illustration of the bordered condition of the "Inconvenient Indian" as identified by Indigenous writer Thomas King in his novels and short stories (Mayer 2021). An illustrated edition of the award winning and bestselling *Inconvenient Indian* (King 2017) is now available with 150 images that add colour and context to the original work (King 2013). The images also provide additional perspective into the transnational politics of contemporary Indigenous culture (Huhndorf 2011), and these images convey insights to how Indigenous North Americans reconfigure the impossible border (Nabokov 2002).

Reece Jones (2012b) has identified "spaces of refusal" where sovereign power meets resistance at the border. Audra Simpson (2014) expands the notion and shows how the "ruse of consent" further complicates these spaces of refusal for Indigenous people in North America and Australia. Beenash Jafri (2020) then takes a cue from Simpson's concept of refusal to link settler colonial relationships with Indigenous people to ongoing practices of diasporic refusal. Jafri writes:

> To elaborate on what this refusal can look like, I turn to South Asian Canadian filmmaker Ali Kazimi's experimental documentary *Shooting Indians: A Journey with Jeffrey Thomas* (1997), a profile of Iroquois (Haudenosaune) photographer Jeffrey Thomas that self-reflexively explores the politics of spectatorship and representation through an examination of Native subjects of Edward Curtis' portrait series. Understanding Shooting Indians' refusal requires not only an analysis of its representational politics, but the contextualization of film as (a) a generative effect of South Asian diasporic artists in Toronto engaging questions of Indigenous sovereignty and relationality through art and community discussion, and (b) as itself opening possibilities for continued conversations and cultural production among South Asian diasporas and Indigenous peoples in Toronto.
>
> *(Jafri 2020, 110)*

Encounters with spaces of refusal at borders in Toronto, at the Canada–U.S. border, and borders more widely, are shared by diasporic and Indigenous communities, and conveyed in their cultural productions.

Indigenous encounters with the border have been portrayed as images of running the "Medicine Line" (Morris 2011) and renditions of entangled resistance in Indigenous art, literature, and film (Rader 2011). Significantly, as outlined in the previous paragraph, and in earlier references in this book, the entangled resistance aligns with other minorities and marginalized peoples as in the film *Frozen River.* Dylan Miner (2014), an Anishnabeg artist whose work has been referenced in the discussion of border culture at Windsor–Detroit, weaves border cultures in *Creating Aztlan: Chicano Art, Indigenous Sovereignty, and Lowriding across Turtle Island.* At the Mexico–U.S. border, intertwined discourses of crisis have encouraged and enabled collaborative performance art at the border wall (Anderson 2020). Matthew Irwin (2017) describes a project by the Postcommodity Art Collective to convey the Indigenous presence on the U.S.–Mexico border at Douglas, Arizona, and Agua Prieta, Sonora. In October 2015, twenty-six yellow, helium filled balloons, each ten feet in diameter, and painted with "scare eyes", were launched at the border to "ward off Western civilization" in an installation named "Repellent Fence". Although this installation, and various other Indigenous art works at North American borders convey serious messages, the approach is often subtle and the humour of "Indians playing Indian" is usually conveyed (Siebert 2015).

Reconfiguring the impossible border for Indigenous North Americans is to engage in *Creative Combat.* Jarrett Martineau's (2015) dissertation at the University of Victoria in Victoria, Canada, explores Indigenous art, resurgence, and decolonization. Not only is the work a study of resistance to ongoing forms of settler colonization such as bordering, but also the thesis traces Indigeneity's "opaque transits", trajectories and fugitive forms in art to illustrate the resistance to performing Indigeneity according to settler colonial logics. Resistance is to commodification as well as to control, and a goal is to "constellate new forms of community". Indigenous art is viewed as "noise to colonialism's signal" and the force of the art gains power through movement and action in the creative combat. The primary action is to turn away from the colonial state and towards one another, and to take out the border.

5.4 Following the line and enhancing the line: The cultural production of border walls

In chapters three and four, our attention to border walls and culture focused on the imagination of border walls and how these imaginaries aligned with or were differentiated from national border constructs. The border studies literature also extends to considerations of the cultural production of border walls, fences, and barriers. This is the subject of the following brief discussion of how border culture emerges from the construction of walls in historical China, and how this cultural production continues to resonate in China and around the world. Also, the discussion addresses the cultural production of the U.S.–Mexico border wall, and explores how "Trump's wall" and its predecessors have altered or galvanized border culture in North America. This discussion develops themes introduced previously in this chapter in the discussion of the wall between Israel and Palestine.

In order to address the question of border culture production in conjunction with border walls, we have narrowed our focus considerably to highlight only one historical, yet persistent, and one contemporary illustration. The literature related to border walls is expanding significantly to signal one of the major research poles within border studies. As elaborated in chapters three and four, most of this work is focused on border walls as manifestations of power, political delineations, social constructs, sites of resistance, and even screams of insecurity. Are border walls—the Great Wall of China, the Berlin Wall, and the Mexico Border Fence among them—simply "great blunders" as suggested by Helmut Langerbein (2009)? In comparing the Great Wall of China and the "Great" Trump Wall, Mimi Yang (2017, 1) suggests that there is a "wall-DNA" in a cultural blueprint, and that by decoding the wall-DNA in American culture we find that the Trump Wall is more a mental than a physical construct. Yet, the Trump Wall, both in its mental and physical incarnations is redefining American cultural identity. And, like the Great Wall of China, the interwoven symbolic and physical manifestations of the Trump Wall may reverberate for a long time to remind people of the potential of "barbarians at the wall" (Villalon 2007) and the exclusionary nature of "White Borders" (Jones 2021).

5.4.1 The Great Wall of China: Reproduction, extension, and commodification of the border

China's Great Wall, based on a cumulative system of walled frontiers, and spanning centuries of construction, adjustment, enhancement, and expansion (Lattimore 1937, Turnbull 2012), persists as *one* artifact to remind us how the idea of a wall once produced is reproduced as concurrent and mutually reinforcing constructs. This cultural blueprint, as identified in the previous paragraph (Yang 2017), is even more durable than the physical manifestation of the wall, because the "wall" is actually a succession of discrete and often geographically distinct constructions built from 221 BC to AD 1644 (Waldron 1983, Turnbull 2012, Jing 2015). Erik Ringmar (2019, 124) concludes that there are many walls but there is no "Great Wall of China". Ringmar views the Great Wall as a mindset existing in the imagination of Europeans who had limited access to China before the twentieth century. Furthermore, he sees walls as limiting access to civilization—"walls cannot talk … they 'stonewall' us"—and the Great Wall became a symbol of a stationary mindset that epitomized China, and may well still do so (Ringmar 2019, 123–124). "Culture may require walls to be erected, civilization requires walls to come down" (Ringmar 2019, 123). Border culture, as represented by the Great Wall of China is more complex and diverse than meets the eye.

The culture of the Great Wall of China is shared at national and international scales. Visitors to China view predominantly the Great Wall, whereas Chinese citizens see a broader manifestation of border history and wall components, as well as the Great Wall. Both Chinese tourists and visitors see the wall that they read about and view in photos and films, and this perspective is not eclipsed by the actual sight and visitation, because the massive scale of the walls and their extent in mountainous terrain allow only a glimpse at ground level. This locality of perspective and border heritage resource access has enabled community participation at World Heritage site engagement points (Su and Wall 2014). Here, global-local relationships may be developed to a degree because of the extensive international visitation, but the governance of the symbolic messages remain Chinese (Su and Wall 2012). Furthermore, the culture of the Great Wall is not shared transnationally because tour groups are guided in distinct languages, and rarely interact.

The Chinese metaphor of the Great Wall has been appropriated and applied in cyberspace to contain messaging in China, and to exclude platforms such as Google and Twitter that are not Chinese or that could allow Chinese to engage more globally. The Great Wall is being reproduced as well in bordering and re-bordering in the Himalayas, western Chinese provinces, Hong Kong and Taiwan, and maritime claims in the South China Sea. The actual Great Wall, or certainly components of it, may be in ruins (Chu and Ju 1993), but the representation has been extended and commodified in many ways throughout China. The paradox is that, whereas the Great Wall remains a strong representation in Chinese culture and politics, the major thrust of China is to move beyond its borders through initiatives like the Belt and Road (Callahan 2018).

5.4.2 Trump's ? border wall

Former U.S. president Trump's border wall, and the decades-long construction of fences and walls along the U.S.–Mexico border, highlights a similar paradox. The Trump Wall was aligned with making America great again, and making the U.S.

number one among nations, but it is also situated between America and the outside world. This is the paradox of gated globalism (Coleman 2005). Leading border studies specialists like Reece Jones (2012a and 2012c) have questioned "Why build a border wall?" It is revealing to examine the justifications in Trump's U.S.–Mexico border wall proposal. After analyzing communicative techniques and strategies in thirty of Donald Trump's speeches between 2016 and 2018, Angela C. Garcia (2019) concludes that the border wall proposal was reformulated into a debate about border security, and the diverse ways of denigrating illegal migrants to the U.S. Another study, "Trump's Twitter tales", illustrates a narrative framing of stories of crime and crisis associated with the border and the wall that was not in line with official statistics but still impacted policy (Schuchs Carr et al. 2020).

Thomas Nail (2013) identifies three types of power at work in the context of the U.S.–Mexico border wall: sovereign exclusion of illegal life, disciplinary detention of surveilled life, and bio-political circulation of migratory life. These political strategies are diverse and may be antagonistic to each other, but Trump managed to weave them into a rhetoric that aligned the power strategies. Melissa W. Wright (2019) counters the proposal for Trump's wall by arguing that the concept denies social justice as well as environmental well-being in the borderlands. The border wall "raises issues that are central to political ecological and human geographic scholarship into governance across the organic spectrum" (Wright 2019, 511). "Border thinking" (Mignolo 2012), and the comprehension and acknowledgement of border culture enables us to frame debates and coalesce strategies for maintaining diversity and preservation in borderlands.

According to Josiah Heyman (2010) understanding U.S.–Mexico border culture requires embracing the challenge of asymmetrical interpretation. Not only is it necessary to comprehend two distinct cultures, and at least one hybridized culture, but also it is important to recognize the asymmetries in the relationships among cultures. Border walls do not aid in simplifying the analysis but rather work to complicate the cultural interrelationships by alternatively and selectively allowing permeability even though theoretically the walls are deemed as barriers. Daniel D. Arreola (2004) illustrates these conditions of the fence and gates of Ambos Nogales through postcard landscape exploration. Ronald Rael (2017) looks beyond the imposition of the border wall to appreciate but critique the architecture. Kenneth D. Madsen (2011) sees the barriers as landscape of domestic political compromise. The photograph of the U.S.–Mexico border wall at its western extent on the Pacific coast in Tijuana captures the power and finality of the wall yet it also conveys the hope and spirit of the cultural interaction at this place (Figure 5.7).

5.5 Queering the line: Taking the border to all kinds of limits

In her novel *Forgetting the Alamo, Or Blood Memory*, Emma Perez (2003, 122) explores the "challenges of excavating the invisible and unheard" in "queering the borderlands". Her protagonist is Micaela Campos, "a *tejana* baby butch

FIGURE 5.7 Pacific End of the U.S.–Mexico Border Wall from the Mexican side. Photo by Victor Konrad.

who must avenge her father's death at the battle of San Jacinto just a month after the fall of the Alamo" (Perez 2003, 122–123). Perez describes how her story "inscribes a gaze on the borderlands that is geographic and spatial, mobile and impermanent" (Perez 2003, 123). This gaze allows and enables transition and transformation. In the contemporary Israeli–Palestinian situation, "sexual politics and most specifically issues concerning queerness, which might initially seem marginal in this context, do in fact play a central role in both facilitating and transgressing the current hostile and oppressive relationship between Israelis and Palestinians" (Hochberg 2010, 493). Critical geographies aim to question the active production of space as heterosexualized, and address the heterosexual bias of geographical theorizing (Oswin 2008). This leads to a "critical reading and deployment of the notion of 'queer space' in geography and it highlights the alternative queer approach inseparable from feminist, materialist, postcolonial and critical race theories" (Oswin 2008, 89). Queer space may then be viewed as border space, and border space is arguably "queered space" (Amilhat Szary 2020). Ursula Biemann (2002) characterizes performing the border as gendered, in transnationalized bodies, with transgressive identities, and in a technologized space. In this section, we introduce the notion of taking the border to all kinds of limits, and how this expands our appreciation and understanding of border culture. We focus on brief discussions of queer borders and bordering, technologies of movement and networks and their impact on borders and culture, the bio-politics of border crossing, and the re-bordered space of disabled and disadvantaged people.

5.5.1 Queer borders and bordering

Borders are made and broken at LGBTQ+ pride parades as discursive and material borders are maintained by marchers and audience, but they wear thin and threaten to break and disrupt the social order as the parades gain momentum and energy (Johnston 2002, 75). Queer bodies become embodied contradictions in the paradoxical performances of pride parades (Johnston 2007). Queer assemblages and queer intersections may then reveal deeper understanding of borders and bordering processes between people, and particularly of the production of border cultures associated with these divisions and binaries (Hall and Jagose 2013). For example, when race is factored in to queer relationships conveyed in film, a "queer matrix of borderline" emerges, with the polarization of "white neurotics" and "black primitives" (Walton 1999, 243). Yet, as Anjali Arondekar (2005, 236) observes, in queer postcolonialities outside the U.S., linking sex and race becomes a "dynamic dilation of difference" with new forms of racisms and imperialisms emerging, thus challenging the translation of previous analytical paradigms of race and queerness. Not only does the queer cultural matrix of borderline shift, but also the nature and visibility of, for example, queer "Arab" and "Muslim" groups is altered.

We will focus briefly on "queering Asia" (Wilson 2006, 1) as an example and a step towards our discussion of the bio-politics of migration. Megan Sinnott (2010) evaluates borders, diaspora, and regional connections in the trends related to Asian queer studies. Several observations ground the work: there is transnational movement of concepts, bodies, and imagery; transnationalism, diaspora, and border crossings are comingled; binaries such as traditional/modern and local/global are sublimated if not transcended. The result is that we find "complex responses to, and extensions of, culturally determined systems of gender, nationalism, capitalist labor and consumer practices, urbanization, and transnational movements" (Sinnott 2010, 17–18). Furthermore, there are connections and commonalities across Asia and within sub-regions that lead to a departure from the national culture framework. Queering Asia, then, has shifted an LGBTQ+ culture in space and time within the continental framework, and established sub-cultures that also cross boundaries and evolve new borders.

5.5.2 The "queer politics of migration": Bio-politics at the border

"The queer politics of migration", Nicholas De Genova (2010, 101) suggests, shows an "affinity between crucial articulation of this radically open-ended politics of migrant presence with the similarly abject and profoundly destabilizing politics of queer presence". Commonalities include irreverence and disaffection for state power, irreversible presence, and intractable challenge of their own intrinsic incorrigibility. Bina Fernandez (2018) extends the argument in a consideration of the pragmatic complexities, indiscretions, and subversions of queer border crossers. Queer border crossers are viewed as transgressors of boundaries who disrupt normative categories, are contradictory and provocative, and appear alien to the majority, but open critical and transformative possibilities (Fernandez 2018, 194). In response to the question of what happens when two inherently unstable signifiers "queer" and "border" intersect, Fernandez (2018, 194–196) offers that modes of inclusion, dissidence, submission, or normalization are produced. Yet, both queer border crossers and all migrants at the border are resisting the hetero-normative imaginary of the nation-state (Otto 2018a and 2018b).

The nation-state now performs the biometric state while it expands neoliberal management of space/time at contemporary borders to govern borders and bodies. According to Benjamin Muller (2010), the creation of the biometric state to mitigate security and risk "elides the border(ing) experience". Suspect(ing) biometrics now prevail to ascertain: Who are you, and where are you going? Are you who you say you are? The articulation of the geopolitics of migration and mobility aims to "bring geopolitics to bear on biopolitics in relation to migration", by "displacing attention on borders to the crossers of borders themselves", and "shifting focus from state-defined subjects (as objects of analysis) to emerging techniques of governance and/or government(ality)" (Hyndman 2012, 243). Jennifer Hyndman's purpose is to reveal the multiple relations of power that produce patterns of geopolitics and oblige people to live in exile and on the edge (Hyndman and Giles 2016). The culture of this existence is epitomized by "invisible lives and silent disasters", securitization at the expense of protection in refugee camps, the indeterminacy and indefiniteness of exile, and the ultimate "coldness" of refugee resettlement after long term exile (Hyndman and Giles 2016). The unsettled border culture of violence and displacement follows the refugee through war, detention, and the "slow violence" of waiting (Hyndman 2019, 3), and this border culture then adheres to the refugee in resettlement and produces multigenerational trauma.

Other spatial contexts emerge for this border culture along the protracted refugee journey from dispersal to resettlement. These refugee spaces constitute an externalization of denial of asylum by governments around the world. A combination of insecurity and fear has "produced political space to advance security measures including the externalization of asylum", and by cutting off access to sites where claims may be made by refugees (Hyndman and Mountz 2008, 249, Maguire et al. 2018). Alison Mountz (2011, 118) calls this space the "enforcement archipelago" where offshore enforcement is practiced at or associated with the margins of the nation-state. Here, at these bordered locations, nation-states may innovate and exercise spatialities of power, and expand the socio-spatial production of borders (Silvey 2008). Also, at these and other spaces where people in migration are bordered, geographies of gender and migration are illuminated by the social construction of scale, politics of inter-linkages between place and identity, and socio-spatial production of additional borders (Silvey 2006). According to Rachel Silvey (2004), feminist advances in migration studies have accrued through a more complete understanding of power, difference, and mobility. Queering the line has become a euphemism for bordering beyond the nation-state where the politics of difference prevail as power shifts to reveal constantly emerging queer geographies.

Border cultures, like many other cultures, produce icons that epitomize and sharpen the values and beliefs of the culture. The border(ed) culture of refugees and asylum seekers gained an icon as "little" Alan Kurdi's body was photographed washed up on a Mediterranean beach. A poignant reminder and symbol of the plight of the powerless refugee, the iconic photo was appropriated by #humanitywashedashore, Ai Weiwei, and Charlie Hebdo in both decontextualizations and recontextualizations of the imagery to confirm and consolidate the iconic status (Mortensen 2017, 1142), but also incensed as well as shocked many, causing them to be strongly denounced. According to Penelope Papailias (2019) we are both seeing and unseeing dead refugee bodies as mourning memes, "spectropolitics", and haunting images. The spectacularization has rendered Alan Kurdi's body unsacred and the subject of virtual voyeurism, thus locking the image into a "sensorium" (after Rancière) (Ibrahim 2018, 1). Here, the body is "trapped in an aesthetic regime re-centering the migrant body as a new type of inhumanity in Europe". The "internet constantly re-appropriates iconic imagery into new artistic and creative formats where images can be stripped from context, re-hashed, and endlessly circulated as cultural artifacts, bearing the burden of history yet being disenfranchised from it" (Ibrahim 2018, 1).

5.5.3 Technologies of movement/networks

One of the factors that contributed to the rapid acceptance and proliferation of the Alan Kurdi icon for the plight of border crossers was the Internet, and its extensive reach in the global population. In the Mediterranean refugee crisis, surveillance and countersurveillance had a mediating effect (Dijstelbloem 2015). Although the Internet enables global communication, it is not without borders, as was illustrated by the fragmentation of the Internet during the Ukrainian crisis in 2014 (Douzet et al. 2020). As Frederick Douzet and Aude Gery (2021, 96) state unequivocally, "Cyberspace is used, first and foremost, to wage wars." Consequently the Internet creates and proliferates borders, provides security, yet wrenches it away, and espouses stability while also constantly destabilizing cyberspace (Cattaruzza 2019). Some countries, China most prominent among them, exclude selected "open" platforms like Google, and replace them with Chinese search systems and online service providers. In addition to this bordering effect, variation in Internet access across the world also creates borders although universal access to the technology is increasing rapidly (Allen and Vollmer 2018).

On the one hand, communication tools change the very essence of how people interact with each other, particularly in generations X, Y, and Z that have grown up with the Internet. For them social networking through the Internet transforms categories of time and space, thus providing a sense of a world without borders (Levickaite 2010). The online culture that is produced is extensive, widely acknowledged, accessible to users, and linguistically consistent. Online tools are scaled from the local to the multinational level of public participation, including otherwise marginalized peoples and communities (Sieber 2003). In institutions such as universities, a cadre of "third space professionals" (first space and second space are faculty and administration) is growing and being enabled by online networking to advance "cross-border" collaborations between and within institutions (Veles et al. 2019). International online distance education is also expanding rapidly and it has a worldwide reach. Although this approach to higher education has the potential to cross borders and cultures, the educational culture produced may be impacted by institutional and cultural imperialism (Sadykova and Dautermann 2009).

This form of online institutional and cultural imperialism is a part of a more extensive and potentially insidious cyber regionalism. In the sparsely populated polar region, cyber regionalism has produced and enhanced scientific, economic, and cultural integration (Sorlin 2016). North American cyber regionalism, according to Alexander Rudolph (2021) may be less benign. Rudolph makes the case for an online cultural demarcation or re-bordering of Canadian culture through increased loss of control of the Internet contributions to culture in Canada. "Rudolph employs cultural-semantic modeling to show the physical reality of the cyberspace, and the 'new' regionalism of active integration and convergence in North America, and particularly between the U.S. and Canada" (Konrad and Kelly 2021b, 26). In a sense, this is the second wave of cultural imperialism from the U.S. impacting Canada. The first wave occurred in the mid to late twentieth century with the diffusion of television, film, and other media from the U.S. to its neighbour. Alexander Rudolph (2021) concludes that, instead of bowing to integration and convergence, Canada is actively engaged in using new media as a form of cultural and linguistic education, not only in *la Francophonie* and Indigenous communities, but also more generally by making content more accessible and expedient through video-sharing platforms, innovation, and preservation of cultural heritage. Border culture in the realm of new media is multidimensional and multiscalar.

New media cultures also extend to the realms of fantasy film and Internet gaming where borders are produced and destroyed with violent ease. In the film *RoboCop 2*, for example, cyborgs are annihilated in an array of "bursting borders and bodies with queer machines" (Allison 2001). Holger Potzsch (2011) traces the discursive production of self as heroic human, and other as less than human, in the film *Black Hawk Down*, and several video games set in the context of war. "Shifting borders" takes place in the game space as well as between the game space and the gallery space (Bailey 2019, 125), and shifting borders extends to multiple territorial contexts where territories are invaded and re-constituted simultaneously, or in manners of sequence (Abrams et al.

2012). The new videogame *Animal Crossing: New Horizons* (2020) is analyzed from a border studies perspective to illustrate how geographical borders may be altered into temporal and cultural dimensions, and it blurs borders between the real and virtual world (Benti and Stadtmann 2021). In summary, video games, similar to recent film and television, seek and create different markets across cultural borders, but they also localize genres and themes (Esser et al. 2016). Brendan Keogh (2021, 116) designates this production as a "cultural field" (following Bourdieu) that is "locally situated and constituted by a contested range of activities and identities implicated in interrelated economic, cultural, and social forces".

5.5.4 Disabled and disadvantaged people at borders

Some production of cultural fields at the border aligns with bio-physical and psychological fields. Disabled and disadvantaged people are characteristically multiply bordered at nation-state boundaries because they must negotiate security apparatus as well as entry restrictions that are not imposed on "the ableist" or non-disabled people (Alshammari 2017). Whereas citizens of the European Union who are disabled are provided with supporting technologies to ensure the requirement of accessibility at EU entry points (Oostveen and Lehtonen 2018), this practice is not universal even throughout countries of the global north. At border crossing points between the U.S. and Canada, and particularly in airports, facilities for disabled people have been developed and upgraded according to accessibility requirements. Yet, for the disabled "incomer" the border remains an "invalidating intersection" (Hughes, B. 2017, 467), and this intersection is not addressed sufficiently in the literature of border studies.

Even more apparent is the lack of attention to disabled and disadvantaged refugees and asylum seekers, although the literature is extensive on forced migration based on an ableist approach. Despite the fact that refugees and asylum seekers originate from countries with the world's highest numbers of disabled people, these people arriving at borders are caught in an epistemological, ontological, and practical invisibility, and they are "cast aside in Eurocentric disability studies" (Pisani and Grech 2017, 2). Maria Pisani and Shaun Grech (2017, 1) go on to say that "disability studies fail to critically engage with issues of sovereignty, borders and bodies beyond the protection of the state", and they call for a "critical interrogation of intersectionality of forced migration and disability studies". In refugee camps and detention centres in the U.S., the intersection of disability and humanitarian confinement has become starkly apparent (Mirza 2014). In Canada, discourses of "risk and protection mask dominant health discourses that construct immigration applicants with disabilities as the 'inadmissible other'" (El-Lahib 2016, 1). In Australia, a country with a long record of immigration restrictions on people with disabilities, disabled refugees and asylum seekers are made invisible within the remote resettlement landscape (Soldatic et al. 2017). In all of these contexts, the border is compounded further for lesbian and disabled women who additionally locate heterosexuality as a boundary at the border (Beckett 2004).

5.6 Conclusions: COVID-19 and the reinforcement of border culture

The current pandemic reveals emphatically that the response to the virus is a form of border politics (Kenwick and Simmons 2020). A culture of "border orientation" is expressed as states make efforts to control the spread of the virus through the use of various symbols and structures. Public opinion about the virus is shaped by the state. Instead of heeding the guidelines of the World Health Organization, and developing a consistent, transnational response to the pandemic, many countries, and most notably the U.S., decided to approach the crisis in their own way and establish a border orientation towards the problem. During the pandemic, governments have consistently externalized the virus which initially was demonized as the China virus, and most recently articulated culturally as British, South African, and Brazilian virus strains or variants. Lenore Manderson and Susan Levine (2020) focus on the risk, fear and fall-out of the COVID-19 pandemic in their editorial in *Medical Anthropology*. They contrast the unprecedented political-cultural reaction of nation-states to contain the virus, with lack of "cultural" norms and sensitivities in the care of the people infected by the virus. Similarly contrasting are nightmares of transmission from privileged to underprivileged bodies (wealthy and healthy versus poor and ill), and underprivileged bodies to privileged bodies (India surge to the Western world). China has inflated the "efficiency" of dictatorship in containment, whereas a combination of Trump's eugenicist policies, with extreme individualism among many Americans, have made the U.S. first a leader in infections, and then a leader in resistance to effective measures to combat the virus. The state has been as much if not more in the way as opposed to showing and leading the way in the confrontation and management of the COVID-19 pandemic.

COVID-19 related behaviours have differed across cultures on scales of optimism–pessimism, general trust in a solution, and conspiracy theories (Jovancevic and Milicevic 2020). Research in Eastern Europe and Latin America illustrates cross-cultural variance in most behaviours except the fear of food shortages and resultant stock-piling and hoarding which is confirmed as a top priority. Another study confirms that culture counts in discerning effects of COVID-19 on mental health in Australia (Furlong and Finnie 2020). Geert Hofstede's (2011) multidimensional construct of culture (1. Power Distance, 2. Uncertainty/Avoidance, 3. Individualism/Collectivism, 4. Masculinity/Femininity, 5. Long/Short-Term Orientation, and 6. Indulgence/Restraint) is utilized to identify which communities are more resilient. Findings reveal that Aboriginal communities are at the highest risk in most dimensions, and Asian communities show the impact of increased racial micro-aggressions and xenophobia. In Sub-Saharan Africa, another study finds that the right cultural fit in the COVID-19 response is locally relevant and culturally appropriate intervention through mobilization and engagement of the diaspora (Renzaho 2020). Again, the solution, not surprisingly, lies in global cooperation and alignment of mitigation strategies, yet this target remains out of focus.

Whereas social distancing has become a global response and mitigation procedure to combat COVID-19, there are cultural differences. In the Swiss Cantons, mobility declines significantly less in German speaking areas (Deopa and Fortunato 2020). With higher trust among people there is a lower reduction in mobility. Ruben Durante et al. (2021) introduce the concept of "asocial" capital accrued in civic culture through social distancing. A study in Italy, carried out between January and May 2020, showed that mobility declined throughout the country but it declined more in areas with higher civic capital. Consistent results were also recorded for Germany. According to Manderson and Levine (2020, 369), social distancing is a form of embodied re-knowledging which also includes other physical manifestations such as bumping elbows in recognition rather than shaking hands. Yet, the "capacity to respond [with social distancing measures] has been uneven along the predictable fault lines of class, race and gender". Those who manage daily schedules and routines effectively to stay distanced, and maintain avoidance, "reek of White privilege" (369). Most of the privileged exhibit the "neoliberal urge to move on with life as usual regardless of the risk" and it appears that the "virus' DNA is coded to attack our strongest neoliberal urges" (370). Manderson and Levine (2020, 370) conclude that the virus is forcing people to act counter-intuitively, not only for protecting themselves, but also to protect the medically and socially vulnerable. This is well illustrated in anti-vaccination sentiment that is at an all-time high in the U.S., with over 40% of Republicans acknowledging that they will never be vaccinated (Levin 2021).

The border culture produced in response to the COVID-19 pandemic is extensive and chilling in its counter-intuitive tenacity. Although various characteristics of this border culture continue to emerge, and become apparent through extensive studies aimed at learning and in many instances re-learning how humans react to threats and disasters of global magnitude, there is confirmation that uncoordinated human response split along statist lines, and other cultural divides, is ineffective and ultimately deadly. The border culture produced in response to the pandemic represents a contrast to the nurturing and connective border cultures commonly associated with globalization trends and transnational interactions. The final chapter of the book will focus on the transnational dimensions of border culture, and explore both the positive and negative implications of the culture revealed through human interaction across boundaries.

References

Abrams, Sandra Schamroth, Hannah R. Gerber, and Melissa L. Burgess. 2012. "Digital worlds and shifting borders." In Bronwyn Williams, and Amy A. Zenger, eds. *New Media Literacies and Participatory Popular Culture Across Borders*. New York: Routledge, 90.

Agamben, Giorgio. 2005. *State of Exception*. Chicago: University of Chicago Press.
Agnew, John. 1994. "The territorial trap: The geographical assumptions of international relations theory." *Review of International Political Economy* 1, (1): 53–80.
Alfonso, Haraldo Dilla, and Camilla Alvarez Torres. 2018. "Economía e intercambio desigual en una región transfronteriza: Arica, Chile - Tacna, Peru." *Estudios fronterizos* 19: 1–20.
Alfonso, Haraldo Dilla, and Camila Alvarez Torres. 2019. *La Vuelta de Todo Eso. Economía y sociedad en la frontera chileno/peruana: el complejo urbano transfronterizo Tacna/Arica*. UNAP. RIL editores.
Allen, William L., and Bastian A. Vollmer. 2018. "Clean skins: Making the e-border security assemblages." *Environment and Planning D: Society and Space* 36, (1): 23–29.
Allison, Anne. 2001. "Cyborg violence: Bursting borders and bodies with queer machines." *Cultural Anthropology* 16, (2): 237–265.
Alshammari, Shahd. 2017. "Troubling academe: Disability, borders, and boundaries." *Journal of Middle East Women's Studies* 13, (3): 458–460.
Amilhat Szary, Anne-Laure. 2012a. "Wall and border art: The politics of art display." *Journal of Borderlands Studies* 27, (2): 213–228.
Amilhat Szary, Anne-Laure. 2012b. "The geopolitical meaning of a contemporary visual arts upsurge on the Canada-U.S. border." *International Journal: Canada's Journal of Global Policy Analysis* 67: 951–962.
Amilhat Szary, Anne-Laure. 2013. "L'artiste passe-muraille? La resistance au passage du mur entre Israel et la cisjordanie. (The artist walking through walls? Resistance and barrier crossings between Israel and the West Bank)." *Espaces Temps.net* Travaux 19.11.2013. http://www.espacetemps.net/articles/artiste-passe-muraille-la-resistance-au-passage-du-murs-entre-israel-et-la-cisjordanie-2/hal-0157684v1.
Amilhat Szary, Anne-Laure. 2020. "A new research agenda to move beyond (a)gendered regions." *Regions and Cohesion* 10, (3): 10–29.
Amilhat Szary, Anne-Laure, and Frédéric Giraut, eds. 2015. *Borderities: The Politics of Contemporary Mobile Borders*. London: Palgrave Macmillan.
Anderson, Britta. 2020. "Embodiment against borders: Discourses of crisis and collaborative performance art on the U.S.-Mexico border wall." *Arizona Journal of Hispanic Cultural Studies* 24, (1): 129–148.
Andreas, Peter. 1996. "U.S.: Mexico: Open markets, closed border." *Foreign Policy* 103: 51–69.
Andreas, Peter. 2012. *Border Games: Policing the U.S.-Mexico Divide*. Ithaca: Cornell University Press.
Anzaldúa, Gloria. 1987. *Borderlands/La Frontera: The New Mestiza*. San Francisco: Aunt Lute Books.
Appadurai, Arjun. 1990. "Disjuncture and difference in the global cultural economy." *Theory, Culture and Society* 7, (2–3): 295–310.
Appadurai, Arjun. 1996. *Modernity at Large: Cultural Dimensions of Globalization*. Minneapolis: University of Minnesota Press.
Araya, Alberto Diaz. 2003. "Problemas y perspectivas sociohistoricas en el norte chileno: análisis sobre la 'Chilenización' de Tacna y Arica." *Si Somos Americanos: Revista de Estudios Transfronterizos* 5, (4): 49–81.
Arendt, Hanna. 2013 [1958]. *The Human Condition*. Chicago: University of Chicago Press.
Arondekar, Anjali. 2005. "Border/line sex: Queer post colonialities, or how race matters outside the United States." *Interventions* 7, (2): 236–250.

Arreola, Daniel D. 2004. "The Fences and Gates of Ambos Nogales: A postcard landscape exploration." In Andrew Grant Wood, ed. *On the Border: Society and Culture between the United States and Mexico*. Latham: Rowman and Littlefield, 43–80.

Armstrong, Karen. 2004. *Remembering Karelia: A Family's Story of Displacement During and after the Finnish Wars*. Oxford: Berghahn.

Autissier, Anne-Marie. 2006. "Quelles priorités pour les politiques culturelles européennes?" *Raison présente* 160, (1): 73–81.

Baba, Marietta L., and Carla Dahl-Jorgensen. 2013. "Language policy in practice: Re-bordering the nation." *International Migration* 51, (2): 60–76.

Bacon, David. 2004. *The Children of NAFTA: Labor Wars on the U.S.-Mexico Border*. Berkeley: University of California Press.

Bahnev, Aleksandar. 2021. "On the occasion of Frederik Barth's 'ethnic groups and boundaries': How ethnic boundaries, ethnicity, and boundaries in social structures are to be viewed." Сборник доклади от годишна университетска научна конференция 2021, Том 8 Научно напрвление "Социални, стопански и правни науки https://www.academia.edu/49263276/ON_THE_OCCASION_OF_FREDRIK_BARTHS_ETHNIC_GROUPS_AND_BOUNDARIES_HOW_ETHNIC_BOUNDARIES_ETHNICITY_AND_BOUNDARIES_IN_SOCIAL_STRUCTURES_ARE_TO_BE_VIEWED.

Bailey, Andrew Remington. 2019. "Shifting borders." *Press Start* 5, (2): 125–136.

Barth, Fredrik, ed. 1969. *Ethnic Groups and Boundaries: The Social Organization of Cultural Difference*. Oslo and Boston: Universitetsvorlaget and Little Brown.

Beckett, Clare. 2004. "Crossing the border: Locating hetereosexuality as a boundary for lesbian and disabled women." *Journal of International Women's Studies* 5, (3): 44–52.

Beecroft, Chris. 1988. "Insite: Art for public places." Catalogue of an exhibition. March-April, 1988, Centre for the Arts Gallery, Hunter Street, Hobart.

Benti, Behailu Shiferaw, and Georg Stadtmann. 2021. "Borders in motion: An application related to the video game animal crossing: New horizons." Europian University Viadrina Frankfurt (Oder) Business Administration and Economics. *Discussion Paper* 423.

Bernard, Anna. 2018. *Rhetorics of Belonging: Nation, Narration and Israel/Palestine*. Liverpool: Liverpool University Press.

Bicer, Nurrat. 2017. "The views of Syrian refugees migrating to Turkey on the Tukish language and culture: Kilis case." *Journal of Education and Training Studies* 5, (3): 97–109.

Bie, Q.L., C.S. Li, and S.Y. Zhoa. 2014. "Evaluation of the effectiveness of border policies in Dehong prefecture of Yunnan, China." *Sustainability* 6, (8): 5284–99.

Biemann, Ursula. 2002. "Performing the border: On gender, transnational bodies, and technology." In Claudia Sadowski Smith, ed. *Globalization on the Line: Culture, Capital, and Citizenship at U.S. Borders*. New York: Palgrave Macmillan, 99–118.

Bigley, James D., Choong-Ki Lee, Jinhyung Chou, and Yooshik Yoon. 2010. "Motivations for war-related tourism: A case of DMZ visitors in Korea." *Tourism Geographies* 12, (3): 371–394.

Bille, Franck ed. 2020. *Voluminous States: Sovereignty, Materiality and the Territorial Imagination*. Durham: Duke University Press.

Blad, Cory, and Philippe Couton. 2009. "The rise of an intercultural nation: Immigration, diversity and nationhood in Quebec." *Journal of Ethnic and Migration Studies* 35, (4): 645–667.

Boedetje, Freerk, Henk van Houtum, and Olivier Kramsch. 2007. "'The shadows of no man's land': Crossing the border in the divided capital of Nicosia, Cyprus." *Geographica Helvetica* 62, (1): 16–21.

Borchard, Edwin M. 1922. "The Tacna-Arica controversy." *Foreign Affairs* 1, (1): 29–48.
Boucher, Vincent, Christophe Cloutier-Roy, and Élisabeth Vallet. 2019. "Frontiérités québécoises: Représentations de la zone transfrontalière québéco-américaine au Congrès des Etats-Unis, 2001–2016." *The Canadian Geographer/Le Géographe canadien* 63, (1): 27–42.
Brady, Lisa M. 2008. "Life in the DMZ: Turning diplomatic failure into an environmental success."*Diplomatic History* 32, (4): 585–611.
Brambilla, Chiara. 2015. "Exploring the critical potential of the borderscapes concept." *Geopolitics* 20, (1): 14–34.
Brambilla, Chiara, Jussi Laine, James W. Scott, and Gianluca Bocchi, eds. 2015. *Borderscaping: Imaginations and Practices of Border Making*. Farnham: Ashgate.
Bray, Zoe. 2004. *Living Boundaries: Frontiers and Identity in the Basque Country*. Bern: Peter Lang.
Bueno-Lacy, Rodrigo, and Henk van Houtum. 2019. "The glocal green line: The imperial cartopolitical puppeteering of Cyprus." *Geopolitics* 24, (3): 586–624.
Burridge, Andrew, Nick Gill, Austin Kocher, and Lauren Martin. 2017. "Polymorphic borders." *Territory, Politics, Governance* 5, (3): 239–251.
Butler, Judith. 2015. 14. "Exercising rights: Academic freedom and boycott politics." In Akeel Bilgrami, and Jonathan R. Cole, eds. *Who's Afraid of Academic Freedom?* New York: Columbia University Press, 293–315.
Callahan, William A. 2018. "The politics of walls: Barriers, flows, and the sublime." *Review of International Studies* 44, (3): 456–481.
Campbell, Howard. 2008. "Female drug smugglers on the U.S.-Mexico border: Gender, crime, and empowerment." *Anthropological Quarterly* 81, (1): 233–267.
Canada, NFB (National Film Board of Canada). 1976. *Between Friends / Entre Amis*. Toronto: McClelland and Stewart.
Caplan, Neil. 2019. *The Israel-Palestine Conflict: Contested Histories*. New York: John Wiley and Sons.
Casaglia, Anna. 2019. "Northern Cyprus as an 'inner neighbor': A critical analysis of European Union enlargement in Cyprus." *European Urban and Regional Studies* 26, (1): 37–49.
Casaglia, Anna. 2020. *Nicosia Beyond Partition: Complex Geographies of the Divided City*. Milano: Edizioni Unicopli.
Casey, Edward S., and Mary Watkins. 2014. *Up against the Wall: Reimagining the U.S.-Mexico Border*. Austin: University of Texas Press.
Cattaruzza, Amael. 2019. *Géopolitique des données numériques: pouvoir et conflits à l'heure du big data*. Paris: Le Cavalier Bleu.
Chacon, Justin Akers, and Mike Davis. 2018. *No One is Illegal: Fighting Racism and State Violence on the U.S.-Mexico Border*. Chicago: Haymarket Books.
Chu, Godwin C., and Yanan Ju. 1993. *The Great Wall in Ruins: Communication and Cultural Change in China*. Albany: SUNY Press.
Cisneros, Josue David. 2014. *The Border Crossed Us: Rhetorics of Borders, Citizenship, and Latina/o History*. Montgomery: University of Alabama Press.
Coleman, Mathew. 2005. "U.S. Statecraft and the U.S.-Mexico border as security/economy nexus." *Political Geography* 24, (2): 185–209.
Collins, Timothy W. 2009. "The production of unequal risk in hazardscapes: An explanatory frame applied to disaster at the U.S.-Mexico border." *Geoforum* 40, (4): 589–601.
Contreras, Yasna, Marcela Tapia, and Nannette Liberona. 2017. "Movilidades y praticas socioespaciales fronterizas entre Arica y Tacna. Del sentido de frontera a la transfrontericidad entre ciudades." *Dialogo andino* 54: 127–141.

Cornell, Stephen. 1992. "Land, labor, and group formation: Blacks and Indians in the United States." In Jean-Robert Rouge, ed. *Frontière et Frontières Dans Le Monde Anglophone*. Paris: Presses de l'Université de Paris-Sorbonne, 37–54.

Correa-Cabrera, Guadalupe, and Victor Konrad, eds. 2020. *North American Borders in Comparative Perspective*. Tucson: University of Arizona Press.

Davis, Jeffrey E. 2010. *Hand Talk: Sign Language among American Indian Nations*. Cambridge: Cambridge University Press.

Diana, Antonella. 2013. "The experimental governing of mobility and trade on the China-Laos frontier: The Tai Lue case." *Singapore Journal of Tropical Geography* 34, (1): 25–39.

Dijstelbloem, Huub. 2015. "Mediating the Mediterranean: Surveillance and countersurveillance at the southern borders of Europe." In Yolande Jansen, Robin Celikates, and Joost de Bloois, eds. *The Inequalities of Migration in Contemporary Europe: Detention, Deportation, Drowning*. London: Rowman and Littlefield, 103–120.

Dear, Michael. 2013. *Why Walls Won't Work: Repairing the U.S.-Mexico Divide*. New York: Oxford University Press.

De Genova, Nicholas. 2010. "The queer politics of migration: Reflections on 'illegality' and incorrigibility." *Studies in Social Justice* 4, (2): 101–126.

De Marchi, Bruna, and Anna Maria Boileau, eds. 1982. *Boundaries and Minorities in Western Europe*. Milan: Franco Angeli.

Dell'Agnese, Elena, and Anne-Laure Amilhat Szary. 2015. "Borderscapes: From border landscapes to border aesthetics." *Geopolitics* 20, (1): 4–13.

Delso, Rodrigo. 2018. "Concrete punishment: Time, architecture and art as weapons in the Israeli-Palestinain conflict." *Political Geography* 66: 57–66.

Deopa, Neha, and Piergiuseppe Fortunato. 2020. "Coronagraben: Culture and social distancing in times of COVID-19." Culture and Social Distancing in Times of COVID-19. June 23, 2020. http://dx.doi.org/10.22139/ssrn.3635287.

Desbiens, Caroline. 2004. "Producing North and South: A political geography of hydro development in Quebec." *The Canadian Geographer/Le Géographe Canadien* 48, (2): 101–118.

Dodds, Klaus. 2013. "'I'm still not crossing that': Borders, dispossession and sovereignty in *Frozen River* (2008)." *Geopolitics* 18, (3): 560–583.

Douzet, Frederick, and Aude Gery. 2021. "Cyberspace is used, first and foremost, to wage wars: Proliferation, security, and stability in cyberspace." *Journal of Cyber Policy* 6, (1): 96–113.

Douzet, Frederick, Louis Petiniaud, Loqman Salamatian, Kevin Limonier, Kave Salamatian, and Thibaut Alchus. 2020. "Measuring the fragmentation of the internet: The case of the border gateway protocol (BGP) during the Ukrainian crisis." In *2020 12th International Conference on Cyber Conflict (CyCon)* v. 1300: 157–182. IEEE.

Dowty, Alan. 2012. *Israel/Palestine*. London: Polity.

Durand, Frederic. 2015. "Theoretical framework of cross-border space production: The case of the Eurotropolis Lille-Kortrik-Tournai." *Journal of Borderlands Studies* 30, (3): 309–328.

Durante, Ruben, Luigi Guiso, and Giorgio Gulino. 2021. "Asocial capital: Civic culture and social distancing during COVID-19." *Journal of Public Economics* 19: 104342.

During, Roel, et al. 2007. "Cultural differences in European cooperation: Learning from INTERREG practice." *Final Report of the INTERACT Project CULTPLAN*. http://www.cultplan.org/downloads/RAPPORT520DEF202.

El-Lahib, Yahya. 2016. "Dominant health discourses in action: Constructing people with disabilities as the 'inadmissible other' in Canadian immigration." *Disability Studies Quarterly* 36, (3).

Ellingwood, Ken. 2009. *Hard Line: Life and Death on the U.S.-Mexico Border.* New York: Vintage.
Esser, Andrea, Iain Robert Smith, and Miguel A. Bernal-Merino, eds. 2016. *Media Across Borders: Localizing TV, Film and Video Games.* New York: Routledge.
Faist, Thomas. 2014. "Brokerage in cross-border mobility: Social mechanisms and the (re)production of social inequalities." *Social Inclusion* 2, (4): 38–52.
Fakhrashrafi, Mitra, Jessica Kirk, and Emily Gilbert. 2019. "Sancturary inter/rupted: Borders, illegalization, and unbelonging." *The Canadian Geographer/Le Géographe Canadien* 63, (1): 84–99.
Farfan, Matthew. 2009. *The Vermont-Quebec Border: Life on the Line.* Chicago: Arcadia.
Feiler, Gil. 1998. *From Boycott to Economic Cooperation: The Political Economy of the Arab Boycott of Israel.* New York: Psychology Press.
Fellner, Astrid M. 2020. "Countermapping corporeal borderlands: Border imaginaries of the Americas." In F. Weber, C. Wille, B. Caesar, and J. Hollstegge, eds. *Geographien der Grenzen. Raume-Grenzen-Hybriditaten.* Wiesbaden: Springer, 287–300.
Fernandez, Bina. 2018. "Queer border crossers: Pragmatic complicities, indiscretions and subversions." In Dianne Otto, ed. *Queering International Law Possibilities, Alliances, Complicities, Risks.* New York: Routledge, 193–212.
Foucher, Michel. 2000. "The geopolitics of front lines and borders." *Geopolitics* 5, (2): 159–170.
Friedman, Lawrence M. 1996. "Borders: On the emerging sociology of transnational law." *Stanford Journal of International Law* 32: 65.
Furlong, Yulia, and Tanya Finnie. 2020. "Culture counts: The diverse effects of culture and society on mental health amidst COVID-19 outbreaks in Australia." *Irish Journal of Psychological Medicine* 37, (3): 237–242.
Gagliardi, Connie. 2020. "Palestine is not a drawing board: Defacing the street art on the Israeli separation wall." *Visual Anthropology* 33, (5): 426–451.
Gagne, Gilbert. 2003. "Cultural sovereignty, identity, and North American integration: On the relevance of the U.S.-Canada-Quebec border." *Quebec Studies* 36: 29–51.
Gagnon, Frederick. 2016. "Right next door: Quebec and the 2014 electoral marketplaces of ideas in New York, Vermont, New Hampshire and Maine." *Quebec Studies* 61: 77–109.
Gandolfo, K. Luisa. 2010. "Representations of conflict: Images of war, resistance, and identity in Palestinian art." *Radical History Review* 106: 47–69.
Ganivet, Elisa. 2019. *Border Wall Aesthetics: Artworks in Border Spaces.* Bielefeld: Transcript Verlag.
Garcia, Angela Cora. 2019. "Bordering work in contemporary political discourse: The case of the US/Mexico border wall proposal." *Discourse and Society* 30, (6): 573–599.
Gómez-Peña, Guillermo. 1991. "A binational performance pilgrimage." *TDR* 35, (3): 22–45.
Gonzalez Miranda, Sergio. 2009. "El Norte Grande de Chile: La definición histórica de sus limites, zonas y líneas de fronteras, y la importancia de las ciudades como geo símbolos fronterizos." *Revista de historia social de las mentialidades* 13, (2): 9–42.
González-Riesle, Alvaro. 2015. "Political psychology of border integration." *LIBERABIT. Revista Peruana De Psicología* 21, (2): 269–298.
Gould, Rebecca Ruth. 2015. "Samud: The palestinian art of existence." *World Policy Journal* 31, (2014): 99–106.
Gregory, Derek. 2004. *The Colonial Present.* Oxford: Blackwell.
Grigoryan, Aleksandr, Knar Khachatryan, and Vahram Ter-Matevosyan. 2019. "Armenia-Turkey border opening: What determines the attitudes of Armenians?" *Caucasus Survey* 7, (1): 25–43.

Guizardi, M., F. Valdebenito, E. Lopez, and E. Nazal. 2015. "Condensaciones en el espacio hiperfronterizo: Apropiaciones migrantes en la frontera norte en Chile." In M. Guizardi, ed. *Las fronteras del transnacionalismo. Límites y desbordes de la experiencia migrante en el centro y norte de Chile.* Santiago: OchoLibros, 254–257.

Hall, Donald E., and Annamarie Jagose, eds. 2013. *The Routledge Queer Studies Reader.* New York: Routledge.

Hataley, Todd, and Scott J. Mason. 2018. "Collective efficiency across borders: The case of Stanstead, Quebec and Derby line, Vermont." *Journal of Borderlands Studies* 33, (3): 433–444.

Henderson, Ailsa. 2007. *Hierarchies of Belonging: National Identity and Political Culture in Scotland and Quebec.* Montreal and Kingston: McGill-Queen's University Press.

Heyman, Josiah. 2010. "U.S.-Mexico border cultures and the challenge of asymmetrical interpenetration." In Hastings Donnan, and Thomas B. Wilson, eds. *Borderlands: Ethnographic approaches to security, power, and identity.* Lanham: University Press of America, 21–34.

Heyman, Josiah. 2018. *The Shadow of the Wall: Violence and Migration on the U.S.-Mexico Border.* Tucson: University of Arizona Press.

Hinderliter, Beth, William Kaizen, Vered Maimon, Jaleh Mansoor, and Seth McCormick. 2011. *Communities of Sense: Rethinking Aesthetics and Politics.* Durham: Duke University Press.

Hochberg, Gil Z. 2010. "Introduction: Israelis, Palestinians, Queers: Points of departure." *GLQ: A Journal of Lesbian and Gay Studies* 16, (4): 493–516.

Hofstede, Geert. 2011. "Dimensionalizing cultures: The Hofstede model in context." *Online Readings in Psychology and Culture* 2, (1): 1–26.

Horacio, Larrain B. 1993. "Pueblo, etnia o nacion? Hacia una clarificación antropológica de conceptos corporativos applicable a las comunidades indigenas." *Revista de Investigaciones Cientiicas y Technologicas y Ciencas Sociales* 2: 19–36.

Hu, Zhiding, and Victor Konrad. 2018. "In the space between exception and integration: The Kokang borderlands on the periphery of China and Myanmar." *Geopolitics* 23, (1): 147–179.

Hughes, Bill. 2017. "Impairment on the move: The disabled incomer and other invalidating intersections." *Disability and Society* 32, (4): 467–482.

Hughes, Jessica Anne. 2017. "Asian extreme as cult cinema: The transnational appeal of excess and otherness." PhD thesis, University of Queensland, Australia.

Hughes, Sara Salazar. 2020. "Unbounded territoriality: Territorial control, settler colonialism, and Israel/Palestine." *Settler Colonial Studies* 10, (2): 216–233.

Huhndorf, Shari M. 2011. *Mapping the Americas: The Transnational Politics of Contemporary Native Culture.* Ithaca: Cornell University Press.

Hyndman, Jennifer. 2012. "The geopolitics of migration and mobility." *Geopolitics* 17, (2): 243–255.

Hyndman, Jennifer. 2019. "Unsettling feminist geopolitics: Forging feminist political geographies of violence and displacement." *Gender, Place and Culture* 26, (1): 3–29.

Hyndman, Jennifer, and Alison Mountz. 2008. "Another brick in the wall? Neo-refoulement and the externalization of asylum by Australia and Europe." *Government and Opposition* 43, (2): 249–269.

Hyndman, Jennifer, and Wenona Giles. 2016. *Refugees in Extended Exile: Living on the Edge.* London: Routledge.

Ibrahim, Yasmin. 2018. "The unsacred and the spectacularized: Alan Kurdi and the migrant body." *Social Media and Society* 4, (4): 1–9.

Insite Art. 2005. "The insight transborder archive." https://insiteart.org/insite-2005/scenarios/the-insight-transborder-archive.
Irwin, Matthew. 2017. "Suturing the borderlands: Postcommodity and Indigenous presence on the U.S.-Mexico border." *InVisible Culture* 26.
Jafri, Beenash. 2020. "Refusal/film: Diasporic-Indigenous relationalities." *Settler Colonial Studies* 10, (1): 110–125.
Jing, Ai. 2015. *A History of the Great Wall of China*. New York: World Scientific. SCPG.
Johnston, Lynda. 2002. "Borderline bodies." In Liz Bondi et al, eds. *Subjectivities, Knowledges, and Feminist Geographies: The Subjects and Ethics of Social Research*. Lanham: Rowman and Littlefield, 75–89.
Johnston, Lynda. 2007. *Queering Tourism: Paradoxical Performances of Gay Pride Parades*. New York: Routledge.
Jones, Reece. 2012a. *Border Walls: Security and the War on Terror in the United States, India, and Israel*. New York: Zed Books.
Jones, Reece. 2012b. "Spaces of refusal: Rethinking sovereign power and resistance at the border." *Annals, Association of American Geographers* 102, (3): 685–699.
Jones, Reece. 2012c. "Why build a border wall?" *NACLA Report on the Americas* 45, (3): 70–72.
Jones, Reece. 2021. *White Borders: The History of Race and Immigration in the United States from Chinese Exclusion to the Border Wall*. Boston: Beacon Press.
Jovancevic, Ana, and Nbojsa Milicevic. 2020. "Optimism, pessimisim, conspiracy theories and general trust as factors contributing to COVID-19 related behaviour: A cross-cultural study." *Personality and Individual Differences* 167: 110216.
Kazimi, Ali. 1997. Shooting Indians: A Journey with Jeffrey Thomas. Documentary Film. *Social Doc*. Accessed November 30, 2019.
Keating, Michael. 1996. *Nations against the State: The New Politics of Nationalism in Quebec, Catalonia and Scotland*. New York: Palgrave-Macmillan.
Kennedy, Beccy. 2016. "Zones of seeing: Artistic, touristic and digital images of the DMZ." *East Asian Journal of Popular Culture* 2, (2): 287–303.
Kenwick, Michael R., and Beth A. Simmons. 2020. "Pandemic response as border politics." *International Organization* 4, (1): 1–23.
Keogh, Brendan. 2021. "The cultural field of videogame production in Australia." *Games and Culture* 16, (1): 116–135.
Kilicbay, Baris, and Mutlu Binark. 2002. "Consumer culture, Islam and the politics of lifestyle: Fashion for visiting in contemporary Turkey." *European Journal of Communication* 17, (4): 495–511.
Kim, Eleana J. 2016. "Toward and anthropology of landmines: Rogue infrastructure and military waste in the Korean DMZ."*Cultural Anthropology* 31, (2): 162–187.
Kim, Ke Chung. 1997. "Preserving biodiversity in Korea's demilitarized zone." *Science* 278, (5336): 242–243.
Kim, Minesong, and Brijesh Thapa. 2018. "The influence of self-congruity, perceived value, and satisfaction on destination loyalty: A case study of the Korea DMZ." *Journal of Heritage Tourism* 13, (3): 224–236.
Kim, Suk-Young. 2011. "Staging the 'cartography of paradox': The DMZ special exhibition at the Korean war memorial, Seoul." *Theatre Journal* 63, (3): 381–402.
Kim, Suk-Young. 2014. *DMZ Crossing: Performing Emotional Citizenship Along the Korean Border*. New York: Columbia University Press.
King, Thomas. 2013. *The Inconvenient Indian: A Curious Account of Native People in North America*. Toronto: Anchor Canada.

King, Thomas. 2017. *The Inconvenient Indian Illustrated: A Curious Account of Native People in North America*. Toronto: Doubleday.

Kizilabdullah, Yildiz, and Tugrul Yuruk. 2018. "The contribution of the religious culture and ethics course on the integration of children of Syrians in Adana, Turkey." *Religious Education* 113, (3): 289–301.

Konrad, Victor. 2015. "Toward a theory of borders in motion." *Journal of Borderlands Studies* 30, (1): 1–18.

Konrad, Victor. 2020. "Belongingness and borders." In James W. Scott, ed. *A Research Agenda for Border Studies*. Cheltenham: Edward Elgar, 109–128.

Konrad, Victor. 2021. "Border cultures: A retrospective. Part 1: A context for border cultures and conversations with the curator." In Victor Konrad, and Melissa Kelly, eds. *Borders, Culture, and Globalization: A Canadian Perspective*. Ottawa: University of Ottawa Press, 107–114.

Konrad, Victor, and Zhiding Hu. 2021. "Expanded border images and aligned border narratives: Ethnic minorities and localities in China's encounters with Myanmar, Laos and Vietnam." In Johan Schimanski, and Jopi Nyman, eds. *Border Images. Border Narratives: The Political Aesthetics of Boundaries and Crossings*. Manchester: Manchester University Press, 127–147.

Konrad, Victor, and Melissa Kelly. 2021. "Culture, Globalization and Canada's Borders." In Victor Konrad, and Melissa Kelly, eds. *Borders, Culture, and Globalization: A Canadian Perspective*. Ottawa: University of Ottawa Press, 7–38.

Konrad, Victor, and Laetitia Rouvière. 2016. "La 'Ligne Verte'." *Diplomatie* 80: 20–25.

Kurki, Tuulikki. 2013. "From Soviet locality to multivoiced borderland: Literature and identity in the Finnish-Russian national borderlands." *Region: Regional Studies of Russia, Eastern Europe, and Central Asia* 2, (1): 95–112.

Kurki, Tuulikki. 2014. "Borders from the cultural point of view: An introduction to writing borders." *Culture Unbound* 6, (6): 1055–1070.

Kurki, Tuulikki. 2018. "Border crossing trauma seen through hyper-naturalist prose and surreal forms of narration." *Mobile Culture Studies: The Journal* 4: 39–56.

Kurki, Tuulikki. 2020. "Materialized narrative of border: Articulating the unspeakable through everyday objects." In James W. Scott, ed. *A Research Agenda for Border Studies*. Cheltenham: Edward Elgar, 129–144.

Kurki, Tuulikki. 2021. "From heroism to grotesque: The invisibility of border-related trauma narratives in the Finnish-Russian borderlands." In Johan Schimanski, and Jopi Nyman, eds. *Border Images, Border Narratives: The Political Aesthetics of Boundaries and Crossings*. Manchester: Manchester University Press, 105–126.

Lagerqvist, Yayoi Fujita. 2013. "Imagining the borderlands: Contending stories of a resource frontier in Muang Sing." *Singapore Journal of Tropical Geography* 34, (1): 57–69.

Laine, Jussi. 2016. "The multiscalar production of borders." *Geopolitics* 21, (3): 465–482.

Langerbein, Helmut. 2009. "Great blunders? The Great Wall of China, the Berlin Wall and the proposed United States/Mexico Border Fence." *The History Teacher* 43, (1): 9–29.

Larkin, Craig. 2014. "Jerusalem's separation wall and global message board: Graffiti, murals, and the art of Samud." *The Arab Studies Journal* 22, (1): 134–169.

Latte Abdallah, Stephanie, and Cedric Parizot. 2015. *Israelis and Palestinians in the Shadows of the Wall: Spaces of Separation and Occupation*. Farnham: Ashgate.

Lattimore, Owen. 1937. "Origins of the Great Wall of China: A frontier concept in theory and practice." *Geographical Review* 27, (4): 529–549.

Lee, Choong-Ki, and Seung-Kon Lee. 2007. "Investigating relationships among perceived value, satisfaction, and recommendations: The case of the Korean DMZ." *Tourism Management* 28, (1): 2014–214.

Lee, Choon-Ki, and James W. Mjelde. 2007. "Valuation of ecotourism resources using a contingent valuation method: The case of the Korean DMZ." *Ecological Economics* 63, (2–3): 511–520.

Lehec, Clémence. 2017. "Graffiti in Palestinian refugee camps: From palimpsest walls to public space." *Articulo-Revue de Sciences Humaines* 15. https://doi.org/10.4000/articulo.3399.

Lehec, Clémence. 2020. *Sur Les Murs de Palestine: Filmer Les Graffitis Aux Frontières de Dheisheh*. Genève: Métis Presses.

León, Luis D. 2014. *The Political Spirituality of Cesar Chavez: Crossing Religious Borders*. Berkeley: University of California Press.

Levin, Bess. 2021. "Thanks to Republican Anti-Vaxxers, the U.S. may never reach COVID-19 herd immunity." *Vanity Fair*. April 21, 2021. htpp://www.vanityfair.com/news/2021/04/republicans-anti-vaccine-herd-immunity.

Levickaite, Rasa. 2010. "Generations X, Y, Z: How social networks form the concept of the world without borders (the case of Lithuania)." *LIMES: Cultural Regionalistics* 3, (2): 170–183.

Levi-Strauss, Claude. 1952. *Race et Histoire*. Paris: UNESCO/Gallimard-Folio Essais.

Lévy, Jacques. 2008. "Topologie furtive." *Espaces Temps.net*. Mensuelles. February 28, 2008. https://www.espacestemps.net/articles/topologie-furtive/.

Long, Joanna C. 2006. "Border anxiety in Palestine-Israel." *Antipode* 38, (1): 107–127.

Lunden, Thomas, and Dennis Zalamans. 2001. "Local cooperation, ethnic diversity and state territoriality: The case of Haparanda and Tornio on the Sweden-Finland border." *Geojournal* 54, (1): 33–42.

McDonald, David A. 2009. "Poetics and the performance of violence in Israel/Palestine." *Ethnomusicology* 53, (1): 58–85.

Maddux, William W., and Adam D. Galinsky. 2009. "Cultural borders and mental barriers: The relationship between living abroad and creativity." *Journal of Personality and Social Psychology* 96, (5): 1047–1061.

Madsen, Kenneth D. 2011. "Barriers of the U.S.-Mexico border as landscape of domestic political compromise." *Cultural Geographies* 18, (4): 547–556.

Maguire, Mark, Ursala Rao, and Nils Zurawski. 2018. *Bodies as Evidence: Security, Knowledge, and Power. Global Insecurities*. Durham: Duke University Press.

Maira, Sunaina. 2021. "The academic boycott movement: A reflection on cross-border solidarity and lockdown." *Human Geography* 14, (3): 374–378.

Man, John. 2010. *The Great Wall*. New York: Random House.

Manderson, Lenore, and Susan Levine. 2020. "COVID-19: Risk, fear, and fall-out." *Medical Anthropology* 39, (5): 367–370.

Marié, Solène. 2020. "At the centre of the edge: The development of cross-border cities between Brazil and Uruguay and France and Germany." PhD. Dissertation, University of Paris 8, Vincennes-St. Denis/Universidade de Brasilia.

Martineau, Jarrett. 2015. "Creative combat: Indigenous art, resurgence, and decolonization." PhD. Dissertation, University of Victoria, Canada.

Masaru, Nishitani, and Nathan Badenoch. 2013. "Why periodic markets are held: Considering products, people, and place in the Yunnan-Vietnam border area." *Southeast Asian Studies* 2, (1): 171–192.

Matthews, Elizabeth, ed. 2011. *The Israel-Palestine Conflict: Parallel Discourses*. London: Routledge.

Mayer, Evelyn P. 2021. "Across borders and cultures: Thomas King's artistic activism." In Victor Konrad, and Melissa Kelly, eds. *Borders, Culture, and Globalization: A Canadian Perspective*. Ottawa: University of Ottawa Press, 233–254.

Medeiros, Eduardo, ed. 2018. *European Territorial Cooperation*. New York: Springer.

Ale Mendoza, Christina Elizabeth. 2018. *Infrastructura Cultural para el Fortalecmiento de la Oferta Cultural en la Ciudad de Tacna 2018*. Tacna: Universidad Privada de Tacna.

Michaelson, Scott, and David E. Johnson, eds. 1997. *Border Theory: The Limits of Cultural Politics*. Minneapolis: University of Minnesota Press.

Middleton, Townsend. 2013. "States of difference: Refiguring ethnicity and its 'crisis' at India's borders." *Political Geography* 35: 14–24.

Mignolo, Walter D. 2012. *Local Histories/Global Designs: Coloniality, Subaltern Knowledges, and Border Thinking*. Princeton: Princeton University Press.

Miner, Dylan. 2014. *Creating Aztlan: Chicano Art, Indigenous Sovereignty, and Lowriding Across Turtle Island*. Tucson: University of Arizona Press.

Mirza, Mansha. 2014. "Refugee camps, asylum, detention and the geopolitics of transnational migration: Disability and its intersections with humanitarian confinement." In Liat Ben-Moshe, Chris Chapman, and Allison C. Corey, eds. *Disability Incarcerated*. New York: Palgrave Macmillan, 217–236.

Mitra, Srimoyee. 2015. *Border Cultures*. London: Black Dog Publishing.

Moffette, David. 2018. *Governing Irregular Migration: Bordering Culture, Labour, and Security in Spain*. Vancouver: UBC Press.

Morris, Kate. 2011. "Running the 'medicine line': Images of the border in contemporary native American art." *American Indian Quarterly* 35, (4): 549–578.

Morrison, Suzanne. 2015a. "Organizing the boycott, divestment and sanctions movement: The case of the 'we divest' campaign." *Conflict, Security and Development* 15, (5): 575–593.

Morrison, Suzanne. 2015b. "The boycott, divestment, and sanctions movement: Activism across borders for Palestinian justice." PhD. Dissertation, London School of Economics and Political Science.

Mortensen, Mette. 2017. "Constructing, confirming, and contesting icons: The Alan Kurdi imagery appropriated by #humanitywashedashore, Ai Weiwei, and Charlie Hebdo." *Media, Culture and Society* 39, (8): 1142–1161.

Mountz, Alison. 2011. "The enforcement archipelago: Detention haunting, and asylum on islands." *Political Geography* 30, (3): 118–128.

Muhamad, Nazlida, Munirah Khamarudin, and Waida Irani Mohd Fauzi. 2019. "The role of religious motivation in an international consumer boycott." *British Food Journal* 121, (1): 199–217.

Muller, Benjamin J. 2010. *Security, Risk and the Biometric State: Governing Borders and Bodies*. New York: Routledge.

Murton, Galen. 2019. "Facing the Fence: The production and performance of a Himalayan border in global contexts." *Political Geography* 72: 31–42.

Nabokov, Peter. 2002. *A Forest of Time: American Indian Ways of History*. Cambridge: Cambridge University Press.

Nahdee, Russell. 2016. "Russell Nahdee: Transcending borders: Visions from the Windsor-Detroit Corridor." *YouTube*. scholar.uwindsor.ca/uwilldiscover/2016/keynotes/3/.

Nail, Thomas. 2013. "The cross-roads of power: Michel Foucault and the US/Mexico border wall." *Foucault Studies* 1, (15): 110–128.

Nail, Thomas. 2016. *Theory of the Border*. Oxford: Oxford University Press.

Nevins, Joseph. 2007. "Dying for a cup of coffee? Migrant deaths in the U.S.-Mexico border region in a neoliberal age." *Geopolitics* 12, (2): 228–247.

Nevins, Joseph, and Allan Nevins. 2002. *Operation Gatekeeper: The Rise of the "Illegal Alien" and the Making of the U.S.-Mexico Boundary*. New York: Psychology Press.

Newman, David. 2001. "From national to post-national territorial identities in Israel-Palestine." *Geojournal* 53, (3): 235–246.
Newman, David. 2002. "The geopolitics of peacemaking in Israel-Palestine." *Political Geography* 21, (5): 629–646.
Newman, David. 2008. "Britain and the academic boycott of Israel." *Israel Journal of Foreign Affairs* 2, (2): 45–55.
Newman, David. 2012. "Borders and conflict resolution." In Thomas Wilson, and Hastings Donnan, eds. *A Companion to Border Studies.* Oxford: Blackwell, 249–265.
Newman, David. 2013. *Territory and Borders.* London: Routledge.
Newman, David. 2016. "The failure of academic boycotts." *Geographical Review* 106, (2): 264–269.
Nicol, Heather N. 2012. "The wall, the fence, and the gate: Reflexive metaphors along the Canada-U.S. border." *Journal of Borderlands Studies* 27, (2): 139–166.
Nicol, Heather N. 2015. *The Fence and the Bridge: Geopolitics and Identity along the Canada-U.S. Border.* Waterloo: Wilfrid Laurier University Press.
Nightingale, Andrea J. 2011. "Bounding difference: Intersectionality and the material production of gender, caste, class and environment in Nepal." *Geoforum* 42, (2): 153–162.
Nilsson, Jan Henrik, Lena Eskilsson, and Richard Ek. 2010. "Creating cross-border destinations: Interregprogrammes and regionalization in the Baltic Sea area." *Scandinavian Journal of Hospitality and Tourism* 10, (2): 153–172.
Oostveen, Anne-Marie, and Pinja Lehtonen. 2018. "The requirement of accessibility: European automated border control systems for persons with disabilities." *Technology and Society* 52: 60–69.
Oswin, Natalie. 2008. "Critical geographies and uses of sexuality: Deconstructing queer space." *Progress in Human Geography* 32, (1): 89–103.
Otto, Dianne, ed. 2018a. *Queering International Law Possibilities, Alliances, Complexities, Risks.* New York: Routledge.
Otto, Dianne. 2018b. "Resisting the heteronormative imaginary of the nation-state: Rethinking kinship and border protection." In Dianne Otto, ed. *Queering International Law Possibilities, Alliances, Complexities, Risks.* New York: Routledge, 236–257.
Papailias, Penelope. 2019. "(Un)seeing dead refugee bodies: Mourning memes, spectro-politics, and the haunting of Europe." *Media, Culture and Society* 41, (8): 1048–1068.
Parodi Revoredo, Daniel, and Sergio Alberto Gonzalez Miranda, eds. 2014. *Las Historias Quenos Unen: 21 relatos para la integración entre Perú y Chile.* Lima: Fondo Editorial, Pontificia Universidad Católica del Perú.
Parry, William. 2011. *Against the Wall: The Art of Resistance in Palestine.* Chicago: Chicago Review Press.
Payan, Tony. 2016. *The Three U.S.-Mexico Border Wars: Drugs, Immigration, and Homeland Security.* Santa Barbara: ABC Clio.
Perez, Emma. 2003. "Queering the borderlands: The challenges of excavating the invisible and unheard." *Frontiers: A Journal of Women Studies* 24, (2–3): 122–131.
Perrin, Thomas. 2013. *Culture et eurorégions. La coopération culturelle entre régions européennes.* Bruxelles: Editions de l'Université de Bruxelles.
Perrin, Thomas. 2015. "Creative regions on a European cross-border scale: Policy issues and development perspectives." *European Planning Studies* 23, (12): 2423–2437.
Phaneuf, Victoria M. 2013. "The Vermont-Quebec border region: Negotiations of identity and logic in the Northeast Kingdom." *Journal of Borderlands Studies* 28, (1): 109–125.

Pisani, Maria, and Shaun Grech. 2017. "Disability and forced migration: Critical intersectionalities." *Red CDPD*. http://repositoriocdpd.net:8080/handle/123456789/1505.

Potzsch, Holger. 2011. "Borders, barriers and grievable lives: The discursive production of self and other in film and other audio-visual media." *Nordicom Review* 32, (2): 75–94.

Prokkola, Eeva-Raisa. 2011. "Cross-border regionalization, the INTERREG III A initiative, and local cooperation at the Finnish-Swedish border." *Environment and Planning A* 43, (5): 1190–1208.

Radan, Peter. 1997. "The borders of a future independent Quebec: Does the principle of *Uti Possidetis Juris* apply?" *Australian International Law Journal* 11: 200–214.

Radan, Peter. 1997. "The supreme court of Canada and the borders of Quebec." *Australian International Law Journal* 171: 200–214.

Radavist. 2021. "Grenzfahrungen." https://theradavist.com/2021/01/grenzfahrungen-borderline-experiences/ Accessed January 18, 2021.

Radcliffe, Sarah, and Sallie Westwood, eds. 2005. *Remaking the Nation: Identity and Politics in Latin America*. London: Routledge.

Rader, Dean. 2011. *Engaged Resistance: American Indian Art, Literature, and Film from Alcatraz to the NMAI*. Austin: University of Texas Press.

Rael, Ronald. 2017. *Borderwall as Architecture: A Manifesto for the U.S.-Mexico Boundary*. Berkeley: University of California Press.

Raivo, Petri J. 2004. "Karelia lost or won–materialization of a landscape of contested and commemorated memory." *Fennia–International Journal of Geography* 182, (1): 61–72.

Rajaram, P. K., and C. Grundy-Warr (2007). *Borderscapes: Hidden Geographies and Politics at Territory's Edge*. Minneapolis: University of Minnesota Press.

Rancière, Jacques. 2015. *Dissensus: On Politics and Aesthetics*. London: Bloomsbury.

Ratner, Steven R. 1996. "Drawing a better line: *Uti Possidetis* and the borders of new states." *American Journal of International Law* 90, (4): 590–624.

Reid, Scott J. 1997. "The borders of an independent Quebec: A thought experiment." *The Good Society* 7, (1): 11–17.

Reinhart, Tanya. 2006. *The Road Map to Nowhere: Israel/Palestine since 2003*. London: Verso.

Reitel, Bernhard, Birte Wassenberg, and Jean Peyrony. 2018. "The INTERREG experiences in bridging European territories: A thirty year summary." In Eduardo Medeiros, ed. *European Territorial Cooperation*. London: Springer, 7–23.

Renzaho, Andre. 2020. "The need for the right socio-economic and cultural fit in the COVID-19 response in Sub-Saharan Africa: Examining demographic, economic, political, health, and socio-cultural differentials in COVID-19 morbidity and mortality." *International Journal of Environmental Research and Public Health* 17, (10): 3445.

Ringmar, Erik. 2019. "Walling, boundaries and liminality: A political anthropology of transformation." In Agnes Horvath, Marius Ion Berta, and Joan Davison, eds. *The Great Wall of China Does Not Exist*. New York: Routledge, 122–135.

Robins, Kevin. 1996. "Interrupting identities: Turkey/Europe." In Stuart Hall, and Paul du Gay, eds. *Questions of Cultural Identity*. London: Sage, 61–86.

Robins, Kevin. 2003. "Peculiarities and consequences of the Europe-Turkey border." In Kevin Robins, ed. *Culture and Cooperation in Europe's Borderland*. Leiden/Boston: Brill/Rodopi, 233–250.

Rodney, Lee. 2017. *Looking Beyond Borderlines: North America's Frontier Imagination*. New York: Routledge.

Rodney, Lee. 2021. "Sight and site on the line: The cultural imaginary of borderlands in North America." In Victor Konrad, and Melissa Kelly, eds. *Borders, Culture, and Globalization: A Canadian Perspective*. Ottawa: University of Ottawa Press, 39–60.

Rogge, Sabine, and Michael Grunbart, eds. 2015. *Medieval Cyprus: A Place of Cultural Encounter.* Munster: Waxman Verlag.

Romero, Fernando. 2008. *Hyperborder: The Contemporary U.S.? Mexico Border and its Future*. New York: Princeton Architectural Press.

Ron, James. 2000. "Savage restraint: Israel/Palestine and the dialectics oflegal repression." *Social Problems* 47, (4): 445–472.

Rouvière, Laetitia. 2019. "Entre souveraineté indigène et sécurité nationale: Négocier la sécurité frontalière et la culture Mohawk à Akwesasne." *The Canadian Geographer/Le Géographe canadien* 63, (1): 57–68.

Rudolph, Alexander. 2021. "North American cyber new regionalism in Canada: Online cultural borderlands and change through new media." In Victor Konrad, and Melissa Kelly, eds. *Borders, Culture, and Globalization: A Canadian Perspective*. Ottawa: University of Ottawa Press, 187–214.

Rumford, Chris. 2012. "Towards a multiperspectival study of borders." *Geopolitics* 17, (4): 887–902.

St. John, Rachel. 2012. *Line in the Sand: A History of the Western U.S.-Mexico Border.* New York: Princeton University Press.

Sadykova, Gulnara, and Jennie Dautermann. 2009. "Crossing cultures and borders in international online distance higher education." *Journal of Asynchronous Learning Networks* 13, (2): 89–114.

Sahin, Sanem. 2011. "Open borders, closed minds: The discursive construction of national identity in North Cyprus." *Media, Culture and Society* 33, (4): 583–597.

Saldana-Portillo, Maria Josefina. 2016. *Indian Given: Racial Geographies across Mexico and the United States*. Durham: Duke University Press.

Saldívar, Jose David. 1997. *Border Matters: Remapping American Cultural Studies*. Berkeley: University of California Press.

Salih, Ruba, and Sophie Richter-Devroe. 2014. "Cultures of resistance in Palestine and beyond: On the politics of art, aesthetics, and affect." *The Arab Studies Journal* 22, (1): 8–27.

Sanders, Douglas. 1995. "If Quebec secedes from Canada, can the Cree secede from Quebec?" *University of British Columbia Law Review* 29: 143.

Sassen, Saskia. 2000. "Spatialities and temporalities of the global: Elements for theorization." *Public Culture* 12, (1): 215–232.

Schimanski, Johan. 2015. "Border aesthetics and cultural distancing in the Norwegian-Russian borderscape." *Geopolitics* 20, (1): 35–55.

Schimanski, Johan, and Jopi Nyman. 2021. *Border Images, Border Narratives: The Political Aesthetics of Boundaries and Crossings*. Manchester: Manchester University Press.

Schimanski, Johan, and Stephen Wolfe. 2010. "Cultural production and negotiation of borders: Introduction to the Dossier." *Journal of Borderlands Studies* 25, (1): 38–49.

Schimanski, Johan, and Stephen Wolfe. 2017. *Border Aesthetics: Concepts and Intersections*. New York: Berghahn.

Schindel, Estela. 2019. "Death by 'nature': The European border regime and the spatial production of slow violence." *Environment and Planning C: Politics and Space*.40, (2): 428–446. 2399654419884948.

Schuchs Carr, Isla A., Deborah A. Sibila, and Beth M. Rauhaus. 2020. "Trump's Twitter Tales: Policy implications of stories of crime and crisis along the Southwest border." *Public Voices* 17, (1): 82–98.

Scott, James C. 2009. *The Art of Not Being Governed*. New Haven: Yale University Press.

Scott, James W. 2013. "Constructing familiarity in Finnish-Russian Karelia: Shifting uses of history and the re-interpretation of regions." *European Planning Studies* 21, (1): 75–92.

Sidaway, James D., and Chih Yuan Woon. 2017. "Chinese narratives on 'one belt, one road' in geopolitical and imperial contexts." *The Professional Geographer* 69, (4): 591–603.

Sieber, Renée E. 2003. "Public participation geographic information systems across borders." *The Canadian Geographer/Le Géographe canadien* 47, (1): 50–61.

Siebert, Monika. 2015. *Indians Playing Indian: Multiculturalism and Contemporary Indigenous art in North America*. Montgomery: University of Alabama Press.

Silvey, Rachel. 2004. "Power, difference and mobility: Feminist advances in migration studies." *Progress in Human Geography* 28, (4): 490–506.

Silvey, Rachel. 2006. "Geographies of gender and migration: Spatializing social difference." *International Migration Review* 40, (1): 64–81.

Silvey, Rachel. 2008. "Managing Migration." In Isabella Bakker, and Rachel Silvey, eds. *Beyond States and Markets: The Challenges of Social Reproduction*. New York: Routledge, 108–121.

Simpson, Audra. 2014. *Mohawk Interruptus: Political Life across the Borders of Settler States*. Durham: Duke University Press.

Simpson, Audra. 2017. "The ruse of consent and the anatomy of 'refusal': Cases from Indigenous North America and Australia." *Postcolonial Studies* 20, (1): 18–33.

Sinnott, Megan. 2010. "Borders, diaspora, and regional connections: Trends in Asian Queer Studies." *The Journal of Asian Studies* 69, (1): 17–31.

Siriphon, Aranya. 2007. "Dress and cultural strategy: Tai Peddlers in transnational trade along the Burma-Yunnan Frontier." *Asian Ethnicity* 8, (3): 219–234.

Sirkeci, Ibrahim, and Jeffrey H. Cohen. 2016. "Cultures of migration and conflict in contemporary human mobility in Turkey." *European Review* 24, (3): 381–396.

Skuban, William E. 2007. *Lines in the Sand: Nationalism and Identity on the Peruvian-Chilean Frontier*. Albuquerque: University of New Mexico Press.

Slack, Jeremy. 2019. *Deported to Death: How Drug Violence is Changing Migration on the U.S.-Mexico Border*. Berkeley: University of California Press.

Slowe, Peter M. 1991. "The geography of borderlands: The case of Quebec-U.S. borderlands." *Geographical Journal* 157, (2): 191–198.

Soldatic, Karen, Kelly Sommers, Anna Buckley, and Caroline Fleay. 2017. "'Nowehere to be found': Disabled refugees and asylum seekers within the Australian resettlement landscape." *Red CDPD*. http://repositoriocdpd.net:8080/handle/123456789/1497.

Sorlin, Sverker, ed. 2016. *Science, Geopolitics and Culture in the Polar Region: Norden Beyond Borders*. London: Routledge.

Sowards, Stacey K. 2019. "Bordering through place/s, difference/s, and language/s: Intersections of border and feminsist theories." *Women's Studies Communication* 42, (2): 120–124.

Sparke, Matthew. 2008. "Political geography—Political geographies of globalization III: Resistance." *Progress in Human Geography* 32, (3): 423–440.

Staudt, Kathleen A. 1998. *Free Trade? Informal Economies of the U.S.-Mexico Border*. Philadelphia: Temple University Press.

Stoffelen, Arie. 2018. "Tourism trails as tools for cross-border integration: A best practice case study of the Vennbahn cycling route." *Annals of Tourism Research* 73: 91–102.

Stoffelen, Arie, and Dominique Vanneste. 2017. "Tourism and cross-border regional development: Insights in European contexts." *European Planning Studies* 25, (6): 1013–1033.

Stoffers, Manuel. 2012. "Cycling as heritage: Representing the history of cycling in the Netherlands." *The Journal of Transport History* 33, (1): 92–114.
Stokes, Martin. 2014. "New Islamist popular culture in Turkey." In Kamal Salki, ed. *Music, Culture and Identity in the Muslim World: Performance, Politics and Piety.* London: Routledge, 15–34.
Strasser, Sabine, and Eda Elif Tibet. 2020. "The border event in the everyday: Hope and constraints in the lives of young unaccompanied asylum seekers in Turkey." *Journal of Ethnic and Migration Studies* 46, (2): 354–371.
Su, Ming Ming, and Geoffrey Wall. 2012. "Global-local relationships and governance issues at the Great Wall World Heritage site, China." *Journal of Sustainable Tourism* 20, (8): 1067–1086.
Su, Ming Ming, and Geoffrey Wall. 2014. "Community participation in tourism at a world heritage site: Mutianyu Great Wall, Beijing, China." *International Journal of Tourism Research* 16, (2): 146–156.
Sufian, Sandra Marlene, and Mark Levine, eds. 2007. *Reapproaching Borders: New Perspectives on the Study of Israel-Palestine.* Lanham: Rowman and Littlefield.
Tapia Ladino, Marcela, and Adriana Gonzalez Gil, eds. 2014. "Regiones fronterizas, migración y las desafíos para los Santiago de Chile: RIL editores."
Thomas, Julia Adeney. 2009. "The exquisite corpses of nature and history: The case of the Korean DMZ." *Asia-Pacific Journal* 43, (3): 1–17.
Toenjes, Ashley. 2015. "This wall speaks: Graffiti and transnational networks in Palestine." *Jerusalem Quarterly* 61: 55.
Topak, Ozgun E. 2014. "The biopolitical border in practice: Surveillance and death at the Greece-Turkey border zones." *Environment and Planning D: Society and Space* 32, (5): 815–833.
Truett, Samuel. 2008. *Fugitive Landscapes: The Forgotten History of the U.S.-Mexico Borderlands.* New Haven: Yale University Press.
Turnbull, Stephen. 2012. *The Great Wall of China, 221BC - AD 1644.* London: Bloomsbury.
Turner, Victor. 1969. *The Ritual Process: Structure and Anti-Structure.* Chicago: Aldine.
Urry, John. 2012. *Sociology beyond Societies: Mobilities for the 21st Century.* London: Routledge.
Vallet, Elisabeth, ed. 2014. *Borders, Fences and Walls: State of Insecurity?* Farnham: Ashgate.
Van Bochove, Marianne. 2012. "Truly transnational: The political practices of middle-class migrants." *Journal of Ethnic and Migration Studies* 38, (10): 1551–1568.
Vandervalk, Sandra. 2020."Line dancing in the borderlands region of Stanstead, Quebec." *Borders in Globalization Review* 1, (2): 111–113.
Vandervalk, Sandra. 2021. "Passing through and living here: Body and self in-between and on edge in the borderlands region of Stanstead, Quebec and Derby Line, Vermont." In Victor Konrad, and Melissa Kelly, eds. *Borders, Culture, and Globalization: A Canadian Perspective.* Ottawa: University of Ottawa Press, 163–186.
Varol, Cigdem, and Emrah Soylemez. 2019. "Socio-spatial network structures in border regions: West and east borders of Turkey." In Xinyue Ye, and Xingjian Liu, eds. *Cities as Spatial and Social Networks.* New York: Springer, 207–225.
Veles, Natalia, Margaret-Anne Carter, and Helen Boon. 2019. "Complex collaboration champions: University third space professionals working together across borders." *Perspectives: Policy and Practice in Higher Education* 23, (2–3): 75–85.
Villalon, Oscar. 2007. "Barbarians at the wall." *The Virginia Quarterly Review* 83, 277.
Waldron, Arthur N. 1983. "The problem of the Great Wall of China." *Harvard Journal of Asiatic Studies* 43, (2): 643–663.

Walton, Joan. 1999. "White neurotics, black primitives, and the Queer Matrix of Borderline." In Ellis Hanson, ed. *Out Takes? Essays on Queer Theory and Film*. Durham: Duke University Press, 243–270.

Wang, Y. X. et al. 2013. "Mobile livelihoods among ethnic minorities in China: Insights from Yunnan." *Norwegian Journal of Geography* 67, (4): 187–199.

Weigand, Heidi, and Colin Howell. 2021. "Sport, globalization, and the bordering process: The Iroquois Nationals lacrosse team and the issue of contested national identities." In Victor Konrad, and Melissa Kelly, eds. *Borders, Culture, and Globalization: A Canadian Perspective*. Ottawa: University of Ottawa Press, 277–292.

Weizman, Eyal. 2007. *Hollowland: Israel's Architecture of Occupation*. London: Verso.

Wells, Chloe. 2016. "Eating Karelia: The geography, history, and memory of Karelian pies." *CARELiCA* 2: 72–82.

Wilson, Ara. 2006. "Queering Asia." *Intersections: Gender History and Culture in the Asian Context* 14, (3): 1–10.

Woodsworth, Paddy. 2008. *The Basque Country: A Cultural History*. Oxford: Oxford University Press.

Wright, Melissa W. 2019. "Border thinking, borderland diversity, and Trump's wall." *Annals, Association of American Geographers* 109, (2): 511–519.

Yang, Mimi. 2017. "Crossing between the Great Wall of China and the 'great' Trump Wall. "*Palgrave Communications* 3, (1): 1–6.

Yiftachel, Oren. 1999. "Ethnocracy: The politics of Judaizing Israel/Palestine." *Constellations* 6, (3): 364–390.

Yiftachel, Oren. 2002. "Territory as the kernel of the nation: Space, time and nationalism in Israel/Palestine." *Geopolitics* 7, (2): 215–248.

Young, Robert Andrew. 1998. *The Secession of Quebec and the Future of Canada*. Montreal and Kingston: McGill-Queen's University Press.

Zhou, C. 2012. "From Yiwu to Menghai: Yunnan border town on the ancient Tea Travel Road." *Urban China* 55: 54–55.

Ziadah, Rafref. 2012. Art for Palestine: 'Re-narrating' history and the present. In Aziz Choudry, Jill Hanley and Eric Shragge, eds. *Organize! Building from the Local for Global Justice*. Oakland, CA: PM Press. 111–122.

6

BORDERS WITH/IN TRANSNATIONAL CULTURE

Border culture is no longer culture at the margins, but rather it is culture at the heart of geopolitics.
Will borders become a bewildering array of binary cues?
Where is home in transnational space?
Dispossession of culture begins in migration and ends in violence at the border.
Rationalization of border culture is counter-productive; the border is in the art!

Introduction: Approaching border culture in globalization, and in a post-globalization world

More than 30 years ago, at a time when Canada, the U.S., and Mexico were building the North American Free Trade Agreement and engaging in the integration of trade, labour, and environment agendas, a smaller and lesser-known transnational project was initiated by Singapore, Malaysia, and Indonesia. In this instance, the city-state of Singapore linked with Johor state in Malaysia and with the Riau Islands of Indonesia in the promotion of transnational economic development, a kind of "next door transnationalism" (Hutchinson and Chong 2016). The Singapore–Johor–Riau Islands (SIJORI) cross-border region is a social construction of distinct polities, a distant shared history, common cultural differences, and, most pervasively, an aligned vision of economic growth and cooperation. Although Singapore has spilled across its boundaries and many Singaporeans now live in adjacent Johor, Malaysia, and numerous Malaysians work in Singapore, citizenship and identity remain guarded in social and cultural communities. Interethnic dissonance prevails, and the borders that matter are both political and cultural. Transnational flows of commerce, finance, technology, and labour are enabled through economic networks, yet transnational integration of society and culture is limited or channelled through ethnic linkages such as the Chinese

DOI: 10.4324/9781003301486-6

FIGURE 6.1 Singapore: Borders *with/in* Transnational Culture. This photo illustrates the Chinatown area of Singapore enclosed by the new city. Photo courtesy of the Singapore Tourism Board.

business community. Cultural integration across the border remains under-developed. Transnational culture in the SIJORI cross-border region is a veneer of integration across imaginary frontiers whereas deeply rooted ethnic communities display the operative borders that sustain cultural islands *with/in* transnational culture (Figure 6.1). The photo illustrates the sharp architectural and cultural distinction between Singapore's Chinatown area and the new city that encloses it.

As Shelley Fisher Fishkin (2005) indicated in her inaugural address as president of the American Studies Association, there has been a transnational turn in American and other regional studies. We agree with this assessment, but we add the corollary that culture has not readily and easily negotiated this transnational turn. Culture is at once driving and responding to the turn. While aspects of economic activity, technological transfer, information sharing, and even social structures have shifted from national contexts to transnational expressions, culture has often been central in these transitions (Appadurai 1996). As Clifford Geertz (2017, 13) reminds us:

> The concept of culture that I espouse ... is essentially a semiotic one. Believing, with Max Weber, that man is an animal suspended in webs of significance he himself has spun, I take culture to be those webs ... and the analysis of it to be therefore not an experimental science in search of law, but an interpretive one in search of meaning.

Geertz (2017, 18, 20) continues "Culture, this acted document, thus is public, like a burlesqued wink or a mock sheep raid. Though ideational, it does not exist in someone's head, though unphysical, it is not an occult entity." "Culture is public because meaning is." "There is, in brief, a human nature as regularly organized, as thoroughly invariant, and as marvellously simple as Newton's universe. Perhaps some of its laws are different, but there are laws; perhaps some of its immutability is obscured by the trappings of local fashion, but it is immutable" (Geertz 2017, 42). This immutability has centred culture in transnationalism, as Appadurai (1996) has argued, and it has enabled the flexibility and adaptability of culture in transnational processes.

Border culture may be viewed as a precept of transnationalism, yet it remains partially rooted in nationalisms, the local and regional cultures that merge into or resist a national culture, and the diasporic dynamics that evolve from it. The transnational imaginary, according to Ramón Saldívar (2006), remains unfulfilled because it has not completed its "trans-sentimental journey" and so the national and transnational remain intertwined but distinguishable. In North America, in particular, transnational approaches to culture remain inherently comparative because incised borders are sustained and distinctive border cultures prevail (Nischik 2016, Correa-Cabrera and Konrad 2020). There are borders with transnational culture, borders in transnational culture, and borders *with/in* transnational culture.

A brief foray into the pedagogy of language and culture may serve to highlight some of the complexities of this multidimensional relationship, and to suggest how language and culture are shifting from a national to a transnational paradigm (Risager 2007). Whereas culture exhibits the stasis of hierarchy, differentiation, and genericism, culture is also a process and a flow (Hannerz 1996). Linguistic complexity and flows are integral parts of this dynamism of culture which encompasses "languaculture" (Agar 1994) and "linguaculture" (Friedrich 1989). Linguaculture includes the single universe of language and culture, and consists of three interrelated dimensions: the semantic-pragmatic, the poetic, and the component of language related to identity (Risager 2012). These interrelated components produce a linguacultural ideology (Friedrich 1989), and may impact how people in a certain community perceive things. For example, American English is more idea-based and Mandarin Chinese is more image-based (Durst-Andersen and Barratt 2019). Languaculture conveys the inextricable relationship between language and culture in which a specific language will shape and influence culture (Agar 2019). These concepts of linguaculture and languaculture help us to discern the double intertextuality of discourse as linguistic and cultural contents engage in transnationalism (Risager 2007, 110). This intertextuality may convey the language and culture nexus in transnationalism (Risager 2007, 185), but it also identifies a space of hybridization where components of both culture and language in two engaging cultural entities are both combined and differentiated in a variety of iterations to constitute the border culture of language.

As we have learned in this book, border culture is culture imagined and produced at boundaries, and in an increasing array of sites where visions, values, identities, and other facets of human distinction meet and increasingly collide. In the mobile world of globalization's flows and interactions, border culture has become at once more elusive in dispersal of imaginaries and productions, and more expressive in resistance to the recidivism of nation-states. Yet, border culture is not merely ubiquitous, and just generally out there everywhere in the world. As we have illustrated in this book, border culture works according to epistemologies of human discourse, narration, spatial behaviour, and social construction, all inclined toward geopolitics. We begin this final chapter by exploring how and why border culture is found at the heart of geopolitics in the transnational world. Then we address how border culture is imbedded in the profusion of border experience in globalization, yet it also clarifies the definition and the meaning of home. We examine how the "suture" of the border both separates and connects transnational space, and the nature of the landscapes that emerge in this bordered geography. We draw attention to the dispossession, violence, and gendering that occur in transnational space. Finally, we conclude both this chapter and the book with a pre-script and post-script addressing culture at the post-humanistic border.

6.1 Border culture at the heart of geopolitics

When Marvel superheroes become world figures, are we not in the transnationalization of U.S. culture? Captain America's empire may be popular culture, but it conveys strong reflections on U.S. identity and post-9/11 geopolitics through the popular culture narratives and metaphors of the nationalist and transnationalist superhero (Dittmer 2005, Dittmer and Hurley 2013). As people everywhere experience the flows of the transnational world, they become dislocated and often relocated in space and place. This experience creates borders, both real and imaginary, borders that are at least unsettling and in some instances pathological. These borders may be enhanced nation-state boundaries or incised differences of race, gender, wealth, and other attributes of human embodiment. Embodied borders may facilitate border management and securitization in a transnational world of flows, but they also assure geopolitical alignment or separation and accompanying resistance, dispossession, and violence. Border culture is embodied as well, and it is mobilized as people move about in their everyday lives as well as materialized in places and spaces at, near, and beyond borders. Wherever people express their identity through language and other facets of culture, they make a statement about who they are and what they believe in. These statements are conveyed electronically and extensively in a transnational world, and the images and other manifestations abut and often collide to create borders, or to enhance borders that already exist. Border culture emerges and grows in these liminal borderland spaces, inevitably encountering, challenging, and/or displacing other aspects of border culture. Border culture is at the heart of geopolitics in a transnational world.

The shifting and expanding conceptualization of the geopolitics of borders and boundaries (Van Houtum 2005) now encompasses increasingly complex encounters of people in a "wider" world that is at once de-territorialized and re-territorialized, de-bordered and re-bordered, mobilized and contained, and globalized and localized. James W. Scott (2005) explores the alternative geopolitics of regional cooperation of the EU in a "wider Europe" of enlargement. A border culture of positive interdependence with the European East and South is forwarded in the European Neighbourhood Policy to develop market logics and accommodate the heterogeneous realities of the expanded transnational partnership. On the other hand, Reece Jones (2009) illustrates how geopolitical boundary narratives linked to the war on terror framed an enemy "other", especially in the Indian case by the demonization of the other as religiously and culturally distinct, and, consequently, moved India to enclose its cultural container with border fencing. The transnational encompasses these antithetical geopolitical currents of containment and cooperation and expresses the currents in efforts to either advance global political society or constrain it. Yet, the transnational is not merely geopolitics of enlargement versus containment. It is also about de-colonialization and "epistemic disobedience" in border thinking to question world powers, and add value to culture (Mignolo 2011). A major impediment to the realization of transnationalism lies in the predominance of fear in geopolitics and everyday life. Rachel Pain and Susan J. Smith (2016) detail how paranoia has led to surveillance and hyper-vigilance in the homeland security state, and how this has led to an everyday life of being monitored, bunkered, patrolled, and fortressed. Consequently, border culture in the transnational world is often associated with and defined by security regimes and resistance to these regimes.

6.1.1 Culture in the transnational world

As we begin this final chapter, our aim is to re-visit briefly themes of citizenship, identity, and migration, introduced in Chapter 4, but to engage with these themes specifically as they relate to border culture production in the transnational world. In 1992, Akhil Gupta and James Ferguson called for a more effective theorization of space and place to take us beyond the representations of "naturally" discontinuous spaces of societies and cultures (Gupta and Ferguson 1992, 6). Culture needed to be theorized as produced across breaks, ruptures, and disjunctions as well as contained within the spaces bounded by these constructs. This shift from the atomized cultural to cultural difference occurred through theorizing space-related concerns of location, displacement, community, and identity in post-modernist and feminist theory (Anzaldúa 1987, Deleuze and Guattari 1988, Foucault 1982, Kaplan 1987). Also, the shift revealed new or revived conceptualizations of surveillance, panopticism, simulacra, deterritorialization, hyperspace, marginality, and of course borderlands. As Gupta and Ferguson (1997, 2) emphasized, the constructions of culture, power, and place are engaged in "changing schemes of categorization and discourses of difference, wherein the intertwining of place making, identity, and resistance interact with meaning and consumption of signs". This is contested cultural production and not consensual, shared, and orderly culture. This cultural production conveys changing spatial and cultural relations, and it engages and extends the politics of difference, particularly in borderland spaces. As Michael Kearney (1991, 52) states, cultural production in these spaces is "ambiguous" and people in these spaces "partake of both [countries] in some ways, and partake of neither in other ways". As "national distinctions decline, ethnicity emerges as a consciousness of difference". Yet, in this reproduced border culture, citizenship requirements become more acute, identities are sharpened, and mobility matters (Amilhat Szary 2013). In this section we focus on illustrations of diasporas beyond borders, and the nature of flows and objects at borders.

6.1.2 Diasporas

In 1995, Michael Kearney positioned diasporas as flows between the local and the global, both producing and operating within transnational space, and participating in deterritorialization. Kearney's (2000) study of transnational Oaxacan Indigenous identity illustrates how Mixtec and Zapotec illegal migrants from Oaxaca, Mexico, produced a third socio-cultural and political space, popularly known as "Oaxacalifornia" in the U.S. The study draws attention to two common characteristics of diasporas: the "home" country, Mexico in this case, attempts to retain political hegemony over the Indigenous communities both at home and abroad; and the migrants construct pan-Mixtec, pan-Zapotec, and more generally pan-Oaxacan identities (Kearney 2000, 173). African diaspora identities in transnational migration are expressed and negotiated as both or either ethnicities and nationalities (Arthur 2010). In Nova Scotia, Canada, African diaspora communities identify as Nigerian, Ugandan, Ghanaian, Liberian, and Sierra Leonean as represented by their diaspora community associations (Musabende 2021). In Toronto and Montreal, and more recently Vancouver, larger African diaspora communities are identifying through religion, gender, and power (Mensah et al. 2013, Creese 2017).

Diaspora is the dispersal of a people from its original homeland, therefore creating potentially multiple border crossings and borderlands (Butler 2001). Also, diasporas illustrate plural identities.

> I remember very clearly being a little girl trapped between two worlds. The one where we spoke English and did American things like eat cookies and sit in a circle in nursery school, and the one of my home, where we spoke a different warmer language, and the aroma of tea brewing was always in the air. And then there was the inbetween place where I would stay with my Danish babysitter who I called grandma, with my friend Chrissy who was Japanese.
>
> *(Reyes Cruz et al. 2009, 787)*

Processes of acculturation and ethno-nationalism contribute to the perpetual motion of the human population and diaspora is one vector of this perpetual motion (Verstraete 2010). Consequently, according to Brian Keith Axel (2004, 26), diaspora needs to be viewed as a "globally mobile category of identification rather than a community of individuals dispersed from a homeland" and the "context of diaspora may be understood through its production of disparate temporalities (anteriorities, presents, futurities) and subjects". Martin Sokefeld (2006, 265) encourages a social movement approach to the study of mobilization in transnational space in order to counter the "essentialist concepts that reify belonging and roots". This approach reveals the chaordic structure of diaspora and the "shared sense of moral co-responsibility of diasporic community". For example, in international Sufi cults, no guiding hand and no command structure is necessary (Werbner 2002, 119). According to Sudesh Mishra (2006) in her book *Diaspora Criticism* there are three pillars of diaspora: a dual territoriality scene, a scene of situational laterality, and a scene of archival specificity. Culture must be situated and sustained, but this location may not be unique as expressed by multi-situated territoriality (Giraut 2013). Dual homeness is more accessible and sustainable in transnational space, and this spread of home challenges national cultures to socio-cultural unity and enables cultural reproduction as transnational entities, thus enhancing multiculturalization (Ben-Rafael 2013, 842). Although this cultural production and reproduction may appear chaotic and incoherent, it represents the complex, attenuated, and interconnected fibre linking cross-national spaces, and moving societies into a new era of globalization and post-globalization. Integration of diasporic populations is only partially accomplished in transnationalism and new "1.5 generations" who maintain both old and new cultures and flourish "in between" in highly mobile diaspora communities (Alonso 2018). The new generations of diasporans create border cultures that reflect their mobility and their comfort in multiple places connected by multiple media. Unfortunately, state practices remain mired in expatriate, closed, and indifferent policies aimed more at managing labour in transnationalism and less in building the global-nation and embracing populations abroad (Ragazzi 2014).

6.1.3 Flows and objects in transnational space

Whereas cultural flows are evident because they are re-inscribed in specific cultural environments in scales from the local to the regional, national and transnational, "spaces of things" constituted of objects appear in transnational space according to multiple logics (Muller and Torp 2009). The resulting complexity of objects in transnational space has focused attention on and exaggerated mobility. The body is a "powerful corrective of exaggerating mobility" because it places the focus on migrants rather than migration, and on the transnational rather than transnationalism, thus offering a more complicated and realistic picture. The embodied approach to transnationalism situates people in transnational space and it "reveals the ever-present valency of place" (Dunn 2010, 1–3). The embodied approach accounts for objects that accompany the body such as signifiers of gender materialized in dress and grooming that extend beyond the national to the transnational. Gendered geographies of power across transnational spaces are constructed on agency that is gained from objects wielded and displayed as well as from other assets (Mahler and Ressar 2001). Illegal and illicit flows combine with criminal things to illustrate the other side of globalization, and they convey a transnationalism based on moving items considered illegal from one state to another (Van Schendel and Abraham 2005). Cattle, arms, drugs, diamonds, exotic species, and more may be legal in one state but not another, illegal in some states but not others, or generally considered illegal, thus creating a geography of illicit flows of things across borders.

Anelynda Mielke and Nadia Pohran (2021) explore the centrality of objects at the border as pivotal contributions in human struggles to assert legitimacy and claim asylum. Their central argument is that borders exist within remotely located symbolic objects as well as within the non-material consciousness of those who interact with borderlines. This may be very evident when the objects are borderlines such as the "lively" Drina River border between Serbia and Bosnia and Herzegovina (Brkovic and Jansen 2018), and also apparent where human bodies inhabit ambiguously bordered spaces, as in the border between Stanstead, Quebec, and Derby Line, Vermont (Vandervalk 2021). Mielke and Pohran discuss a case of sanctuary that occurs geographically distant from the border. They focus not on the geographical cohabitation or conflict along a physical border, but rather a struggle that is crucially and inarguably a border struggle. Drawing "on Ranajit Guha (1983) and subaltern theories of what constitute politics, and on Jacques Rancière (1999) and also Bruno Latour (2004) to establish the centrality of objects", Mielke and Pohran (2021, 86) establish and strengthen their own argument that borders also exist in bordering *things* (see also Sundberg 2008, Mazzara 2018 for Mexico–U.S. and Mediterranean contexts). Also, the study is informed by the "politics of visibility", or spectacle, in an image or set of images observed by an audience, either remotely or in person. The authors focus on a case of a Montreal asylum seeker—Abdelkader Belaouni, a blind, diabetic migrant— who took refuge in a Catholic church in order to stay in Canada.

> The lived experience of Belaouni illuminates the importance of physical objects, *things*, and the church as a place of refuge from the controlling and policing efforts of the official border, as well as the significance of spectacle, as defined above. The case of Belaouni supports our theoretical argument that borders are not, in fact, limited to physical borderlines. Moreover, his case points toward a new era of representation in which image capture and spectacle are central. The reproduction and representation of objects further augments their significance at borders (already places of heightened spectacle, observation, and representation). Our emphasis on things and spectacle draws from and contributes to a growing body of scholarship on

> materiality (Demetriou and Dimova 2019, Dimova and Demetriou 2019), making a case for the significance of materiality and objects to border studies.
>
> *(Mielke and Pohran 2021, 86)*

In the Mediterranean context, the Sea Memory Museum in Zarzis, Tunisia, portrays a diversity of objects lost and recovered in the sea migrations, including shoes and other items of clothing. A repository of items collected is illustrated in a "night view" to signify the end of their ownership and utility (Figure 6.2). In the failing light, the items—bottles, floats, and more—mesh in the stacks of similar type and purpose, and lose their identity associated with the people dependent on them.

Tuulikki Kurki (2020) traces materialized narratives of border in the articulation of unspeakable aspects of bordering through everyday objects. By combining selected theories and methods of material culture research and narrative analysis, Kurki problematizes the objects that people interact with and carry across borders as "complementary instruments for conceptualizing borders" (Kurki 2020, 129). She sees the object embodying alternative and non-narrative knowledge about borders through the materiality of the object, in addition to the object's embedded narrative knowledge. Thus, the object may speak with multiple voices. Kurki (2020, 131) draws our attention to an important shift that underlies the materialized narrative:

> Followed by the material turn of the 1990s, humanistic and sociological research has brought forward the relationships between material culture, objects, and humans (Kinnunen 2017, 33–34). The concept of a new materialism aimed at formulating this relationship differently from former traditions of modernist thought that stressed the divide between material and non-material spheres of culture (Dolphijn and Van der Tuin 2012, 85–86). In new materialism, the divide between two dimensions is surpassed, and the material and non-material are studies "in their entanglement" (Dolphijn and Van der Tuin 2012, 91). However, the original theorization of these relationships can be traced back to older sociological theories, formulated for example in Pierre Bourdieu's *Outline of a Theory of Practice* (1977), Michel de Certeau's *The Practice of Everyday Life* (1984), and later, as stressed by Dolphijn and Van de Tuin (2012, 86–87), in the works of Latour, Lyotard, and Deleuze.

This theoretical backgrounding aligns with the conceptual framework for bordering things outlined by Mielke and Pohran above, and also illustrated in the work of Sundberg and Mazzara cited above. Kurki continues: "A challenge in research is to reach the non-narrative knowledge embedded in the materiality and visuality of the object, as well as in the human interaction with the object"

FIGURE 6.2 Night View, Sea Memory Museum Series by Alessandro Brasile, Zarzis, Tunisia. Photo by permission of Alessandro Brasile.

(2020, 135). She offers several methods for making this non-narrative information visible, and for interpreting traces of the contemporary past of borders and mobilities. These include the idea of the "trace" as envisioned by archaeologists and geographers (see discussion of David Lowenthal's *The Past is a Foreign Country* in Chapter 4). Also included are objects as embodiments of individual and cultural memory, and objects as memory storage. In addition, an object carried across borders may become an instrument to embody knowledge of the border, as is well illustrated by those who use cameras to document crossings, sides, and changes. Finally, arts-based methods are used to examine material objects related to borders and bordering as discussed in Chapter 5 of this book. Tuulikki Kurki's development of a research agenda for exploring materialized narratives of border promises to establish a firm grounding for the "archaeology of experiencing contemporary objectscapes" (2020, 139) related to the border.

6.2 The profusion of border culture experience

Alejandro Morales (1995) writes about people desperately running across the border from Mexico to an imagined utopia in the U.S., only to discover that southern California is a profusion of cultural enclaves and a multitude of othernesses. Focused aspiration and vision, so critical in migration into the unknown, are confronted by heterotopia, and the confusion caused by confronting multiple borders. According to Manuel M. Martin-Rodriguez (1995), the global border emerges in transnationalism and cultural hybridism as conveyed by Alejandro

Morales in his work *The Rag Doll Plagues*. Drawing from Gilles Deleuze and Felix Guattari (1988), and their notions of becoming and deterritorialization, Martin-Rodriguez explores the engagement of language usage, minority discourses, cultural hybridism, and the relation between vernacular and hegemonic cultures in the Americas. He determines that in transnationalism minor languages erode, and that there is even a rejection of dialect and *patois*. From a border studies perspective we may interpret that minority language is relegated to an apportioned space and bordered within the transnational. Yet, minority language in transnational space remains becoming and retains a dynamic as long as it is exercised. Resurgence may be possible as in the case of some Indigenous languages in the Americas. The reterritorialization of minority language is also possible as cultural space is appropriated, and then marked and defended with language and other cultural manifestations.

A sense of struggle prevails within transnationalism's tableau of cultural interaction. Crossing borders is not easy, particularly in the face of hegemonic cultural presence and intransigence. Peter McLaren (2002) defines the predatory culture of the "white terror" that is bent on annulling the concept of the border by imposing other borders. As Liam O'Dowd (2010) explains, the struggle with borders, the shifts from a "borderless world" to a "world of borders" are not new, and these perceived encumbrances are due in part to the problem of epochal thinking, and also a lack of critical historical sensitivity in border studies. Contradictory meanings and changing significance of borders, border regions, and territoriality arise in struggles toward homogenization and hegemony (Anderson and O'Dowd 1999). Bordered culture and the resultant hybridity and plurality of culture in transnationalism will have its discontents (Brah and Coombes 2000). Border theatre will ensue from the clash of security and resistance to produce more border culture (Amoore and Hall 2010). However, the transnational space is not only a space of border struggle but also a cultural space of integration and a site of the "postborder city" as described for "Bajalta California" (Dear et al. 2003). The energy of change and creativity reforms border space and place.

Circuits of global contemporary art offer an illustration of how old and traditional borders of art are being replaced in a transnational art world. Mobile circuits of generating value and gaming the art market, and diffuse developments that lack cohesion and accountability in art discourse currently prevail (Horowitz 2014). Major players, Damien Hirst and Sotheby's among them, create and navigate the shifts. Also, the exhibitions that create contemporary art—biennials, triennials, and *DOCUMENTAS*—both are part of the waves and circuits, and help to establish canons, legitimacy, and hegemony (Gardner and Green 2016). Global art is then linked into the politics of mobility through the "(trans)cultural" shifts in the international contemporary art system (Rodriguez 2011).

These ideas are explored in "Borders: The topos of/for a post-politics of images?" (Amilhat Szary 2021). Beyond the classic figurative/non-figurative duality, this sense of multiplication opens up a possibility of thinking about works that have been created and relate to—or are situated on—the lines of geopolitical structuring formed by international boundaries in a global perspective. It is their intense proliferation that suggests the possibility of seeking a comprehensive overview of works composed around the borders that are closing—especially the most visible (and, paradoxically, the most aesthetic) ones, namely the new walls. But this approach is also valid for the other types of borders, those that are opening up, and for which artistic intervention is often a way of transforming artifacts of passage and control into cultural heritage. Therefore, the link between art and politics can be analyzed within the framework of the "hyper-territorialization" of contemporary borders.

Border art takes us from site to location through the "inter-visualization" in deeds. It is not simply because the image is on the line or among the network of border checkpoints, or because it depicts one or the other that it becomes geopolitical. Understanding, as Jean Cristofol (Parizot et al. 2014) asks us to, how the border becomes "a 'field' of artistic intervention and not just an aspect of landscape" means considering visual products at the borders not only as single and separate acts but as an iterated object related to the border condition globally. Something essential is at stake in "inter-visuality"—this implicit link between images anchored in their location on borders around the world.

This inter-visuality linked to the location of the works—that is, their functional context, rather than the specificity of their site, the uniqueness of their position—undoubtedly creates the conditions for the renewal of a political regime of images. The artists who operate at the borders are presumably responding to the *visible* order of official images by using *visual* complexity and seeking to restore a form of opacity to geopolitical images that makes it possible to imbue them with forms of resistance to the dominant order (Didi-Huberman 1990).

Art accomplishes transcultural shifts by enacting small-scale resistances against the status quo in the social domain through the mobility of agents, and the mobility of subjectivities, and displacements of imaginaries. Art conducts "transcultural negotiations emerging from the inclusion of the politics of identity and multiculturalist points of view within the global art system" (Rodriguez 2011, 313). The geopolitics of subjectivity, representational systems, and aesthetic legitimizing strategies all play roles in characterizing hybridization, locating the periphery, establishing marginality, and enforcing subalterity within globalizing discourses to help visualize the transnational. Circuits of global contemporary art encompass the motion and the re-imagined terrain of the transnational.

6.2.1 The borders away from the border: Border culture of world cities

Global or world cities may be characterized as components of "survival circuits" in transnational space (Sassen et al. 2002). Global cities are the centres in a new geography of centres and margins (Sassen 2018) in which old borders of the state give way to novel borderings to de-nationalize what has been constructed historically (Sassen 2005). Saskia Sassen (2005) proceeds to emphasize that global processes also take place and make place at subnational levels, and that at all scales, new types of borders manifest. Aihwa Ong (1997) has argued that the cultural politics of modern Chinese transnationalism has bolstered "ungrounded empires" where "flexible citizenship" (Ong 1999) is the central cultural logic of transnationality. Whereas considerable attention and debate have been focused on the de-bordering and re-bordering processes at play in globalization, the terrain of the transnational geographies created has seen less attention because this terrain is seismic and metamorphic, in the process of becoming but not sufficiently realized, evasive of governance, socially de-stabilized, and culturally convoluted. Our focus in this book has been to reveal some of the understanding that has been gained about border culture more generally, but we have not focused specifically on the border culture emerging in world cities. This focus is the subject of a different book. Yet, it is necessary to introduce and to characterize border culture in these sites because global cities are gateways in globalization, and generators of re-globalization, rescaling, and representation (Short et al. 2000).

World cities, according to Peter J. Taylor (2000, 2001) are global service centres joined in an interlocking network. These world cities operate within their own world system, a system distinct from the global template of nation-states, and the number of world cities and the complexity of the world cities system are both expanding in globalization (Knox and Taylor 1995). The world city hypothesis has been criticized because the criteria for ranking these urban places have privileged cities in the global north and forced major urban places from the global south off the map. Doreen Massey (2007, 9–15), for example, questions why some cities like Calcutta or Lagos are not in the world city ranking whereas others like Zurich are. These cities are beyond borders in one sense (Kenny and Madgin 2015), contributing to a transnationalism of urbanization, and the cities have their own internal and external borders that are parallel, intersect, and subvert other sorts of boundaries (Wilson 2014). In globalization, there has been a metamorphosis of city borders as the city has become diffused (Lazzarini 2015).

> As pure extension, a place anywhere in the city refers to anywhere, elsewhere, outside. However, the elsewhere outside the city no longer corresponds to the countryside: it is the outside of an indefinite city stretching and reaching out to other cities, eventually absorbing them and overcoming differences and distance. For all of these reasons, the impact of global processes and particularly the crossing of borders have led to a proliferation of images and metaphors, new terms and concepts for describing the spatial specificity of this post-metropolis.
>
> *(Lazzarini 2015, 181)*

Although the reference in this instance is to Los Angeles, similar descriptions could be offered to capture the limitlessness of other world cities, and the cultural diffusion inherent in and emanating from these urban places. The cities are shaped by centrifugal, exogenous forces constantly related to and operating with their borders. Edward Soja (1999, 154–155, 1996, 238) refers to this edge city or post-metropolis as exopolis.

The border culture imagined and produced in each exopolis is at once hyper-distinct from and hyper-connected to the global urban constellation. As Manuel Castells (1996, 436) suggests the world cities are "globally connected and locally disconnected, physically and socially". World cities are relocated in space and time, and becoming something else. The border culture associated with world cities reflects at once the intricacies of spatially compacted cultural imaginaries and manifestations, the attenuated connections of culture across time and space in diasporas and migration chains, expansion and extended expression of cultural imaginaries across borders of time and space, new hybridities adjacent to and intertwined with resistant, traditional cultural entities, and all associated with the energy of motion and evolution. These "transcultural cities" (Hou 2013, 3–4) feature spaces of border crossing and negotiation, and they may be characterized in various ways ranging from an emphasis on distinctive cultures and origins—"ethni Cities" (Roseman et al. 1996), "ethnoscapes" (Appadurai 1990, 7) or landscapes that are constituted in this shifting urban world, "Kaleido-scapes" that describe hybrid urban morphologies of local vernaculars and imported global elements (Nasser 2004b), or "mongrel cities" in which difference, otherness, fragmentation, splintering, multiplicity, heterogeneity, diversity, and plurality prevail (Sandercock 2003, 1). Despite growing cultural diversity, social and spatial barriers between different ethnic groups persist, and in North American cities, immigrants who move to the suburbs sustain the racial and ethnic lines that commonly delineate the inner city (Hou 2013, 5). Hou (2013, 7) goes on to argue that the model of multiculturalism is no longer sufficient or adequate: the dynamic reality of immigrants and immigration eludes assimilation and pluralism (Martin and Midgely 2003); transnational cultures challenge the traditional claims of citizenship (Nasser 2004a); "identities are multiple and cannot be subsumed under an ethnic umbrella" (Sandercock and Brock 2009, 22); and, in planning practice, strategies of consultation and participation are "disconnected from the complex intercultural relations that actually exist between people" (Wood and Landry 2008, 252).

"Transcultural placemaking" is a "framework that embodies ideas … that recognize the instability of culture(s) and the emergent nature of cultural formation and reconstitution in the shifting terrains of today's cities" (Hou 2013, 7). Its components are: to address both intercultural exchanges and cultural *trans*-formation; to view cultures as mutually influenced, constituted, and transformed; to recognize the importance of trans-locality and trans-location in processes of identity formation and placemaking beyond fixed and singular locations; to focus on the capacity and agency of individuals and communities to adapt and transform urban cultural landscapes; and, to address transcultural processes and understanding as a building block for more inclusive democracy and critical embrace of diversity. Hou (2013, 7) concludes that, "most importantly, it highlights the instrumentality of placemaking as a vehicle for cross-cultural learning, individual agency, and collective actions".

> Transcultural placemaking implies similar subjectivity on the part of migrants and migrant communities while addressing the full complexity and scope of change faced by cities and their occupants. It recognizes

> that cultural boundaries can be porous, and cultural practices can be reinvented, and, at best, self-determined.
>
> *(Hou 2013, 8)*

By locating transcultural placemaking "by nature in a state of in-between, on the move, and yet to settle", Jeffrey Hou (2013, 11) resonates an argument that we have forwarded in this book, and is often articulated in border studies, wherein border cultures are in a process of *becoming*. People engaged in transcultural placemaking occupy multiple worlds with multiple forms of knowledge. Culture and identities evolve, new interactions and influences emerge, and new spatial expressions manifest. These spaces may be hybrid and messy, sometimes invite fear, may become precarious, and are then threatened by institutional forces indifferent and hostile to their existence. Overall, as Hou (2013, 11) concludes, transcultural placemaking "calls for a process-driven focus that supports continuing adaptation and change. It calls on planners and designers to question the static and reifying notion of culture and place." Furthermore, these everyday places of border culture offer space for participation and engagement, renewal of citizenship, culture and identity negotiation and reconstitution, and an enriched understanding of place and justice.

Although most cities, and certainly most world cities, are historically situated away from nation-state boundaries, there are many instances where urban development and expansion has produced border cities (Sohn and Lara-Valencia 2013). Border cities are found in Africa, Asia, Europe, and the Americas, and several prominent instances have been discussed in this book. Whereas border cities were characteristically directed by nation-states as stewards of the border and arbiters of cross-border commerce and migration, with the advent of transnationalism and globalization, border cities have become more linked and unified with the result that they are now often referred to as twinned and binational places (Sohn and Lara-Valencia 2013). Henk Van Houtum and Huib Erneste (2001, 101) reflect on this intertwining of cities across borders and refer to these cities as "spaces of (in)difference" where linkages and connections are crafted to counter the border effect, and to benefit from its resources (Amilhat Szary and Giraut 2015, Sohn 2020). Consequently, border cities are places where the enhanced opportunity for interaction through expanded transnational forces, and the availability of urban infrastructure, labour, capital, and agency, create and mobilize intersection and interaction. Cultures are connected, sometimes coalesce, sometimes resist, but in all instances are activated and often evolve into new forms and expressions. In this book, we have traced these border culture changes in places as diverse as Arica, Chile, and Tacna, Peru; Hekou, China, and Lao Cai, Vietnam; and Detroit, U.S., and Windsor, Canada.

6.2.2 Border culture at once a manifestation and an imaginary

In the global city, a study illustrates that youth develop imaginaries and utopian fantasies of urbanization, and struggle to relate these geographies of emotion with the material city of daily experience (Dillabough and Kenelly 2010). One strategy is to generate distinctive language forms and vocabularies; another is to claim and legitimize space through marking belonging with graffiti. On the Mexico–U.S. border, imagined and material culture are intertwined in the folklore of the Texas–Mexico border (Paredes 1995). Recently, the figure of the border has become central in the rhetorical culture of alienization and fence logic of the Minuteman Civil Defense Corps, and other self-proclaimed border keepers (De Chaine 2009). In this instance the border is a civic imaginary and it is political and cultural abjection. The border has been dislodged from its consensus meaning and understanding, and it has become a dynamic conception, which we have seen subverted in many ways in the rhetoric of the more recent Trump administration.

Border culture is revealed as both an imaginary and a manifestation in the ancient virtue of hospitality in American immigrant literature and culture (Manzanas Calvo and Sanchez 2016). The ideal of hospitality, transported in culture and revealed in identity, becomes multiply bordered in transnationalized American society through attenuation of differences between hosts and guests, and belonging and non-belonging as home is accentuated as either within or outside the body politic. The virtue of hospitality, generally proclaimed as a human universal, has become a device for dividing space in contemporary American culture. Border culture in this instance is at a crossroads between imaginary and manifestation, and between space and border theory. As Canadian journalist Scott MacKenzie (1996, 1) proclaimed about the border between Quebec and Ontario, visualizing the border is both imaginary and real, a veritable "line in the snow". Producing transnational space involves the extra-territorial reach of state power within international migration, wherein techniques of control are physical, symbolic, and imaginative (Collyer and King 2015).

6.2.3 Culture integral to borders in motion

The mobile nature of culture is well documented. Pilgrimage is reframed as cultures in motion (Coleman and Eade 2004); Chicana and Latina popular culture is conveyed as "Locamotion" (Habell-Pallan 2005). Migrant cartographies identify new cultural and literary spaces in a postcolonial Europe (Ponzanesi and Merolla 2005). Cultures in motion may be mapped through identifiable and apparent "key" contacts that occur between the cultures, and the imprints, such as social transformations, scientific breakthroughs, and the dissemination of powerful political notions, that manifest through cultures in motion and contact (Stearns 2001). Michael David McNally (2000) relates how Ojibwe singers convey a Native culture in motion through hymns of grief to document memory, negotiation, and cultural criticism.

Borders are also in motion. We have engaged extensively with the theory of borders in motion (Amilhat Szary and Giraut 2015, Konrad 2015) and this theoretical focus has become a central component in theory of the border (Nail

2016). Further theoretical exploration of borders in motion has captured the dynamic processes of relational motion (Ptak et al. 2020). Among the relationships of borders in motion, the intertwining of culture and borders requires attention to the spaces or zones of transition, interaction, and identity to document the border crossings of culture (Konrad 2014). Border culture in motion is a shape-shifter on a journey across boundaries.

Kathy Burrell (2008) illustrates how this traverse across borders may be materialized by recording the material culture and spaces of mobility of migrants from post-socialist Poland to the United Kingdom. Her approach is to articulate the furnishing of the journey. Passports, car and coach travel, suitcases, and laptops are among the components of material culture in motion apparent at border crossings. Another illustration is found in the multiple citizenship formations developed across migration sites by Chinese migrants in their patterns of migration, immigration, and re-migration (Ong 1999, Ho 2018). These variants of citizenship in the globalization of culture are predicated on extensive and effective communication networks and systems in order to extend beyond tradition and borders (Mohammed 2011). The intersection of mobile cultures and human mobility also engages metacultural discourses and imaginaries. Among the Maasai of Tanzania, imaginaries and social relations concerning mobility are materialized in moveable material culture, enacted in body motions and decoration, and inculcated in defined ways and traditions (Salazar 2010).

In order to develop a more nuanced understanding of these metacultural discourses and imaginaries, particularly in emergent societies, we will require more effective mappings of cultural encounters (Schimanski and Wolfe 2007). Traditionally, narrative has marked boundaries but spatial stories also address the medial and aesthetic phenomena of borders and portray the landscapes of borders and bordering in detail, and in "poetics de-limited" (Schimanski and Wolfe 2007). Rethinking border culture requires a firm grounding in knowledge of images and narratives on the border, but it also calls for more extensive exploration of forms of the border, zones of living with the border, and migrations crossing the border (Schimanski and Nyman 2021). This will draw us deeper into understanding the geographies of creativity wherein mobility and culture are intertwined with each other, and engaged with locality, labour, intervention, and method (De Dios and Kong 2020). Also, rethinking border culture in motion will require attention to the cultural psychology of borders, and specifically how borders impact the tensional integrity (tensegrity) of cultural dialogue (Marsico and Tateo 2017).

Toward resolving border culture: Cultures of post-globalization and post-humanistic borders

Resolving the nature and process of border culture will gain imperative as humans move into an era when the world is exhibiting signs that societies have transitioned from globalization into something decidedly different that we may call, temporarily at least, *post-globalization* (Konrad 2021). The urgency to clarify border culture in globalization and post-globalization derives from the proliferation and unsettling nature of more and more imposing borders. Also, the fluidity and shifting characteristics of borders make border cultures that are always becoming and more difficult to resolve. Another call for attention derives from the acknowledgement that humans have entered a post-humanistic era (Nail 2019), in which people have encountered the limitations of nature and sparred with natural laws. In response, states and societies have propped up borders and emphasized boundaries. From one perspective: "This 'border turn' is reactionary, and antithetical, a time when we need to be mindful of the branded border and anxious of our belongingness both within and beyond borders" (Konrad 2020, 2021, 1). Other perspectives may attribute the renewed emphasis on borders as barriers as merely a component response in transnationalism, or a result of reshuffling the world order.

Cultures of post-globalization and post-humanistic borders are exemplary of the prevailing in-betweenness of the border world and the punctuated significance of both anchors and currents in border culture constructs. In this conclusion, we discuss six anchors and currents that are apparent as border cultures form and re-form in post-globalization and a post-humanistic world. Likely, there are other components that expedite or sustain border culture and border culture change, but the following are apparent in our research and they are offered as initiation points in the exploration of border culture emerging in post-globalization and post-humanistic borders. Brief discussions will focus first on anchoring components: finding and staying *home* in transnational space; exemplifying the *suture* as an agent of separation and integration; and foregrounding *women* and, more generally, non-binary people (Amilhat Szary 2020a), at the border and of the border. Among the numerous currents in creating and sustaining border culture, two are fundamentally disturbing and they need to be addressed. One is *dispossession* and the other one is *violence*. A final component, one that has been addressed at various points in this book, is the *cultural landscape* which serves to both document the flow of border culture and identify its prominences. We end with a re-consideration and re-visitation of the cultural landscape of borders, and we convey how a careful reading of this cultural landscape positions and prepares the reader to ascertain and comprehend border culture.

6.3 Finding and staying *home* in transnational space

In the houses of our fairy tales, we enter through the door or even through the chimney. Windows and sometimes shutters complete this set of controlled openings that allow us to delimit the private from the public sphere in a fairly dichotomous fashion. In Western style contemporary houses, electric wires, a family telephone cable and a television antenna connect each living unit to the outside world through a series of networks which materially appears through a suitable infrastructure. Today, not only architecture provides for complex flow circulations to ventilate homes better,

> but in particular, all sorts of waves pass through our walls without our having to provide them with openings. Televisions work with satellite packages, and every member of the household has his or her own telephone, which may be served by a variety of operators. Wireless electronic devices display a number of networks to which access is no longer physical but regulated through codes. The issue of access is the negative of borders which are occupying increasing space in our daily lives.
>
> *(Amilhat Szary 2015, 7 [translated from French])*

During the COVID-19 pandemic, most people around the world were obliged to find or at least designate a home and stay there in order to comply with social distancing and quarantine protocols. Home, and in some instances multiple homes, have become even more familiar as people have spent more time at home and constructed revised routines around the centre of home life. The culture of home, at least temporarily, has become enlarged and pervasive. The pandemic has reminded us of the sanctuary and utility of home, and we have responded by refining, enlarging, and investing in our home space. This renewed focus on home offers the opportunity to explore the culture of home, and to visualize how bordering at home operates in multiscalar contexts from the local, where home and community are reinforced, to the national, where home is even more bordered from the foreign, and to the transnational, where home is currently more restricted and constricted. For migrant communities in Canada from China and India, for example, home has been restricted to a place in China or India, or Canada. There is an expansion and also a contraction of home in transnational space. Yet, "those who are confined, are also the most mobile!" (Amilhat Szary 2020b). Mobility has evolved and enlarged through new teleconferencing technologies to sustain and even to enlarge connectivities.

Expansion or relocation of home in transnational space has been documented in Chinese migration to Germany (Leung 2004). Migrants have established integrated communities that are less apparent and visible than traditional "China towns". Similarly, Brazilians in Gort, Ireland, have combined transnational practices with a placed-based identity to create home as an anchored place in transnational space (Sheringham 2010). On the other hand, for Burkinabe (migrants from Burkina Faso) sent "home" during recent hostilities in Cote d'Ivoire, to a place most had never seen, home is an active process of placement in everyday life, rather than an abstract notion of belonging based on citizenship and identity (Bjarnesen 2013). Home in transnational space may be more fragile due to the potential of displacement or dispossession wielded by the "host" nation-state. Finding and staying home, creating and re-creating home, are aspects of border culture in the space of becoming. The culture process of home at and across boundaries requires attention in a combined approach of metaphorical geographical research and border studies (Collyer and King 2015). Finding home becomes an imperative in post-globalization as massive shifts in population challenge nation-state migration controls, and as humans encounter a post-humanistic world where the space available for home is becoming more limited.

6.4 The *"suture"* // and the scar: Border separation and integration

Scholars who have studied the border have coined many terms and derived several metaphors to capture border conditions and particularly the combined agency of border separation and integration. Prominent among these are the "Janus" face of the border (Van Houtum et al. 2005) and the "suture" (Salter 2012). We have selected the suture for closer scrutiny because, as Mark B. Salter suggests, the trope of the suture moves beyond the binary division of the border to capture dualism and the space of exception introduced by Giorgio Agamben (2005). The suture envisioned by Salter is expressed as // and it conveys a digital stop and gateway appropriate in contemporary articulation of the meaning of border. How does this device extend beyond the geophysical analogue of the suture zone, as for example in the Border Ranges fault of southern Alaska (Fisher and von Huene 1984)? The analogue conveys the same metaphor but without introducing the questionability and ambiguity of the border as a "zone of indistinction" (Gurkas 2018), where time and space, territory and politics, and identity and culture all are recalibrated. Here, the abstraction of the border enables a state of exception, and spectacles of migrant "illegality" (De Genova 2013) and terror (Gurkas 2018) enlarge in the space of exception, and provide dimension and substance to the border. Here, fingerprints and iris scans, barcodes on items, and other electronic traces delimit the border and dislodge the cultural content of identity at the border. Border culture, however, does remain and manifest and resist in many ways, as we have explained in this book. By emphasizing "sovereign power and bare life" (Agamben 1998), the border analyst foregrounds legal structures and biopolitical significance but misses the albeit messy yet potentially revealing aspects of border culture. For example, Leila Whitley (2017) illustrates how a focus on Agamben's perspective in border and migration scholarship does not articulate racism and actually displaces it. Our point is not to diminish the contribution of Agamben's thinking to critical border studies, or align against the agenda of critical border studies (Parker and Vaughan-Williams 2016), but to call for a balanced assessment of border dynamics and include more sensitive and detailed reading of border culture.

Accordingly, the metaphor of the scar may be appropriate to encompass a broader and culturally more sensitive understanding of border dynamics.

> The idea of the scar seems to me to be better suited to the interpretation I hope to convey here. For most often, a scar is a synonym of reparation, where the contact between tissues is reconstituted and the trace is minimal;

> but when you require "stitches" to keep everything that has been lacerated together, the redness and grain of the skin show that it is impossible to return to before.
>
> *(Amilhat Szary 2015 [translation from French])*

Annamarie Jagose (2019) illustrates how the slash and the suture operate to appreciate "Post/colonialization in *Borderlands/La Frontera: The New Mestiza*". A radically new utopic hybridization is realized by foregrounding figures of the border and the mestiza. These figures become emblematic in duality through illustration of the political radicalness of hybridization, and the corollary of political conservatism of separatism and classificatory demarcation. The slash and suture emphasize that there is no escape from hybridization, and in effect, colonial power. The "mestiza is not transcending but figuring the fundamental irresolution of the legislative border" (Jagose 2019, 212). Border culture will not help us to solve the border, but understanding border culture may help to resolve human interaction with the border.

6.5 *Feminization* of the border and *foregrounding women and LGBTQ+* at the border

The feminization of survival in globalization, and in the eras which may follow, is a prominent theme embraced by social theorists (Sassen 2018). Households and even entire communities worldwide have become dependent on women for survival (Sassen 2000), and this condition has been exemplified by women refugees at Mediterranean borders (Schmoll 2020). In another example, female foreign domestic workers from other Asian countries gravitate to Singapore where opportunities and high wages abound (Yeoh and Huang 2000). The pattern is replicated in more extensive "home" and "away" relationships of domestic workers between the Philippines and Canada, for example. Feminization of the border is apparent in Asian cross-border marriage migration (Yang and Lu 2010). In Korea, men seek women marriage partners of foreign origin to enhance their economic and social standing (Lee 2012). In Xishuangbanna, Yunnan's southernmost extension into Southeast Asia, Dai minority women cultivate a highly feminized and youthful image consistent with their cosmological understanding of women's role (Komlosy 2009). This stance is not simply a passive submissive nod to Han Chinese fantasy of women, but rather evidence of ongoing negotiation and accommodation of the Dai in their borderland context.

Yet, the feminization of the border, and most specifically labour migration across borders, also needs to be viewed and understood as violence against women (Piper 2003). Cross-border movements of women in trafficking and prostitution emphasize the prominences and the boundaries of gender difference (Kapur 2017). Undocumented migration is feminized in many global contexts, but perhaps most evidently at the U.S.–Mexican border (Ruf 2009). In protracted situations of waiting at the border or in migrant camps, there is a feminization of asylum (Hyndman and Giles 2011). Maria Socorro Tabuenca Cordoba (2011) details a chilling account of the femicide in Ciudad Juarez at the Mexico–U.S. border. A decade ago, during the height of the drug and gang violence, more than 900 women died in sexual serial killings, and more died at the hands of organized crime in the city. The extensive writings of Cordoba and her colleague Debra A. Castillo (2002) document the precarity of border women in displacement, dispossession, and violence, but also in their solidarity and resolve to sustain home, family, and community. Given the insights into feminization of the border and the foregrounding of women at the border, and the broader role of feminization of circuits of survival in globalization and post-globalization, this stark reality requires new and renewed attention in order to understand border culture.

6.6 Migration at the border as *dispossession*

> So let us make the border a place of warning. Invisible borders are no longer "on the edge of politics" but constitute "essential objects of political action", the philosopher Etienne Balibar reminded us twenty years ago. They have become the "undemocratic condition of democracy" (Balibar 2022)... "What is the future of political systems that see both the conditions of citizen ownership and the perimeters of their systems shake at the borders? When the opposition between a "protective inside" and a potentially dangerous outside" is eroding, when citizenship is defined by exclusion rather than inclusion, how can we continue to define and construct the "common good", and on what scale(s)? For the time being, international borders remain the backbone of a citizenship that is itself the foundation of democracy ... The way our borders flicker highlights the uncertain future of our political systems. Without further reflection, it may soon be said that these killing borders are where we have admitted that we have lost our humanity.
>
> *(Amilhat Szary 2015, 150–151 [translated from French])*

Although one may argue that all migration involving permanent dislocation and relocation of space, of residence, of home, and ultimately of citizenship, is dispossession, the degree and intensity of dispossession at the border impacts refugees, asylum seekers, people of colour, and women more directly and emphatically (Washington 2020). At the U.S.–Mexico border, Alejandro Lugo (2008) articulates this dispossession as culture of fragmented lives and assembled parts. In Tucson, Arizona, the frontier is more than a metaphor, it is racial governance throughout colonization, dispossession, and resistance, in which there is an overall devaluation of non-white territorial and economic relations, and the displacement and dispossession of communities of colour (Launius and Boyce 2021). Histories of belonging(s) at the border characteristically engage narratives of territory, possession, and dispossession (Cons 2012), yet these narratives are conveyed with bias and manipulated by power. Dispossession of women and their identification as liminal figures diminishes them at borders. This dispossession has deep roots in Western societies, for example, the diminishment of "economic woman" as opposed to "economic man" in nineteenth century British culture (Rappoport and Dalley 2013), and the demeaning of anxiety and jealousy in nineteenth century French culture (Belenky 2008).

Current media attention on Uyghur dispossession in far western China emphasizes the plight of bordered Indigenous cultures living within and across state boundaries. In his dissertation, Darren Byler (2018) explores the process of "spirit breaking" and the tools of "terror capitalism" employed by the Chinese government to dispossess the Uyghur. Terror capitalism constitutes the use of passbook systems, technological surveillance, urban cleansing, and mass internment camps to shape self-representation among the Uyghur and the Han Chinese. A form of human engineering ensues. The discourse of terror justifies more state investment in controls, and this investment employs millions of state security workers. On the other hand, the Uyghur use this cultural production and bordering to refuse Chinese development. Another recent dissertation focuses on dispossession in Detroit. Matthew J. Irwin (2020) illustrates how the border is the organizing structure in Indigenous dispossession and in the racialization of labour in Detroit. Dispossession is articulated as a social process and discourse produced and replicated in the built environment through locating (siting), seeing (sighting), and discussing (citing) the role of the border in dispossession. A third dissertation, this one written by Michelle Braiden (2014) at Concordia University in Montreal, focuses on the nomos or legal devices utilized as border-making practices by the League of Nations to dispossess Indigenous peoples in South America's Chaco War. In all of these instances, as Klaus Dodds (2013) illustrates for Akwesasne on the Canada–U.S. border (see detailed discussion in Chapter 4), dispossession of Indigenous territory and culture reverberates as sovereignty is tested constantly, and border space and place evolve.

Juanita Sundberg (2008) shows how the material evidence of undocumented crossings along the U.S.–Mexico border helps to dispossess the migrants. These objects—identity documents, personal mementos—emphasize those who do not belong, and differentiate them from those who do belong. Although these items may be viewed as waste and disposable, the items also signify culture left behind and this is the essence of dispossession (Lucas 2002). Non-humans are also actors at the border. Sundberg (2011) advances a post-humanist political ecology to broaden our understanding of boundary enforcement impacts and dispossession of territory and habitat in the U.S.–Mexico borderlands. Representing dispossession at the border and in the borderlands is consequently very extensive and inclusive of human and non-human components, historical and contemporary renditions, imaginaries and manifestations. Representing dispossession, in one instance through imaging the great Irish famine and diaspora, is accomplished most effectively through conveying visual culture (Kelly 2018).

In many instances, culture is placed in balance; some culture is left behind at the border, and other culture is gained. The border may operate like a comb to remove loose aspects of culture and to align cultural strands with/in a different polity, society, and cultural milieu. Yet, in some instances, states of dispossession emerge where precarious coexistence is the norm (Biner 2020). In southeastern Turkey, for example, the Kurdish region is in a persistent state of dispossession with both tangible and intangible effects of dispossession evident among the disenfranchised Kurdish population, and the remains of violence still unfolding.

6.7 Border *cultures of violence*

Whereas the border may seal out some violence, the border also creates cultures of violence that accompany the dispossession and displacement, the arbitrary division, the confrontation and resistance, and the trauma, all focused at the border line. There is the violence of borders and the violence of borderlessness (Megoran 2020). All of these conditions produce a culture of violence in Kurdish borderlands extending from Turkey to Iran, yet the cultures of violence are both abated and fuelled by global pan-Kurdish solidarity (Kurdayeti) in times of war and trauma (Gourlay 2018). Similar structures have supported cultures of violence in Northern Ireland through loyalist mobilization in the late twentieth century (Burke 2020). More recently, the terrorist group Boko Haram fashioned and wielded a culture of violence across borders in central Africa (MacEachern 2018). Borders in globalization have become catalysts and flashpoints of violence and criminality (Pickering and McCulloch 2012), and an immense literature has focused on aspects of borders and violence. In the cultural imaginary of violence, the "vampire nation" looms larger in popular culture and at the borders of reality (Longinovic 2011).

Only a small fraction of this attention has focused, however, on the cultures of violence at borders and in borderlands, and how cultures of violence emerge and impact life in border regions. At the beginning of the twenty-first century, a study of identity fragmentation through violence in the Balkans and Macedonia specified a border culture of violence as central to understanding identity fragmentation (Sheleva 2003). More recently, cultures of border violence have been deconstructed to reveal underlying connections and commonalities, particularly as related to global migrations and asylum seekers. Ozgun E. Topak (2021) examines border violence and migrant subjectivities beyond the general designations of victims and criminals to reveal that migrant subjectivities are abject, religious, nomadic, and dissident, thus expanding understanding and perhaps informing empathy. Hunger strikes of asylum seekers are better understood when viewed as embodiment of border violence (Pellander and Horsti 2018). Knowing border violence requires an intersectional and decolonial approach to comprehend the interconnection of systems of oppression, mutually reinforcing and multipliable, with other forms of violence and domination (Tofighian 2020). In Australia, according to Omid Tofighian, border violence is rooted in colonial imaginary and it pervades socio-political structures and institutions. Although recognition of cultures of violence is implicit in the many studies focusing on violence along the U.S.–Mexico border (see for example Staudt 2009, Slack and Whiteford 2011, Payan 2016), the nature and impact of these cultures of violence also requires theorization and articulation of cultural facets of crime and trauma.

Tuulikki Kurki (2021) and a few other border specialists are exploring the impact of border-related trauma narratives. Their work is focused on the Finnish–Russian borderlands in both historical and contemporary contexts, and it reveals the invisibility of the trauma narratives despite their elaborations of heroism and the grotesque. Recently, Vamik D. Volkan (2018), a leading scholar in the study of traumatized societies, has focused his attention on the psychology of border trauma. This attention to trauma as a border culture of violence signals the need for more extensive investigation in a broader range of border contexts including border art (Bennett 2005).

Violence and trauma also constitute the essence of games, and specifically the popular series of videogames called *Borderlands*. The borderlands of "playfulness" are violent and dangerous (Pichlmair 2008), and someone needs to fall (Shirley 2011). As Kaitlin Tremblay (2017) proclaims in the title of her book on the *Borderlands* game, this *Ain't No Place for a Hero*. Indeed, racism and sexism are commonplace in video games and in the gaming world (Nakamura 2019). There are few signs of a post-racial society and gender tolerance and acceptance in gaming culture. Yet, as Felicity Amaya Schaeffer (2018, 1005) claims "spirit matters" as she foregrounds Gloria Anzaldúa "cosmic becoming across human/nonhuman borderlands" and communing with shapes to suggest a realization beyond violence in the game of *Borderlands*.

6.8 *Cultural landscapes* in transnational space

Although the shapes in the game *Borderlands* are created digitally, they do constitute cultural landscapes, and these cultural landscapes form a component of contemporary transnational space. Contemporary transnational space, however, is an accumulation and amalgam of some extraordinary cultural landscapes amid a vast expanse of ordinary landscapes. Cultural landscapes of and at the border may be embellished with walls and fortifications to render them extraordinary, but with expansion of border walls and fences worldwide, even these border landscapes are made ordinary. On the other hand, some border culture landscapes appropriated from nature, Niagara Falls for example, may remain extraordinary indefinitely. The point of all of this is to convey that the cultural landscapes of borders are always in the process of becoming, in a variegated fashion, with prominences, within a vast expanse of ordinary, everyday, border culture experience. As a final step in this book toward situating border culture with/in transnational space, our objectives are to complete the conversation on borders and culture by returning the discourse to border landscapes, and re-engaging culture and border landscapes in a post-humanistic world. There are three steps:

re-visit the interpretation of ordinary landscapes, insert aesthetics and politics, and, simultaneously enlarge the aperture to embrace the fluorescence of culture surrounding borders and focus border culture within post-humanistic limits.

In 1979, Don Meinig published an exceptionally influential book *The Interpretation of Ordinary Landscapes: Geographical Essays*. The volume included contributions by J.B. Jackson, who influenced the perspective on vernacular landscapes (1984), and prominent geographers who extended attention to ordinary landscapes: Pierce Lewis, David Lowenthal, Marwyn Samuels, David Sopher, Yi Fu Tuan, and Don Meinig. This work, combined with W.G. Hoskins' BBC film *The Making of the British Landscape* inspired generations of anthropologists, historians, and geographers to study and revere cultural landscapes. The passion for cultural landscape interpretation was fuelled periodically by enthusiasts and scholars, among them Dennis Cosgrove (1998) in geography and Amos Rapoport (1992) in anthropology, but the original seed was planted firmly and landscape studies became central in cultural geography, and impacted research in the disciplines of anthropology, architecture, and history, and influenced research in other social sciences and the humanities.

When *The Geography of Border Landscapes* (Rumley and Minghi 2014) was first published in 1991, border studies had recently been rejuvenated in geography and introduced in other fields. Since then, border landscapes have offered an organizing framework or focus for numerous extensive studies of border regions. Included in this broad reach of regional studies of borders are Janet Sturgeon's (2007) work on the Akha in China and Thailand, Michelle Brym's (2013) studies of integration and division in border landscapes on the EU periphery, Aimee Edith Joyce's (2014) focus on border landscapes of religion and mobility on the Polish–Belarusian frontier, and Kenneth D. Madsen's (2011) research on barriers of the U.S.–Mexico border as landscapes of domestic political compromise. All of these works invoke and convey the border cultural landscape, yet they embrace and endeavour to reveal the politics of border culture.

At this juncture, we re-engage with Don Mitchell's (2003) point that cultural landscapes are not just landscapes but landscapes where justice is defined and wielded. The corollary for border culture landscapes is obvious provided the politics of boundaries, yet we cannot simply allow politics to pervade and immerse the cultural essence of border landscapes. Here, we engage the aesthetics of borders, reveal the interaction of aesthetics and politics and articulate this interaction as borderscapes (Dell'Agnese and Amilhat Szary 2015). Borderscaping embraces the imaginaries and practices of border making (Brambilla et al. 2015, 2016). This minted term of borderscape merges the interaction of politics and some aspects of culture, yet it also compresses and moulds culture at the border, thus socially mediating the meaning of culture (Schein 2006). As Don Meinig (2008) reminds us, in the study of the cultural landscape, we also need to view geography as an art. This calls for re-visiting as well as re-visioning border culture landscapes.

How do we do this? In border studies, and particularly in the study of border culture, we need to inventory and then communicate what Nick Megoran (2012) has referred to as the biography of the border. Megoran has drawn extensively from border culture and border landscape at the Uzbekistan and Kyrgyzstan boundary to document a biography with historical depth and cultural expression (Megoran 2017). Then, we place the biography in cultural-ecological context (Grichting and Zebich-Knos 2017) to re-engage the "uncommon ground" of cultural landscapes and environmental values (Strang 2020). Cultural landscapes are intertwined with environmental change (Head 2017), and they are viewed as a bridge between culture and nature (Taylor and Lennon 2011) in the field of heritage studies where cultural landscape studies have experienced a resurgence (Roe and Taylor 2014). This approach has been exemplified in a recent integrative historical–cultural–environmental heritage study and plan for the Niagara border region between the U.S. and Canada (Cafarella et al. 2021).

Border culture has become a matter for preservation at and beyond the border. Cultural landscapes at the border and in the borderlands are constantly being altered to produce new assemblages which in turn become something bordered. Some of these bordered cultural landscapes are sustained and even preserved in the face of further flows as culture walls. The cultural landscapes of borders encompass the politics of division, and the cultural imaginaries and productions revealed in aesthetic representations, all engaged somehow and to some degree with the border environs. More evident in a post-humanistic era, extending beyond the initial flourish and exhilaration of globalization, is a growing realization that humans have extended beyond the limitations of nature, and overstepped our bounds. Whether this realization will be expressed in a revised and more sensitive border culture remains to be seen. The culture of the post-humanistic border may be viewed as a pre-script for human–nature relationships; alternatively, the culture of the post-humanistic border may be a post-script for human relations. As Jacques Rancière (2020) writes in *The Edges of Fiction*, we may move from "the shores of the real" to "the edge of nothing and the all".

References

Agamben, Giorgio. 1998. *Homo Sacer: Sovereign Power and Bare Life*. Stanford: Stanford University Press.

Agamben, Giorgio. 2005. "State of exception." *Nova srpska politička misao* 12, (01+04): 135–145.

Agar, Michael. 1994. "The intercultural frame." *International Journal of Intercultural Relations* 18, (2): 221–237.

Agar, Michael. 2019. *Culture: How to Make It Work in a World of Hybrids*. Latham: Rowman and Littlefield.

Alonso, Alexandra Delano. 2018. *From Here and There: Diaspora Policies, Integration, and Social Rights Beyond Borders*. Oxford: Oxford University Press.

Amilhat Szary, Anne-Laure. 2013. "Cultura de Fronteras." In Beatriz Nates Cruz, ed. *Frontera, Fronteras*. Manizales, Colombia: Editorial Universitaria de Caldas, 43–60.

Amilhat Szary, Anne-Laure. 2015. *Qu'est-ce qu'une frontière aujourd'hui?* Paris: Presses Universitaires de France.

Amilhat Szary, Anne-Laure. 2020a. *Géopolitique Des Frontières. Découper La Terre, Imposer Une Vision Du Monde.* Paris: Le Cavalier Bleu.

Amilhat Szary, Anne-Laure. 2020b. "Those who are confined, are also the most mobile!" *BorderObs.* June 5, 2020. Luxemburg http://cbs.uni-gr.eu/en/resources/borderobs#.

Amilhat Szary, Anne-Laure. 2021. "Borders: The topos of/for a post-politics of images?" In Johan Schimanski, and Jopi Nyman, eds. *Border Images, Border Narratives.* Manchester: University of Manchester Press, 151–167.

Amilhat Szary, Anne-Laure, and Frederic Giraut, eds. 2015. *Borderities: The Politics of Contemporary Mobile Borders.* New York: Palgrave Macmillan.

Amoore, Louise, and Alexandra Hall. 2010. "Border theatre: On the arts of security and resistance." *Cultural Geographies* 17, (3): 299–319.

Anderson, James, and Liam O'Dowd. 1999. "Borders, border regions and territoriality: Contradictory meanings, changing significance." *Regional Studies* 33, (7): 593–604.

Anzaldúa, Gloria. 1987. *Borderlands/La Frontera: The New Mestiza.* San Francisco: Aunt Lute Books.

Appadurai, Arjun. 1990. "Disjuncture and difference in the global cultural economy." *Theory, Culture & Society* 7, (2–3): 295–310.

Appadurai, Arjun. 1996. *Modernity at Large: Cultural Dimensions of Globalization.* Minneapolis: University of Minnesota Press.

Arthur, John A. 2010. *African Diaspora Identities: Negotiating Culture in Transnational Migration.* Lantham: Lexington Books.

Axel, Brian Keith. 2004. "The context of diaspora." *Cultural Anthropology* 19, (1): 26–60.

Balibar, Etienne. 2002 [2001]. "World borders, political borders." *PLMA* 117, (1): 68–78.

Belenky, Masha. 2008. *The Anxiety of Dispossession: Jealousy in Nineteenth Century French Culture.* Lewisburg: Bucknell University Press.

Bennett, Jill. 2005. *Empathic Vision: Affect, Trauma, and Contemporary Art.* Stanford: Stanford University Press.

Ben-Rafael, Eliezer. 2013. "Diaspora." *Current Sociology* 61, (5–6): 842–861.

Biner, Zerrin Ozkm. 2020. *States of Dispossession: Violence and Precarious Coexistence in Southeast Turkey.* Philadelphia: University of Pennsylvania Press.

Bjarnesen, Jesper. 2013. "Diaspora at home? Wartime mobilities in the Burkhina Faso-Cote D'Ivoire transnational space." PhD. Dissertation, Uppsala University.

Bourdieu, Pierre. 1977. *Outline of a Theory of Practice.* Cambridge: Cambridge University Press.

Brah, Avtar, and Annie Coombes. 2000. *Hybridity and its Discontents: Politics, Science, Culture.* New York: Psychology Press.

Braiden, Michelle. 2014. "The nomos of border-making practices: The Chaco War, League of Nations and Indigenous dispossession." PhD. Dissertation, Concordia University, Montreal.

Brambilla, Chiara, Jussi Laine, James W. Scott, and Gianluca Bocchi, eds. 2015. *Borderscaping: Imaginations and Practices of Border Making.* Aldershot: Ashgate.

Brambilla, Chiara, Jussi Laine, and Gianluca Bocchi. 2016. *Borderscaping: Imaginations and Practices of Border Making.* London: Routledge.

Brkovic, Carna, and Stef Jansen. 2018. "A lively border: Bosnia and Herzogovina and Serbia on the shifting banks of the Drina." In David Montgomery, ed. *Everyday Life in the Balkans.* Bloomington: Indiana University Press, 230–238.

Brym, Michelle. 2013. "Border landscapes on the EU periphery: Examples of integration and division between Polish and Ukrainian cities." *Focus on Geography* 56, (3): 84–94.

Burke, Edward. 2020. "Loyalist mobilization and cross-border violence in rural Ulster, 1972–1974." *Terrorism and Political Violence* 34, (6): 1057–1075.

Burrell, Kathy. 2008. "Materializing the border: Spaces of mobility and material culture in migration from post-socialist Poland." *Mobilities* 3, (3): 353–373.

Butler, Kim D. 2001. "Defining diaspora, refining a discourse." *Diaspora: A Journal of Transnational Studies* 10, (2): 189–219.

Byler, Darren. 2018. "Spirit breaking: Uyghur dispossession, culture work and terror capitalism." PhD. Dissertation, University of Washington.

Cafarella, Scott, Joel Konrad, and Rebecca Sciarra. 2021. "A biocultural planning approach for managing transborder cultural heritage landscapes." In Victor Konrad, and Melissa Kelly, eds. *Borders, Culture, and Globalization: A Canadian Perspective.* Ottawa: University of Ottawa Press, 293–317.

Castells, Manuel. 1996. *The Rise of the Network Society.* Oxford: Blackwell.

Castillo, Debra A., and Maria Soccoro Tabuenca Cordoba. 2002. *Border Women: Writing from La Frontera.* Minneapolis: University of Minnesota Press.

Certeau, Michel de. 1984. *The Practice of Everyday Life* (Translated by Steven Rendell) Berkeley: University of California Press.

Coleman, Simon, and John Eade, eds. 2004. *Reframing Pilgrimage: Cultures in Motion.* London: Psychology Press.

Collyer, Michael, and Russell King. 2015. "Producing transnational space: International migration and the extra-territorial reach of state power." *Progress in Human Geography* 39, (2): 185–204.

Cons, Jasar. 2012. "Histories of belonging(s): Narrating territory, possession, and dispossession at the India-Bangladesh border." *Modern Asian Studies* 46, (3): 527–558.

Cordoba, Maria Soccoro Tabuenca. 2011. "Ciudad Juarez, femicide, and the state." In Gabriela Polit Dueñas, and María Helena Rueda, eds. *Meanings of Violence in Contemporary Latin America.* New York: Palgrave Macmillan, 115–147.

Correa-Cabrera, Guadalupe, and Victor Konrad, eds. 2020. *North American Borders in Comparative Perspective.* Tucson: University of Arizona Press.

Cosgrove, Dennis. 1998. "Cultural landscapes." In Tim Unwin, ed. *A European Geography.* London: Routledge, 65–81.

Creese, Gillian. 2017. *The New African Diaspora in Vancouver.* Toronto: University of Toronto Press.

Dear, Michael, Gustavo Leclerc, and Jo-Anne Berelowitz, eds. 2003. *Postborder City: Cultural Spaces of Bajalta California.* New York: Psychology Press.

De Chaine, D. Robert. 2009. "Bordering the civic imaginary: Alienization, fence logic, and the minuteman civil defense corps." *Quarterly Journal of Speech* 95, (1): 43–65.

De Dios, Anjeline, and Lily Kong. 2020. *Handbook of the Geographies of Creativity.* Oxford: Edward Elgar.

De Genova, Nicholas. 2013. "Spectacles of migrant 'illegality': The scene of exclusion, the obscene of inclusion." *Ethnic and Racial Studies* 36, (7): 1180–1198.

Deleuze, Gilles, and Felix Guattari. 1988. *A Thousand Plateaus: Capitalism and Schizophrenia.* London: Bloomsbury.

Dell'Agnese, Elena, and Anne-Laure Amilhat Szary. 2015. "Borderscapes: From border landscapes to border aesthetics." *Geopolitics* 20, (1): 4–13.

Demetriou, Olga. 2019. "Materiality, imbrications, and the Longue Durée of Greco-Turkish borders." In Olga Demetriou, and Rozila Dimova, eds. *The Political Materialities of Borders: New Theoretical Directions.* Manchester: University of Manchester Press, 16–35.

Demetriou, Olga, and Rozita Dimova. 2019. "Preface." In Demetriou, Olga, and Rozita Dimova, Eds. *Political Materialities of Borders: New Theoretical Directions.* Manchester: University of Manchester Press, xi–xvii.

Didi-Huberman, George. 1990. "Le disegno de Vasari, ou le bloc-note magique de l'histoire de l'art." *La Part de l'œil* 6: 31–51.

Dillabough, Jo-Anne, and Jacquiline Kenelly. 2010. *Lost Youth in the Global City: Class, Culture, and the Urban Imaginary.* London: Routledge.

Dittmer, Jason. 2005. "Captain America's empire: Reflections on identity, popular culture, and post 9/11 geopolitics." *Annals, Association of American Geographers* 95, (3): 626–643.

Dittmer, Jason, and Andrew Hurley. 2013. *Captain America and the Nationalist Superhero: Metaphors, Narratives, and Geopolitics.* Philadelphia: Temple University Press.

Dodds, Klaus. 2013. "'I'm still not crossing that': Borders, dispossession, and sovereignty in *Frozen River* (2008)." *Geopolitics* 18, (3): 560–583.

Dolphijn, Rick, and Iris Van der Tuin. 2012. *New Materialism: Interviews and Cartographies.* Ann Arbor: Open Humanities Press.

Dunn, Kevin. 2010. "Embodied transnationalisms: Bodies in transnational spaces." *Population, Space and Place* 16, (1): 1–9.

Durst-Andersen, Per, and David Barratt. 2019. "Idea-based and image-based linguacultures: Evidence from American English and Mandarin Chinese." *Language and Culture* 6, (2): 351–387.

Fisher, Michael A., and Roland Von Huene. 1984. "Geophysical investigation of a suture zone: The border ranges fault of Southern Alaska." *Journal of Geophysical Research: Solid Earth* 89, (B13): 11333–11351.

Fishkin, Shelley Fisher. 2005. "Crossroads of cultures: The transnational turn in American studies: Presidential address to the American Studies Association, November 12, 2004." *American Quarterly* 57, (1): 17–57.

Foucault, Michel. 1982. "The subject and power." *Critical Inquiry* 8, (4): 777–795.

Friedrich, Paul. 1989. "Language, ideology, and political economy." *American Anthropologist* 91, (2): 295–312.

Gardner, Anthony, and Charles Green. 2016. *Biennials, Trienniels, and Documenta: The Exhibitions that Created Contemporary Art.* New York: John Wiley and Son.

Geertz, Clifford. 2017. *The Interpretation of Cultures: Selected Essays*, 3rd ed. New York: Basic Books.

Giraut, Frédéric. 2013. "Territoire multi-situé, complexité territoriale et postmodernité territoriale: des concepts opératoires pour rendre compte des territorialités contemporaines?" *L'espace géographique* 42, (4): 293–305.

Gourlay, William. 2018. "Kurdayeti: Pan-Kurdish solidarity and cross-border links in times of war and trauma." *Middle East Critique* 27, (1): 25–42.

Grichting, Anna, and Michele Zebich-Knos, eds. 2017. *The Social Ecology of Border Landscapes.* New York: Anthem Press.

Guha, Ranajit. 1983. *Elementary Aspects of Peasant Insurgency in Colonial India.* Delhi: Oxford University Press.

Gupta, Akhil, and James Ferguson. 1992. "Beyond 'culture': Space, identity, and the politics of difference." *Cultural Anthropology* 7, (1): 6–23.

Gupta, Akhil, and James Ferguson, eds. 1997. *Culture, Power, Place: Explorations in Critical Anthropology.* Durham: Duke University Press.

Gurkas, Ezgi Tuncer. 2018. "Border as 'zone of indistinction': The state of exception and the spectacle of terror along Turkey's border with Syria." *Space and Culture* 21, (3): 322–335.

Habell-Pallan, Michelle. 2005. *Loca Motion: The Travels of Chicana and Latina Popular Culture*. New York: New York University Press.

Hannerz, Ulf. 1996. *Transnational Connections: Culture, People, Places*. London: Routledge.

Head, Lesley. 2017. *Cultural Landscapes and Environmental Change*. London: Routledge.

Ho, Elaine Lynn-Ee. 2018. *Citizens in Motion*. Stanford: Stanford University Press.

Horowitz, Noah. 2014. *Art of the Deal: Contemporary Art in a Global Financial Market*. Princeton: Princeton University Press.

Hou, Jeffrey, ed. 2013. *Transcultural Cities: Border Crossing and Placemaking*. London: Routledge.

Hutchinson, Francis E., and Terence Chong, eds. 2016. *The SIJORI Cross-Border Region: Transnational Politics, Economics and Culture*. Singapore: ISEAS-Yusof Ishak Institute.

Hyndman, Jennifer, and Wenona Giles. 2011. "Waiting for what? The feminization of asylum in protracted situations." *Gender, Place and Culture* 18, (3): 361–379.

Irwin, Matthew J. 2020. "(Sī'tĭng) Detroit: Vision and dispossession in a Midwest Bordertown." PhD. Dissertation, University of New Mexico.

Jackson, John Brinckerhoff. 1984. *Discovering the Vernacular Landscape*. New Haven: Yale University Press.

Jagose, Annemarie. 2019. "Slash and Suture: Post/colonialism in borderlands/La Frontera: The New Mestiza." In Sueja Gunew, ed. *Feminism and the Politics of Difference*. London: Routledge, 212–227.

Jones, Reece. 2009. "Geopolitical boundary narratives, the global war on terror and border fencing in India." *Transactions of the Institute of British Geographers* 34, (3): 290–304.

Joyce, Ainee Edith. 2014. "Border landscapes: Religion, space and movement on the Polosih Belarusian frontier." PhD. Dissertation, Goldsmiths, University of London.

Kaplan, Caren. 1987. "Deterritorializations: The rewriting of home and exile in western feminist discourse." *Cultural Critque* 6: 187–198.

Kapur, Ratna. 2017. "Cross-border movements and the law: Renegotiating the boundaries of difference." In Kamala Kempadoo, Jyoti Sanghera, and Bandana Pattannarik, eds. *Trafficking and Prostitution Reconsidered*. London: Routledge, 25–41.

Kearney, Michael. 1991. "Borders and boundaries of state and self at the end of empire." *Journal of Historical Sociology* 4, (1): 52–74.

Kearney, Michael. 1995. "The local and the global: The anthropology of globalization and transnationalism." *Annual Review of Anthropology* 24, (1): 547–565.

Kearney, Michael. 2000. "Transnational Oaxacan Indigenous identity: The case of Mixtecs and Zapotecs." *Identities: Global Studies in Culture and Power* 7, (2): 173–195.

Kelly, Niamh Ann. 2018. *Imaging the Great Irish Famine: Representing Dispossession in Visual Culture*. London: Bloomsbury.

Kenny, Nicholas, and Rebecca Madgin, eds. 2015. *Cities Beyond Borders: Comparative and Transnational Approaches to Urban History*. Aldershot: Ashgate.

Kinnunen, Vauras. 2017. *Things on the Road: A Sociological Research about Object Relations when Moving*. Rovaniemi: University of Lapland.

Knox, Paul, and Peter J. Taylor, eds. 1995. *World Cities in a World System*. Cambridge: Cambridge University Press.

Komlosy, Anouska. 2009. "Feminization, recognition, and the cosmological in Xishuangbanna." In Siu-Keung Cheung, Joseph Tse-Hei Lee, and Lida V. Nedilsky, eds. *Marginalization in China*. New York: Springer, 123–143.

Konrad, Victor. 2014. "Borders and culture: Zones of transition, interaction and identity." *Eurasia Border Review* 5, (1): 41–57.

Konrad, Victor. 2015. "Toward a theory of borders in motion." *Journal of Borderlands Studies* 30, (1): 1–17.

Konrad, Victor. 2020. "Belongingness and borders." In James W. Scott, ed. *A Research Agenda for Border Studies*. Oxford: Edward Elgar, 109–128.

Konrad, Victor. 2021. "New directions at the post-globalization border." *Journal of Borderlands Studies* 36, (5): 713–726.

Kurki, Tuulikki. 2020. "Materialized narratives of the border: Articulating the unspeakable through everyday objects." In James W. Scott, ed. *A Research Agenda for Border Studies*. Oxford: Edward Elgar, 129–144.

Kurki, Tuulikki. 2021. "From heroism to grotesque: The invisibility of border-related trauma narratives in the Finnish-Russian borderlands." In Johan Schimanski, and Jopi Nyman, eds. *Border Images, Border Narratives: The Political Aesthetics of Boundaries and Crossings*. Manchester: Manchester University Press, 105–126.

Launius, Sarah, and Geoffrey Alan Boyce. 2021. "More than metaphor: Settler colonialism, frontier logic, and the continuities of racialized dispossession in a Southwest U.S. City." *Annals, Association of American Geographers* 111, (1): 157–174.

Latour, Bruno. 2004. "From Realpolitik to Dingpolitik or how to make things public." In Bruno Latour, and Peter Weibel, eds. *Making Things Public: Atmospheres of Democracy*. Cambridge: MIT Press, 14–43.

Lazzarini, Anna. 2015. "Metamorphosis of city borders." In Chiara Brambilla, Jussi Laine, James W. Scott, and Gianluca Bocchi, eds. *Borderscaping: Imaginations and Practices of Border Making*. Aldershot: Ashgate, 195–204.

Lee, Hyunok. 2012. "Political economy of cross-border marriage: Economic development and social reproduction in Korea." *Feminist Economics* 18, (2): 177–200.

Leung, Maggi Wai-Han. 2004. *Chinese Migration in Germany: Making Home in Transnational Space*. Frankfurt: IKO.

Longinovic, Toma. 2011. *Vampire Nation: Violence as Cultural Imaginary*. Durham: Duke University Press.

Lucas, Gavin. 2002. "Disposability and dispossession in the twentieth century." *Journal of Material Culture* 7, (1): 5–22.

Lugo, Alejandro. 2008. *Fragmented Lives, Assembled Parts: Culture, Capitalism, and Conquest at the U.S.-Mexico Border*. Austin: University of Texas Press.

MacEachern, Scott. 2018. *Searching for Boko Haram: A History of Violence in Central Africa*. Oxford: Oxford University Press.

MacKenzie, Scott. 1996. "A line in the snow: Visualizing borders imaginary and real." *Public* 16: 1–9.

McLaren, Peter. 2002. "White terror and oppositional agency: Towards a critical multiculturalism." In Peter McClaren, ed. *Critical Pedagogy and Predatory Culture*. London: Routledge, 131–158.

McNally, Michael David. 2000. *Ojibwe Singers: Hymns, Grief, and a Native Culture in Motion*. Oxford: Oxford University Press.

Madsen, Kenneth D. 2011. "Barriers of the U.S.-Mexico border as landscapes of domestic political compromise." *Cultural Geographies* 18, (4): 547–556.

Mahler, Sarah J. and Patricia R. Ressar. 2001. "Gendered geographies of power: Analyzing gender across transnational spaces." *Identities* 7, (4): 441–459.

Manzanas, Calvo, Ana Maria, and Jesus Benito Sanchez. 2016. *Hospitality in American Literature and Culture*. New York: Routledge.

Marsico, Giuseppina, and Luca Tateo. 2017. "Borders, tensegrity and development in dialogue." *Integrative Psychological and Behavioural Science* 51, (4): 536–556.

Martin, Philip, and Elizabeth Midgley. 2003. "Immigration: Shaping and reshaping America." *Population Bulletin* 58, (2) (June).
Martin-Rodriguez, Manuel M. 1995. "The global border: Transnationalism and cultural hybridism in Alejandro Morales's 'The Rag Doll Plagues'." *Bilingual Review/La Revista Bilingue* 20, (3): 86–98.
Massey, Doreen. 2007. *World City*. London: Polity.
Mazzara, Federica. 2018. "Objects, debris and memory of the Mediterrasnean passage: Porto M in Lampedusa." In Gabriele Proglio, and Laura Odasso, eds. *Border Lampedusa*. London: Palgrave Macmillan, 153–173.
Megoran, Nick. 2012. "Rethinking the study of international boundaries: A biography of the Kyrgystan-Uzbekistan boundary." *Annals, Association of American Geographers* 102, (2): 464–481.
Megoran, Nick. 2017. *Nationalism in Central Asia: A Biography of the Uzbekistan-Kyrgystan Boundary*. Pittsburgh: University of Pittsburgh Press.
Megoran, Nick. 2020. "'Go anywhere I damn well please'? Towards an anarchist vocational ethics of international borders." In James W. Scott, ed. *A Research Agenda for Border Studies*. Oxford: Edward Elgar, 183–200.
Meinig, Donald W. ed. 1979. *The Interpretation of Ordinary Landscapes: Geographical Essays*. New York: Oxford University Press.
Meinig, Donald W. 2008. "Geography as an art." In John Agnew, and Nuala C. Johnson eds. *Culture and Society: Critical Essays in Human Geography*. New York: Routledge, 49–63.
Mensah, Joseph, Christopher J. Williams, and Edna Aryee. 2013. "Gender, power, and religious transnationalism among the African diaspora in Canada." *African Geographical Review* 32, (2): 157–171.
Mielke, Anelynda, and Nadya Pohran. 2021. "Bordering things: Objects and subjugated struggle at the border." In Victor Konrad, and Melissa Kelly, eds. *Borders, Culture, and Globalization: A Canadian Perspective*. Ottawa: University of Ottawa Press, 85–106.
Mignolo, Walter D. 2011. "Geopolitics of sensing and knowing: On (de)coloniality, border thinking and epistemic disobedience." *Postcolonial Studies* 14, (3): 273–283.
Mishra, Sudesh. 2006. *Diaspora Criticism*. Edinburgh: University of Edinburgh Press.
Mitchell, Don. 2003. "Cultural landscapes: Just landscapes or landscapes of justice?" *Progress in Human Geography* 27, (6): 787–796.
Mohammed, S. Nick. 2011. *Communication and the Globalization of Culture: Beyond Tradition and Borders*. Oxford: Lexington Books.
Morales, Alejandro. 1995. "Dynamic identities of heterotopia." *Bilingual Review/La Revista Bilingue* 20, (3): 14–27.
Muller, Michael B., and Cornelius Torp. 2009. "Conceptualizing transnational spaces in history." *European Review of History – Revue europeenned'histoire* 16, (5): 609–617.
Musabende, Alice. 2021. "The roles of cultural communities in African immigrant retention." In Victor Konrad, and Randy Widdis, eds. *Borders, Bordering and Borderlands in Atlantic Canada*. Victoria: Borders in Globalization ebooks, 119–146.
Nail, Thomas. 2016. *Theory of the Border*. Oxford: Oxford University Press.
Nail, Thomas. 2019. "Kinopolitics: Borders in motion." In Rosi Braidotti, and Simone Bignall, eds. *Posthuman Ecologies: Complexity and Process after Deleuze*. New York: Roman and Littlefield, 183–203.
Nakamura, Lisa. 2019. "Gender and race in the gaming world." In Mark Graham, and William H. Dutton, eds. *Society and the Internet: How Networks of Information and Communication are Changing Our Lives*. Oxford: Oxford University Press, 127–145.

Nasser, Noha. 2004a. "From multicultural urbanities to the postmodern cosmopolis: A praxis for urban democracy." *Built Environment* 30, (1): 4–16.

Nasser, Noha. 2004b. "Southall's Kaliedo-scape: A study in the changing morphology of a West London suburb." *Built Environment* 30, (1): 76–103.

Nischik, Reingard M. 2016. *Comparative North American Studies: Transnational Approaches to American and Canadian Literature and Culture*. New York: Palgrave Macmillan.

O'Dowd, Liam. 2010. "From a 'borderless world' to a 'world of borders': Bringing history back in." *Environment and Planning D: Society and Space* 28, (6): 1031–1050.

Ong, Aihwa. 1997. *Ungrounded Empires: The Cultural Politics of Modern Chinese Transnationalism*. New York: Routledge.

Ong, Aihwa. 1999. *Flexible Citizenship: The Cultural Logics of Transnationality*. Durham: Duke University Press.

Pain, Rachel, and Susan J. Smith. 2016. *Fear: Critical Geopolitics and Everyday Life*. New York: Routledge.

Paredes, Americo. 1995. *Folklore and Culture on the Texas-Mexican Border*. Austin: University of Texas Press.

Parizot, Cedric, Anne-Laure Amilhat Szary, Gabriel Popescu, Isabelle Arvers, Thomas Cantens, Jean Cristofol, Nicola Mai, Joanna Moll, and Antoine Vion. 2014. "The antiAtlas of borders, a manifesto." *Journal of Borderlands Studies* 29, (4): 503–512.

Parker, Noel, and Nick Vaughan-Williams, eds. 2016. *Critical Border Studies: Broadening and Deepening the "Lines in the Sand" Agenda*. London: Routledge.

Payan, Tony. 2016. *The Three U.S.-Mexico Border Wars: Drugs, Immigration, and Homeland Security*. Santa Barbara: ABC-CLIO.

Pellander, Saara, and Karina Horsti. 2018. "Visibility in mediated landscapes: The hunger strike of asylum seekers as an embodiment of border violence." *Political Geography* 66: 161–170.

Pickering, Sharon, and Jude McCulloch, eds. 2012. *Borders and Crime: Pre-crime, Mobility and Serious Harm in an Age of Globalization*. New York: Palgrave Macmillan.

Pichlmair, Martin. 2008. "Venturing into the borderlands of playfulness." *Technoetic Arts* 6, (2): 207–212.

Piper, Nicola. 2003. "Feminization of labor migration as violence against women: International, regional, and local nongovernmental organization responses in Asia." *Violence Against Women* 9, (6): 723–745.

Ponzanesi, Sandra, and Daniella Merolla, eds. 2005. *Migrant Cartographies: New Cultural and Literary Spaces in Post-Colonial Europe*. Oxford: Lexington Books.

Ptak, Thomas, Jussi Laine, Zhiding Hu, Yuli Liu, Victor Konrad, and Martin Van der Velde. 2020. "Understanding borders through dynamic processes: Capturing relational motion from South-West China's radiation center." *Territory, Politics, Governance* 10, (2): 200–218.

Ragazzi, Francisco. 2014. "A comparative analysis of diaspora policies." *Political Geography* 41: 74–89.

Rancière, Jacques. 1999. *Disagreement: Politics and Philosophy*. Minneapolis: University of Minnesota Press.

Rancière, Jacques. 2020. *The Edges of Fiction*. Cambridge: Polity.

Rapoport, Amos. 1992. "On cultural landscapes." *Traditional Dwellings and Settlements Review* 3, (2): 33–47.

Rappoport, Jill, and Lana L. Dalley. 2013. *Economic Women: Essays on Desire and Dispossession in Nineteenth Century British Culture*. Colombus: Ohio State University Press.

Reyes Cruz Mariolga, Claudio Moreira, and Desiree Yomtoob. 2009. "Transgressive borders: A performative diaspora in three movements." *Qualitative Inquiry* 15, (5): 787–805.

Risager, Karen. 2007. *Language and Culture Pedagogy: From a National to a Transnational Paradigm*. Toronto: Multilingual Matters.

Risager, Karen. 2012. "Linguaculture." *The Encyclopedia of Applied Linguistics*: 1–4.

Rodriguez, Joaquin Barriendos. 2011. "Global art and the politics of mobility: (Trans) Cultural shifts in the intenational contemporary art system." In Mieke Bal and Miguel Hernandez-Navarro, eds. *Art and Visibility in Migratory Culture*. Brill: Rodopi, 313–334.

Roe, Maggie, and Ken Taylor, eds. 2014. *New Cultural Landscapes*. New York: Routledge.

Roseman, Curtis C., Gunter Thiem, and Hans-Dieter Laux, eds. 1996. *EthniCity: Geographic Perspectives on Ehnic Change in Modern Cities*. Lanham: Rowman and Littlefield.

Ruf, Martina. 2009. "The feminization of undocumented migration at the U.S.-Mexican border as represented in Latino/a literature." PhD. Dissertation, University of Vienna.

Rumley, Dennis, and Julian V. Minghi, eds. 2014 [1991]. *The Geography of Border Landscapes*. New York: Routledge.

Salazar, Noel B. 2010. "Towards an anthropology of cultural mobilities." *Crossings: Journal of Migration and Culture* 1, (1): 53–68.

Saldívar, Ramón. 2006. *The Borderlands of Culture: Americo Paredes and the Transnational Imaginary*. Durham: Duke University Press.

Salter, Mark B. 2012. "Theory of the: // The suture and critical border studies." *Geopolitics* 17, (4): 734–755.

Sandercock, Leonie. 2003. "Planning in the ethno-culturally diverse city: A comment." *Planning Theory & Practice* 4, (3): 319–323.

Sandercock, Leonie, and Samara Brock. 2009. "Inventing a multicultural nation: Canada's evolving story." In Leonie Sandercock, and Giovanni Attili, eds. *Where Strangers Become Neighbours: Integrating Immigrants in Vancouver, Canada*. Dordrecht: Springer, 3–33.

Sassen, Saskia. 2000. "Women's burdern: Counter geographies of globalization and the feminization of survival." *Journal of International Affairs* 53, (2): 503–524.

Sassen, Saskia. 2005. "When national territory is home to the global: Old borders to novel borderings." *New Political Economy* 10, (4): 523–541.

Sassen, Saskia. 2018. *Cities in a World Economy*, 5th ed. Thousand Oaks: Sage.

Sassen, Saskia, Barbara Ehrenreich, and Arlie Russell Hochschild. 2002. "Global cities and survival circuits." In Janice A. Radway, Kevin Gaines, Barry Shank, and Penny Von Eschen, eds. *American Studies: An Anthology*. New York: Wiley-Blackwell, 185–193.

Schaeffer, Felicity Amaya. 2018. "Spirit matters: Gloria Anzaldúa's cosmic becoming across human/non-human borderlands." *Signs: Journal of Women in Culture and Society* 43, (4): 1005–1029.

Schein, Richard. 2006. "Cultural landscape studies: Reception and social mediation of meaning." *The Journal of the Society of Architectural Historians* 65, (1): 17–18.

Schimanski, Johan, and Jopi Nyman, eds. 2021. *Border Images, Border Narratives: The Political Aesthetics of Boundaries and Crossings*. Manchester: Manchester University Press.

Schimanski, Johan, and Stephen Wolfe, eds. 2007. *Border Poetics De-limited*. Hannover: Wehrhahn.

Schmoll, Camile. 2020. *Les damnées de la mer. Femmes et frontières en Méditerranée*. Paris: La Découverte.

Sheleva, Elizabeta. 2003. "Border cultures/Cultures at the border." *Identities: Journal for Politics, Gender and Culture* 2, (1): 123–139.

Sheringham, Olivia. 2010. "A transnational space? Transnational practices, place-based identity and the making of home among Brazilians in Gort, Ireland." *Portuguese Studies* 26, (1): 60–78.

Scott, James W. 2005. "The EU and 'wider Europe': Toward an alternative geopolitics of regional cooperation?" *Geopolitics* 10, (3): 429–454.

Shirley, John. 2011. *Borderlands: The Fallen*. New York: Simon and Schuster.

Short, John Rennie, Carrie Breitbach, Steven Buckman, and Jamey Essex. 2000. "From world cities to gateway cities: Extending the boundaries of globalization theory." *City* 4, (3): 317–340.

Slack, Jeremy, and Scott Whiteford. 2011. "Violence and migration on the Arizona-Sonora border." *Human Organization* 70, (1): 11–21.

Sohn, Christophe. 2020. "Borders as resources: Towards a centering of the concept." In James W. Scott, ed. *A Research Agenda for Border Studies*. Oxford: Elgar, 71–88.

Sohn, Christophe, and Francisco Lara Valencia. 2013. "Borders and cities: Perspectives from North America and Europe." *Journal of Borderlands Studies* 28, (2): 181–190.

Soja, Edward. 1996. *Thirdspace: Journeys to Los Angeles and Other Real-and-Imagined Places*. Oxford: Blackwell.

Soja, Edward. 1999. *Postmetropolis: Critical Studies of City and Region*. Oxford: Blackwell.

Sokefeld, Martin. 2006. "Mobilizing in transnational space: A social movement approach to the formation of diaspora." *Global Networks* 6, (3): 265–284.

Staudt, Kathleen. 2009. *Violence and Activism at the Border: Gender, Fear and Everyday Life in Ciudad Juarez*. Austin: University of Texas Press.

Stearns, Peter N. 2001. *Cultures in Motion: Mapping Key Contacts and their Imprints in World History*. New Haven: Yale University Press.

Strang, Veronica. 2020. *Uncommon Ground: Cultural Landscape and Environmental Values*. New York: Routledge.

Sturgeon, Janet C. 2007. *Border Landscapes: The Politics of Akha Land Use in China and Thailand*. Seattle: University of Washington Press.

Sundberg, Juanita. 2008. "'Trash talk' and the production of quotidian geopolitical boundaries in the USA-Mexico borderlands." *Social and Cultural Geography* 9, (8): 871–890.

Sundberg, Juanita. 2011. "Diabolic Caminos in the desert and catfights on the Rio: A posthumanist political ecology of boundary enforcement in the United States-Mexico borderlands." *Annals, Association of American Geographers* 101, (2): 318–336.

Taylor, Ken, and Jane Lennon, eds. 2011. *Managing Cultural Landscapes*. New York: Routledge.

Taylor, Peter J. 2000. "World cities and territorial states under conditions of contemporary globalization." *Political Geography* 19, (1): 5–32.

Taylor, Peter J. 2001. "Specification of the world city network." *Geographical Analysis* 33, (2): 181–194.

Tofighian, Omid. 2020. "Introducing Manus prison theory: Knowing border violence." *Globalizations* 17, (7): 1138–1156.

Topak, Ozgun E. 2021. "Border violence and migrant subjectivities." *Geopolitics* 26, (3): 791–816.

Tremblay, Kaitlin. 2017. *Ain't No Place for a Hero: Borderlands*. Toronto: ECW Press.

Vandervalk, Sandra. 2021. "Passing through or living here: Body and self in-between and on edge in the borderland region of Stanstead, Quebec, and Derby Line, Vermont." In

Victor Konrad, and Melissa Kelly, eds. *Borders, Culture, and Globalization: A Canadian Perspective*. Ottawa: University of Ottawa Press, 163–186.

Van Houtum, Henk. 2005. "The geopolitics of borders and boundaries." *Geopolitics* 10, (4): 672–679.

Van Houtum, Henk, Olivier Kramsch, and Wolfgang Zierhofer, eds. 2005. *B/Ordering Space*. Aldershot: Ashgate.

Van Houtum, Henk, and Huib Erneste. 2001. "Re-Imagining spaces of (in)difference: Contextualizing and reflecting on the intertwining of cities across borders." *Geojournal* 54, (1): 101–105.

Van Schendel, Willem, and Itty Abraham, eds. 2005. *Illicit Flows and Criminal Things: States, Borders, and the Other Side of Globalization*. Bloomington: Indiana University Press.

Verstraete, Ginette. 2010. *Tracking Europe: Mobility, Diaspora, and the Politics of Location*. Durham: Duke University Press.

Volkan, Vamik D. 2018. *Immigrants and Refugees: Trauma, Perennial Mourning, Prejudice, and Border Psychology*. London: Routledge.

Washington, John. 2020. *The Dispossessed: A Story of Asylum at the U.S.-Mexico Border and Beyond*. London: Verso.

Werbner, Drina. 2002. "The place which is diaspora: Citizenship, religion and gender in the making of chaordic transnationalism." *Journal of Ethnic and Migration Studies* 28, (1): 119–133.

Whitley, Leila. 2017. "The disappearance of race: A critique of the use of Agamben in border and migration scholarship." *Borderlands* 16, (1): 1–23.

Wilson, Thomas M. 2014. "Borders: Cities, boundaries, and frontiers." In Donald M. Nonini, ed. *A Companion to Urban Anthropology*. Oxford: Blackwell, 103–119.

Wood, Phil, and Charles Landry. 2008. *The Intercultural City: Planning for Diversity and Advantage*. New York: Routledge.

Yang, Wen-Shan, and Melody Chia-Wen Lu, eds. 2010. *Asian Cross-Border Marriage Migration: Demographic Patterns and Social Issues*. Amsterdam: Amsterdam University Press.

Yeoh, Brenda S. A., and Shirlena Huang. 2000. "'Home' and 'away': Foreign domestic workers and negotiations of diasporic identity in Singapore." *Women's Studies International Forum* 23, (4): 413–429.

INDEX

Note: The index entries in **bold** are the numerous sub-titles in the book. The items in *italics* are titles of books, museum exhibitions, etc.

For Product Safety Concerns and Information please contact our EU representative GPSR@taylorandfrancis.com Taylor & Francis Verlag GmbH, Kaufingerstraße 24, 80331 München, Germany